D1559753

Sexing the Citizen

SEXING THE CITIZEN
Morality and Masculinity in France,
1870–1920

JUDITH SURKIS

Cornell University Press

ITHACA AND LONDON

First published 2006 by Cornell University Press

Printed in the United States of America

Library of Congress Cataloging-in-Publication Data
Surkis, Judith.
    Sexing the citizen : morality and masculinity in France, 1870–1920 / Judith Surkis.
        p. cm.
    Includes bibliographical references and index.
    ISBN-13: 978-0-8014-4464-7 (cloth : alk. paper)
    ISBN-10: 0-8014-4464-0 (cloth : alk. paper)
        1. Masculinity—Political aspects—France—History.   2. Masculinity—Moral and ethical aspects—France—History.   3. Marriage—Political aspects—France—History.   4. Marriage—Moral and ethical aspects—France—History.   5. Sex role—Political aspects—France—History.   6. Sex role—Moral and ethical aspects—France—History.   7. Citizenship—France—History.   8. France—History—Third Republic, 1870–1940.   I. Title.
    HQ1090.7.F8S87   2006
    305.310944'09034—dc22

2006009534

Cornell University Press strives to use environmentally responsible suppliers and materials to the fullest extent possible in the publishing of its books. Such materials include vegetable-based, low-VOC inks and acid-free papers that are recycled, totally chlorine-free, or partly composed of nonwood fibers. For further information, visit our website at www.cornell press.cornell.edu.

Cloth printing   10 9 8 7 6 5 4 3 2 1

For My Parents

Contents

Acknowledgments   ix

Introduction: Regular Love and Republican Citizenship   1

PART I   AFFECTIVE GOVERNMENT   17

1. Moral Education, the Family, and the State   21
2. Liberal Discipline   43

PART II   THE BACHELOR'S VICE   69

3. Wasted Youth   73
4. Life and the Mind   104

PART III   ÉMILE DURKHEIM AND DESIRABLE REGULATION 125

5. The Limits of Desire   133
6. The Sacralization of Heterosexuality   161

PART IV   PRESERVING MEN   185

7. Venereal Consciousness and Society   189
8. Hygienic Citizens   212

Epilogue   243

Bibliography   249
Index   271

Acknowledgments

The French literary critic Roland Barthes famously appealed to the metaphor of the network to describe textual composition. The web of intellectual, affective, and financial support that makes writing and thinking possible is not, however, merely metaphorical. I have had the chance to be sustained by just such a network in the many years that I have devoted to this project. And it is a privilege and a pleasure to acknowledge some of the individual strands that contributed to its fabrication.

I could not have asked for a more supportive and engaged adviser and mentor than Dominick LaCapra, under whose direction I began this project at Cornell University. His ongoing devotion to his students and to creating intellectual community was nothing less than exhilarating. At each and every stage of my work, I have been guided by his critical insights, his subtle suggestions, his attentive readings, and repeated re-readings. He is a model and inspiration for my own teaching and thinking. While Ithaca, New York, is not known for a comfortable climate, Cornell offered a very warm environment in which to develop as a graduate student. Michael Steinberg and Nelly Furman provided endless advice and comfort. Members of the European History faculty—Isabel Hull, Steven Kaplan, Peter Holquist, and Rachel Weil—were all remarkable for their intellectual commitment and critical support.

Clio surely smiled on me when I began my undergraduate studies at Brown University; it was there that I encountered Joan Scott on my first day and Carolyn Dean in my last year. Joan's intellectual generosity is immeasurable; a crucial reader and sensitive interlocutor at many decisive moments, she repeatedly helped me shape this book into its final form. Carolyn's advice and attention have been equally vital; her unparalleled ability to distill arguments and tease out their implications pushed me to be ever more rigorous in my conceptualizations. I owe a great debt to them both.

Many sources provided the material means necessary to this work. Funding from the Fulbright and Mary K. Sibley foundations, the Council on European Studies, the Cornell University Einaudi Center pre-dissertation, Western Societies, and Mario Einaudi Dissertation Research Grants, as well as the generous support of the Cornell History Department were crucial in the years spent researching and writing my dissertation. A research leave from Harvard University gave me much needed time to complete my manuscript. And a Nancy L. Buc Fellowship at the Pembroke Center for Research and Teaching on Women offered me an opportunity to return to Brown and a genial environment in which to think and write. Many thanks are in order to Elizabeth Weed, David Konstan, and my fellow fellows Timothy Bewes and Dicle Kogacioglu for that intellectually exciting, productive, and laughter-filled year.

Much of my research on this book was conducted in Paris at the Bibliothèque nationale, both in its old and new incarnations. In addition to its extraordinary resources, this institution was a vital scene of intellectual community. During my time in France, seminars at the École des hautes études en sciences sociales with Francine Muel-Dreyfus and many discussions with Gisèle Sapiro helped to orient my research and writing. Audiences and participants in the Cornell European History Colloquium, the Society for French Historical Studies, and the Nottingham History Seminar gave helpful feedback. Special thanks to Karen Adler, Joshua Cole, Jan Goldstein, Patricia O'Brien, Miranda Pollard, Christophe Prochasson, and Vanessa Schwartz for their comments and suggestions. Harvard University has been a wonderful place in which to complete my work on this book. The resources offered by the Center for European Studies, the collections of the Widener and Houghton Libraries, my colleagues and friends in the History Department, and my students all contributed to making it possible. Thanks as well to my colleagues in the Program in Women, Gender, and Sexuality Studies, Afsaneh Najmabadi and Brad Epps, who have been crucial and supportive interlocutors.

Cornell University Press made the experience of turning my manuscript into a book a truly delightful one. John Ackerman's support of this project, his expansive knowledge, and his sense of humor have been indispensable. Teresa Jesionowski and Herman Rapaport provided expert editorial assistance. Thanks also to Julie F. Nemer for preparing the index.

During the years spent at work on this book I have been sustained by extraordinary camaraderie and kinship. In Ithaca and Paris, I was very lucky to meet colleagues—Karen Adler, Jackie Clarke, Tracie Matysik, Jennifer Milligan, Camille Robcis, Todd Shepard, Suzanne Stewart-Steinberg—who would also become conference buddies, attentive readers, and cherished friends. They have enriched my work and my life in more ways than I can express. From Paris to Cambridge and beyond, the spirited wit of Juliette Cadiot, Serguei Emmeline, Peter Gordon, Lisa Randall, Olivier Samour, Cindy

Skach, Orla Smyth, Molly Watson, Gillian Weiss, and Zina Yourovskaya made sure I never forgot how to laugh. Many thanks to the Guitton family for offering a home away from home in France. And much gratitude to my own family for making sure that we remain very close even when I live afar. Rachel, Robert, and Oliver are endless sources of perspective, cheer—and postcards of aquatic mammals. In dedicating this book to my parents, I offer a small token of all that I owe them. Antoine Guitton has lived with this book for almost as long as I have; I can only begin to thank him for being an endless source of companionship, playfulness, and understanding.

J.S.

Introduction

Regular Love and Republican Citizenship

> That the union of the sexes is the first germ of association and, in
> general, of sociability, cannot be misrecognized.
> —Alfred Fouillée, *Les éléments sociologiques de la morale* (1905)

Conjugal love is a very seductive metaphor for sociability. It is premised
on an enduring and harmonious union of different, yet complementary
bodies and souls. It represents a triumph of altruism over egotism by bringing two beings together to create an entity larger than themselves. Dedicated, at least in theory, to reproduction, it is on the side of life and creativ-
ity. Ethical, selfless, life-affirming, and yet also pleasurable, marriage
appears to offer a fine model of the good life. By pairing desire and discipline, satisfaction and structure, conjugality is a particularly powerful figure
for the happy reconciliation of individual and social interests. This conception of marriage as a social ideal—indeed, as an institution which at once
signifies and produces individuals' socialization—implicitly consigns persons who cannot or do not marry to asociality. This threat of social abjec-
tion, and the at once material and symbolic precariousness it entails, help to
constitute the normative force of conjugality.

In turn-of-the-century France, philosophers and sociologists frequently
invoked the conjugal family as a metaphor for social integration and, indeed, as its very source. This book examines and seeks to explain the powerful hold of married love on the social imagination of French policy makers and moralists from the Third Republic's beginnings in the 1870s
through World War I. For republican thinkers like Alfred Fouillée, the exemplary solidarity of marriage was premised on a belief both in the fundamental sexual difference between men and women and on the complementarity of their natures and desires.[1] They imagined married heterosexuality
as a motor and manifestation of civilizational and moral progress. Developments that effaced the difference between men and women were hence seen
as signs of atavism or decadence. As Fouillée remarked elsewhere: "The dif-

---

1. Alfred Fouillée, *Les éléments sociologiques de la morale,* 2nd ed. (1905), 112.

I

ference between the sexes cannot and must not be suppressed by the progress of institutions and moeurs; indeed, in superior organisms and in superior societies the division of functions only becomes more accentuated."[2] Understood as a source and sign of social order and morality, the conjugal organization of sexual difference could also operate as an index of cultural superiority. How and why did republican politicians and professionals make marriage so central to their conception of modern society? And what, in turn, can this tell us about how such idealizations of heterosexuality shape what it means to have a socially valuable and viable life? This book endeavors to answer these questions.

The Third Republic was an enduring regime founded on the principle of universal male suffrage. After the Revolution of 1789, the capacity to exercise individual autonomy conditioned access to active citizenship. Qualifying for suffrage, as a result, was not, or not simply, a political right, but also a normative construction, built on the presumption that citizens were able to think and act independently of others. As a result, with the radicalization of the Revolution in 1792, the oxymoronic category of "passive citizen" was abolished, while women nonetheless remained excluded from political rights. Under the more restricted suffrage regimes of the first half of the nineteenth-century, however, individual men's wealth and qualities granted full citizenship. In 1848, the short-lived Second Republic established universal male suffrage, only to curtail it in 1850. And, while Louis-Napoleon removed these restrictions after his coup d'état, the very meaning of suffrage was constrained under his authoritarian regime. In part as a reaction to the regime, republicans and liberal political thinkers and actors worked to elaborate new understandings of citizenship and civic belonging. However, only in the wake of the Second Empire's defeat in 1870, and after the adoption of a new Constitution in 1875, did all male citizens have regular and repeated occasions on which to exercise their political rights. Because individual autonomy was the theoretical precondition of active citizenship, and because all adult French men had become citizens, autonomy now appeared to be not an attribute of some wealthy or talented men, but as a trait of masculinity itself. It is in this sense that, in the Third Republic, the citizen became sexed.[3]

2. Alfred Fouillée, *Tempérament et caractère selon les individus, les sexes et les races* (1895), 258–59. All translations are my own, unless otherwise indicated.
3. For accounts of the evolution of the concept of citizenship, see Rogers Brubaker, *Citizenship and Nationhood in France and Germany* (1992); Sudhir Hazareesingh, *From Subject to Citizen: The Second Empire and the Emergence of Modern French Democracy* (1998); James R. Lehning, *To Be a Citizen: The Political Culture of the Early Third Republic* (2001); Pierre Rosanvallon, *Le sacre du citoyen: histoire du suffrage universel en France* (1992); Joan W. Scott, *Only Paradoxes to Offer: Feminism and the "Rights of Man" in France, 1789–1940* (1996); William H. Sewell, "Le citoyen/la citoyenne: Activity, Passivity, and the Revolutionary Concept of Citizenship," in *The French Revolution and the Creation of Modern Political Culture*, ed. Colin Lucas (1988).

According to the tautological arguments which founded their exclusion, women were denied access to full citizenship on the principle that they were incapable of acting independently; this exclusion actually produced the very dependence that women were imagined to embody. Despite repeated efforts by feminists to negotiate the paradox of this political exclusion and to demonstrate their capacity for reasoned independence by other means, women would obtain the right to vote in France only in 1944. By structurally and discursively positioning them as objects of state and familial solicitude, the Third Republic gave women certain social rights and protections—such as limitations on their work week and access to education—without granting them direct political representation. These reforms were, for the most part, enacted not in the name of women as rights-bearing individuals, but as social goods, necessary for the health of families, and hence the moral and physical strength of nation. They were based not on women's capacities, but on their presumed vulnerability and victimization. Women, whose interests were conceived as equivalent to those of families, stood in for the needs of society as a whole. Femininity marked bodies that required care, that is, persons who could not care for themselves, in part because they had to care for others, and children in particular. This social logic both granted women new protections and underwrote the ongoing regulation of their bodies, desires, and destinies. As a result, despite some clear improvements in women's legal status and the expansion of their professional possibilities, their status as individuals remained vexed.[4]

Conjugal complementarity became one way to organize and explain men and women's sexual difference, not just as a natural principle, but also as a socially necessary one, as in fact, generative of sociality itself. The logic of sexed citizenship in the Third Republic established women as at once different from and complementary to men. It bound together gender ideals—proper masculinity and femininity—with a specifically social and moral account of sexuality. Imagined as drawn together by forces of mutual attraction, men and women, in theory, entered their unions freely. Conjugality, according to this model, was based ideally on neither financial nor social advancement, but on sexual desire. As an expression and extension of this heterosexual desire, marriage consolidated the citizen's masculinity. It instituted both men's sexual difference from women and a kind of free choice, purportedly cleaved from worldly considerations. It also, and just as

4. On women's postrevolutionary exclusion from citizenship see Geneviève Fraisse, *Reason's Muse: Sexual Difference and the Birth of Democracy* (1994); Carla Hesse, *The Other Enlightenment: How French Women Became Modern* (2001); Lynn Hunt, *The Family Romance of the French Revolution* (1992); Joan B. Landes, *Women and the Public Sphere in the Age of the French Revolution* (1988); Rosanvallon, *Le sacre*; Scott, *Only Paradoxes*. On the development of "social rights" in general and, especially those of women, see Elinor A. Accampo, Rachel G. Fuchs, and Mary Lynn Stewart, eds., *Gender and the Politics of Social Reform in France, 1870–1914* (1995); Jacques Donzelot, *L'invention du social: Essai sur le déclin des passions politiques* (1994); Susan Pedersen, *Family, Dependence, and the Origins of the Welfare State: Britain and France, 1915–1945* (1993).

importantly, bound men to the social interests embodied by women. In marriage, then, citizens were both theoretically independent *and* articulated to the social order.

This socialization of citizens in and through marriage took on particular importance for a republican elite who, while committed to the principle of universal suffrage, also sought to guarantee the moral character of the men who had newly acceded to political rights. These men's political emancipation depended on a wider project of moral reform. Thus, as many historians have signaled, prominent republicans' vision of a new political and social order entailed the creation of a universal system of primary education for the "popular classes."[5] As one such reformer remarked in a series of lectures on the relationship between education and democracy, "I would say, gentlemen, that the universal education decreed by the Third Republic will create in this country, a moral and social revolution whose importance will be, at the very least, equivalent to the one achieved by the establishment of universal suffrage: the two are corollaries, reliant each upon the other."[6] The relationship between moral regeneration and republican politics had been well established by republican elements of civil society under the Second Empire. Efforts to elaborate this moral vision coincided with their political critiques of the authoritarianism, excess, and corruption of that regime.[7] After the radical revolt of the Parisian working classes in the Commune, republicans were even more concerned to marry, as it were, political and moral reform. This joint vision remained central to their efforts both to delegitimate the clerical and monarchist adversaries who resisted democratic reform and to address the problems of social inequality so violently raised in the Commune.

How could republicans guarantee that men would be at once autonomous and socialized, men, that is, who freely chose, in the words of the prominent republican pedagogue Ferdinand Buisson, to "behave according to the norms of their time and country's civilization"?[8] I argue that the effort to moralize men's sexuality was, in the Third Republic, a terrain on which social reformers and critics both articulated and putatively resolved this classic liberal paradox. If the regulation of women was central to the

5. See, for example, Katherine Auspitz, *The Radical Bourgeoisie: The Ligue de l'enseignement and the Origins of the Third Republic, 1866–1885* (1982); Rosanvallon, *Le sacre*; Phyllis Stock-Morton, *Moral Education for a Secular Society: The Development of Morale Laïque in Nineteenth-century France* (1988); Eugen Weber, *Peasants into Frenchmen: The Modernization of Rural France, 1870–1914* (1976).

6. Eugène Spuller, "La République et l'enseignement (1884)," in *Éducation de la démocratie: Troisième série de conférences populaires*, ed. Eugène Spuller (1892), 30–31.

7. Hazareesingh, *From Subject to Citizen*, 240; Philip Nord, *The Republican Moment: Struggles for Democracy in Nineteenth-century France* (1995), 191; Judith F. Stone, *Sons of the Revolution: Radical Democrats in France, 1862–1914* (1996), 47.

8. Ferdinand Buisson, ed., *Dictionnaire de pédagogie et d'instruction primaire, 1re partie* (1887), vol. 1, s.v. "École," 762.

constitution of a viable and productive social order, so, too, was that of men. Men's sexuality, I suggest, was conceived as a locus of specific social and political problems.

In this book, I argue that discussions of the regulation of the passions, instincts, and desires associated with men's sexuality anchored wider debates about the meaning of moral autonomy, the nature of civilization and social progress, and the normative regulation of social life. Debates about the nature of men's sexual drives and how they could and should be ordered were in this sense also debates about the foundations of morality and the stakes of republican political and social reform. Because they hinged on conceptions of conjugality as a sign and guarantor of social order and progress, these debates, in turn, had important implications both for how women's sexual and social roles were ideally imagined and for the figuration of sexual deviance as a troubling symptom of social disorder. These connected concerns are not reducible to the predicament presented by the citizen's sexuality. The problematic status of the male self nonetheless contributed to contemporary fears of and fascination with women and men who did not conform to the gender and sexual prescriptions of conjugality.

I aim here to offer a historically specific argument about the ways in which republicans imagined marriage as an institution for the social and sexual regulation of men. Social reformers and theorists at the end of the nineteenth-century notably discussed the historicity of marriage and, as a corollary, marriage's contribution to history. They regularly speculated about its role in the advancement of progress and "civilization." These accounts reflected general preoccupations with modernity, in other words, with the significant social, economic, political, and technological developments that characterized the era. New knowledge of other cultures that developed in tandem with nineteenth-century imperial projects and civilizing missions structured and helped to constitute contemporary understandings of marriage; ideas about conjugal marriage and its relationship to civilization in turn shaped those policies in notable ways. The exclusion of colonial subjects from citizenship was, in part, based on these presumptions. The difference between indigenous "moeurs" and civilized domestic arrangements were often invoked to explain and justify that exclusion. Sociologists, ethnographers, demographers, and hygienists, meanwhile, began to write their own histories of marriage and described the conjugal family as at once force and symptom in the evolution of "humanity." Sociologist Émile Durkheim, a thinker who plays an important role in my story, would hence claim that the "conjugal family," and the affective and sexual bonds that it implied, was not a transhistorical social form. In his view, it was new to Western modernity and an important corollary to the decline of traditional society and the rise of an implicitly male modern individual.[9]

9. Émile Durkheim, "La famille conjugale (1892)," in *Textes 3*, ed. Victor Karady (1973).

Theorists and historians of liberalism have examined the different ways in which the imagination of men's freedom entailed an exclusion of women from politics and public political debate, inscribing them in a position of subordination exemplified by the marriage contract. As described by political theorist Carol Pateman, this "sexual contract" was a (disavowed) founding presupposition of the modern social contract. It instituted both heterosexuality and women's submission at the origin of political modernity and reconstituted "patriarchy" in new terms.[10]

Like all models, Pateman's account is both instructive and limiting. Its greatest weakness lies in the static terms in which it poses the transfer from old to new and imagines historical change in terms of epistemological rupture. It ultimately risks reifying the very order that it seeks to critique (which is, of course, the danger inherent in all theories of "patriarchy"). Historians, while more attentive to context, have rehearsed aspects of this model. Lynn Hunt, like Pateman, appealed to Sigmund Freud's account of the killing of the primal father by the "band of brothers" in her suggestive discussion of the shift from a patriarchal to a fraternal social order in the French Revolution. Hunt thus stressed the "unifying functions" of revolutionary family romances over and against "their effects of difference or fragmentation," and she examines the "powerfully unifying features of the political imagination" as it was reconstructed in and by stories about gender and the family. Hunt herself has, more recently, sought to revise this overly schematic and totalizing position.[11] What is more, current work on the innovations and contestations of revolutionary reforms of marriage and family law has brought to light just such effects of "difference or fragmentation."[12] How can we account for the extent to which the social organization and regulation of gender and sexuality remained subject to debate and

10. Fraisse, *Reason's Muse*; Carol E. Harrison, *The Bourgeois Citizen in Nineteenth-century France: Gender, Sociability, and the Uses of Emulation* (1999); Hesse, *The Other Enlightenment*; Isabel V. Hull, *Sexuality, State, and Civil Society in Germany, 1700–1815* (1996); Hunt, *The Family Romance*; Linda Kerber, "The Paradox of Women's Citizenship: The Case of Martin vs. Massachusetts, 1805," *American Historical Review* 97, no. 2 (1992); Landes, *Women and the Public Sphere*; Dorinda Outram, *The Body and the French Revolution: Sex, Class, and Political Culture* (1989); Carole Pateman, *The Sexual Contract* (1988); Rosanvallon, *Le sacre*; Scott, *Only Paradoxes*; Sewell, "Le citoyen/la citoyenne"; Nancy Leys Stepan, "Race, Gender, Science, and Citizenship," *Gender and History* 10, no. 1 (1998); Rachel Weil, *Political Passions: Gender, the Family, and Political Argument in England, 1680–1714* (1999).

11. Hunt, *The Family Romance*, 196. In her more recent efforts to defend the legacy of the Revolution from what she sees as the joint excesses of antitotalitarian and feminist critiques, Hunt has highlighted the imaginative ways in which Revolutionaries attempted to remake the family. See Lynn Hunt, "Male Virtue and Republican Motherhood," in *The French Revolution and the Creation of Modern Political Culture*, ed. Keith Michael Baker (1994). And Lynn Hunt, "Forgetting and Remembering: The French Revolution Then and Now," *American Historical Review* 100, no. 4 (1995): 1130–33.

12. Suzanne Desan, *The Family on Trial in Revolutionary France* (2004); Jennifer Heuer, *The Family and the Nation: Gender and Citizenship in Revolutionary France, 1789–1830* (2005).

change in the wake of the political modernity inaugurated by the French Revolution? Were the terms and bases of the sexual contract so clearly fixed? Or was the very instability of the normative identities that it presumed integral to how sexuality became an important modality of modern political and social power? In examining the sexualization of political subjects as an ongoing process rather than as a singular event, I emphasize how instability and incoherence were part of how gender and sexual norms were both elaborated and transformed. I argue that the imagined threat of deviance at the heart of individual subjects and society as a whole gave regulation a reason for existing.[13]

My analysis of this dynamic is indebted to Michel Foucault's influential account of the history of sexuality. His first volume of the *History of Sexuality* emphasized how sexuality, especially in the nineteenth century, was regulated by multiple strategies. In that work, he famously elaborated on different ways—the medicalization of women's bodies, concerns over children's sexuality, the political investment in population growth, and new attention to sexual perversions—that sexualities were both constituted and controlled. Foucault inverted the commonsense logic which held that these discussions of sexuality sought to control an inherent, intimate, and volatile characteristic of individuals—their "sex"—in order to claim instead that, "the deployment of sexuality, with its different strategies, was what established this notion of 'sex.'" In so doing, he showed that "sex" was not a fixed substance or a primal cause lodged within the subject, but a composite and imaginary category, an "artificial unity," whose seeming "autonomous agency," he suggested, was a conceptual effect of the very technologies whose appearance he cataloged.[14]

My account of the "sexing" of the citizen similarly understands sex as an artificial and speculative unity between diverse physical, mental, and emotional qualities. Rather than assuming masculinity, which is to say, the attributes of men's "sex" as a coherent entity which became fixed, for example, in the Revolution of 1789, with the Napoleonic Civil Code in 1804, with men's universal suffrage in 1848, or with the advent of the Third Republic in 1870, I examine the processes by which this "sex" was continually imagined and re-imagined. I thus do not chronicle the emergence of a single, dominant model of a liberal, modern, and implicitly male individual, but examine instead how masculinity was repeatedly reorganized and rearticulated. My approach here differs, as well, from Robert Nye's account of the enduring relationship between a largely stable biological notion of sex and

13. On how incoherence and instability are themselves sites of power with respect to sexuality see Janet Halley, "Reasoning about Sodomy: Act and Identity in and after Bowers v. Hardwick," *Virginia Law Review* 79, no. 7 (1993): 1747–49; Eve Sedgwick, *Epistemology of the Closet* (1990), 10–11.
14. Michel Foucault, *The History of Sexuality, Volume I: An Introduction*, trans. Robert Hurley (1980), 154–55.

bourgeois codes of honor in the nineteenth century.[15] In investigating discussions of children's moral education, demographers' denunciation of bachelorhood, sociologies of the family, or medical accounts of syphilis as a social disease, I show how masculinity, as an amalgam of a certain kind of body, a modality of desire, and a quality of mind, was contingently constituted and regularly reconfigured. While masculinity was tautologically conferred on men by male citizenship, its meaning remained unstable. Recent histories of masculinity often highlight its constitutive uncertainty. They do not, however, always explain the relationship between such precariousness and certain men's material and symbolic power.[16] *Sexing the Citizen,* by contrast, demonstrates how instability, rather than undermining masculinity as a regulatory political and social ideal, actually lent it its force.

The suggestion that uncertainty was part and parcel of how masculinity was constituted as a powerful social norm may appear to be counterintuitive. Historians, especially in the wake of the "linguistic" and "cultural turns," have frequently worked under the assumption that the revelation of the contingency and constructedness of meaning destabilizes and on some level demystifies it. This attachment to destabilization and denaturalization has had particular purchase in fields such as the history of gender, sexuality, and race. Scholars working in these domains are understandably invested in demonstrating that these categories of difference are based not in nature, but in culture, that the very meaning of nature is culturally constructed, and that hierarchically ordered differences are, ultimately, effects of power—especially when legal determinations of right are based on them.[17] While this is no doubt true, I want to suggest that the instabilities that haunt such socially constituted categories are not, of necessity, delegitimating. They can,

---

15. Robert A. Nye, *Masculinity and Male Codes of Honor in Modern France* (1993). It also differs from accounts of "hegemonic" and "subordinated" masculinities, by pointing to the constitutive instability of the norm itself. For a discussion of this model, see John Tosh, "Hegemonic masculinity and the history of gender," in *Masculinities in Politics and War,* ed. Stefan Dudnik et al. (2004).

16. For an analysis and critique of this problem, see Toby L. Ditz, "The New Men's History and the Peculiar Absence of Gendered Power: Some Remedies from Early American Gender History," *Gender and History* 16, no. 1 (2004). This is not to say that the study of masculinity is, or should be, reducible to this project. For an important account of the multiple directions taken by the study of masculinity in recent years, including that of masculinity without men, see Robyn Wiegman, "Object Lessons: Men, Masculinity, and the Sign Women," *Signs* 26, no. 2 (2001).

17. See, for example, the pathbreaking work Thomas Laqueur, *Making Sex: Body and Gender from the Greeks to Freud* (1990). On the linguistic and cultural turns see Victoria E. Bonnell, Lynn Hunt, and Richard Biernacki, eds., *Beyond the Cultural Turn: New Directions in the Study of Society and Culture* (1999); Lynn Hunt, ed., *The New Cultural History* (1989); Dominick LaCapra, "History, Reading, and Critical Theory," in *History and Reading: Tocqueville, Foucault, French Studies* (2000); Joan W. Scott, *Gender and the Politics of History* (1988); Ronald Grigor Suny, Patrick Brantlinger, and Richard Handler, "Review Essays: What's Beyond the Cultural Turn?" *American Historical Review* 107, no. 5 (2002); John Toews, "Intellectual History after the Linguistic Turn: the Autonomy of Meaning and the Irreducibility of Experience," *American Historical Review* 92, no. 4 (1987).

in fact, motivate and justify efforts to police the boundaries of these admittedly unstable, but nonetheless effective norms.[18]

In this book, I focus primarily on contemporary concerns about men's sexual desire as at once a condition of and problem for their socialization. That is, I emphasize policies and pedagogies that targeted men, not women. Because they figured conjugality as a matrix of sociality, these reformist visions were nonetheless conceptually dependent on idealized models of femininity. The projects I describe thus paralleled efforts to define and regulate women's socially productive and reproductive roles. New schooling laws sought to wrest girls' minds from the hands of the Catholic Church and hence, at least in part, to promote greater conjugal solidarity. New protective legislation aimed to preserve working women's bodies and the well-being of children and the family. Debates about the regulation of prostitution and perceived population decline focused new attention on women who appeared to resist or refuse their purportedly naturally assigned roles. The increasing visibility of feminism and "new women"—professionals, consumers, and social reformers—in the public sphere drew attention to the inadequacy and instability of naturalist assumptions about femininity. In different ways, these developments revealed that "nature" could not serve as a sufficient ground and guarantee for the social organization of sexual difference. They, at the same time, contributed to the emergence of new approaches to and arguments for the moral, and indeed, social necessity of those differences. While I concentrate here on public debates and policies aimed at forming male citizens, my account demonstrates how efforts to know and discipline men's sexual desire were intimately bound up with concerns about women and the nature of their desires.[19]

18. For an account of the simultaneous instability and force of gender as a norm, see Judith Butler, *Undoing Gender* (2004), 40–43.
19. On the complicated construction of femininity and the regulation of women in this period, see, for example, Accampo, Fuchs, and Stewart, eds., *Gender and the Politics;* Judith Coffin, *The Politics of Women's Work: The Paris Garment Trades, 1750–1915* (1996); Joshua Cole, *The Power of Large Numbers: Population, Politics, and Gender in Nineteenth-century France* (2000); Caroline Ford, *Divided Houses: Religion and Gender in Modern France* (2005); Rachel Fuchs, *Poor and Pregnant in Paris: Strategies for Survival in the Nineteenth Century* (1992); Jo Burr Margadant, *Madame le professeur: Women Educators in the Third Republic* (1990); Angus McLaren, *Sexuality and Social Order: The Debate over the Fertility of Women and Workers in France, 1770–1920* (1983); Jean E. Pedersen, *Legislating the French Family: Feminism, Theater, and Republican Politics, 1870–1920* (2003); Michelle Perrot, "The New Eve and the Old Adam: Changes in French Women's Condition at the Turn of the Century," in *Behind the Lines: Gender and the Two World Wars*, ed. Margaret Randolph Higonnet et al. (1987); Mary Louise Roberts, *Disruptive Acts: The New Woman in Fin-de-siècle France* (2002); Sylvia Schafer, *Children in Moral Danger and the Problem of Government in Third Republic France* (1997); Ann-Louise Shapiro, *Breaking the Codes: Female Criminality in Fin-de-siècle Paris* (1996); Debora Silverman, "The 'New Woman,' Feminism and the Decorative Arts in Fin-de-siècle France," in *Eroticism and the Body Politic*, ed. Lynn Hunt (1991); Mary Lynn Stewart, *Women, Work, and the French State: Labour Protection and Social Patriarchy, 1879–1919* (1989); Lisa Tiersten, *Marianne in the Market: Envisioning Consumer Society in Fin-de-siècle France* (2001). For discussions of analogous developments

The projects I describe coincide, as well, with the emergence of new ways of thinking about sexuality and about sexual deviance. The regulation and policing of such deviance, and especially of male same-sex activity continued through the nineteenth century despite the fact that sodomy was decriminalized at the time of the French Revolution and by the Napoleonic Penal Code of 1810. And, in the last third of the century, scientific experts, in France and elsewhere, increasingly submitted the nature and causes of sexual perversion to intense scrutiny. These medical and psychiatric approaches to sexual pathology notably worked to unsettle the presumptive relationship between the sexed body and cross-sexual desire, even as they attempted to fix the normality of that relationship all the more firmly. In studying individuals whose sexual comportments did not conform to that supposedly assigned by their biological "sex," these doctors developed accounts of the sexual instinct as a locus of potential aberration and deviation. While appealing to nature as the ground and origin of properly masculine and feminine desires, they simultaneously revealed the contingency and unreliability of that ground. Sexologists nonetheless sought, at least initially, to maintain the coherence of their categories by appealing to the model of inversion. Male inverts were hence thought to express a fundamentally feminine nature, and hence desire, while female inverts were understood to be masculine. These inquiries turned the relationship between the sexed body and the organization of desire into a scientific and social problem. As historians have well demonstrated, this instability did not, however, delegitimate normative ideas about masculinity and femininity or the model of heterosexuality that, increasingly, served to lend them coherence. It rather fueled efforts to more effectively police those norms.[20]

---

elsewhere: Kathy Peiss, *Cheap Amusements: Working Women and Leisure in Turn-of-the-Century New York* (1987); Judith Walkowitz, *City of Dreadful Delight: Narratives of Sexual Danger in Late-Victorian London* (1992).

20. On the policing of homosexuality, see Leslie Choquette, "Degenerate or Degendered? Images of Prostitution and Homosexuality in the French Third Republic," *Historical Reflections/Reflexions Historiques* 23, no. 2 (1997); Scott Eric Gunther, "The Elastic Closet: Legal Censure and Auto-censure of Homosexuality in France" (Ph.D. diss., New York University, 2001); William Peniston, *Pederasts and Others: Urban Culture and Sexual Identity in Nineteenth-century Paris* (2004); Michael David Sibalis, "The Regulation of Male Sexuality in Revolutionary and Napoleonic France, 1789–1815," in *Homosexuality in Modern France*, ed. Jeffrey Merrick et al. (1996); Victoria Elizabeth Thompson, "Creating Boundaries: Homosexuality and the Changing Social Order in France, 1830–1870," in *Homosexuality in Modern France*, ed. Jeffrey Merrick et al. (1996). On the emergence of sexology see Antony Copley, *Sexual Moralities in France, 1780–1980: New Ideas on the Family, Divorce, and Homosexuality* (1989); Arnold I. Davidson, *The Emergence of Sexuality: Historical Epistemology and the Formation of Concepts* (2001); Carolyn J. Dean, *The Frail Social Body: Pornography, Homosexuality, and Other Fantasies in Interwar France* (2000); Nye, *Masculinity and Male Codes;* Vernon A. Rosario, *The Erotic Imagination: French Histories of Perversity* (1997). On related developments beyond the borders of France see Ed Cohen, *Talk on the Wilde Side: Toward a Genealogy of a Discourse on Male Sexualities* (1993); Harry Oosterhuis, *Stepchildren of Nature: Krafft-Ebing, Psychiatry, and the Making of Sexual Identity* (2000); Jennifer Terry, *An American Obsession: Science, Medicine, and Homosexuality in Modern Society* (1999).

In this book, I apply these insights to debates about the morality of citizens in order to explore how, for elite professional men in government and civil society, the citizen's heterosexual masculinity was at once presumed and problematic. In order to demonstrate how this was the case, I examine efforts to understand and contain men's deviance, not in sexological studies, but in philosophical, pedagogical, literary, and scientific debates about how to prepare young men for citizenship. In these discussions of students and soldiers, adolescents and bachelors, "perversion" most often appears as an unspecified threat to the socially idealized relationship between masculinity and conjugality, not as an overt object of inquiry or detailed classification. They do not, in other words, deploy the terminology of sexologists, including the nascent opposition between "heterosexuality" and "homosexuality." These thinkers and reformers tend to treat same-sex vice obliquely, by shrouding it in euphemism. Indeed, the very vagueness of this menace, as a latent peril for all potential citizens, is a central component of the dynamic I describe. It reproduced the association of homosexuality with hiddenness, a haunting secrecy that was constitutive of its imagined threat to normative heterosexuality.[21] In outlining and analyzing these debates, my focus is hence not on the contested and often contradictory meanings of "homosexuality" as a distinctive pathology, but on the complex and contingent construction of conjugality and of the masculinity that it was supposed to guarantee. I aim, in the process, to historicize how heterosexuality emerged as an idealized model of "normal" sexual identity.[22]

I argue that philosophers and educators, writers and demographers, sociologists and hygienists, conceived conjugal heterosexuality and the familial model that it implied not or not just as a natural institution, but as a crucible of sociality; they saw the family, and mothers in particular, as vital to the moralization of children, and marriage as a way to anchor male individuals in the social order. My contention is not that men, including married men, always strictly adhered to the conjugal norm. Indeed, the same autonomy that created the citizen's imagined need for marriage also allowed him to occasionally and even regularly violate its prescriptions. This seeming paradox is not, or not simply, a contradiction between "ideology" and "practice." It is rather demonstrative of the very regulatory dilemma that the conjugal norm sought to address.

By placing this social regulatory dynamic at the center of my story, I also seek to displace the causal framework of "crisis" that has been operative in much historical writing about gender and sexuality in turn-of-the-century France and fin-de-siècle European culture more generally. That is, I do not argue that a formerly stable, bounded, liberal male individual was suddenly dislodged from a sense of sovereign self-assuredness and mastery in the wake of the transformations of turn-of-the-century culture and politics.[23] I

21. Dean, *The Frail Social Body*, 140–42.
22. Jonathan Katz, *The Invention of Heterosexuality* (1995).
23. Both Christopher Forth and Mary Louise Roberts pose new questions to the "crisis" model, while nonetheless invoking it. See Christopher E. Forth, *The Dreyfus Affair and the*

instead show how the risk of social and sexual deviance was integral to how contemporaries imagined the male individual and his relationship to a rapidly changing environment in the first place. Masculinity, and the gender and sexual order that organized it, were, I argue, contingent norms, constituted by ever-present possibilities of abnormal deviation. The contemporary rhetoric of "crisis" and the tropes that were used to articulate it—depopulation, exhaustion, déclassement, criminality, disease, and racial degeneration—were not threats to a presumptively stable male subject. They can be seen, instead, as expressions of a precariousness that constituted the force of masculinity as norm. My account does not paradoxically imply that elite bourgeois men were powerless. I rather show how instability fueled the regulatory logic by which an idealized masculinity and a specific configuration of social and political power were articulated and maintained.

As I am interested in citizenship as a socially normative and not as a purely legal category, I do not focus exclusively on state discourses. I instead examine how official theory and policy intersected with the work of civil actors in a variety of arenas—education, literature, social science, and medicine. Historians have well demonstrated how the vital associational life that grew up under the Second Empire and continued to flourish under the Third Republic was a kind of laboratory for the theory and practice of republican citizenship.[24] This book builds on these insights in order to explain how the interaction between state and society constituted the gendered conception of citizenship in significant ways. According to the solidaristic social and political philosophy of the era, the state, as a social organ among others, depended on the initiative and impetus of intermediary bodies for direction and inspiration. In their planning commissions and policy proposals, state representatives frequently appealed to the authority of the academic, literary, scientific, and social scientific milieus from which they, as

Crisis of French Manhood (2004); Roberts, *Disruptive Acts*. Further examples of this "crisis model" may be found in Annelise Maugue, *L'identité masculine en crise au tournant du siècle, 1871–1914* (1987); Robert A. Nye, *Crime, Madness, and Politics in Modern France: The Medical Concept of National Decline* (1984); Daniel Pick, *Faces of Degeneration: A European Disease, c. 1848– c. 1918* (1989); André Rauch, *Le premier sexe: Mutation et crise de l'identité masculine* (2000). In a wider European context, see Bram Dijkstra, *Idols of Perversity: Fantasies of Feminine Evil in Fin-de-siècle Culture* (1986); John C. Fout, "Sexual Politics in Wilhelmine Germany: The Male Gender Crisis, Moral Purity, and Homophobia," *Journal of the History of Sexuality* 2, no. 3 (1992); Angus McLaren, *The Trials of Masculinity: Policing Sexual Boundaries, 1870–1930* (1997); Carl E. Schorske, *Fin-de-siècle Vienna: Politics and Culture* (1981); Elaine Showalter, *Sexual Anarchy: Gender and Culture at the Fin-de-siècle* (1990). For critical discussions of the rhetoric of crisis, see Gail Bederman, *Manliness and Civilization: A Cultural History of Gender and Race in the United States, 1880–1917* (1995), 6; Edward Ross Dickinson, "The Men's Christian Morality Movement in Germany, 1880–1914: Some Reflections on Politics, Sex, and Sexual Politics," *Journal of Modern History* 75, no. 2 (2003); Ditz, "The New Men's History."

24. Auspitz, *The Radical Bourgeoisie;* Harrison, *The Bourgeois Citizen;* Janet A. Horne, *A Social Laboratory for Modern France* (2000); Nord, *The Republican Moment*.

often as not, emerged. At the same time, civil actors had a concrete interest in framing their discussions in terms that were relevant to the state. Pedagogy, as a terrain on which social expertise coincided with the political project of the Republic, frequently served as a point of both collaboration and potential conflict. And, because the very object of schooling was the formation of proper citizens, pedagogy was a privileged arena for the discussions of both the norms of citizenship and its potential deviations. I thus take the problem of schooling, that lieu par excellence of normalization, as a point of entry into this wider set of debates.[25]

In order to understand how educational projects both relied on and instituted idealized conceptions of masculinity, I focus on their profound interest in the problem of male desire. Rather than presuming the coherence and self-evidence of that desire, I examine how social reformers variously made men's desire into a problem in the first place. I highlight how pedagogical theories and policies imagined men's sexuality as simultaneously productive and disruptive, as both a source of sociality and social progress, and as a potentially deviant and antisocial force. Conjugal heterosexuality, I argue, offered one way to affirm and regulate men's desire, and hence resolve the dilemma it appeared to pose, while also accounting for and organizing women's social and reproductive roles.

In part 1, I examine how the architects of the new primary schooling, instituted in 1882, sought to moralize future citizens. I argue that this system of "free, mandatory, and secular" primary schooling entailed simultaneously emancipatory and regulatory ends. The project was libratory in its effort to displace clerical education and to free sons from the tyrannical oppression of "fathers." Republicans did not, however, want to destroy the family. Their vision of "liberal" as opposed to "authoritarian" discipline explained how the proper schooling of affect, alongside reason, could guarantee that future citizens would be at once free and "solidary" with society, and implicitly with the family as well. And because primary education targeted the "popular classes" rather than the nation's elite, educational theorists suggested that appeals to "primary" sentiments would guarantee the accessibility of their programs. Conjugal heterosexuality, founded on a gendered complementarity between "reason" and "affect," conveniently reconciled these aims. At the same time, affect, as they understood it, was unreliable and given over to potential excess. Rather than undermining their efforts however, this sentimental uncertainty justified the regulatory aims of state education. My discussion of pedagogical reformers' efforts to bring primary schooling to the native Arab and Kabyle populations in Algeria brings these dynamics into sharp relief. Republican schooling aimed to liberate these subjects from the purportedly perverse passions of Islam and the degraded character of their domestic life. As a condition of eventual eman-

25. On "normal schools" and normalization, see Georges Canguilhem, *Le normal et le pathologique* (1966), 175.

cipation, with the illusory promise of assimilation that this entailed, "adaptive" education in Algeria affirmed the universality and righteousness of the normative vision of the properly masculine republican citizen.

Part 2 moves from the world of primary education to that of secondary schooling. In these two chapters, I focus on the figure of "the bachelor" as a vexed creature in turn-of-the-century pedagogical debates over how best to form the nation's elite citizens. Bachelors, in the sense both of youths who had recently been granted their *baccalauréat* and unmarried men in general (the two, as I show, were not unrelated), were a symptom of perverse tendencies paradoxically produced by the very institutions that were supposed to form the nation's male elite. According to its critics, the monastical character of lycée life distorted adolescent conceptions of sexual difference and risked giving rise to abnormal sexual comportments. Upon graduation, these young men were overeducated and underemployed, at once adult and yet unprepared or unwilling to marry. As an embodiment of dissipation and waste, the bachelor provided a convenient way to depict mechanisms of social and sexual deregulation purportedly exacerbated by lycée education itself. Young men's failed social integration expressed related concerns about the potentially unsettling effects of social progress, which is to say, the democratization, rationalization, individualism, and materialism associated with the fin-de-siècle republican political order itself. Advocates and adversaries of the meritocratic aims of republican secondary schooling similarly pointed to bachelorhood, and the sexual excess and impotence it represented, as a sign of a problem that needed fixing. The perception of this conflict fueled efforts to reform secondary education and informed discussions of who should make up the nation's elite at the very moment, in the 1890s, when the Republic was on shaky ground.

The work of sociologist and prominent republican academic Émile Durkheim is the focus of part 3. As a beneficiary of and participant in the republican educational establishment, his work was closely aligned with its moral and social aims. Like many of the figures discussed in part 2, Durkheim analyzed the mechanisms of deregulation that disturbed the modern social order, including those that gave rise to the alienation and anomie of the male bachelor. He did not, however, see this apparent conflict between male individuals and society as an inevitable and irremediable effect of modernity in general or of modern democracy in particular. Durkheim nonetheless sought to affirm such core republican ideals as secularism, equality, and right by recasting the ideal relationship between society and citizen as one of mutuality and dependence, rather than divergence and conflict. The ideal of conjugal marriage became one important way for Durkheim to explain how men could be at once socially contingent and still masculine. In his major works and in his occasional writings, Durkheim described marriage as a fundamentally social rule upon which men, as subjects of potentially deregulated desire instantiated by the bachelor, relied in order to fend off anomie and to achieve, in turn, happiness and social wholeness. Durkheim's insistence on the cultural constitution of sexual norms is revealed with particular clarity in his writing on the "origins of the incest taboo." In this article, which is at the core of my analysis in chapter 6, Durkheim categorically refused to see the prohibition on incest as an extension of natural aversions between blood relations. In the process of revealing the social origins of the taboo, and the equally contingent reasons for its perpetuation, Durkheim affirmed men and women's sexual difference and heterosexuality as quasi-sacred social norms.

While the advent of Durkheim's social scientific thinking about men's sexuality is the focus of part 3, I concentrate, in part 4, on hygienic approaches to it. I explore how venereal disease experts, in their efforts to battle this "social danger," located syphilis, and the sexuality that it signified, at the intersection between individual bodies and the social body. As a consequence, their efforts to prevent and treat the disease posed men's sexual desire as a regulatory problem. Many of these experts conceived men's heterosexual desires to be natural and normal and, for that very reason, a potential source of social risk represented by syphilis and its "carrier," prostitution. In drawing up proposals for both "sanitary" and "moral" prophylaxis, hygienists did not so much seek to "repress" men's sexual desires as to protect them, or to help men to protect themselves, from the corrupting force of disease. Because adult men's sexual privacy was surrounded by legal protections, such as the absolute principle of medical secrecy, their efforts focused, initially, on "minors" such as adolescents, soldiers, and colonial subjects. This distinction between adult and minor, between citizens and those who were not or not yet citizens, allowed hygienists to adopt a flexible approach to fighting venereal disease. With the advent of World War I, and the mass mobilization of citizens and the disruption of conventional gender relations that it entailed, the scope of their project expanded considerably. According to the hygienic conception of citizenship that emerged in the wake of the war's hecatombs, the exigency of rebuilding the nation placed new limits on the rights of male citizens, and, in particular, made men's reproductive health a moral as well as sanitary imperative. Because these purported restrictions acted in the name of the monogamous reproductive family, however, they confirmed, rather than undermined, the citizen's normative masculinity.

Debates about how best to form male citizens in the Third Republic did not presume that men were automatically capable of simultaneously acceding to both autonomy and social attachment. Masculinity, like citizenship itself, required schooling. As a result, these at times competing and contradictory pedagogical endeavors understood the masculinity tautologically conferred on men by their status as citizens to be contingent and unstable. This volatility is revealed most clearly in educators' discussions of men's sexuality. Such discussions, I contend, condensed wider concerns about the difficult articulation of the citizen's freedom and his social responsibilities. They implicitly framed arguments about the extent and limits of democracy itself. In appealing to conjugality as the framework in which men's desire could be at once expressed and contained, policy makers and social reformers reconciled their libratory and regulatory projects. At the same time, they figured men and women's difference and sexual complementarity as fundamental to a harmonious social and political order.

In outlining their projects of moral and social education, policy makers, social scientists, and cultural critics repeatedly posed men's sexual desire as a regulatory problem. For these figures, male desire was consistently ambivalent. When properly oriented and contained, it could be a vital source of sociality. However, when unduly repressed or overly unconstrained, it might act as a force of disorder. Pedagogical debates hence articulated the administration of men's sexual desire as a dilemma of proper government. These accounts of masculinity both presumed potential deviance and sought to guard against it. This imagined risk animated and underwrote republican pedagogical endeavors. Conjugality, meanwhile, in reconciling men's freedoms and their social attachment, was central to how they ideally resolved this dilemma.

PART I

AFFECTIVE GOVERNMENT

School: Role of the school.— . . . the school is an essentially social
organ which prepares individuals for the society in which they must
live. It is an institution which is necessary in order to enact a transition between the family and the state, in order to ensure that new
generations are molded not according to whims, whether individual
caprice or narrow familial beliefs, but rather in view of the communal life which will follow, and according to the needs of society . . .
For individuals, the school represents an aid offered by society in
order to make them into men who behave according to the norms of
their time and country's civilization.
        —Dictionnaire de pédagogie et de l'instruction publique, 1887

The four volumes of the *Dictionnaire de pédagogie et de l'instruction
publique* edited by philosopher and director of primary education Ferdinand Buisson, stand as a monument to the extensive project of educational
reform initiated soon after republicans acceded to power in the Third Republic.[1] They testify to the immensity of the endeavor undertaken by republican reformers who viewed this national system of free, obligatory, and
secular education as a necessary complement to the government's new commitment to the universal suffrage of its male citizenry. The formation of
proper men and citizens was integral to their educational project. At the
Congrès pédagogique, organized in 1883 by the Ministry of Education, Undersecretary Durand proclaimed to his audience of normal school directors:
"What must be developed in the child are not only the faculties of mind, but
also the man himself, the whole man, the physical man and the moral man.
In other words, the instruction must turn the child into a man, into a citi-

---

1. Ferdinand Buisson, ed., *Dictionnaire de pédagogie et d'instruction primaire, 1ʳᵉ partie*,
vol. 1 (1887), s.v. "École," 762. See also Pierre Nora, "Le *Dictionnaire de pédagogie* de Ferdinand Buisson: Cathédrale de l'école primaire," in *Les lieux de mémoire: La République*, ed.
Pierre Nora (1984).

zen."[2] The theorization and implementation of a new vision of the "whole man" was part and parcel of these reformers' project. As Durand's speech made clear, the acquisition of knowledge was not the unique focus of the new primary schooling. The school was also charged, according to the *Dictionnaire,* with forming its pupils according to the exigencies of "communal life." As a "social organ," it was designed to surmount the particularities of individual desire and the parochialism of familial religious faith. The new national education aimed *both* to create self-governing citizens and men who would adapt to "communal life" and the "needs of society." The goals of this project, as described by republican reformers themselves, were at once emancipatory and regulatory.

This articulation of libratory and moral aims was a central concern for the republican politicians and thinkers who had contested the authoritarianism of the Second Empire and who came to power with the emergence of the truly "republican" Republic in 1877. Once in control, they needed a model of government to supplement their already well-honed critique of authoritarianism.[3] They were faced with the quandary of how to legitimate the state and its domain of action without reproducing the undemocratic order they sought to replace. In particular, they needed to explain and encourage willing adherence to the regime without reducing the Republic's new citizens to servile subjects. State-run schools, equipped with new teachers, who were armed with new pedagogical methods were indispensable to the realization of this political and social vision. In an analogy that was frequently employed by the republican reformers themselves, the young Republic's own maturation was tied to this instruction, which would lead students from childhood dependence to *l'âge d'homme* or majority. Their developmental pedagogical vision was, in short, a philosophy of government.

My analysis shows that the moralizing aims of this republican pedagogical project depended on an understanding of subjectivity that was structured by gendered and sexual social norms. Masculinity, as the distinctive trait of the active citizen, both conferred social, political, and sexual privilege *and* prescribed a set of social comportments for which married love often served as a metonym. School reformers hence sought to liberate the male child from patriarchal authority without fundamentally undermining the family. Their model of moralization, in turn, rested upon an implicit model of sexual complementarity. A close examination of this model helps explain how republican education was designed as an agent of both emancipation and discipline. In their accounts of the moral formation of male cit-

2. "Le Congrès pédagogique de 1883," *Revue pédagogique* 2, no. 4 (1883): 344.
3. For an overview of the Republican oppositional alliances under the Second Empire, see Philip Nord, *The Republican Moment: Struggles for Democracy in Nineteenth-century France* (1995). See also Katherine Auspitz, *The Radical Bourgeoisie: The Ligue de l'enseignement and the Origins of the Third Republic, 1866–1885* (1982); Sudhir Hazareesingh, *From Subject to Citizen: The Second Empire and the Emergence of Modern French Democracy* (1998). On the tensions inherent in this project, post-1870, see James R. Lehning, *To Be a Citizen: The Political Culture of the Early Third Republic* (2001).

izens, republican pedagogues described affect as a necessary "companion" to reason; their vision of the proper administration of sentiment, ideally structured in and by conjugality, played a crucial role in their theory of "liberal" as opposed to "authoritarian" pedagogy.[4] This project to moralize the future male citizen simultaneously relied on an idealized model of femininity in order to sustain its coherence and efficacy. Thus, while republicans were newly interested and invested in girls' education, they also insisted on its compatibility with women's wifely and maternal destinies.

Republican pedagogues sought to develop a model of state authority that, while different from a patriarchal one, could guarantee that men "behave according to the norms of their time and country's civilization." The figure of the adolescent articulated in important ways the political stakes of the republican moral project; adolescence, as a metonym for the problem of liberal government, staged a dynamic between discipline and liberation. The identification of the newly constituted government's problematic authority with the figure of the adolescent served a political function. It distinguished the new state from preceding authoritarian regimes, which were largely associated with a patriarchal authority enshrined in the Napoleonic Civil Code. It also legitimated reformers' claims to the exigency of their educational project. Reformers relied upon the promise and potential embodied in youthful vitality. At the same time, they sought to discipline the affective tendencies, such as excess and passion, that they associated with male youth. While contemporary sexologists endeavored to catalogue and classify the diverse causes and forms of deviance, pedagogues hinted at, often without clearly specifying, a seemingly universal risk of deviant sexuality that haunted male adolescents. In their efforts to enact school reforms, republican moral theorists aimed at once to mobilize and regulate the passionate forces of youth. In so doing, they imagined and invoked the ambivalent experience of puberty as a common, indeed "universal" masculine trait.

In examining the formulation and implementation of the republican pedagogical project in the French metropole and in Algeria, I demonstrate how its purportedly libratory and socially normative aspects were closely intertwined and mutually constitutive. More specifically, I show how the "liberal discipline" of republican moral education freed up affect, both in the family and in the "crisis" of puberty, in order to better harness it toward political, moral, and socially productive ends. The extension of schooling to the native populations of Algeria operated as a kind of limit case for the stated goals of republican pedagogy, one that, I argue, served to shore up some of its core claims and aims in and through its application in "adapted" form. In advocating for this education, republican reformers confirmed the "universality" of their secular morality.

4. For a highly original account of the relationship between emotional and political regimes, see William M. Reddy, *The Navigation of Feeling: A Framework for the History of Emotions* (2001).

I Moral Education, the Family, and the State

With the advent of the Third Republic, reformers such as Minister of Public Instruction Jules Ferry famously endeavored to wrest control of primary schools from the hands of clerics and, more broadly, the forces of political reaction. According to republican narratives of pedagogical emancipation, clerical educators and the past authoritarian governments that had supported them, exercised control through fear and violence. Republican schooling, by contrast, sought to develop children's willing, as opposed to fearful, attachment to the laws and principles that would make them into good citizens. If clerical schooling was, for these reformers, "authoritarian," that of the new republican state would be adamantly "liberal."

This chapter argues that affect was central to how pedagogical theorists and philosophers imagined this new approach to teaching. Sentiment, they claimed, was essential to how children developed a capacity to reason, and hence how they eventually acceded to moral and political freedom. In opposing their "liberal" pedagogy to "authoritarian" methods of teaching and government, these thinkers and policy makers conceived of affect, not as a quality that needed to be mastered by an autonomous will, but rather as the ground out of which children's ability to will developed in the first place. This approach to childhood and adolescent development relied on a specific model of the conjugal family as a locus for both the production and the regulation of sentiment and desire. As a result, the social and socializing function of conjugal marriage was, I suggest, deeply implicated in the at once political and moral aims of republican schooling.

Republican School Reform

New legislation, passed in 1882, established a system of secular state-run primary schools by supplanting the 1850 Falloux law, which had led to a growth of confessional primary education under the Second Empire.[1] Education, as a vital tool of socialization, could no longer be consigned to the care of the new government's ideological adversaries. These schools were, at the same time, designed to integrate the potentially revolutionary working-classes, now armed with the vote, into the republican fold. While serving a politically and socially integrative function, the schools were also mechanisms of social reproduction, which effectively limited possible trajectories for social ascension. Primary schooling targeted the popular classes and was sharply distinguished from the secondary education reserved for elites (which prepared entry into lycées and ultimately, higher education). The separate sequences of diplomas and degrees virtually blocked passage from one to the other. Republican primary schooling reform thus aimed to bring about moral not social emancipation. And, as histories of the conflicts surrounding the implantation of republican schooling demonstrate well, it was in no way ideologically or politically neutral.[2]

The architects of the new system anticipated the potential for popular resistance to the new state-imposed program, an opposition, which they frequently associated with the parochial economic and religious convictions of "the family." As a result, they made primary schooling not simply "free" and "secular," but also "mandatory." The 28 March 1882 law, which instituted the reforms, both outlined the contents of primary education programs and delineated procedures for enforcing obligation. According to these strictures, fathers (or legal guardians) had to declare where the child would be attending school at the town hall. In cases of repeated failure to comply or a child's delinquent attendance, municipal school commissions could call the father in "to remind him of the text of the law and explain to him his duty," post his name on the door of the town hall, and eventually report him to the police.[3] On March 29, the very day after the passage of

1. Antoine Prost, *Histoire de l'enseignement en France, 1800–1967* (1968), 172–90. And Sarah A. Curtis, *Educating the Faithful: Religion, Schooling, and Society in Nineteenth-century France* (2000); Laura S. Strumhinger, *What Were Little Girls and Boys Made Of? Primary Education in Rural France, 1830–1880* (1983). For an account that complicates a facile opposition between the clerical Empire and the secular Republic, see Caroline Ford, *Divided Houses: Religion and Gender in Modern France* (2005), 135–37.

2. Some of the major signposts in the enormous literature on the history of French education in the Third Republic include Jean-François Chanet, *L'école républicaine et les petites patries* (1996); Maurice Crubellier, *L'enfance et la jeunesse dans la société française, 1800–1950* (1979); François Furet and Mona Ozouf, *Lire et écrire: L'alphabétisation des Français de Calvin à Jules Ferry* (1977); Robert Gildea, *Education in Provincial France, 1800–1914: A Study of Three Departments* (1983); Raymond Grew and Patrick J. Harrigan, *School, State, and Society: The Growth of Elementary Schooling in Nineteenth-century France* (1991); Françoise Mayeur, *Histoire générale de l'enseignement et de l'éducation en France: De la Révolution à l'École républicaine*, vol. 3 (1981); Mona Ozouf, *L'École, l'église, et la République, 1871–1914* (1963); Prost, *Histoire de l'enseignement*; Eugen Weber, *Peasants into Frenchmen: The Modernization of Rural France, 1870–1914* (1976).

3. Ferdinand Buisson, ed., *Dictionnaire de pédagogie et d'instruction primaire, 1re partie*, vol. 2 (1887), s.v. "Lois scolaires," 1705–1706. On family politics in debates about mandatory

the 1882 law, Ferry, Minister of Public Instruction, issued a circular to police prefects urging them to establish the adequate administrative machinery to address this new responsibility.[4]

Because the municipal commissions were local rather than centralized bodies, these disciplinary measures were applied unevenly.[5] Indeed, as many recent historians have pointed out, local and community sentiments played a considerable role in the alacrity with which the Republic's schooling project was realized. The *Dictionnaire de pédagogie,* the encyclopedic resource devoted to the nation's new primary schooling, indicated in an article on "Obligation" that the continued presence of "reactionary" elements on the commissions, namely, the clerics whose presence had been allowed by the Falloux law, hindered police enforcement. Republican reformers were, it noted, also concerned that fathers, especially from the popular milieus targeted by the legislation, might be particularly averse to giving up the additional family income derived from their children's labor.[6] Advocates of obligatory schooling were, however, ambivalent about using police force to implement and extend the Republican project. Were legal constraints, they asked, actually conducive to a desired increase in school attendance? They feared that strict repression might do more harm than good. Ferdinand Buisson, the author of the *Dictionnaire*'s article on *"Fréquentation scolaire,"* remarked: "Mightn't this confrontation, on the contrary, actually make them more hostile? Won't children, who almost always agree with their parents, come to school as if it were forced labor, arriving with a bad attitude, with a desire to misbehave; won't they be a constant nuisance in class, and destined for punishment? What is more, the most extreme form of discipline would be an expulsion, which they would perceive more as deliverance than as punishment."[7] Republicans, in other words, feared that excessive state repression could produce perverse political effects. Ideally, the laws on obligation were to be self-effacing. In the words of Paul Janet, the philosopher responsible for drawing up the new secular moral education program for primary schools and instructors, "the law works to make

schooling: Véronique Antomarchi, *Politique et famille sous la Troisième République, 1870–1914* (2000), 74–78.

4. Buisson, ed., *Dictionnaire,* vol. 2, s.v. "Obligation," 2135. See also Edmond Benoit-Lévy and F.-B. Bocandé, *Manuel pratique pour l'application de la loi sur l'instruction obligatoire* (1882); Jules Valabrègue, *Commentaire sur l'obligation de l'instruction primaire à l'usage des maires, des commissions municipales scolaires et des directeurs des établissements d'instruction* (1883).

5. See, for example, an inspector's report from the year following the law's adoption: "Les notes d'inspection et les rapports des inspecteurs primaires," *Revue pédagogique* 10, no. 1 (1883). And Jean Peneff, *Écoles publiques, écoles privées dans l'Ouest, 1880–1950* (1987), 91.

6. Buisson, ed., *Dictionnaire,* vol. 2, s.v. "Obligation," 2135. Article 15 of the 28 March 1882 law did allow for a significant "softening" of the regulation in giving municipal commissions the right to grant special dispensations.

7. Ibid., s.v. "Fréquentation scolaire," 1108.

itself unnecessary."[8] These reformers privileged a "liberal" approach to discipline at the level of both the individual pupil and the institution. Their suspicion of forceful coercion structured much of the pedagogical theory and moral philosophy that legitimated and subtended the reforms themselves.

Coercion, they believed, could only strengthen the reactionary forces that claimed to protect fathers against incursions on the part of the centralized republican state. Conservative Catholics had, for much of the nineteenth century, framed the fight to maintain clerical influence over schools as a defense of the *père de famille*'s right to educate his own children. Relying on the Civil Code's definition of *puissance paternelle* ("In marriage, a father exercises la *puissance paternelle;* he surveys the child and directs his/her education"), they claimed that theirs was a protected right to choose the education of their children.[9] By deploying a competing notion of individual "liberty"—one explicitly linked to divinely sanctioned paternal right—these traditionalists fashioned a rhetorical weapon that could effectively be wielded against republican reformers who similarly represented themselves as agents of liberty. Defenders of the "liberty to teach" figured the Church, not as authoritarian, but as the true advocate of individual liberties in the face of a tyrannical and invasive Republic.[10]

According to these conservative Catholics, republicans threatened the stability of the family and hence society as a whole by supplanting the authority of the father. Despite the clearly class-specific goals of primary schooling, the reforms violated, in their view, the at once sacred and legal principles on which private, paternal authority—as distinguished from that of the state—was founded. It comes as no surprise that holdovers from the government of "Moral Order" who continued to dominate the Senate expressed vocal resistance to the 1882 law's articles on "Obligation." They depicted the new infringement on the family as tantamount to political Terror. In response, Ferry tried to explain that the reforms were geared toward so-

8. P. Janet, "L'enseignement laïque et obligatoire apprécié par M. Paul Janet," *Revue pédagogique* 1, no. 5 (1882): 446.

9. On the Civil Code and the post-Revolutionary restoration of paternal authority see Jean Delumeau and Daniel Roche, eds., *Histoire des pères et de la paternité* (1990); Suzanne Desan, *The Family on Trial in Revolutionary France* (2004); François Ewald, ed., *Naissance du Code civil: La raison du législateur* (1989); Marcel Garaud, *La Révolution française et la famille* (1978); Jean-Louis Halpérin, *L'impossible Code civil* (1992); Jennifer Heuer, *The Family and the Nation: Gender and Citizenship in Revolutionary France, 1789–1830* (2005).

10. Defenders of the father's right to choose the education of his children would often cite with horror Danton's claim that all children belonged to the Republic before their parents. See, for example, Alfred des Cilleuls, *Histoire de l'enseignement libre dans l'ordre primaire en France* (1898), 540–41. See also Père Frédéric Rouvier, *La révolution maîtresse d'école: Étude sur l'instruction laïque, gratuite et obligatoire* (1880); C. Saint-Maurice, *Pétition à MM. les députés contre l'instruction obligatoire, par un ami de l'instruction* (1880); Jean Sansterre (ouvrier agricole), *Qu'est-ce que l'enseignement laïque, gratuit et obligatoire? La vexation, l'absurdité, le despotisme* (1880). And Yves Déloye, *École et citoyenneté: L'individualisme républicain de Jules Ferry à Vichy; Controverses* (1994), 52–59.

cial order, not revolution. He answered the critiques of senators such as the Duc de Broglie, with explanations of how the law was aimed at exclusively "refractory" (i.e., popular or working-class) and not bourgeois fathers.[11] He played on the senators' class anxieties in order to justify the state's intervention into the affairs of *certain* families: "At once unjust and unjustified is the worry that this law is not composed against those classes most resistant to instruction—classes who are the unique concern of all the legislators who have proclaimed the primary schooling as obligatory; instead, it is feared that it will serve as some kind of war machine, targeting the children of the bourgeoisie; destined to penetrate the intimacy of the domestic foyer and to install, within these same families, under a pretext of civic instruction, some kind of irreligious instruction and some sort of impious and Jacobin enterprise."[12]

In the speech that followed, Ferry insisted that in order to effectively enforce compliance on the part of the popular classes, and especially those fathers, who out of either ignorance or selfishness refused to educate their children, the language of the law had to establish a mechanism of surveillance. Ferry explained that the law's abstract wording masked its implicit social aims: "You should understand that the legal weapon that we aim to secure will never be directed against *l'éducation des châteaux* or bourgeois families . . . We do not aim to intervene between you and your children; we want, however, to make sure that a supposed family 'education' does not become a last resort for those who resist primary schooling."[13] Ferry's speech intimated that the behavior of certain fathers should and could be subject to governmental regulation. These fathers did not have the right to construct a strict division between public law and private, domestic morality. In effect, not all fathers could be trusted *qua* fathers to properly educate their children.[14] The Ferry legislation established that citizenship posed limits on the rights of fathers—and particularly on those fathers who were newly given suffrage. For its critics, the law set a dangerous precedent. Whether or not bourgeois fathers were the actual targets of school reform, the law threatened a conservative vision of patriarchal right as at once natural and divinely sanctioned.

This conflict between the right of the state to educate its future citizens

11. For a materialist account of anticlericalism, see Sanford Elwitt, *The Making of the Third Republic: Class and Politics in France, 1868–1884* (1975), 170–229.

12. Speech made in the Senate, 14 June 1881, Jules Ferry, *Discours et opinions de Jules Ferry*, ed. Paul Robiquet, vol. 4 (1896), 166.

13. Ibid., 172.

14. On critiques of working-class fathers and the "shift in the definition of parenthood from right to obligation," see Sylvia Schafer, *Children in Moral Danger and the Problem of Government in Third Republic France* (1997), 40. Similar questions arose in debates over the Naquet divorce law of 1884: Theresa McBride, "Divorce and the Republican Family," in *Gender and the Politics of Social Reform in France, 1870–1914*, ed. Elinor A. Accampo et al. (1995), 78–80.

and that of fathers to educate their own children converged in debates over the reform legislation's proposed program in secular moral and civic education. The very first line of the first article of the 28 March law instituted this new course of study (while the previous regulations of 1833 and 1850 called for "moral and religious" education).[15] The actual duties to be inculcated by these classes were almost identical to those that had been listed in the past. In the new program, however, the catechism would no longer serve as the primary pedagogical instrument. And, in the wake of the legislation's passage, a flurry of new secular moral education textbooks was published. Phyllis Stock-Morton and Yves Déloye have given detailed treatment to the substance of these courses and the debates provoked by their implementation.[16] My goal in this chapter is otherwise. I investigate the at once philosophical and political framework in which republicans sought to legitimate the moralizing mission of the republic's secular schools. I emphasize how the reformers' moral vision was deeply implicated in a pedagogical technology, and, in particular, a model of "liberal discipline," which sought to foster subjects who were capable of moral self-regulation. In the process, republican pedagogy negotiated the conflict between the family and the state, exacerbated by the reforms, through a gendered division of educational practices and roles.

In devising a compulsory course program in moral and civic education, the state articulated a set of moral ground rules that conformed to the secular politics of the regime itself. The new programs and pedagogy fostered an idea of the subject, and eventual citizen, as morally self-governing rather than as held in by external religious or political constraints.[17] To what principles, to what authority could the neutral state and the instructors that served as its agents appeal in order to ground the rules that pupils were urged to discover within themselves? Where would this authority be located? How, in turn, did republican pedagogues frame the relationship between the state's role in the shaping of children into future citizens and the rights of those citizens who happened also to be fathers?

In his well-known "Lettre adressée aux instituteurs," Jules Ferry explained how teachers were expected to execute their new role. The neutrality of public instruction established by the 1882 legislation was guaranteed by a careful distinction between "private" religious education and the pub-

---

15. For the texts of these laws, see Buisson, ed., *Dictionnaire*, vol. 2, s.v. "Lois scolaires," 1705–1706, 1684–1686, and 1687–1694, respectively.

16. Déloye, *Ecole et citoyenneté*; Phyllis Stock-Morton, *Moral Education for a Secular Society: The Development of Morale laïque in Nineteenth-century France* (1988). See also Jean Baubérot, *La morale laïque contre l'ordre moral* (1997); Laurence Loeffel, *La question du fondement de la morale laïque sous la IIIe République (1870–1914)* (2000); Claude Nicolet, *L'idée républicaine en France (1789–1924): Essai d'histoire critique* (1994). For an excellent contemporary analysis of the new textbooks, see Émile Boutroux, "Les récents manuels de morale et d'instruction civique," *Revue pédagogique* 2, no. 4 (1883).

17. On the of teaching self-discipline, see Déloye, *École et citoyenneté*, 25–27, 41–47.

lic morality promulgated by the state. In circumscribing the sphere of parental and clerical control as proper to the "private" realm, Ferry cleaved moral duty from religious conviction; he claimed that "religious instruction belongs to the church and family, moral instruction to the school."[18] The legitimacy of the republican schooling project thus depended upon the clarity of this distinction between "private" and "public" morality. Despite this formal separation, however, the careful circumscription of roles was at times difficult to uphold—as Ferry's own definition of morality revealed. For, in one of his early speeches to the Senate, Ferry famously announced that the state sanctioned morality was nothing more than "the good old morality of our fathers, ours, yours; for we only have one."[19] In other words, despite his figuration of the family as the scene of "private" morality, Ferry also invoked fathers as a repository of transhistorical moral principles. While Ferry sought to delimit the role of parents (and implicitly the Church), he appealed to the family in order to underwrite his own moral vision. Indeed, he imagined the instructor as an "auxiliary" of the father: "You are at once the auxiliary, and to some extent, the replacement of the *père de famille*: speak to his child as you would want your child spoken to."[20] Moral lessons, he urged, should not be overly abstract or based primarily on a textbook; the teacher was supposed to address his pupils not in the dry manner of a state official, but rather in the intimate, sentimental manner of a father.[21]

Ferry's description of moral instruction displayed the ambivalence between paternity and the new schooling. He suggested that instructors should use paternal affection as an exemplar and guide. And yet, the instructor, as an auxiliary, also *replaced* fathers. Republican pedagogical theory legitimated this displacement by highlighting the concomitant dangers of the father's affective and emotional investments in his children. As the *Dictionnaire de pédagogie*'s entry "Père" indicated, paternal moral authority, because of its lack of objectivity, was also suspect. The article described how "one of the most frequent and generalized phenomena of contempo-

18. See "Lettre adressée aux instituteurs (17 November 1883)" in Ferry, *Discours*, 259. For a related discussion of "the separation between the family and the Church," see Rémi Lenoir, *Généalogie de la morale familiale* (2003), 222–23.

19. Speech given 10 January 1881, in Ferry, *Discours*, 142. This statement is often taken as indicative of Ferry's transhistorical vision of morality. Historians have not noted how it is in tension with Ferry's implicit distinction between public and private education. See Jean-Marie Mayeur, "Jules Ferry et laïcité," in *Jules Ferry, fondateur de la République*, ed. François Furet (1985), 145; Theodore Zeldin, "The Conflict of Moralities: Confession, Sin, and Pleasure in the Nineteenth Century," in *Conflicts in French Society: Anticlericalism, Education, and Morals in the Nineteenth Century*, ed. Theodore Zeldin (1970).

20. "Lettre adressée aux instituteurs (17 November 1883)" in Ferry, *Discours*, 261. Philosopher and deputy Auguste Burdeau similarly described the instructor as a substitute for fathers, as "a government authorized representative of fathers of families." In A. Burdeau, *Devoir et patrie: Notions de morale et d'éducation civique* (1893), 36–37.

21. Ferry, *Discours*, 264.

rary society is the misunderstanding between fathers and sons," a misunderstanding produced by the fact that "it is as if there is a pane of glass between them; without being able to avoid one another, they remain at a distance, irritated and reciprocally incapable of expressing themselves openly."
Here then, the father, because unable to communicate with his son, is quite
the opposite of a model teacher: "He is after all his father, and he finds it
suffocating to not be able to respond directly, to act as if he did not have the
right and duty to command. So, despite himself, he commands, and all is
lost. Their two souls do not interpenetrate; instead their two wills collide."[22]
Like all affect, paternal feeling is ambivalent. Its investments could both en-
able closer communication and produce divisive conflict. The architects of
the new primary schools, on the one hand, associated paternal authority
with bad, "disciplinary" education—the reactionary, repressive, and parochial mode of instruction that they so fervently criticized. On the other
hand, they depicted fatherly, and familial affection more generally, as integral to a liberal model of education diametrically opposed to the mechanical and authoritarian methods associated with clerical institutions. In
Ferry's vision, the school would be a "house of education and no longer a
mere instrument of discipline."[23]

In order to negotiate the ambivalence surrounding paternal authority and
affect, republican educational theorists granted mothers and maternal affection a pivotal pedagogical role. According to their theories, maternal affection facilitated and encouraged learning, without provoking a confrontation
between virile wills. In his speech to *instituteurs* and several *institutrices,*
Ferry suggested that the only way to assure regular school attendance was to
"make students love school, and to make work attractive."[24] For Ferry,
women's maternal natures were crucial to creating such appeal:

> Messieurs, I am profoundly convinced of women's natural superiority in the
> domain of teaching; this superiority, believe me, becomes more and more evi-
> dent each and every day. There are fathers who are capable of showing tender-
> ness, the devotion and delicateness of a mother; there are teachers—and it is
> the case with all great pedagogues—who have something maternal about them;
> but as a general rule, education springs most profoundly from maternal senti-
> ment; the spouse and mother who becomes a teacher brings to teaching the ad-
> vice and revelations of her own precious experience; the unmarried *institutrice*
> finds in the children of others, satisfaction for this maternal sentiment, this
> great instinct of sacrifice which all women carry in themselves, which nature
> has profoundly engraved in your hearts, Mesdames, and which lends your so-
> cial activities nobility, dignity, and force.[25]

22. Buisson, ed., *Dictionnaire*, vol. 2, s.v. "Père," 2256.
23. Ibid., vol. 1, s.v. "Enseignement primaire," 871. The citation is taken from Ferry's address to the Congrès pédagogique delivered on 19 April 1881 in Ferry, *Discours*, 249.
24. Ferry, *Discours*, 248.
25. Ibid., 254. On Ferry's vision of femininity and women's social role, see Françoise
Mayeur, "La femme dans la société selon Jules Ferry," in *Jules Ferry, fondateur de la
République*, ed. François Furet (1985).

This appeal to maternal affect served a variety of strategic ends. It helped to differentiate properly republican pedagogy from the mechanistic disciplinary methods associated with confessional schooling.[26] The privileging of sentiment as a wellspring of education also helped reformers to parry accusations of tyrannical Jacobinism. The family—through the figure of the mother—was here integrated into the process of children's moral formation. This appeal to maternal instinct further granted women, including single women, a secular social mission which could counter the appeal of a religious vocation. Reformers' appeals to a presumed substratum of natural affective sentiments simultaneously helped to explain how children—especially of the popular classes—could be started on the path to moral maturity. Because children would learn to love school in the home, they would go voluntarily. Republican pedagogues hence worked with a developmental model, which presumed that an education that targeted the lower social orders needed to commence with "primary" affects, rather than reason itself. They conceived of affect as crucial to the child's eventual acquisition of reason. At the same time, they warned against the potential excesses to which passionate and emotive tendencies might be subject. The tensions inherent in the problematic dialectic that they established between the role of sentiment and the role of reason in moral autonomy were made apparent in their depiction of a liminal figure—torn between passion and will and on the threshold between the family and civil society, dependence and independence—the adolescent.

The Republic from Child to Man

The "crisis of puberty" was, since Jean-Jacques Rousseau's *Emile,* a commonplace in pedagogical thinking and writing. These longstanding concerns about adolescent development had specific resonance in the context of Third Republic educational reform.[27] In an oration on the "Present duty of youth," Ferdinand Buisson thus described both the promise and peril of adolescence. At "that critical hour that separates childhood from youth," he noted, "the child has grown all at once: tall, slim, slender, one would say a man." And yet, he warned, "This large and fatigued child's body is lanky and awkward, at times the heart beats until breaking, at times the spirit seems disturbed, troubled either by feverishness or an invincible lassitude and languor which saps the very source of life." For Buisson, puberty represented a "rupture in equilibrium." It was "Always a serious crisis, even

26. On the rigorous discipline of confessional education, see Curtis, *Educating,* 82–103.

27. See Jean-Jacques Rousseau, *Emile or On Education,* trans. Allan Bloom (1979), Book IV. On the ambivalent construction of a modern concept of adolescence in the early Third Republic, see Kathleen Alaimo, "Shaping Adolescence in the Popular Milieu: Social Policy, Reformers, and French Youth, 1870–1920," *Journal of Family History* 17, no. 4 (1992); Agnès Thiercé, *Histoire de l'adolescence* (1999). And, in a broader context, John R. Gillis, *Youth and History: Tradition and Change in European Age Relations, 1770–Present* (1974), 95–131.

mortal if it is aggravated." As such, adolescence was fundamentally ambivalent, at once risky and full of potential. In this "crisis of growth," he
claimed, "nothing resembles more a wasting disease than the one that
makes a man a man."[28]

Buisson went on to draw a striking analogy between the crisis of puberty
and the growing pains of the new Republic. It, too, in his view "has grown
a bit hastily." Like the adolescent boy, the Republic itself was "formed but
still weak," and thus in need of "a hygienic regimen that will lend it blood,
flesh and muscles."[29] In this address, Buisson explained that while furnished
with a mature legislative skeleton, the Republic remained wanting in the
life-blood of an adult citizenry. In referring to an ambivalent efflorescence
of potency associated with adolescence, Buisson's metaphor is a strong one.
What should we make of the specter of impotence that appeared to haunt
the advent of virility? Puberty here is volatile, characterized by tendencies
toward excess and overflow, which constitute at once its powerful promise
of growth and its menacing danger. Buisson bound the fate of the Republic
to that of its youth, suggesting that a proper navigation of the Scylla and
Charybdis of "feverishness" and "invincible lassitude" was essential to the
health of both. His organicist vision linked the dangers of implicitly sexual
excess to political failure. The youthful male body was at once necessary in
order to fill out the malnourished republican skeleton, but also dangerous
to the extent that it remained undisciplined. He understood the training of
those vital drives, which might both spur growth and undercut it, as an explicitly political problem.

Ferdinand Buisson was an exemplary liberal Protestant advocate of the
Republic. He studied philosophy at the Sorbonne under Paul Janet and received his university diploma in 1866. In the same year, he obtained his first
academic post as a philosophy professor in Neuchâtel, Switzerland, where
he spent four years of voluntary exile in the last years of the Second Empire.
In Geneva, he encountered other like-minded republicans and liberal
Protestants, including Jules Barni, a student of Victor Cousin who translated Kant's oeuvre into French and authored an important text, *La morale
dans la démocratie*, in 1869. Like Barni, Buisson returned to France only
after the 1870 defeat. He soon assumed important government posts in the
arena of education, serving as the secretary of the Commission de statistique de l'enseignement primaire, Inspector-General, and eventually director of Primary Education for a period of seventeen years. During his tenure
as director from 1879 to 1896, he worked closely with Jules Ferry to develop and institute the new system of free, obligatory, and secular primary
education. He assumed the chair of pedagogy at the Sorbonne in 1896 and

28. Ferdinand Buisson, "Le devoir présent de la jeunesse," in *Morale sociale*, ed. Emile
Émile Boutroux (1899), 241–41.
29. Ibid., 241.

went on to participate in the foundation of the Ligue des droits de l'homme, to serve as representative in the National Assembly and, at the very end of his life, received the Nobel Peace Prize. During his initial period of government service, Buisson assumed editorship of and wrote numerous articles for the *Dictionnaire de pédagogie,* a document testifying to the close relationship between his liberal Protestantism and his commitment to republican educational principles.[30]

Buisson's brand of liberal Protestantism was an important inspiration for the Republic's moral pedagogy, which aimed both to reconcile reason and faith and to integrate the popular classes into the republican fold. His notion of *foi laïque,* or secular faith, provided a positive foundation for republican instruction. Buisson had been a student of the spiritualist historian of philosophy Paul Janet at the Sorbonne in the 1860s, and his theorization of a secular religiosity coincided well with the traditions of French moral education that had been established by thinkers such as Victor Cousin and Charles Renouvier.[31] A harsh critic of the Empire, he devoted himself to articulating a nonauthoritarian moral foundation for the new regime. Buisson's theory of education, and, in particular, his conception of "intuitive" instruction, exemplifies how republican pedagogy tried to explain how young subjects could accede to universal moral tenets on the basis of their own free will.

Buisson's account of the role of "intuition" in education remained a key reference for authors of moral education texts throughout the 1880s. Buisson drew on Victor Cousin's psychologized conception of "intuition," which served to revise Kant's moral categories. As a number of scholars have well noted, Cousin's eclecticism continued to influence theorists of moral education in France through the first decades of the Third Republic—that is, until subjective psychology was supplanted by solidarist theories of the "social" as the foundation of moral laws. Buisson participated in nineteenth-century French efforts to revise Kant's strict division between

30. For biographical information on Buisson, see Christophe Charle, *Dictionnaire biographique des universitaires aux 19ᵉ et 20ᵉ siècles: La Faculté des lettres de Paris,* vol. 1 (1985), 38–40. On Buisson as a founding theorist of *laïcité,* see Pierre Hayat, *La passion laïque de Ferdinand Buisson* (1999); Loeffel, *La question du fondement,* 23–83. See also Jean-Marie Mayeur, *La question laïque, 19ᵉ–20ᵉ siècle* (1997), 73–88; Philip Nord, *The Republican Moment: Struggles for Democracy in Nineteenth-century France* (1995), 91–113. On Barni, see Jules Barni, *La morale dans la démocratie suivi du Manuel républicain: Présentation de Pierre Macherey* (1992).

31. It is important that, while Paul Janet inscribed himself within the spiritualist lineage of Cousin, he was also responsible for initiating a serious study of Kant at the Sorbonne in the 1860s. This may account for the extent to which Buisson's thought is marked by elements of both eclecticism and neo-Kantianism. On Cousin and eclecticism, see Jan Goldstein, *The Post-Revolutionary Self: Politics and Psyche in France, 1750–1850* (2005); John I. Brooks, *The Eclectic Legacy: Academic Philosophy and the Human Sciences in Nineteenth-century France* (1998); William Logue, *From Philosophy to Sociology: The Evolution of French Liberalism, 1870–1914* (1983). For the impact of Janet's psychology, see Déloye, *École et citoyenneté,* 90–91. On Renouvier, see William Logue, *Charles Renouvier: Philosopher of Liberty* (1993).

pure and practical reason. Unlike Kant, for whom intuition (or sense-perception) pertained solely to the work of pure—and not practical—reason, Buisson highlighted its role in the development of moral faculties. While Kant banished empirical considerations from his account of moral autonomy, Buisson's evolutionary psychology conceived of virtue as an extension of subjective experience. In drawing up the official program in moral education in 1882, Buisson's teacher, Paul Janet, similarly appealed to the "intuitive method" and similarly took recourse to a psychologized understanding of moral development.[32]

"Intuition" as a universal foundation for human moral judgment served as the cornerstone of Buisson's theory of education. Like Kant, he assumed intuition—the mind's ability to perceive and order appearances in space and time—to be a priori. Buisson, however, appealed to this capacity in order to explain how morality originates inside the human subject. Because based on the senses, intuition was, for Buisson, a universal aptitude, which was accessible even to the popular classes. It hence played a central role in his effort to democratize instruction.[33] The article he consecrated to it in the *Dictionnaire de pédagogie* stated: "Since sensual intuition is the simplest, easiest form of intuition, it is this form that should most be put to use in elementary instruction." This appeal to the senses was based on class assumptions. "Inherent to the human spirit itself," wrote Buisson, "it constitutes an ultimately accessible and legitimate mode of affirmation which should thus serve as the very method of popular education."[34] Buisson's universalistic claims rested on this direct relation between intuition and the senses. Because founded on "intellectual activity in its instinctive state," this moral education would speak to pupils of all classes.

In a significant departure from Kant, Buisson suggested that moral faculties could be derived from this quasi-instinctual basis. For Kant, moral decision was not and could not be founded on empirical considerations; in his view, "freedom of choice is this independence from being determined by sensible impulses."[35] Kant saw humans as composite characters or "rational *natural* beings, who are unholy enough that pleasure can induce them to

32. P. Janet, "Nouveau programmes d'études dans les écoles normales primaires: Plan d'un cours de psychologie," *Revue pédagogique* 8, no. 7 (1881). In the Restoration and July Monarchy, Cousinian psychologism and spiritualism served conservative and elitist political interests by providing a critique of the more explicitly "materialist" psychology associated with a radical, republican left. See Goldstein, *The Post-Revolutionary Self*; Jan Goldstein, "Foucault and the Post-Revolutionary Self: The Uses of Cousinian Pedagogy in Nineteenth-century France," in *Foucault and the Writing of History*, ed. Jan Goldstein (1994). In the context of the Third Republic, it was precisely this "idealist" aspect that allowed pedagogues such as Buisson to articulate a positive content for the new program in moral and civic education. See Jean-Louis Fabiani, *Les philosophes de la république* (1988); Logue, *From Philosophy*, 81.
33. See, for example, the speech given at the 1878 World Exhibition in Paris: Ferdinand Buisson, *Conférence sur l'enseignement intuitif (31 août 1878)* (1897).
34. Buisson, ed., *Dictionnaire*, vol. 2, s.v. "Intuition," 1375.
35. Immanuel Kant, *The Metaphysics of Morals*, trans. Mary Gregor (1996), 13.

break the moral law"; they hence relied on the categorical imperative in order to properly govern themselves.[36] Inner freedom, for him, was contingent on the mastery of sensibly determined affects; it required "being one's own *master* in a given case, and *ruling* oneself, that is subduing one's affects and *governing* one's passions."[37] The rational component of the human made possible—indeed, it demanded—this administration of sensible affect. By contrast, for Buisson, self-mastery was born of the very natural and sensible drives, which were, in Kant's formulation, subjected to rational government.

At once intrinsic and nearly natural, intuition did a certain amount of ideological work for Buisson. Principally, it explained how and why education could be made accessible to all. It also guarded against the charge of republican tyranny by figuring moral learning as spontaneous rather than imposed from without. Formed in a liberal Protestant milieu, Buisson repudiated the artificial intermediaries and the mechanical methods of catechism that he associated with clerical instruction. By recourse to the spontaneous activity of intuition, liberal education encouraged rather than reviled nature.[38] As the *Dictionnaire de pédagogie*'s article "Discipline" explained, schooling should in no way resemble military training or that of animals. While authoritarian approaches "deform the child's nature" rather than "form character," the notice insisted, "the system of discipline which best fits the child teaches him to control himself."[39] The intuitive method aimed to encourage such self-government.

Buisson turned toward contemporary theories of evolutionary psychology in order to explain the complex process by which the young subject acceded to reasoned judgment. For example, he appealed to Théodule Ribot's work on sentiment and will in an account of "the education of the will," given as the conclusion to his course on the science of education at the Sorbonne in 1899.[40] While trained as a philosopher, Ribot became a great advocate of experimental psychology and went so far as to employ biological evidence to support his theories. In making use of Ribot, Buisson expressed interest in the role of biological forces in psychic evolution. In using the idiom of "force," however, Buisson's theory maintained a metaphysical aspect—an analysis frequently made of Ribot's work as well.[41]

36. Ibid., 145.
37. Ibid., 166.
38. Buisson, *Conférence*, 13–14.
39. Buisson, ed., *Dictionnaire*, vol. 1, s.v. "Discipline," 716.
40. Ferdinand Buisson, "Éducation de la volonté: Leçon de cloture du cours de pédagogie," *Revue pédagogique* 35, no. 10 (1899).
41. While Ribot insisted that his experimental psychology was to be sharply distinguished from spiritualist and neo-Kantian metaphysics, historians have shown that, precisely because Ribot had been trained as a philosopher and never actually practiced psychological experiments, his work was largely perceived to be in the domain of philosophy by fellow philosophers. See John I. Brooks, "Philosophy and Psychology at the Sorbonne, 1885–1913," *Journal of the History of the Behavioral Sciences* 29, no. 2 (1993); Brooks, *The Eclectic Legacy*, 67–

Delivered to a group of students preparing for careers in secondary or university education rather than primary schooling, this lecture placed more emphasis on will than intuition. Buisson's account nonetheless hinged on the developmental possibilities inherent in "sensibility" itself. The body's ability to learn how to rule its initially ungovernable reactions constituted the first, most humble step in the progressive evolution of the will. In contradistinction to Kant's strict division between reasonable will and natural passion, Buisson's self-governing *volonté* originated in the very sensibilities that it eventually learned to control. He imagined the living body to possess an originary "force" that fueled the will's own formation. In this developmental model, self-control derives from an initial set of unruly and inchoate organic reactions. Progressive stages of self-training repeat themselves in ever higher registers, engaging the subject in a movement of self-negation and dialectical self-overcoming; initial forces, through repetition, develop into their opposite by learning to master the primitive energies from which they originate. Repetition of muscular movements gives way to corporeal control, sensation to the mastering of sensation, sentiment to a mastering of sentiment, etc. Buisson thus described a stage in this process: "Just like motor activity, sensibility develops itself through repetition; it becomes able to sense things that it was previously incapable of feeling; to classify, grade, modify, attenuate or amplify, to group primitive sensations."[42] According to this liberal pedagogical model, the capacity for self-government emanated from the body's own potential energies:

> Who must will? The schoolmaster or the pupil? Both of them do. But the schoolmaster's will is entirely aimed at arousing that of the pupil. Here there are two possible methods: one fixes upon an immediate result which is only apparently satisfactory—it plies the pupil's will under the schoolmaster's authority; the other's goal is incomparably more difficult—plying the pupil's will under a self-respecting, self-given law. Herein lies the great difference between authoritarian and liberal education. Exterior action and interior action constitute two systems by which the child, and eventually men, may be governed.[43]

Proper instruction encouraged self-rule rather than imposing government from without—a principle, which gave way to a fundamentally political distinction between two modes of education. In other words, the question of

---

96; Dominique Merllié, "Les rapports entre la *Revue de métaphysique* et la *Revue philosophique*: Xavier Léon, Théodule Ribot, Lucien Lévy-Bruhl," *Revue de métaphysique et de morale*, no. 1–2 (1993). On Ribot's influence on the development of child psychology and theories of children's moral development, Katharine H. Norris, "Reinventing Childhood in Fin-de-siècle France: Child Psychology, Universal Education, and the Cultural Anxieties of Modernity" (Ph.D. diss., University of California, Berkeley, 2000).

42. Buisson, "Éducation de la volonté," 322.

43. Ibid., 329. See also Buisson, ed., *Dictionnaire*, vol. 1, s.v. "Discipline," 716. For a discussion of the violence of clerical school discipline and its republican critics, see Jean-Claude Caron, *À l'école de la violence* (1999).

how to instruct youth was for Buisson and his colleagues in the Ministry of Public Instruction, a problem of government *tout court*.

The child did not, however, arrive at this stage of self-government without outside influence; an exterior force was in play here, but a rather soft one. For, it was the child's mother who, in Buisson's narrative, best embodied this liberal mode of education in its first stages. Figuring the child as a burgeoning plant, Buisson suggested that the mother acts as an attentive "gardener," intervening in order to "trim, weed, and clean. How to go about this? Should one impose one's will, choice and orders? A well-informed mother would never think of it; instead, she adroitly solicits the child's nascent will."[44] She encourages the child to follow its natural course and to blossom on its own. "Wait. Allow this little barely visible shoot to grow up on its own: it is a nascent will; don't touch it, even to help it out of the ground; leave everything up to the sun, the rain, the cool nights, the nourishing soil, and the mysterious sap which makes it grow."[45] Buisson suggested an intimate relationship between proper mothering and the immanent self-government of the future citizen; naturally tender and caring, this republican mother guaranteed the nearly autonomous development of the child's own will.

At the same time, maternal affect was ambivalently sexualized; according to Buisson, the mother "seduces" the child into self-control, drawing out (his) natural capacity for self-government: "When does this phase of moral apprenticeship begin? No one can say, for it begins long before the child is even aware; the mother says: 'one must, one must not,' and makes him understand, miraculously! The not yet existent will, is already solicited, attracted, molded, and won over by thousands of seductions—through speech, play, examples, caresses and threats, love and fear, mechanical imitation and nervous excitement, without even speaking of the secret influence of heredity."[46] The mother's alluring education of the child's will was diametrically opposed to an authoritarian model implicitly associated with clerical education; instead of imposing rules from without, she seduced forth the child's will, encouraging (his) natural desire to be independent. The fate of the girl child in this dynamic, meanwhile, remained unclear. Was she, too, "seduced" by her mother and with what implications for the development of her will? Buisson's account leaves these questions unanswered.

In Buisson's narrative, the early moral education provided by mothers was indispensable to the proper development of the child's burgeoning will. Ferry's schooling legislation addressed this exigency by reforming early childhood education. A decree of 2 August 1881 brought nursery schools

44. Buisson, "Éducation de la volonté," 324.
45. Ibid., 328.
46. Ibid., 329.

under the purview of the Ministry of Public Instruction. Before this official pronouncement, *salles d'asile* had been state regulated, initially by a 5 March 1833 circular and later by a 22 March 1855 decree. They functioned, however, as local, charitable institutions frequently run by prominent women philanthropists and only loosely subject to state inspection. The reform established a uniform program for nursery schools, renaming them *écoles maternelles* and giving women the exclusive rights to work as teachers and *directrices*. While the *salles d'asile* had similarly employed women teachers, this invocation of *maternity* as central to the teaching process was new. As Jean-Noël Luc has analyzed, it delegitimated women religious and hence served an explicitly anticlerical function.[47] A 25 January 1882 circular starkly contrasted the new *écoles maternelles* with the old, stating, "the *école maternelle*, as we now conceive of it, no longer resembles the *salle d'asile* of old, the refuge where one was satisfied to keep children and to keep them mechanically occupied . . . it is a real house of education."[48] According to the Conseil supérieur d'instruction publique, the *école maternelle* provided a crucial transition between home and school, as the name itself indicated: "It should preserve the affective gentleness and indulgence of the family, and at the same time, initiate the child into the work and regularity of the school."[49] Of course, to the extent that the school "imitated" maternal practice, it both relied on a parental model for its legitimacy and also potentially undercut that model. Ministry of Public Instruction officials, such as inspector-general of nursery schools Pauline Kermogard, attempted to address just such fears. Would the development of the *école maternelle* in fact encourage mothers to become selfish and irresponsible, to hand over the care of their young to the state rather raise them themselves? Kermogard recommended that the nursery school be developed in moderation, that it be "proscribed everywhere where, unnecessary, it would encourage laziness among mothers and multiplied where it can be proven that a mother cannot take care of her child, and everywhere also, where the child might suffer from the immorality of the family."[50] Educa-

47. See Jean-Noël Luc, *L'invention du jeune enfant au 19ᵉ siècle: De la salle d'asile à l'école maternelle* (1997); Jean-Noël Luc, ed., *La petite enfance à l'école, 19ᵉ–20ᵉ siècles: Textes officiels présentés et annotés* (1982); Bonnie Smith, *Ladies of the Leisure Class: The Bourgeoisies of Northern France in the Nineteenth Century* (1981), 123–61. See also Buisson, ed., *Dictionnaire*, vol. 2, s.v. "Maternelles (écoles)," 1862–1877. On the perceived threat of women religious to both the family and the state, see Ford, *Divided Houses.*

48. In "Circulaire aux préfets relative à la création d'écoles publiques de tout ordre et d'emplois dans ces écoles, 25 janvier 1882," in *La petite enfance*, ed. Luc, 163. Contemporaries criticized the *salle d'asile* as a failure because it "annihilates the individuality, crushes the spontaneity and the activity of the child." In Marie Matrat, "Histoire de l'éducation enfantine publique," in *Les écoles maternelles*, ed. Marie Matrat et al. (1889), 29.

49. Ideally, the school would "imitate as much as possible the practices of an intelligent and devoted mother." Buisson, ed., *Dictionnaire*, vol. 2, s.v. "Maternelles (écoles)," 1873.

50. Pauline Kermogard, "Les écoles maternelles," in *Les écoles maternelles*, ed. Marie Matrat et al. (1889), 58. Jacques Donzelot figures such women as responsible for the emasculation of working-class fathers. He does less to analyze the way in which the feminization of "social

tional reformers, in other words, sought to allay fears that their moralizing programs contained seeds of social disruption and demoralization.

Buisson's invocation of the maternal role in childhood education reflected a more general current in republican pedagogy. In a speech delivering prizes to women normal school students in 1883, Buisson commented: "It is not impossible to create a real course of instruction destined to form, at the same time, future *institutrices* and future mothers. We make no distinction between one and the other, firmly believing that things will not be better than the day when there will be in every *institutrice* a mother, and in every mother an *institutrice*." As a result, girls' schooling would not be based on boys' instruction, for between them there was "a profound difference, not of degree, but of kind."[51] Vice-rector of the Academy of Paris and administrative president of the elite institution for training women secondary school teachers, Octave Gréard proclaimed in his famous work on the history of girl's education: "What is incontestable is that neither their destination, nor their natures are the same [as men's]. The goal of education is to perfect within the order of nature. We should fortify woman's reason, which is a common good, but without harming those gifts which are her own."[52] Her "sensibility" was precisely one of the gifts. And it had to be preserved, given its importance for the proper development the child's will. These arguments for the crucial social function of women's role as both wife and mother cut both ways. They were, of course, deployed in order to extend girls' education and hence the training of women teachers in the early 1880s, and thus made challenging careers open to women. But they also perpetuated assumptions about women's difference from and complementarity to men and institutionalized them in new ways.[53]

Pedagogues often insisted that a schoolmistress rather than a schoolmaster conduct the first years of schooling. Among them, the principal of the Lycée Montaigne asserted, "This individuality, still in its germlike state, needs to be cared for with the greatest solicitude in order that it may bloom at ease. With a man, it would risk opposition, as men have a tendency to affirm their force, a desire to mold the children in their own image, to recreate themselves. . . . While a woman, on the other hand, when in the presence of a young boy in whom she already sees a growing young man, feels

---

work" also affected women. See Jacques Donzelot, *The Policing of Families*, trans. Robert Hurley (1979), 45–46.

51. Ferdinand Buisson, "Distribution des prix aux cours normaux de la Société pour l'instruction élémentaire (28 juillet 1883, à la Sorbonne)," in *Conférences et causeries pédagogiques*, ed. Musée pédagogique (1888), 75, 79.

52. Octave Gréard, "De l'éducation des filles," *Revue pédagogique* 1, no. 6 (1882): 552.

53. Jo Burr Margadant, *Madame le professeur: Women Educators in the Third Republic* (1990), 24–36; Karen Offen, "The Second Sex and the Baccalauréat in Republican France, 1880–1924," *French Historical Studies* 13, no. 2 (1983). See also Linda Clark, *The Rise of Professional Women in France: Gender and Public Administration* (2000); Katrin Schultheiss, *Bodies and Souls: Politics and the Professionalization of Nursing in France, 1880–1922* (2001).

more disposed by her sentiment of respect, to allow the child's nature to develop without constraints and with a relative independence. As a result, she is better at clearing the way for this emerging personality, affirming it and guaranteeing its future development."[54] Using the same organicist rhetoric as Buisson, Principal Kortz suggested that women provided a fertile environment for the growth of the young boy's individuality. Like the author of the article on the father in the *Dictionnaire de pédagogie,* he was wary of men's tendency to deform the young male child's will. Kortz's representation of the teacher/student dyad intimated that because women were not endowed with men's forceful character, woman's sentiment freed up the potential self-governing man born into the child, affirming and assuring its eventual emergence. Unlike the schoolmaster, the mother did not pose a threat to the maturing will because she seemed to lack one of her own. Here, as elsewhere, the relationship between the mother and the girl-child is left in abeyance. Did mothers also encourage the efflorescence of girls' individuality? And with what implications for their presumptive future roles as mothers? The question is studiously avoided by theories of liberal education which relied upon such naturalized conceptions of motherhood in order to assure that young boys would become autonomous and will-bearing citizens. They focused, instead, on the eminently social and socializing role of this purportedly natural maternal function. Meanwhile the problem posed by "bad mothers," while seemingly disruptive of this naturalist assumption, justified efforts to regulate women's parental and maternal roles.[55]

In Buisson's account, the child's individuality, bathed in an affective maternal glow, blossoms unmarred by external constraints. In this formulation, the child's willingness to become independent partially relies upon a desire different in nature from the intellectual abstraction characteristic of rational consciousness. Unlike Kant, for whom will and reason were synonymous, Buisson insisted that the "will cannot be reduced to a superior desire which victoriously opposes itself to more base desires, a reasonable desire, which silences animal ones. We easily concede that the will cannot be reduced to a cold and dry operation of understanding." In essence, he claimed, "One does not desire in a vacuum; one desires because and to the extent that one loves."[56] The self-governing will was partly but not exclu-

54. M. Kortz, "Rôle de la femme dans ses classes," in *L'éducation morale dans l'université (École des hautes études sociales, 1900–1901),* ed. Alfred Croiset (1901), 87–88.

55. This attachment of women's social role to their maternal nature was a long-standing tenet of republican motherhood, which can be traced back to Rousseau. On Revolutionary republican motherhood, see Lynn Hunt, "Male Virtue and Republican Motherhood," in *The French Revolution and the Creation of Modern Political Culture,* ed. Keith Michael Baker (1994). On "bad mothers," see Joshua Cole, *The Power of Large Numbers: Population, Politics, and Gender in Nineteenth-century France* (2000), chap. 6; Schafer, *Children in Moral Danger;* Sylvia Schafer, "Between Paternal Right and the Dangerous Mother: Reading Parental Responsibility in 19th-century French Civil Justice," *Journal of Family History* 23, no. 2 (1998).

56. Buisson, "Éducation de la volonté," 336.

sively comprised of the "cold and dry" operations of reason. It was always also supplemented by a different desire—a sort of "love" which acts as a motive force and affective ground for the more rational kind of willing.

This dynamic sheds light on Buisson's discussion of the simultaneous promise and peril of adolescence, when the equilibrium between reason and base or animal desires is even more fragile than in the young child. Buisson viewed the will as composite, as at once fueled by passion and as the very negation of passion. "Psychology reveals that the will has two aspects; it acts either as an impulsive or as an inhibitive force. These two functions, one stimulating, the other repressive, would appear to be opposed; one appears as a rush of desire and spirited by passion; the other as a knowledge-able veto and reasoned resistance to our initial whims, the result of choice, comparison and calculation."[57] A strange synthesis of two agonistic forces, Buisson's will was in constant motion, pushing forward and pulling back on itself. The very spiritedness that provided the will's impetus also subjected it to a constant threat of losing control. This persistent menace kept it in motion. Because the will relied as much on desire and passion as on reasoned resistance and rational calculation, a principle of excess was inscribed within the heart of the rule-bound subject. On one level, Buisson exposed a logic implicit in the Kantian model of the subject—namely, that the very possibility of willing was constituted by the ability of the subject, and in particular of the masculine subject, to control his natural passions through the use of his reason.[58] And yet, Buisson's model was slightly different. Desire and passion were not simply negated or excluded (and through this negation, constitutive of the subject's ability to will); their affirmative, excessive force supplemented and gave positive form to the very will responsible for carrying out the negation.[59]

The problem that then emerged for Buisson was how to distinguish good, productive impulses from dissolute, bad ones. Pedagogy played an important role here in "arousing vibrant forces, blowing up courage and initiative, provoking a healthy and happy excitement in the organism which will translate into prompt, hardy, lively actions, perhaps even temerity—but of the kind that almost always succeeds in youth."[60] It encouraged the vital, organic potential of the future man so gently respected in his early years by the mother. But was it possible to stimulate the good virile excess that lent itself to "temerity" without also soliciting less socially desirable, and implicitly "feminine" or devirilizing traits? This very difficulty made adoles-

---

57. Ibid.

58. For a discussion of this dynamic in Kant, see Isabel V. Hull, *Sexuality, State, and Civil Society in Germany, 1700–1815* (1996), 247–48.

59. What Buisson describes is hence closer to a model of sublimation than one of outright repression. On "sublimation" and the self-governing subject as theorized by Freud, see Judith Butler, *The Psychic Life of Power* (1997); Suzanne R. Stewart, *Sublime Surrender: Male Masochism at the Fin-de-siècle* (1998).

60. Buisson, "Éducation de la volonté," 336–37.

cence, with all of its burgeoning drives, a moment of both great hope and danger. The natural, vital aspects of the future citizen so desperately needed to fill out the Republic's lanky skeleton, could also menace that ordered structure. While encouraging the efflorescence of potency, education had to discipline these drives in order to ensure the emergence of the proper type of subject; not all natural instincts were to be encouraged. As Buisson explained, "We should not forget that next to those instincts that we call good, there develop in youths, equally strong ones that we might call bad: while they are, like nature, in reality, neither good nor bad, they nonetheless exist and struggle with one another. It is thus our goal to intervene in order to defend the weak ones against the strong, the elite against the masses, those more delicate and complex penchants, those which are truly human, against the blind and gross appetites of pure animality."[61] Buisson employed a language of class and civilization in order to describe this hierarchy of instincts. The social and civilizing mission of republican education (i.e., moralizing "the masses" and civilizing "savagery") was here enacted within the subject himself.[62] In the case of the adolescent, schooling channeled the passionate desires that arose in puberty toward productive social ends. Buisson assumed that this disorderly potential—one that he associated metaphorically with the very "masses" that he endeavored to moralize—existed at the heart of the subject. Only external intervention could prevent the higher, more delicate drives from being drowned out by a crowd of gross appetites. The school played its essential role here. Once the mother has helped the child's natural will to emerge, the initial stage gave way; she was succeeded by the *instituteur*.

The child could now confront the differently constituted authority of the *instituteur* without risking deformation. According to Buisson, "With growth, and the natural development of the intelligence, education can begin to appeal directly to willful effort. The schoolmaster, who has replaced the mother, represents an authority which imperiously demands rather than pleading, surprising or persuading."[63] Buisson's vision of pedagogical evolution assumed a gendered division between a masculine force of "imperious" authority and a more feminine force of "pleading" and "persuasion."[64] The masculine authority of the schoolteacher offered a corrective to the potential excesses of the mother's instruction, which, as we have

61. Ibid., 328.

62. For an account of a similar dynamic in the thought of republican moralist Charles Renouvier, see Alice Bullard, *Exile in Paradise: Savagery and Civilization in Paris and the South Pacific, 1790–1900* (2000).

63. Buisson, "Éducation de la volonté," 329.

64. On the feminine connotations of "persuasion," see Joan W. Scott, *Only Paradoxes to Offer: Feminism and the "Rights of Man" in France, 1789–1940* (1996), 108. On the normative assumption of this renunciation and its potential failure, see Paul Seeley, "O Sainte Mère: Liberalism and the Socialization of Catholic Men in Nineteenth-century France," *Journal of Modern History* 70, no. 4 (1998).

seen, was implicitly sexualized and potentially unruly. While a mother's natural capacities played a crucial role in the initial growth of the child, she—and by extension the "family"—was disqualified from carrying out the higher stages of moral education.

The successful schooling of children depended, in the view of prominent pedagogical reformers such as Ferry and Buisson, on a productive partnership between mothers and the state. The family's role in schooling was, however, confined to the affective and sentimental environment provided by the mother. Once the child developed sufficient independence, he was ready to encounter the forceful will of the *instituteur*. As mothers did not have the same civil or political rights as fathers, this account smoothed over some of the difficulties provoked by discussions of the father's right to educate his children.[65] This seamless story of pedagogical evolution relied on a mother whose lack of autonomy and tendency toward sentimental excess made her eventual substitution by the *instituteur* eminently less problematic than that of a rights-bearing father.

Buisson's appeal to the role of sensibility and instinct in children's schooling served a number of related ideological functions. It helped him to promulgate a "liberal" pedagogical model that was strongly opposed to the authoritarian and mechanical procedures of clerical schooling. The recourse to sensible intuition rather than abstract reason alone explained how this education would reach the popular classes who were its primary target. By assigning mothers—and metonymically the family—a central and yet circumscribed place in children's moral development, Buisson sidestepped the problem posed by paternal authority, while also granting women a role in the secular mission of the state. This model's coherence relied both on the figuration of mothers as fonts of an always ambivalent sentiment and seduction and on an obfuscation of the pedagogical relationship between mothers and their daughters. Meanwhile, the dynamic between the mother and the teacher constructed the relationship between the family and the state as one of collaboration between feminine and masculine principles, rather than as a conflictual struggle between male wills (as a partnership between fully developed male wills appeared to be unimaginable). This gendered compact similarly structured the child's own development. In cultivating the child's immanent and natural drives, the mother assured that moral development would occur as a spontaneous process. The emergence of a truly republican will relied on a passage through an initial ambivalent instinctual and affective phase, whose youthful vigor and temerity were contiguous with "gross" and "animal" tendencies. The capacity to desire

---

65. On the extent to which the regulation of women presented fewer contradictions to republicans precisely because they were not citizens with rights to protect, see Rachel Fuchs, "France in Comparative Perspective," in *Gender and the Politics of Social Reform in France, 1870–1914,* ed. Elinor A. Accampo et al. (1995).

helped to found but always also threatened to thwart the eventual development of a proper republican citizen.[66] At once promise and peril, these forces of nature inherent in the child continued to pose a menace through adolescence—where vitality, as we have seen in Buisson's plea to youth, emboldened and endangered the health of the Republican body. Their cultivation and encouragement also called for a "liberal" form of discipline.

66. On the wider political resonance of anxieties surrounding women and crowds, especially in relation to the Paris Commune, see Susanna Barrows, *Distorting Mirrors: Visions of the Crowd in Late-Nineteenth-century France* (1981); Gay Gullickson, *Unruly Women: Images of the Commune* (1996). And, during the Dreyfus Affair, Christopher E. Forth, *The Dreyfus Affair and the Crisis of French Manhood* (2004).

2 *Liberal Discipline*

Republican reformers allotted affect and sensibility an important role in their liberal pedagogy. Feelings that they variously described as "sentiment," "desire," and "love" were, in their view, essential to children's ethical apprenticeship. These affective tendencies accounted for how an implicitly male child developed a capacity to will, and in turn, to willingly embrace moral laws. This recourse to sentiment, however, installed a risky principle at the heart of the very subject that educational reformers sought to cultivate. Because affect was prone to excess and deviation, this model of men's moral subjectivity contained within itself an instability that required ongoing oversight and administration.

Contemporary accounts of the "crisis" of adolescence both articulated this perpetual risk of deviance and explained how a liberal, as opposed to authoritarian pedagogical strategy, might best manage it. In their efforts to delegitimate conservative and clerical opponents, school reformers suggested that force and tyranny exacerbated male subjects' potential vices, vices that they frequently articulated in implicitly sexual terms. The logic of their arguments hinged on a representation of the boundary between the normal and the abnormal, regular and irregular sexuality, as fragile and volatile, rather than as firm or fixed. This chapter explores how pedagogues' notion of liberal discipline aimed to recuperate otherwise ambivalent affects toward practical moral ends. Their educational ethics, I contend, were based on a logic of conjugality, a complementary pairing between reason and sentiment ideally embodied in married love. As a framework for disciplining young men, this logic simultaneously relied on the presumption that women were men's "auxiliary and companion." This moral psychology, in turn, neatly intersected with a philosophy of government.

By conceiving of puberty as a sentimental crisis common to all young men, educational reformers sought to generalize their moral pedagogy. This "universalist" notion of adolescence is pronounced in the work of philosopher and educator Henri Marion, the first holder of a prestigious post in the Sciences of Education at the Sorbonne. His moral philosophy, I argue here, exemplified the nexus between a normative model of the masculine subject, conjugality, and republican theories of government. These ideas about adolescence as a "universal" regulatory crisis and the moral value of conjugality informed republican efforts to extend schooling to native Arab and Kabyle populations in Algeria. This universalistic model of morality, I suggest, did not simply underwrite the "civilizing mission," but was actually legitimated in and produced by it.

Perverse Potentials

Similar to Ferdinand Buisson, the neo-Kantian philosopher and republican pedagogue Henri Marion drew an intimate association between adolescence and political crisis. Marion described puberty as "a great disturbance, a sudden evolution, which is at times so feverish that it resembles a revolution." His analogy rendered explicit a number of Buisson's less overt assumptions about the relationship between nascent sexual desires and the child's transition to adulthood. With "the appearance of a new function, destined to perpetuate the species," Marion indicated, "our mental powers, like our organic energies, are modified in their equilibrium and are now oriented toward different needs." Marion likewise viewed puberty as a simultaneous promise and threat for male youth. "How could it not be important for morality whether or not this crisis ends well?" he wondered. Adolescence epitomized and exacerbated the equivocal moral tendencies that he identified at the heart of all subjects. Indeed, Marion remarked, "there is no other time in life when moral growth is more active; and no other when deviations are so dangerous, when the least incidents can have great implications."[1]

Marion's optimistic discussions of republican moral progress were structured by the perpetual menace of a dangerous reversal. This perverse potential lurking inside all future citizens legitimated the republican moral project by underscoring how the proper administration of passions was central to social order. Adolescence articulated in important ways the political stakes of republican moral education.

For Marion, adolescence was the crucible of morality, the moment when either good moral habits or bad dissolute ones established their foothold in the subject. In his view, a deviant possibility haunted all youth. "The spirit gets used to what is frequently presented before it; it trains itself little by little with those thoughts that at first shocked it." As a result, Marion

1. Henri Marion, *De la solidarité morale: Essai de psychologie appliquée*, 2nd ed. (1883), 151–52.

claimed, "This is how we find, in an unhealthy entourage or in bad reading, on the one hand, maxims which justify the worst that passion suggests to us and, on the other, the excitation of our latent passions." For Marion, who notably speaks here in the first person plural, this risk of a latent, unspecified perversion ("the worst") at the hands of bad books and friends was universal. Healthy moral apprenticeship, meanwhile, relied on an identical psychic mechanism, which simply worked in reverse. Edification and perversion were flip sides of the same coin. "In these cases," he suggested, "the ideas, images, and maxims imprinted upon the spirit, instead of coming to excuse and then excite the worst irregularities of sensibility, rather awaken their opposite and fortify the heart's generous sentiments. In a word, the good instincts (of which no man is entirely stripped) find aid in the spirit's good habits, just as base instincts find accomplices in its bad ones."[2] Importantly, then, rather than imagining deviance to be the result of individual pathology, he invoked this fragile coming of age as a universal experience, whose sheer generality legitimated the republican political and moral project. Abnormal sexuality thus appears in Marion's account as a pedagogical and hence social, rather than a uniquely individual problem.

Like Buisson, Marion played a foremost role in establishing the institutional and philosophical foundations of republican education. Trained at the École normale supérieure in the 1860s, he became a philosophy professor at lycées in Pau, Bordeaux, and eventually at Henri IV in Paris. In 1880, he was elected to serve on the Conseil supérieure de l'instruction publique as the representative of philosophy professors. And, as contributor to Buisson's *Dictionnaire de pédagogie,* he was responsible for the article "Psychology." In 1882, Jules Ferry asked him to create a course of psychological and moral instruction at the new École normale supérieure at Fontenay, the elite training institution for women normal school instructors. He was called away in 1883 to a post, specially created for him, in the Science of Education at the Sorbonne. Becoming titular in 1887, he served until his death in 1896, at which time Buisson, and eventually Émile Durkheim, in 1902, replaced him.[3]

Active in the foundation of these new pedagogical institutions and courses of instruction, Marion defended the state's right to play a part in the moral and civic education of its citizens, at both the primary and secondary schooling levels. He thus asserted in his conclusion to *De la solidarité morale,* his doctoral dissertation published in 1880, that national education "figures among the chief interests of the community, and hence one of the

2. Ibid., 127–28.
3. Christophe Charle, *Dictionnaire biographique des universitaires aux 19ᵉ et 20ᵉ siècles: La Faculté des lettres de Paris,* vol. 1 (1985), s.v. "Marion (François, Henri, Marie)," 131–32. See also Ferdinand Buisson, "Leçon d'ouverture du cours de science de l'éducation, faite à la Sorbonne le 3 décembre 1896," *Revue pédagogique* 29, no. 12 (1896); Félix Pécaut, "Henri Marion à Fontenay-aux-Roses," *Revue pédagogique* 28, no. 5 (1896).

legitimate attributions of the State." As "supreme regulator and dispenser of instruction," the state possessed a "powerful means by which to act upon public morality."[4] As a committed proponent of a liberal model of education, however, Marion insisted that external constraint be kept to a minimum. Like Buisson, he drew a close association between political and moral repression and the production of vice. And he, too, explained the difference between liberalism and authoritarianism in psychological terms. Authoritarian regimes, he wrote, "delude themselves if they believe that it is possible to improve [their subjects] by always holding them back; instead, they should give them as much of a sense of dignity and duty as possible; and then, allow them to govern themselves as much as possible. Continual repression, violent and defiant power, which is exercised through spying and threats shows contempt for people and only profits those in charge. It can only engender great vice."[5] Marion echoed Enlightenment-style critiques of tyranny as perverse and perverting. His analogous discussion of the dangers of *sexual* repression illustrates well how his account of authoritarianism drew on a moral psychology.

Marion did not explicitly theorize the relationship between political and sexual repression. His description of the disturbances caused by the suppression of sexual appetites nonetheless resonated with his wider critique of "absolutism." We have already seen how he associated the fiery passions of adolescence, linked to the "new function, destined to perpetuate the species," with revolutionary ferment. In his view, the excessive "repression" of the appetites which "preside over" these functions was a form of "violence" against nature. He used a politically charged rhetoric in order to describe the probable reaction to such repression. Nature, he claimed, "would energetically reclaim its rights and foment fearsome rebellions." Unable to achieve their proper end, the needs associated with the sexual organs persist, albeit in a "denatured" and "disorderly" form. The order produced by repressing this function is thus deceptive, leading to a confusion and disequilibrium that seethes beneath the surface. The danger was all the greater as control could never be absolute. For, he explained, "Once a tendency has known its end, obstacles can only exasperate it. This is what makes an unintelligent repression of natural inclinations, once they have awakened, so dangerous. In themselves legitimate, these inclinations can, in receiving a moderate satisfaction, become regulated and remain innocent: they take the irregular and torrential course of passion when they must find their exit, between those obstacles, insufficient to contain them, and which serve only to triple their force."[6] "Irregular" passion here results from the mismanagement of what is presumed to be a natural sexual inclination. The ambiva-

4. Marion, *De la solidarité morale*, 343–44.
5. Ibid., 255–56.
6. Ibid., 131–32.

lent potential of adolescent sexuality thus staged a general problem surrounding the moral government of all male youth.

Marion's theory of political power and his theory of sexuality converged in his discussion of adolescence. Nowhere is this connection more clear than in Marion's chapter devoted to "imitation and moral contagion," where he appeals to psychology in order to explain the moral promise and danger associated with the "moral solidarity" of individuals living together in close-knit communities. For Marion, this contagion was, like adolescence itself, ambivalent; it was at work in "the influence of good movements of the soul and, in the same way, the bad seductions and stains acquired through contact with vice, in any dense milieu in which they arise."[7] In order to illustrate this "moral contagion," Marion described the proliferation of perversity, and of same-sex vice in particular, in secondary school dormitories or *internats*.

Marion's account of moral contagion makes clear how contemporary theories of adolescence were closely linked to concerns over sexual deviance. Thus, as the criminal anthropologist, Dr. Alexandre Lacassagne, suggested in his often-cited encyclopedia article "*pédérastie*," the "modifications of humor and excitations of puberty" were notable causes of same-sex vice. Dr. Maurice Legrain similarly urged that it was "at puberty" that individuals found "their definitive psychic sexual formula." He hence signaled the "important role of education, especially for the sexually undecided, and, it must be said, the responsibility of the social state in the production of certain sexual monstrosities."[8] And, while turn-of-the-century sexologists hotly debated the relationship between "perversion" and "perversity," between the relative significance of "congenital" and "accidental" sexual deviance, for pedagogues like Marion, the risk of the occasional fall into vice, at the hands of "an unhealthy entourage and bad reading," was clearly designated as a primary object of concern. The generalized threat that it appeared to pose spoke to wider educational, moral, and social concerns. Marion was interested not in the degeneration and congenital aberration of sexual instincts, but in their social mismanagement. His understanding of adolescent sexuality at once presumed and confirmed the fragility of the boundary between the normal and the abnormal. This fragility, as Robert Nye has similarly noted, did not, however, imply greater tolerance toward sexual aberration. It, instead, drove the logic of regulation.[9]

7. Ibid., 187.

8. Alexandre Lacassagne, *Dictionnaire encyclopédique des sciences médicales,* ed. Raige-Delorme et al., vol. 22 (1865–1889), s.v. "Pédérastie," 239–59. Dr. Maurice Legrain, *Des anomalies de l'instinct sexuel et en particulier des inversions du sens génital* (1896), 45. See also Florence Tamagne, "Adolescence et homosexualité: Pratiques, discours et représentations (1850–1945)," *Adolescence* 19, no. 1 (2001); Agnès Thiercé, *Histoire de l'adolescence* (1999), 85–91.

9. For a contemporary discussion of both "congenital" and "accidental" perversion, and of sexual inversion, in particular: Dr. Laupts, *Perversion et perversité sexuelles* (1896). On

Like those of his contemporaries, Marion's argument drew on a notorious report, made by Henri Saint-Claire Deville to the Académie des sciences morales in July 1871 titled "L'internat et son influence sur l'éducation et l'instruction de la jeunesse."[10] Marion followed Saint-Claire Deville's account of the perverse effects of isolating young boys together in harsh and lifeless institutions, far away from contact with their families—and, most important, from members of the opposite sex. The unfortunate result of this segregation was sexual disorder and indiscipline as "the sexual instincts, in these conditions, become fatally exalted and unruly, despite all surveillance." In other words, the boys "naturally" sought to satisfy their exaggerated sexual instincts with one another. The only corrective to this euphemistically named "most shameful vice" lay in the domestic foyer, in "the sweet and regulated liberty of family life, which is the best form of discipline."[11] Reformers such as Marion thus charged the Napoleonic lycées' military-style disciplinary regime with producing subjects that were either servile or insubordinate, and in any case, incapable of self-administration and hence proper manhood and citizenship. Associated with unruliness and devirilized excess, the homosexual deviance bred by the harsh discipline of the *internat* was a symptom and symbol of authoritarian mismanagement. It provided a countermodel to the emancipated, heterosexual masculinity that would emerge out of the liberal model of education advocated by such reformers as Marion.

Marion's privileging of a "liberal" as opposed to "authoritarian" discipline played an instrumental role in reforms undertaken in the late 1880s to correct the excesses of the existing administrative and educational structure of lycées.[12] The reforms were wide-ranging, addressing academic course load, "hygiene" (including a reorganization of sleeping conditions in dormitories), the introduction of "physical education," and a new system of punishments and recompenses, all in the interest of promoting the kind of "liberal discipline" advocated by Marion. In a letter addressed to secondary

---

"Laupts," the pseudonym of Georges St. Paul, see Vernon A. Rosario, *The Erotic Imagination: French Histories of Perversity* (1997), 88–98. On sexual aberration and the stigmatization of male homosexuality, see Robert A. Nye, *Masculinity and Male Codes of Honor in Modern France* (1993), 98–126. On the coexistence and instability of "universalist" and "minoritizing" accounts of homosexuality, see Eve Sedgwick, *Epistemology of the Closet* (1990), 46–48. On degeneracy theory in fin-de-siècle France, see Robert A. Nye, *Crime, Madness, and Politics in Modern France: The Medical Concept of National Decline* (1984); Daniel Pick, *Faces of Degeneration: A European Disease, c. 1848– c. 1918* (1989).

10. Henri Saint-Claire Deville, "L'internat et son influence sur l'éducation et l'instruction de la jeunesse," *Revue scientifique de la France et de l'étranger* 1 (2e série), no. 10 (1871). Lacassagne and Laupts similarly cite this article.

11. Marion, *De la solidarité morale*, 201–2.

12. See, for example, Octave Gréard, *L'esprit de discipline dans l'éducation—Mémoire présentée au Conseil académique dans la séance du 26 juin 1883* (1883); Henri Marion, "Règles fondamentales de l'enseignement libéral: La méthode active," *Revue pédagogique* 12, no. 1 (1888); Henri Marion, *L'éducation dans l'université* (1892). I discuss these reforms at greater length in chapter 3.

school teachers and administrators announcing the recent spate of reforms, Leon Bourgeois, Minister of Public Instruction, condemned the dangerous effects of "purely repressive discipline," which, he claimed "no longer has *droit de cité* in our houses of education." Such discipline, he claimed, "relies on defiance, only uses constraint and is satisfied by an apparent order and external submissiveness, beneath which compressed bad instincts hide, without being corrected, only to burst forth later." For Bourgeois and other members of the Conseil supérieur de l'instruction publique, liberal discipline "seeks, by contrast, to improve the child rather than to contain him, to win him over rather than submit him. It seeks to touch the core, the conscience, and to obtain not a surface tranquility which will not last, but an inner order . . . it seeks to teach him to govern himself."[13] For these reformers, "moral education" was the primary means by which, this "inner order" and autonomy would be obtained.

As Yves Déloye has argued, models of self-government played an essential role in the republican conception of citizenship, and likewise in the pedagogical theory that sought to inculcate this ideal. Primers thus extolled "moderation" and castigated excess in all its forms, such as violence, drunkenness, and debauchery. The subject's ability to achieve moral independence was, as Déloye remarks, a "fundamentally political" question.[14] The crisis of puberty embodied the problem of self-moderation. And, as a crucible of self-government, adolescence received increasing attention from republican social scientists, pedagogues, and psychologists from the 1880s onward.[15]

In Marion's view, the revolution instantiated by puberty inspired "lively sentiments" of an ambivalent sort. Specifically, the noblest aims carried the threat of a precipitous fall, or as he wrote, "the different forms of love are of unequal value. High aspirations can become fatally bound up with gross and exigent appetites." Marion expressed particular concern about the devirilizing potential of debauchery, the debasement of subjects who become enslaved to these implicitly sexual passions which, "in debilitating and depressing the organism . . . enervate courage, stir up the spirit, and render one insensitive to higher pleasures." Marion nonetheless warned against outright repression and its concomitant risk of perversion. "Repressed or counteracted in its élan, deviated from its course," he claimed, "this flow of

13. Ministère de l'instruction publique, "Enseignement secondaire: Instructions et règlements," *Bulletin administratif du ministère de l'instruction publique*, no. 922 (supplément) (1890): 424.
14. Yves Déloye, *École et citoyenneté: L'individualisme républicain de Jules Ferry à Vichy; Controverses* (1994), 88–94.
15. See Kathleen Alaimo, "Shaping Adolescence in the Popular Milieu: Social Policy, Reformers, and French Youth, 1870–1920," *Journal of Family History* 17, no. 4 (1992); Kathleen Alaimo, "Adolescence, Gender and Class in Educational Reform in France: The Development of *Enseignement Primaire Supérieur*, 1880–1910," *French Historical Studies* 18, no. 4 (1994); Agnès Thiercé, *Histoire de l'adolescence* (1999).

tenderness might become corrupted." The passage into adulthood was tricky, sown with hazards as "the worst and best come in pairs, so close to one another, that a minor event can lead us from one to the other."[16] However, as the moment when sentiment explodes, puberty also provided, in his view, an unparalleled opportunity for schooling self-discipline. Marion suggested that the subject's intelligent will was spurred into action by the "inner fire" of the imagination: "It is heated up and expands; this is a moment of decisive growth for the intelligence as well." While "the irredeemable perversions in judgment are never to be more feared," he urged that "the spirit's excitement, the true and just will, never have the same opportunity to develop." In sum, he proclaimed, "It is a singular occasion for the will to affirm itself and to feel finally adult."[17] Called to duty by an ever-present threat of self-loss, the nascent will affirmed itself in learning to control the ambivalent sentiments heating up the inner self. The capacity for self-government that ideally emerged in adolescence at once issued from and negated the powerful emotions that appeared in the wake of puberty. The dynamic to which Marion alludes resembles that sketched by Buisson in his discussion of the push and pull of the will's impulsive and inhibitive forces. Because intelligence operates "under the influence" of inner turmoil, it derives its force from the very fire it endeavors to extinguish. This deviant potential obliges the adolescent to put his house in order.[18]

Marion's notion of virtue was founded on a vision of the young subject as capable of self-control. Clearly reflecting the neo-Kantianism in which he was schooled, Marion's idea of the ethical subject presupposed a universal and a priori capacity for reasoned judgment. He argued against a materialist determinism that would entirely deprive man of this capacity.[19] In principle, Marion excluded affect from ethics; like Kant, he was suspicious of love as a motivation for moral action. He wrote, for example, "Love in itself is capable of at once the most and least moral behavior. In either case, it disposes the individual to self-forgetting and self-sacrifice. This cannot but be dangerous. For morality relies on self-possession in order to behave according to the law; it would thus appear to exclude the self-loss [*aliénation de la personnalité*] in which it gives itself over to the mercy of others, renouncing self-direction."[20] Love's capacity for the extremes of self-sacrifice contained within it an essential threat, namely, a total abdication of self-control. Self-government was, in other words, impossible if there was no self in place to govern.

16. Marion, *De la solidarité morale*, 152–53.
17. Ibid., 153–54.
18. On imagination and self-regulation in republican political thought, see Jan Goldstein, *The Post-Revolutionary Self: Politics and Psyche in France, 1750–1850* (2005), 60–63; Joan W. Scott, "The Uses of Imagination: Olympe de Gouges in the French Revolution," in *Only Paradoxes to Offer: Feminism and the "Rights of Man" in France, 1789–1940* (1996), 19–56.
19. Marion, *De la solidarité morale*, 29.
20. Ibid., 173.

The Promise and Danger of Love

The complementary logic of conjugality was one important way in which the ethical potential of affect could be organized and regulated. The pairing of affect and reason in the productive partnership of men and women in marriage mobilized and controlled morally valuable sentiment. By integrating affect into ethics, conjugality both avoided the perverse risks of authoritarianism and held the potential misjudgments of "love" in check. This model of heterosexuality, in other words, exemplified the sort of "liberal" discipline embraced by Marion. Indeed, it offered an account of how sentiment was an essential component of practical morality. At the same time, because "love" was ambivalent, and hence capable of both good and bad, it required ongoing oversight and regulation.

Marion associated the ethical vagaries of love not only with adolescents, but also with women. In contrast to the adolescent boys in whom the threat of excess ideally provoked the emergence of a stolid will, women, for him, embodied the dangers of a pure sentiment unchecked by reasonable moderation. They were, in his view, capable of both the "most and least moral behavior." Marion was, in fact, considered to be an expert on girls' education, as he had taught the very first courses in psychology and morals at the new elite normal school for women at Fontenay.[21] He drew on this experience when composing his lecture series on girls' education delivered at the Sorbonne. In those lectures, Marion claimed that in woman "it is the faculty of the heart that dominates." At once equal and yet different, men and women complemented one another. He thus claimed that "women's proper role is to perfect and soften life—private life above all, but by way of that, at least indirectly, public life as well."[22] Marion suggested that women's virtue was largely founded on heart-felt instincts and habits rather than on the reasoned principles which informed the moral action of men. Women epitomized the unreliable and immoderate character of love. "I admit," he wrote, "that woman is an instinctual being; this is at once her strength and weakness. Love and devotion are, in the same way, her triumph; but love does not constitute in itself a rule, nor can it find such a rule within itself. For love, because excessive in its zeal, is naturally agitated, violent, indiscreet, jealous and unjust. It can only be moral if it remains just." In a surprising and arguably progressive gesture, he used this very claim, *not* to disqualify

21. Pécaut, "Henri Marion."

22. Henri Marion, *L'éducation des jeunes filles* (1902), 3–4. These lectures were published posthumously. While Marion here recalls Rousseau in, for example, his "Letter to the Republic of Geneva," he nonetheless criticized Rousseau's Sophie. He argued that woman should be educated, not exclusively for *men's* happiness, but rather with a view toward the ideals that exceed the well-being of the couple, namely, the family, the nation, and humanity (5). See also Jean Baubérot, *Laïcité 1905–2005: Entre passion et raison* (2004), 199–201.

women from education but to explain why they needed to read more philosophy! Even if it was not their dominant trait, women were clearly capable of reason. Indeed, concluded Marion, girls had an even greater need than boys to be trained in the icy-hard discipline of the categorical imperative: "It must be presented in its cold majesty to boys and girls alike, but even more so to girls, so that they may learn how to orient their hearts in this sense; to find their greatest joy in the very justice of which they are declared incapable, or better in love, which is their law, but a love founded upon justice." He urged, in a version of the argument that he made in 1881 before the Conseil supérieur de l'instruction publique, that women "need to know that they should not, in either action or moral judgment, follow their nerves and impressions alone, nor even the unreflective impulses of their hearts."[23] Marion appealed to a gendered complementarity between reason and sentiment in order to defend a philosophically grounded moral education for girls. These gendered presuppositions also informed his theory of ethical action, as outlined in his moral education textbook, first published in 1882 and regularly re-edited for decades to come.

According to this textbook, an a priori universal capacity to reason rendered all subjects capable of self-government, of heeding, that is, the dictates of the categorical imperative. Marion explained how moral compliance, while based on a command, was also free and willing. The subject's relationship to self-given law was, in his view, dual, based in part on obligation and in part on desire or sympathy. This ambivalent law was at once "imperious" and "attractive," as, he suggested, "the two things are not at all contradictory." While "the moral law appears more as a commandment when one departs from it," he claimed that "when one does something in accordance with the law, . . . its attractive and lovable character appears." In such cases, "one is thus lifted and drawn toward it by a natural movement; it speaks to us with an engaging voice, which truly seduces the heart and will."[24] Marion's description of the "attractive" side of the law recalls Buisson's account of the maternal presence in the evolution of the child's moral education; the "hardly visible ideal" is attractive, seductive, and even lovable. This imagined role of affect seems to be at odds with a vision of the law as dictated by imperious rules. Indeed, the suggestion that the subject is

23. Marion, *L'éducation des jeunes filles*, 122–23. Janet and Marion both recommended that girls be taught the categorical imperative, Jules Simon claimed that such philosophical training would "create quibbling, debating, ungovernable women." See also Henri Marion, "L'enseignement moral dans l'école primaire et dans les écoles normales," *Revue pédagogique* 1, no. 1 (1882): 20–21. And Françoise Mayeur, *L'enseignement secondaire des jeunes filles sous la Troisième République* (1977), 222–24. As his critique of convent education makes clear, Marion's claim was also informed by his anticlericalism (134). For a discussion of the limitations on girls' training in philosophy, see Jan Goldstein, " 'Saying I': Victor Cousin, Caroline Angebert and the Politics of Selfhood in Nineteenth-Century France," in *Rediscovering History: Politics, Culture, and the Psyche*, ed. Michael Roth (1994); Jan Goldstein, *The Post-Revolutionary Self*, 321–24.

24. Henri Marion, *Leçons de morale* (1882), 37.

guided into conformity by a "natural movement," the intimation that the will is "seduced" by the "engaging voice" of the rule, seems out of step with Marion's insistence upon reason, to the exclusion of "love," as a moralizing force. Here, the law's purportedly desirable character grounds Marion's claim that the subject's compliance is free and willing. In essence, the subject's adherence is autonomous precisely because he is attracted to and seduced by the law. But is a will so seduced still autonomous?

Marion insisted that this dual vision of moral ideals as at once commanding and attractive was not inherently contradictory. He claimed that while reason alone served as an ethical guide, happiness and pleasure were not excluded entirely from the realm of moral action. As in Kant, gratification could appear as a sort of surprise aftereffect and only in inverse proportion to the degree to which it was sought: "It accompanies, supports, acts as an auxiliary and recompense—a recompense which is more merited and assured to the extent that it is not anticipated and sought for."[25] Arriving on the scene after the fact, this reward is theoretically differentiated from virtue's chosen ends. And yet, despite this careful effort at circumscription, happiness as mere "accompaniment" to virtuous action resisted such containment; it was ultimately difficult for Marion to dissociate this reward from the ethical act itself.

While Marion was wary of the potential perversions of sentiment in its unmoderated, and one might add, "feminine" state, he rehabilitated affect for ethical action, by pairing it with unfeeling "duty." He proposed a "light critique" of Kantian doctrine, which he attempted to "soften," by making love a necessary companion to Kant's "cold justice."[26] Marion thus wrote, "Kant usually speaks of love with defiance and bad humor, as he is largely fearful of the deviations of sentiment. These deviations are indeed to be feared to such an extent that it is perhaps better to eliminate love, as he does, at least provisionally, from morality in order to clarify a notion of pure obligation. But once this notion is clearly seized, it is also appropriate to recall that love serves as duty's auxiliary and companion."[27] While potentially dangerous because subject to deviations in its pure state, love, when matched with duty, becomes a force of constancy and commitment. Alluding to a sort of conjugal relation between the two aspects of morality,

25. Ibid., 63.

26. Ibid., 115–16. Although not indicated in Marion's reductive account, "moral pleasure" is a similarly difficult issue in Kant's own work. See J. B. Schneewind, *The Invention of Autonomy: A History of Modern Moral Philosophy* (1998), 508–30.

27. Marion, *Leçons de morale*, 116. Marion's formulation recalls eclectic accounts of moral satisfaction. Cousin described the role of sentiments such as "sympathy and kindness" as the "happy auxiliaries, the assuring and beneficial witnesses to the harmony of virtue and happiness." In Victor Cousin, *Du vrai, du beau et du bien* (1853), 385–86. Paul Janet, likewise questioned Kant's failure to adequately account for moral sentiment. "We only protest against Kant's exaggeration, which entirely excludes sentiment from the domain of morality." Janet nonetheless added that, "one must guard against falling into effeminate tenderness." Paul Janet, *La morale* (1874), 457–58.

Marion wondered whether it was "really necessary to separate virtue and happiness in this way, to accept a provisional divorce between the two of them."[28] He instead imagined reason and affect as dual fonts of morality, linked together by a figurative marriage. Marion's very conception of ethical action was hence structured by a conjugal logic, wherein feminized affect, when paired with the imperious dictates of reason, at once explained and founded free and willing adherence to moral laws. This complementarity was, in other words, the very ground on which he constructed his "liberal" account of moral discipline. This same logic structured his argument that women needed to be trained in philosophy.

Marion upheld, in Kantian fashion, the universal and transcendent duties of "man toward man." Operative between a "Frenchman" and a "savage" or two Parisians, such principles, in theory bound all persons together, regardless of distinctions between "language, race, origin, or belief."[29] He suggested, however, that in concrete social contexts, the "affectionate sentiments" of solidarity between speakers of the same language or members of the same family could act as "auxiliaries to the moral sense."[30] While highly suspect for Kant, these sentiments were, for Marion, indispensable aids in the apprenticeship of moral action.[31] What is more, if these feelings of solidarity, in theory, simply augmented universal principles, his account of moral life in the context of family and country, actually reversed the order of priority between them. He thus claimed that, "the *patrie* provides the best schooling in humanity, the family in patriotism." "General duties" were learned in the heart of the family, contained in and by its "special duties." And, in an atmosphere characterized by "very profound natural sentiments," family members' ethical actions were spurred by feelings of "solidarity," not reasoned understanding. In such contexts, he claimed, "Duty appears to us as charming and luminous, rather than as rigorous and austere. One naturally and joyfully obeys; one becomes accustomed to finding pleasure in obedience."[32]

Marion's model of the family was, of course, a very particular one, namely the monogamous and reproductive "conjugal" family. He considered other forms documented among "savage" tribes—polyandry, polygamy, and matriarchy—to be states of confusion or arrested development and not families "properly speaking." In contrast to these improper families, the conjugal family was at once a motor and measure of "civilization." "What we must demonstrate," he wrote, "is its [the family's] moral

28. Marion, *Leçons de morale*, 117.
29. Ibid., 211.
30. Ibid., 299.
31. By contrast, for Kant, the misanthrope who forces himself to be a philanthropist has an impeccable moral character. See Immanuel Kant, *Groundwork of the Metaphysics of Morals*, trans. H. J. Paton (1956), 66.
32. Marion, *Leçons de morale*, 299–300.

value and its role in the history of civilization. It is an undeniable fact that wherever it appears, it appears as a beneficial institution. A people's degree of civilization can be measured by the solidity of its family spirit and its respect for domestic virtues."[33] The conjugal family thus guided the moral development of *civilization* itself as well as the individuals that comprised it. Primed by filial, fraternal, and paternal affections, the citizen-to-be carries out his obligations happily and willingly. "Whether mere citizen or magistrate, either in peace or war," Marion claimed, "he will be marvelously prepared by family life, to deploy, in whatever form, the spirit of discipline, knowledge and sacrifice which makes nations great and prosperous."[34] The family was, in other words, the arena in which society's male members first learned to appreciate and enjoy responsibility.

Woman was notably excluded from Marion's discussion of the citizen-to-be; in contrast to her male counterparts, her domestic role would not prepare her for a wider public purpose. Women were nonetheless vital to family solidarity, as the relationship between husband and wife exemplified the mutual dependence that, for Marion, characterized all forms of sociality. In his vision, both marriage partners were endowed with identical moral obligations and hence with moral equality. This equality was, in turn, integral to how the affective relations established in marriage and the family contributed to the development of practical morality. Marion lamented that, "unfortunately this truth is not yet recognized by all; in many countries, the woman is for man more of a slave than a companion. A man, who violently imposes his authority, rather than establishing it with gentility and goodness, is an unsupportable tyrant. Brutality, which is always repulsive, is odious in marriage, which must, in its essence, be a society of peace and love."[35] This invocation of an asocial, implicitly uncivilized marital brutality shored up the "truth" of Marion's vision by providing a marked contrast to the "peace and love" achieved by conjugality. The equanimity and affection of conjugality is founded on an "equality" which "does not exclude, but rather presupposes, a difference of attributes. There is neither superiority nor inferiority, simply profound difference. In essence identical, these duties are called by different names." This vision of the conjugal family presumed that fundamentally different and distinctly gendered attributes were assigned to discrete individuals who ideally cooperated. Numbering among the wife's virtuous duties was "voluntary obedience to a reason more mature than her own."[36] The contract secured between man and wife was a first, necessary step toward establishing an environment of moral solidarity

33. Ibid., 300. See also Henri Marion, *Leçons de psychologie appliquée à l'éducation* (1882), 184–85.
34. Marion, *Leçons de morale*, 300.
35. Ibid., 304.
36. Ibid., 305–6. See also the discussion of marriage in Marion, *De la solidarité morale*, 159–61.

in the heart of the family. The conjugal family thus provided a model for how affect coexisted with reason—in a necessary and yet necessarily subordinated position.

Within this atmosphere of mutual affection and responsibility, the child would learn to fulfill his duties "naturally."[37] As in Buisson, this initial moral instruction in the heart of the family guaranteed the "liberal" character of republican education. For, in Marion's view, the family "reveals to us the ideal of social relations; in the family, we find a clearer idea, a more succinct and warmer sentiment of what human relations should be in general, and civic relations in particular."[38] At the same time, the feminine excesses of love epitomized the dangers inherent in a pure affect unrestrained by the forces of reason. While the associative relations of domestic life enabled the development of autonomy, they also posed a threat, a menace which justified an eventual intervention on the part of the teacher—and hence the state.

Marion wrote in the conclusion to his *Leçons*: "The *instituteur* must, in part, continue the work begun by the family, collaborating above all with parents; in any case, he must always aim to have them as his auxiliaries. But how often must he correct the family education!" Marion focused on the "popular" family targeted by the new program of primary education. He urged that, even in the best-case scenario, the original instruction acquired in the heart of the family remained inadequate, precisely because it was "sentimental," based more on routine than on reasoned reflection.[39] Since Marion associated routine and sentiment with women, the family was feminized here. As a corrective to such unreflective and feminine habit, the teacher provided a formal articulation of the routinized principles acquired in the family; he supplemented an initial, sentimental education with reason. In other words, "he must awaken and ceaselessly excite the child's reflection and cultivate his reason. For, this is generally not done in the family."[40] As in Buisson, only the teacher could offer the ultimate training in reason so necessary for the emergence of a proper republican citizen.

Marion was, at the same time, wary of the potential excesses which haunted the loftiest and most reasonable republican ideals, namely, "liberty," "equality," and even rationality itself. In a section devoted to "civic duties," he interrogated the latent immoderation to which "idealism"—or the "instinct for the best"—might be subject. While Marion charged the in-

---

37. On the emergence of the pedagogical vision of the family as ideally ordered by an "affective contract," in which the eventual emancipation of (male) children was the organizing principle, see Lynn Hunt, *The Family Romance of the French Revolution* (1992); Pierre Rosanvallon, *Le sacre du citoyen: Histoire du suffrage universel en France* (1992), 114–16. On the father as educator, see Jean Delumeau and Daniel Roche, eds., *Histoire des pères et de la paternité* (1990), 259–78.

38. Marion, *Leçons de morale*, 299.

39. Ibid., 390–91.

40. Ibid., 392.

structor with inspiring such flights of idealism among his pupils, he simultaneously expressed hesitation about the violent extremes to which such ardor could lead:

> It is unfortunately true that such formidable awakenings of the instinct for the best, for the love of right, give all passions an occasion to explode. The instinct of equality, while noble and responsive to a certain sentiment of right, is not exempt from egotism: it can become easily blinded, jealous, and violent. The inebriation with liberty can engender the gravest disorders. All the virtues that extend from the spirit of independence harbor certain vices, into which it is always to be feared that it might hurry and fall. When one breaks with tradition and custom, it is never halfway, and never for just a moment. The spirit of examination and reform, the vertigo of rationality, in carrying society away, almost necessarily exceeds its goal and cannot help but do evil . . . The best is thus the enemy of the good.[41]

Marion here described the pathology of reason in terms of instinct. Left to its own devices, it might be tempted by excess and, in a sense, transformed into a perverse passion characterized by egotism, drunkenness, violence, vice, and vertigo. Even the virtue of autonomy, the "spirit of independence," could turn willy-nilly into dangerous vice. He suggested that the "love of tradition" could operate as a limiting factor on the "vertigo of rationality" and hence proposed "evolution" as opposed to "revolution" as a the ideal mode of moral progress. The progressive moral development of the child, initially in the heart of the family, and then in the hands of the state, provided the framework for just such an "evolution." The family at once enabled and limited the extent of pedagogical progress.

The complementarity between affect and reason in Marion's pedagogical and moral vision relied on an implicitly gendered and heterosexual logic. In order to organize and explain their relationship to one another, Marion gendered the component aspects of ethical action. This gendering both articulated and explained their cooperation, whether in the heart of the subject or in the dynamic between the family and the school. As for Buisson, the appeal to affective impulses in the development of morality served several ideological functions. It explained how and why subjects embraced their duties spontaneously, without the violent intervention of an external authority. It allotted an important moral role to the family, while also explaining why the domestic environment had to be closely regulated and eventually supplanted by the school. The school's own potential excesses were, in turn, held in check by the family. Marion thus summoned affective forces as a ground and motivation for the spontaneous character of moral action and posed their regulation and moderation as a problem requiring constant vigilance.

41. Ibid., 334.

The problem posed by puberty reflected an analogous logic. Because the "regular," heterosexual, organization of adolescent desires was haunted by its possible failure, they too required proper oversight and care. More specifically, while authoritarian methods of obtaining moral conformity exacerbated potential perversion exemplified by same-sex vice, "liberal" discipline emancipated the future citizen by constituting him as properly heterosexual. Masculine autonomy and heterosexuality, emancipation and sexual regulation, were, in other words, mutually constitutive and together, provided the ground of ethical action. In order to maintain its coherence, this account of masculine moral apprenticeship relied on the figuration of women, with their naturalized, but always also excessive sentiment, as man's "auxiliary and companion." Only in this way could the conjugal family be the origin and model "of what human relations should be in general, and civic relations in particular." This family and the heterosexual pairing of affect and reason that it embodied was, according to Marion's account, not simply an attribute of "civilized" moral development, but actually its agent. In order to understand how this vision of the conjugal family as a secular moral ideal was consolidated and generalized, I now turn to contemporary debates about the extension of schooling to the native population in Algeria.

Family Morality, Adolescence, and Assimilation in Algeria

In his 1892 report to the Senate on the primary instruction of Algerian indigènes, Senator Émile Combes dismissed claims that native males suffered from a uniquely debilitating "crisis of puberty." "No," he wrote, "puberty doesn't weaken the native's intelligence. Combes admitted that "when not contained by moral constraints," puberty "lets sensible desires predominate over the taste for instruction." He asserted, however, that "our youth traverses the same trial, resists by the same means, and fails for the same reasons." For Combes, this apparently universal crisis, rather than posing an obstacle to moral instruction, demonstrated its very necessity. "Far from there being an incompatibility between this crisis and our instruction," he wrote, "I maintain that our teaching moderates it." In sum, the French educational system "retains the rush of desires by a sage direction given to ideas, at the same time that it surrounds the young man by an affectionate surveillance, which preserves him, as much as possible, from temptation and occasions for failure."[42]

The menace of puberty, according to Combes, justified the extension of the secular republican moralizing mission to Algeria's native inhabitants. In

42. Émile Combes, *L'instruction primaire des indigènes: Rapport fait au nom de la commission chargée d'examiner les modifications à introduire dans la législation et dans l'organisation des divers services de l'Algérie* (1892), 114.

contrast to the settler population, reformers like Combes, Ferry, and Buisson advocated for the education of the Arab and Kabyle population. By arguing in favor of this schooling, these reformers consolidated the "universal" truth of their secular morality and pedagogy. As we have seen, the reason-based principles of practical morality were, for pedagogues such as Marion, transcendent and universal, applicable to all without regard to "language, race, origin, or belief." At the same time, the "special duties" learned in the heart of the family were an important part of how children embraced these general principles. How could children learn in places like Algeria where the conjugal family was thought to be lacking? While advocating in favor of indigenous education, school reformers also explained that because native family morality was degraded and deficient, their native charges needed specially "adapted" forms of education.

The Ferry laws instituting free, secular, and obligatory primary education were extended to Algeria by decree in 1883, and subsequently modified by further texts in 1887. The laws applied to settlers, whether of French or other European nationality, and, at least on paper, to native inhabitants throughout the territory. The decree provided for the specific "needs" of the native population by initially restricting obligation to native boys and eventually doing away with it altogether, providing for instruction in native languages by native instructors, and varying the type of school according to the administrative status of communes. The law remarkably required all communes to establish schools and to pay for their construction when they did not already exist. Settlers, who were primarily interested in guarding local funds for themselves and in maintaining a supply of uneducated and inexpensive native labor, predictably resisted applying the decree's provisions to the Arab and Kabyle natives. They initially had little incentive to do so, given the relative absence of metropolitan oversight or intervention. As the settler population benefited from considerable support in Parliament, the progress of primary schooling in Algeria did not receive close scrutiny from metropolitan officials and administrators until the early 1890s. When the Parliament turned its sights on the "Algerian situation" in 1892, the settlers' opposition to native schooling became even more pronounced and dogmatic.[43]

Claims regarding the native adolescent's alleged crisis of puberty were the stock and trade of these *colons*.[44] Settlers and their advocates often cited a notorious statement by Ernest Renan, to the effect that "around the age of

43. Charles-Robert Ageron, *Les Algériens musulmans et la France (1871–1919)*, vol. 1 (1968), 337–42; Hubert Desvages, "L'enseignement des musulmans d'Algérie sous le rectorat de Jeanmaire: Le rôle de l'école," *Mouvement social* 70 (1970); Louis Rigaud, "L'école en Algérie (1880–1862)," in *L'école en Algérie: 1830–1862*, ed. Association "Les Amis de Max Marchand de Mouloud Ferdoun et de leurs Compagnons" (2001), 29; Yvonne Turin, "Instituteurs et colonisation en Algérie au 19e siècle," *Revue historique* 234, no. 2 (1965).
44. Ageron, *Les Algériens musulmans*, 535.

ten or twelve years, the Muslim child, who has been up until that moment rather aware, becomes all of a sudden a fanatic, full of a stupid pride in the possession of an absolute truth, pleased by that which makes him inferior as if it were a privilege."[45] Opponents of indigenous instruction associated this "crisis" with all that made the Algerian native radically different and inassimilable, namely, religious fanaticism, extreme pride, and excessive sensuality. Indeed, they suggested that these "passions" were all interconnected. Deputy Joseph-Gaston Pourquéry de Boisserin denounced the "dream of realizing at a gallop the progress of a people whose revealed religion . . . gives them the hope of perpetually satisfying their passionate pleasures in this world and beyond."[46] Those in favor of extending schooling to the native population parried these charges in an effort to defend their educational enterprise. The 1892 Combes report to the Senatorial Commission, by contrast, argued that the "crisis" of puberty was not a phenomenon restricted to natives. Combes viewed the "crisis" of male youth as universal.

In order to combat the potentially disruptive effects of puberty, school reformers recommended measures analogous to those taken in the metropole, namely, the "liberal" discipline of a moral education combining "sage direction" and "affectionate surveillance." Combes returned to the question several times in his report, precisely because, in his view, "one of the most widespread preconceptions is the claim that, around the age of puberty, the intelligence of the native goes through a crisis that constitutes a veritable arrest in development." He sought to controvert this claim: "The intelligence of the native develops like that of the French. If, around the age of fifteen or sixteen, some of them become lazy or seem to fall off from their studies, the cause is not a failure of the mind, but reasons of another order, among which the Rector [Jeanmaire] principally signals a lack of surveillance. This case demonstrates a general rule, which states that the student, whatever his race or nationality, needs to be protected from the temptations and the new impulses which are derived from the physiological modifications inherent in puberty."[47] Combes universalized the "crisis of puberty" and used it to derive a "general rule" regarding the need to "protect" adolescents from their burgeoning drives. Secular moral education appeared as an at once necessary and universalizable solution to this general problem of male youth.

The application of this "general rule" nonetheless depended on specific or "adaptive" methods in order to protect youth from temptation and fail-

45. Ernest Renan, *L'islamisme et la science (conférence faite à la Sorbonne le 29 mars 1883)* (1883), 2–3. See, for example, Senator Dide's speech in "Discussion d'une interpellation sur la situation de l'Algérie," *Journal Officiel: Sénat; Débats* 30 (1891): 113.

46. Joseph-Gaston Pourquéry de Boisserin, "Rapport fait au nom de la commission du budget chargé d'examiner le projet de loi portant fixation du budget général de l'exercice 1895 (Ministère de l'intérieur, Service de l'Algérie)," *Journal Officiel: Documents parlementaires; Chambre; Session Ordinaire*, no. 906, 28 July 1894 (1895): 39.

47. Combes, *L'instruction primaire des indigènes*, 66–67. See also Maurice Halbwachs, "L'indigénat et l'enseignement public en Algérie," *Revue internationale de l'enseignement* 44, no. 9 (1902): 223–24.

ure. The rector of the Academy of Alger, Charles Jeanmaire, proclaimed in a deposition before the Senatorial Commission that in order for indigenous instruction to be effective, Algerian natives needed to be "inculcated with a morality that conforms to their minds [*leur esprit*]."[48] Ferdinand Buisson, when asked by Jules Ferry for his opinion on the natives' purported "crisis of puberty," suggested that it resulted from the "disorientation" created by overly complex programs of instruction. He urged that "Up until now, the teaching has not been very accessible to the native; it has to be made simple and to be placed above the scruples of race and religion."[49] Extrapolating from Buisson, one might say that this adapted education both raised the native above the implicitly particularistic scruples of his "race and religion" and, in remaining "simple," kept him in his place.

Despite the settlers' dogged opposition to their efforts, metropolitan school reformers like Buisson and Ferry had a hearty advocate in Jeanmaire, who was appointed to his post as Rector in 1884 in order to put the new legislation into place. In the face of relentless resistance, Jeanmaire remained committed to extending primary schooling to the native population. A student of the École normale supérieure, Jeanmaire was, like Buisson and Marion, agrégé in philosophy. He gained his doctorate in 1882 from the Faculty of Letters in Lyon, with a thesis devoted to *L'idée de la personalité dans la psychologie moderne*. His thesis bore the hallmarks of contemporary pedagogical theory, hailing moral education as a "veritable education of the person." His conclusion, for example, urged that: "To know what the good is does not suffice, it must be done; to do it is not enough, it must be done freely, that is to say, it must be loved, it must be wanted."[50] Jeanmaire's spiritualist conception of personality, and especially of the development of individual conscience and will, informed the approaches toward native education that he initiated in the late 1880s. The new curriculum programs for natives he adopted in 1890 illustrate his allegiance to contemporary theories of moral education and "liberal discipline." According to the approach spelled out in the program, the new schooling was as much directed to moralization as learning. "Knowledge" in and of itself constituted a "double-edged sword," which might become "a danger to society if not accompanied by a parallel moral development." With a program of instruction directed as much to the "heart" and "will" as to the "intelligence," the manual proclaimed, "the Arab who goes to school will be recognized not by what he knows, but by what he does; he will distinguish himself from other natives by his more scrupulous probity and gentler moeurs."[51]

48. Commission d'étude des questions algériennes. Sénat, *Dépositions du 1er mai au 20 juillet 1891* (1891), 189.
49. Ibid., 173–74.
50. Charles Jeanmaire, *L'idée de la personnalité dans la psychologie moderne* (1882), 417.
51. *Plan d'études et programmes de l'enseignement primaire des indigènes en Algérie* (1890), 113.

The benefits of this liberal approach would be manifold, particularly in the realm of discipline. According to a logic that, as we have seen, suffused liberal pedagogical thinking, discipline unlike "authoritarian" force, cultivated sentiment rather than imposing external signs of order. Thus, in the moral vision outlined by the 1890 program, "The teacher who knows how to gain children's affections [*s'attacher l'enfance*] can exercise extraordinary influence. Affection rather than fear: that is the most solid foundation for the teacher's authority and of school discipline." Fear, while it might create a momentary, external appearance of order, always risked creating "indocile" and even "rebellious" characters. The goals of this affectionate approach were eminently political, namely, to solicit pupils' eventual willing compliance to French rule. The new program urged: "France does not want to make Arabs into resigned subjects, but into citizens who accept its authority because they recognize it to be equitable and necessary, and into men who follow the correct and generous impulses of their conscience."[52] Citizenship did not refer here to the actual rights and responsibilities accorded to voting members of the polity, but rather to an "enlightened" disposition toward French law and authority. As benevolent as Jeanmaire and his colleagues may have believed their intentions to be, this "citizenship" remained limited, as was well illustrated by the section of the curriculum devoted to "Duties toward France" (and *not* it should be noted *la patrie*). It would cover: "Protection accorded by France to Algeria; insurance of order and justice and realization of progress; obedience; appreciation; necessity of paying taxes."[53] In other words, the program's reference to "citizens" may have served more to obscure the subjection, albeit "enlightened," that this moral education program was designed to produce.[54]

In her important study of the history of the Algerian teaching corps, Fanny Colonna provocatively interrogates the benevolent intentions of the liberal-minded reformers that brought metropolitan schooling methods to the *indigènes*. She criticizes previous accounts of the "neutrality" of this policy and questions whether "rather than proving the neutrality of the school in Algeria, the transposition of methods and of the French schooling project does not prove the, one might say, colonial character of the school in France?"[55] In other words, the ideological mechanisms of domination that remained implicit in metropolitan schooling were rendered explicit in a colonial context in which the pretext of citizenship rights did not mask its

52. Ibid., 114.
53. Ibid., 123.
54. On the exclusion of Algerian "Muslim" subjects from citizenship, see Laure Blévis, "La citoyenneté française au miroir de la colonisation: Étude des demandes de naturalisation des 'sujets français' en Algérie coloniale," *Genèses*, no. 53 (2003). On the legal status of colonial subjects more generally, see Emmanuelle Saada, "Citoyens et sujets de l'empire français: Les usages du droit en situation coloniale," *Genèses*, no. 53 (2003).
55. Fanny Colonna, *Instituteurs algériens: 1883–1939* (1975), 69. Here, Colonna seeks to take distance from the arguments of Ageron and Desvages.

subjugating effects.[56] From Colonna's perspective, the subjugating tactics of metropolitan schooling and its imperialist incarnation were parts of a whole.

Alice Conklin has similarly sought to understand the articulation of republicanism and colonialism implicit in the "civilizing mission" and has argued that republican universalism and imperialism were not in fact "a contradiction in terms." Like Colonna, she examines the institution of an adapted form of republican schooling in French West Africa as an exemplary instance of this intersection. For Conklin, the republicans' colonial "civilizing mission" depended as much on visions of a "shared humanity" as on a discourse of racialized difference.[57] She suggests that republican universalism did not contradict but rather underwrote French imperial projects in the early Third Republic. Colonna and Conklin's insights may be taken further. Did universalist ideals simply precede and hence serve to justify "the civilizing mission"? Or, did projects to extend secular morality to Algeria's colonial subjects actually help reformers to cast their moral vision in universal terms? We have already seen how in making arguments in favor of indigenous schooling republican reformers reaffirmed the universal character of puberty as a moral and regulatory crisis. They would similarly confirm the moral value of the conjugal family by demonstrating its absence in Algeria. Reformers' "adaptive" programs reflected this underlying ambivalence; they constructed native Algerians simultaneously as different and as capable of progress toward moral ideals.[58]

The case of Ferdinand Buisson may be taken as exemplary. As the primary schooling system's apostle of secular faith, he embraced the extension of republican schooling to North Africa. A triumphal tone pervades his report on an 1887 mission, undertaken with Marcelin Berthelot, Minister of Public Instruction, to Algeria and Tunisia to inspect the progress of the republic's newest schools. Buisson hailed the closure of religious schools, the notorious *zaouia,* which he saw as "foyers of fanaticism" and "preparatory

56. Ibid., 72. Eugen Weber has made the inverse argument. In drawing an analogy between the "internal colonization" of the peasantry and imperial project overseas, he endeavors to credit the "natives" with greater autonomy, not to reveal the "true" subjection of metropolitans. In Eugen Weber, *Peasants into Frenchmen: The Modernization of Rural France, 1870–1914* (1976), 485–96. Alice Bullard has extended this analogy in her juxtaposition of the moralization of Communards and savages in New Caledonia. See Alice Bullard, *Exile in Paradise: Savagery and Civilization in Paris and the South Pacific, 1790–1900* (2000).

57. Alice L. Conklin, "Colonialism and Human Rights, A Contradiction in Terms? The Case of France and West Africa, 1895–1914," *American Historical Review* 103, no. 2 (1998): 441. And Alice L. Conklin, *A Mission to Civilize: The Republican Idea of Empire in France and West Africa* (1997). On the conflict between republican and religious visions of the "civilizing mission": James P. Daughton, "The Civilizing Mission: Missionaries, Colonialists, and French Identity, 1885–1914" (Ph.D. diss., University of California, Berkeley, 2002).

58. It is important here to draw a distinction, at times obscured in Conklin's analysis, between the universal moral ideals articulated by republican reformers and universal rights. Schooling was not, or not simply, a "right"; it was also a tactic of moralization and *mise-en-valeur.*

schools for insurrection."[59] He proclaimed that the French schools' mounting success with the native population could be directly traced to their recently instituted neutrality. The secular schools succeeded where, in Buisson's view, religious ones had been doomed to fail. Indeed, for Buisson, "If *laïcité* did not already exist in France, it would have had to be invented for our African possessions." Buisson found confirmation of the universal truth of his secular moral vision in its extension to Algeria and Tunisia; its purported universality was, for him, realized in this transposition. However, *laïcité* did not preclude recourse to "adapted" means, namely, in specially designed courses and course manuals, in short, in "indigenous schools specifically conceived of and organized for the indigenous child."[60] With this combination of a purportedly neutral and hence universalizable message and an "adapted" pedagogy, secular education would successfully supersede the violence of earlier imperialist tactics. "We now know," wrote Buisson, "how to penetrate the Islamic world: we should resolutely penetrate it, not with iron and fire, not to bring a war of race or religion, but in order to light up [*faire luire*] those eternal truths which shine with the same brilliance in all ages and under all skies which belong neither to the Jew, the Christian, or the Muslim, because they belong to humanity: law, reason, justice, work, and liberty."[61] In transplanting republican schools to Algeria, the architects of school reform could demonstrate the transcendent truth of their secular morality and of the liberal pedagogy that accompanied it. It became "universal" in and through this transplantation. Thus, as Paul Bernard, the director of the École normale d'Alger wrote, the teacher is "a pioneer of Western civilization, a secular missionary of French influence."[62]

As their recourse to "adaptive" strategies well demonstrates, republican educators sought to overcome the particular "defects" of native children. These failings were, in their view, especially pronounced in the domain of morality. The 1890 program of study stated: "It should be remarked that there are certain virtues that seem to us natural because we drank them with our mother's milk [*suçer avec le lait*] and which are lacking in Arab tradi-

---

59. Ferdinand Buisson, "Nos pionniers en Afrique," *Revue pédagogique* 10, no. 6 (1887): 493. See also Paul Bert, *Lettres de Kabylie: La politique algérienne* (1885), 71.

60. Buisson, "Nos pionniers." 494. Buisson notably celebrated the increased production of school reading manuals specially adapted to the needs of the children of "workers, farmers, employees, artisans, shop-keepers, in short, the masses" in the metropole as well. He highlighted the "care taken to exactly adapt to the needs of a particular public" and cited as exemplary "the difference which one tends to draw between books designed for little girls and those designed for boys." Ferdinand Buisson, "Les nouveaux livrets de morale," *Revue pédagogique* 28, no. 4 (1896): 302.

61. Buisson, "Nos pionniers," 511.

62. Paul Bernard, "Une excursion scolaire en Grande-Kabylie," *Revue pédagogique* 42, no. 1 (1903): 43. For a detailed account of the "adaptive" programs, see Paul Bernard, "L'enseignement primaire des indigènes musulmans d'Algérie," *Revue du monde musulman*, no. 1 (1906).

tion."[63] As this remark intimates, reformers found the deficiencies of the Arab family and the fanaticism of the Muslim faith to be responsible for the sorry moral character of native pupils. The director of the École normale in Constantine, who helped to draft the 1890 program, declared in an article on "moral instruction for young Muslims" that "if the young Arab child is filled with vice it is because of the gross morality that he drank with his mother's milk in the family and which he later learned to venerate, early on, in the mosque." He continued, "There is no question that, when it comes to the sentiments and comportment of Arab students, one would be wrong to count on the native predisposition of the child, or even the influence of the family, and especially the dictates of religion. An obstacle is raised, there where one should find assistance."[64] In Algeria, the Arab family and the purported (im)morality of Islam—regularly equated with patriarchy, polygamy, and the subjugation of women and children—could not be relied upon as auxiliaries in the child's moral development.[65]

For school reformers, the chronic failings of the Arab family did not however render indigenous schooling irrelevant or even dangerous, as their settler opponents frequently argued, but rather lent greater urgency to their civilizing mission. Thus, wrote the director Lacabe-Plasteig, "These examples do not prove anything against either the aptitude of Arabs, or the educational value of instruction." Administrators, indeed, argued that schooling would eventually bring about a moral reform of the family. In the meantime, instructors would take on a double duty. As Auguste Burdeau wrote in his report to the Chamber of Deputies on the 1892 budget for Algeria, "The teacher will have to do that which, elsewhere, the family and the entourage do with him or in his place: give the child the first principles and habits of a new morality and new civilization."[66]

Discussions of the degraded the state of the Arab family frequently functioned for French administrators as a metonym for the generally degraded character of indigenous society. Pro-settler discourse regularly denounced the moral failings of the Muslim family in order to demonstrate the absolute difference and inferiority of the natives, their utter impermeability to French "civilization." In his report on the 1894 budget for Algeria to the Chamber of Deputies, Pourquéry de Boisserin, a deputy from the Vaucluse and a fervent advocate of settler interests, concluded a lengthy discussion of native practices of polygamy and divorce (which in his view amounted to

63. *Plan d'études,* 120. The program itself refers to "defects" (74).
64. Lacabe-Plasteig, "Instruction des indigènes: L'enseignement de la morale aux jeunes musulmans," *Bulletin universitaire de l'Académie d'Alger* 1, no. 11 (1898): 367–68.
65. See, for example, Étienne Cécile Edouard Villot, *Moeurs, coutumes, et institutions des indigènes de l'Algérie,* 3rd ed. (1888).
66. Auguste Burdeau, *L'Algérie en 1891: Rapport et discours à la Chambre des députés* (1892), 210. For a discussion of Burdeau's report, see: James R. Lehning, *To Be a Citizen: The Political Culture of the Early Third Republic* (2001), 139–44.

the same thing) as follows: "After reading this account of the situation that exists among the Muslim populations of Algeria, our eyes must be opened and we must have the courage to measure . . . the abyss that separates these populations from the mœurs, ideas, and tendencies of our civilization."[67] Critics of the native family focused their attention on the purportedly servile and subjugated position of women as the most pronounced symptom of its depravity.[68] Pro-settler arguments regarding the futility of metropolitan attempts to "assimilate" the natives through education frequently invoked the position of women as an insurmountable obstacle. In the Senate discussion of the Algerian situation in 1891, Senator Dide proclaimed that "One assimilates a people by the practices of sociability of which the woman is a necessary agent, but here the woman escapes us; she is sequestered and imprisoned; you cannot count on her influence."[69] Senator Jacques from Oran urged: "The first thing to do if it were possible would be to save [*relever*] the woman, to give her a situation which would permit her to raise her children, to give them the instruction, to give them that education which always leaves traces in the spirit and character of the child; for if a man is honest, if he is good, most of the time it is because of the principles that were inculcated in his youth. However the Arab family, the indigenous family does not exist. The Arabs are, from this point of view, in an absolutely inferior state."[70]

Of course, these arguments were mobilized *not* out of an interest to improve the situation of native women, but rather to discredit the "assimilationist" goals of metropolitan school reformers. Indeed, settlers and their advocates claimed elsewhere that the schooling of native women was dangerous, as it threatened to overturn the very family structure that they so ardently denounced. The writings of the vociferous critic of assimilation, Louis Vignon, professor at the École coloniale and former cabinet chief of the Undersecretary of State of the Navy and Colonies, are here exemplary. In his immense tome titled *La France en Algérie,* Vignon wrote: "Does France want, in trying to steal these women [*prendre les femmes*], to disorganize indigenous society . . . to pursue *a work of revolution* in disorganizing the family as it exists? Of course, this Muslim family is badly organized for us, 'civilized' Europeans; but do we have a mission to change it and above all, are we strong enough?"[71] Critics of metropolitan schooling efforts claimed that this instruction would only provoke local resistance and perhaps worse, render girls undesirable for marriage (to other natives, of

67. Pourquéry de Boisserin, "Rapport," 51.

68. For a good discussion of these dynamics, see Julia Clancy-Smith, "Islam, Gender, and Identities in the Making of French Algeria, 1830–1963," in *Domesticating the Empire: Race, Gender, and Family Life in French and Dutch Colonialism,* ed. Julia Clancy-Smith et al. (1998). See also Lehning, *To Be a Citizen,* 145–52.

69. "Discussion d'une interpellation sur la situation de l'Algérie," 113.

70. Ibid., 185.

71. Louis Vignon, *La France en Algérie* (1893), 458.

course) and hence lead to an increase in prostitution.[72] Even the most adamant metropolitan reformers were wary of the untoward effects of extending schooling to indigenous girls.[73]

In contrast to settlers who appealed to arguments about Algerian women's subjugation in order to prove the native's profound inassimilability, school reformers mobilized them to legitimate their mission. Emile Combes, in his 1892 report on public instruction for the Senatorial Commission on the situation in Algeria, proclaimed that while "it was not the moment for [him] to destroy these native customs, despite the repulsion they inspire," they nonetheless should not be held up as obstacles to the government's proposed "work of instruction and moral emancipation."[74] He affirmed that "In any case, it is incontestable that the condition of the native women must improve by the effect of education alone. When the youth of both sexes has breathed the pure and fortifying air of the French school, when it has taken up moral ideas more elevated than its current ones, more noble and disinterested sentiments, new relations will be established between husband and wife, relations derived from the ideas and sentiments stimulated in their souls by our teaching, and this even without the prior intervention of legislation."[75] Given the relative absence of provisions for girls' schooling, this reform was initiated among male youth, who were most often figured as the source of the problem. As one school inspector remarked: "When the Arab has acquired instruction, he will, perhaps one day, a longtime off, desire not to have one or several women as instruments of pleasure or as domestic utilities, but to have a companion who is worthy of him."[76] Another author explained: "When the Algerians of the male sex have been freed by our instructors of the false ideas that cloud their minds, they will not hesitate to recognize that their women should not be left in an inferior state."[77]

School reformers upheld this injunction to inspire companionate marriage and its corollary, monogamous heterosexual desire, as a central aim of native schooling in Algeria. Yet they also perpetually postponed its realiza-

72. See the article written by a noted author of moral education textbooks for girls: Mme Clarisse Coignet, "À propos de l'instruction des indigènes en Algérie," *Revue pédagogique* 18, no. 4 (1891). And, Rector Jeanmaire's response: Jeanmaire, "Sur l'instruction des indigènes en Algérie," *Revue pédagogique* 19, no. 7 (1891).

73. An article on the 1883 decree published in the *Revue pédagogique* explained that "it would be imprudent to outstrip the progress of moeurs . . . any woman brought up in our schools would have difficulty finding a husband among the natives: she would be doomed to celibacy or even worse." In A. Bernard, "L'instruction des indigènes algériens et le décret du 13 février 1883," *Revue pédagogique* 4, no. 3 (1884): 209. See also Maurice Wahl, "L'instruction des indigènes en Algérie," *Revue pédagogique* 2, no. 1 (1883): 22–23.

74. Combes, *L'instruction primaire des indigènes,* 167.

75. Ibid., 171.

76. Gustave Benoist, *De l'instruction des indigènes dans la province de Constantine* (1886), 23.

77. Bernard, "L'instruction des indigènes algériens et le décret du 13 février 1883," 210. See also *Plan d'études,* 120.

tion into an ever-receding future.[78] Their efforts in the realm of sexual and family morality may be read as metaphor for the republican "civilizing mission" more generally. They also reveal how republican educators actively forged a connection between "civilization" and companionate marriage. Their calls to reform native male desire did not simply ratify a pre-existing idea of "civilized" sexual morality. It actually helped them to produce that morality, as expressed in and by companionate marriage, as a *universal* norm and ideal.[79]

In their discussions of the family and puberty as central sites and stakes in the introduction of republican education in Algeria, reformers both reconfirmed and extended claims that pervaded their accounts of liberal pedagogy in the metropole. The debates around the schooling of natives reveal how this effort worked to "universalize" their secular moral vision. They confirmed their understanding of puberty, and the gendered and developmental account of male sexuality that it implied, as a "universal" regulatory crisis whose moral management required specific measures of "liberal discipline." Reformers, in turn, generalized conjugality, and the heterosexual complementarity it presumed, as an affective locus for children's moral instruction precisely by pointing to its absence and lack in native Algerian families. In so doing, they set forth an idealized vision of a civilized sexual and social order. In gauging the Algerian natives against this moral, sexual, and social norm, republican reformers produced indigenous difference at the same time that they held out the possibility of assimilation.[80]

The ethical value of sentiment thus played an important role in ideas of liberal pedagogy, both in the metropole and in the strategies that were adapted to the native population in Algeria. It explained how subjects would embrace, rather than resist, moral and social norms. Recourse to affect, in other words, helped reformers to theoretically solve the seeming paradox of liberal government and, in the Algerian context, imperial rule. Sentiment was crucial to how pedagogues and politicians imagined and instituted subjects who would "behave according to the norms of their time and country's civilization." But, affect did not simply explain this free and willing acceptance. Because it was always subject to the menace of deviation or excess, it also required regulatory oversight and intervention.

78. On this logic of perpetual deferral, see Blévis, *La citoyenneté française*, 26.

79. On racialized discourses of "civilization" and the construction of normative gender and sexual identities, see Gail Bederman, *Manliness and Civilization: A Cultural History of Gender and Race in the United States, 1880–1917* (1995). On the production and regulation of "desire" in imperialist discourse and practice, see Ann Laura Stoler, *Race and the Education of Desire: Foucault's History of Sexuality and the Colonial Order of Things* (1995); Ann Laura Stoler, *Carnal Knowledge and Imperial Power: Race and the Intimate in Colonial Rule* (2002).

80. For an analogous discussion of how "assimilationism" produces racial and gender difference: K. H. Adler, *Jews and Gender in Liberation France* (2003).

PART II

THE BACHELOR'S VICE

French education is faulty at its base because it has forgotten this point, which is everything. In no school does one learn love, its nobility, its duties. . . . One cultivates reason, the mind, intelligence. . . . No teaching addresses itself to this power, difficult to define, which, in us, solicits heroism, lifts us above ourselves and everything else, commands actions which are, in appearance, contrary to our most immediate interests.

—Jean Aicard, *Le pavé d'amour*

In his 1892 novel, *Le pavé d'amour,* Jean Aicard, the prolific Provençal writer and future member of the Académie française, condemned French secondary schools for teaching youth about reason, while failing to instruct them in "love." He accused the lycée of being a factory that prepared students for the *baccalauréat,* but left them hopelessly unschooled in matters of the heart. The novel's young protagonist proclaimed: "Without love . . . there is no real courage, no beautiful audacity, no heroism. We are beaten in advance!" He urged later: "This is the origin of all pessimism, all the deviations of thought: impossible love, countered and deviated, at the very age that commands it!"[1] According to Aicard's formulation, an overemphasis on reason in French secondary education was responsible for the demoralization of contemporary youth, both their individualism and alienation. As the next two chapters show, he was not alone. Aicard's novel was quite timely; it invoked recent efforts to reform the emasculating effects of the lycée's mechanical and military regime and cited statistics on the declining birth rate as evidence of the devirilization paradoxically produced by the institution responsible for forming the nation's male elite. His account of the perverse effects of secondary schooling on "love" needs to be understood within a wider context. Such discussions of young men's deviance, of their

1. Jean Aicard, *Le pavé d'amour* (1892), 20, 45.

failure to assume socially productive and reproductive roles, expressed larger concerns about the socially unsettling effects of "modernity," the democratization, rationalization, and materialism associated with the fin-de-siècle republican political order.

Debates surrounding the reform of secondary education in the 1890s coincided with the first major political crises of the Third Republic. The government of Jules Ferry, architect of France's primary education reform, fell in March 1885. The result of reaction to a colonial policy widely perceived as diversionary, the end of Ferry's second ministry symbolically concluded the initial, optimistic phase of the Third Republic. It was the advent of an age of greater ministerial instability, as well as political and financial crisis. The wellspring of enthusiasm on the part of both nationalists and the nascent socialist movement for the populist authoritarian General Boulanger would menace the parliamentary Republic in the late 1880s. In the early 1890s, the regime was further troubled by the Panama Canal scandal in which several government representatives were implicated. The incident was heavily exploited by a growing chorus of critics of the parliamentary elite. The years 1892–1894 were also marked by a series of anarchist attacks that culminated in the assassination of Sadi Carnot, the president of the republic. These turbulent episodes set the stage for the national crisis that would ensue, at the end of the decade, around the Dreyfus Affair. While the Republic remained standing, the rosy blush of youth had warn off; its ideal of creating a cohesive national community—perhaps best embodied in its educational philosophy—was tarnished. France was at once riven by internal conflicts and increasingly threatened by the menacing forces outre-Rhin. This "coming of age" was far from tranquil—accompanied by the rise of more vocal and virulent nationalist and socialist as well as anarchist opposition to the Republican status quo.

In the wake of the events that weakened the Republic's legitimacy, political and pedagogical reformers; novelists and literary critics; and a host of social scientists interrogated the state's ability to effectively form and morally discipline its future citizens, particularly those who were primed to become the nation's elite. How, they wondered, could the nation assure that its citizens were both self-governing and still anchored in the social order? As a particularly dense and politically charged nexus, debates on secondary school reform both articulated and addressed this question. My account of the "crisis of secondary education" builds on the work of other scholars who have carefully reconstructed the political, social, and intellectual context of these reforms.[2] My emphasis is different to the extent that I highlight

---

2. Viviane Isambert-Jamati, "Une réforme des lycées et collèges: Essai d'analyse sociologique de la réforme de 1902," *Année sociologique* 20 (1969); Viviane Isambert-Jamati, *Crises de la société, crises de l'enseignement: Sociologie de l'enseignement secondaire français* (1970); Victor Karady, "Les professeurs de la République: Le marché scolaire, les réformes universitaires et les transformations de la fonction professorale à la fin du 19e siècle," *Année sociologique* 47–48 (1983); Detlef K. Muller, Fritz Ringer, and Brian Simon, eds., *The Rise of*

how gender and sexual norms were implicated in these visions of how best to form the French nation's male elite. In part 1, we saw how primary school reformers sought to balance affect and reason in the moral education of the nation's popular classes. My discussion of secondary schooling reveals a similarly pervasive concern with the relationship between men's citizenship and their "filiation," between their reasoned autonomy and their affective responsibility to the past and future of their families, and implicitly to the past and future of France.

While offering contrasting and at times opposed policy proposals, pedagogical reformers and their contemporary critics expressed uniform concern about the state-run lycée. They debated whether it might be not an engine of social progress but a perverse machine ultimately destructive of a well-regulated social order. Liberals and conservatives, socialists and reactionaries accented the deleterious effects of secondary schooling on young men's desires, and hence on the future of the French family and nation.

A number of related figures functioned in their writings as metonyms for this potential waste and devastation: the repressed student; the unemployed *bachelier;* the unmarried man; and the childless bureaucrat.[3] These characters represented different incarnations of the same problem, namely, a contemporary failure to adequately integrate male youth into the institutions responsible for social production and reproduction, that is, work and family.

Historians have well indicated how the "new woman" embodied a perceived threat to a well-organized and regulated social order. Here, I examine how these "bachelors" represented an analogous, if different problem. For, if the new woman's individualism transgressed the rules of conventional femininity, these youths posed the problem, and hence helped to articulate, the extent and limits of men's individualism. In their case, an excess of individualism could, in fact, appear as a feminizing trait. The excess of will represented by "voluntary bachelorhood" paradoxically signaled these men's weakness and failure, as they sought, according to one observer, "to be exonerated from all public and private responsibilities in order to live with greater ease, in giving free reign to their most disorderly impulses."[4]

the Modern Educational System: Structural Change and Social Reproduction, 1870–1920 (1987); Fritz Ringer, *Fields of Knowledge: French Academic Culture in Comparative Perspective* (1992); John E. Talbott, *The Politics of Educational Reform in France, 1918–1940* (1969); Georges Weill, *Histoire de l'enseignement secondaire en France (1802–1920)* (1921).

3. On contemporary anxieties surrounding the bachelor, see Jean Borie, *Le célibataire français* (1976). Concerns about bachelorhood were, of course, not unique to the turn of the century. See Jean Claude Boulogne, *Histoire du célibat et des célibataires* (2004). On critiques of celibacy and bachelorhood in the Enlightenment and Revolution, see Carol Blum, *Strength in Numbers: Population, Reproduction, and Power in Eighteenth-century France* (2002), 21–60, 155–63; Suzanne Desan, *The Family on Trial in Revolutionary France* (2004), 55–56; Patrice Higonnet, "The Harmonization of the Spheres: Goodness and Dysfunction in the Provincial Clubs," in *The French Revolution and the Creation of Modern Political Culture*, ed. Keith Michael Baker (1994), 122–24. For the interwar period, see Kristen Stromberg Childers, *Fathers, Families, and the State in France, 1914–1945* (2003), 73–78.

4. Pierre Garnier, *Célibat et célibataires: Caractères, dangers et hygiène chez les deux sexes* (1889), 228.

These young men suffered, according to contemporary critics, from anomie, which is to say, excessive because unbounded sexual and professional desires. Their figuration as deviant or perverse distinguished them from, and hence worked to consolidate, a normative model of the male citizen as at once autonomous and socialized. A most often implicit, and at times explicit, concern with same-sex vice pervaded these accounts. Contemporary anxieties over homosexuality intersected here with debates about the socialization of citizens and the menace of its failure. As instantiations of a counternorm, which is to say of the "abnormal," these figures were overdetermined and contradictory, embodying at once sexual excess and impotence, passivity and rebelliousness, individualism and massification, hyper-rationality and irrationality, animality and artifice.[5] At the same time, as the progeny of France's political and social modernity, they indicated the precariousness and fragility of that norm.

5. On the "abnormal": Georges Canguilhem, *Le normal et le pathologique* (1966); Michel Foucault, *Les anormaux: Cours au Collège de France, 1974–1975*, ed. François Ewald and Alessandro Fontana (1999).

3 Wasted Youth

In his famous study of the history of childhood, Philippe Ariès describes the nineteenth century as the golden age of the boarding school in French secondary education. From the end of the eighteenth century, he argues, a new understanding of adolescence as a stage apart from both childhood and adulthood contributed to a model of schooling that upheld the moral and pedagogical value of separating youths from their families. While Jesuit and Jansenist schools had already articulated this ideal earlier in the eighteenth century, Napoleon's remodeling and centralization of the secondary educational system in the early nineteenth century generalized the practice and further introduced an explicitly military-style regime of discipline that would come to characterize the state-run institutions for the century to come. These boarding schools allowed families to send their children to lycées that were frequently far from home, and hence permitted a certain democratization of access as well as an eventual decline of aristocratic modes of home schooling. Based on statistics from the nation's most prestigious secondary institution, the Lycée Louis-le-Grand in Paris, Ariès argues that the percentage of students who were boarders in the *internat* progressively rose throughout the century, reaching its apogee in the Second Empire.[1]

By 1890, however, the *internat* was an institution that everyone loved to hate. Liberals and conservatives alike heaped infamy on this perverse mode

---

1. Philippe Ariès, *Centuries of Childhood: A Social History of Family Life*, trans. Robert Baldick (1960), 269–85. Durkheim provides a history of the *internat* in the *longue durée* of state centralization and the development of a French "passion for order" in Émile Durkheim, *L'évolution pédagogique en France* (1990), 132–45. See also Jean-Claude Caron, "Young People in School: Middle and High School Students in France and Europe," in *A History of Young People in the West*, vol. 2, *Stormy Evolution to Modern Times*, ed. Giovanni Levi et al. (1997). For a discussion of Napoleon's reforms, see Georges Weill, *Histoire de l'enseignement secondaire en France (1802–1920)* (1921), 17–48.

of educational organization. Critics charged that this schooling regime separated boys from the moralizing influence of their families, isolated them in promiscuous dormitories, and subjected them to a harsh disciplinary order that provoked a seething hatred of authority, and at times outright revolts or "mutinies," while also encouraging them to passively accept that same authority.[2] Émile Boutroux, a prominent professor of philosophy at the Sorbonne, remarked in one government inquiry, "What I have been able to observe myself is that the regime of the lycée does not sufficiently form character. The children remain pupils, passive and easy to lead; at the same time they are undisciplined and hate rules. They often have their own morality, in which the notions of good and evil are disturbed."[3] For republicans, the principles of social order that reigned supreme inside the walls of these at once military and monastic institutions in no way resembled the nation's new political and social ideals. How, they wondered, could the state leave its future elite in the hands of such authoritarian and potentially perverse institutions? The danger was, of course, even worse in their view when the institutions were run by clerics rather than state-appointed professors. Meanwhile, for increasingly vocal critics of the Republic, the *internat* represented all the dangers of an at once tyrannical and democratic state that, in pursuing its abstract, philosophical ideals, was responsible for destroying the natural order of families and the social fabric of the nation.

The ongoing debate about the *internat* condensed contemporary concerns about the future of men's education in France and, by extension, the future of France *tout court*. Because most members of the cultural elite had passed through this institution, it was a topic on which they all had something to say.[4] This chapter takes these debates as an entryway into the complex concerns about the relationship between education and democracy, knowledge and morality, individual liberty and sociality, and the state and the family that they distilled. I juxtapose two apparently opposed perspectives on the relationship between elite education and democracy. On the one hand, I show how republican pedagogues aimed to alter the "authoritarian" character of the lycée by reforming the *internat*. On the other, I examine how two prominent conservative critics of the republican state, Hippolyte Taine and Maurice Barrès, attacked the nation's secondary schools as a way to reveal the perverse effects of republican democracy. I do so both in order to map the terrain of contemporary political differences and to reveal shared concerns about normative masculinity, citizenship, and social integration.

2. For an account of these revolts, see R. H. Guerrand, *Lycéens révoltés, étudiants révolutionnaires au 19ᵉ siècle* (1969); Agnès Thiercé, *Histoire de l'adolescence* (1999), 95–99.
3. *Enquête sur l'enseignement secondaire: procès-verbaux des dépositions*, vol. 1 (1899), 330.
4. See, for example, the survey by Jean Rodes, "Enquête sur l'éducation," *Revue blanche* 28 (1902).

The Modernization of Secondary Education

While the Ministry of Public Instruction under Ferry and subsequent ministers undertook a radical overhaul of the nation's system of primary education in the 1880s, they left the regime of secondary education nearly in tact. With the exception of piecemeal curricular adjustments, elite schooling remained in the first decades of the Third Republic much as it had been since Victor Duruy's reforms in the 1860s.[5] By 1890, however, the effects of the modernizing reforms enacted under the liberal Empire were making themselves felt. The ranks of those, issued largely from middle-class or petit-bourgeois families, who had undertaken studies in the more practically oriented "special" track of lycée education had begun to swell. State-run institutions, all the while, faced ongoing competition from private, which is to say, clerically run lycées. New questions emerged about the adaptation of classical studies, with their emphasis on Greek and Latin, both to the Republic's democratic ideals and to the exigencies of the modern world. Raoul Frary, in his notorious *La question du Latin*, denounced the ill effects of classical education and its paradoxical production of *déclassés*, who sought entry into state administration or liberal professions rather than embarking on careers in more "productive" métiers such as agriculture, industry, or commerce.[6] What did it mean to shape a democratic elite? How could schools best meet the nation's needs in order to better compete in an international arena? A veritable tidal wave of works in the late 1880s and 1890s by figures inside and outside the academy debated the past and future of French secondary education. The government itself eventually tackled the question, undertaking substantial public inquiries in parliamentary commissions, and issuing two sets of reforms, one in 1890 and another in 1902.

Scholars have treated the history of this "crisis" in some depth, highlighting how debates about the content of respective course programs, and the generalization of the *baccalauréat* degree, revealed significant social and academic tensions surrounding France's democratization and modernization.[7] They have amply described the effects of the 1890 reform that re-

5. See Sandra Horvath-Peterson, *Victor Duruy and French Education: Liberal Reform in the Second Empire* (1984).
6. Raoul Frary, *La question du latin*, 2nd ed. (1885).
7. Viviane Isambert-Jamati, "Une réforme des lycées et collèges: Essai d'analyse sociologique de la réforme de 1902," *Année sociologique* 20 (1969); Viviane Isambert-Jamati, *Crises de la société, crises de l'enseignement: Sociologie de l'enseignement secondaire français* (1970); Detlef K. Muller, Fritz Ringer, and Brian Simon, eds., *The Rise of the Modern Educational System: Structural Change and Social Reproduction, 1870–1920* (1987); Fritz Ringer, *Fields of Knowledge: French Academic Culture in Comparative Perspective* (1992); John E. Talbott, *The Politics of Educational Reform in France, 1918–1940* (1969). See also Victor Karady, "Les professeurs de la République: Le marché scolaire, les réformes universitaires et les transformations de la fonction professorale à la fin du 19ᵉ siècle," *Année sociologique* 47–48 (1983); Antoine Prost, *Histoire de l'enseignement en France, 1800–1967* (1968), 254–75;

named the "special," more vocational track of secondary study, by calling it "modern." This reform, while not going so far as to put the modern program on par with the "classic" one, allowed "modern" students to sit for the *baccalauréat*. While addressing a similar nexus of issues surrounding the "modernization" of the lycée, I focus here less on the arguments about curricula and more on debates about the "disciplinary" regime of the state-run lycée. I am interested in how the near universal denunciation of the perverse moral effects of the school's military-style discipline and of the boarding schools or *internats* operated in these arguments and, further, what it revealed about normative constructions of men's moral and sexual subjectivity in the early Third Republic. If, as André Rausch has intimated, these reforms broke with an earlier model of "heroic" virility, they nonetheless rearticulated a vision of the properly masculine citizen.[8]

It is not surprising that when Republicans undertook initiatives to modernize and liberalize the nation's secondary schooling they set their sights on the authoritarian regime of the lycée and the *internat*. We have already seen in part 1 how primary school reformers were concerned about the morally perverse effects of authoritarianism. Boarding institutions provided an extreme case of such excessive discipline, whose effects were all the more dangerous given that the future elite of the nation was at stake. Since the state itself was responsible for administering this elite education, its implication in the perceived "crisis" was very great indeed. In his report on the reforms undertaken by the Conseil supérieur de l'instruction publique, Minister Léon Bourgeois urged that the "Conseil wanted for the disciplinary regime of the lycée to be a school of character. It is for this reason that it has manifested a preference for a liberal discipline and a movement away from a purely repressive discipline." In the case of lycée students, the urgency was particularly pronounced: "Moral and civic education, which is a pressing necessity at all levels, which primary schools strive to give to all, is doubly necessary for those who have not only themselves to govern, but who, by their words, in the press, in books, and their social influence, constitute public spirit and lead opinion."[9] These reforms addressed the moral fiber not just of elite subjects, but also that of the nation as a whole.

The Ministry of Public Instruction began its study of possible reforms of secondary educational institutions when it convened a commission, presided over by veteran education minister Jules Simon, in 1888. Four subcommissions examined questions of modern and classical curricula, hygiene and the disciplinary regime of state institutions. The responses they gath-

Pierre Rosanvallon, *Le sacre du citoyen: Histoire du suffrage universel en France* (1992), 490–504; Weill, *Histoire de l'enseignement*.

8. André Rauch, *Le premier sexe: Mutation et crise de l'identité masculine* (2000), 210.

9. From the report by the subcommission on "discipline," authored by Henri Marion. Cited in Ministère de l'instruction publique, "Enseignement secondaire: Instructions et règlements," *Bulletin administratif du ministère de l'instruction publique*, no. 922 (supplément) (1890): 424, 597.

ered from the rectors of regional academies (the administrative units that governed state educational institutions) had a common theme, which could be summed up by the report from the rector from Nancy. He admitted that it would be impossible to do away entirely with the system of the *internats,* given their pragmatic necessity. He made it clear, however, that these boarding schools were not educational goods in and of themselves. Rather, they needed serious reform. "We might cheer up the near captivity of children," he suggested, "by taking away from discipline its most rigorous and narrow aspects, so that our lycées and *collèges* no longer seem to be prisons or caserns or convents; they should be branches of the family home."[10] At the end of the nineteenth century, long before Michel Foucault penned *Discipline and Punish,* pedagogues depicted these institutions as commonly geared toward the production of "docile bodies."[11] But Third Republic reformers did not want the nation's new elite to be docile. Quite the contrary.

The *internat* had already undergone an assault of sorts at the end of the Second Empire in a famous text by the liberal Catholic critic, Victor Laprade, entitled *L'éducation homicide.* One of the earliest advocates in France of physical education, Laprade derided the "mortifying" and essentially devirilizing effects of monastic-style education. He condemned both state-run and religious institutions for privileging the development of the mind, to the utter detriment of the body. At stake for Laprade was the nation's virility and vitality. "We don't want a feminized youth," he warned, "and yet that is exactly what the *collège* produces by compressing muscular life and exasperating the nervous system."[12] In other words, docility was precisely the problem.

In the wake of France's defeat in the Franco-Prussian War and the radical revolt of the Paris Commune, Laprade's critiques found an echo among colleagues in the academy and government. Henri Saint-Claire Deville, a chemistry professor at the Sorbonne and the École normale supérieure, denounced the grave menace of same-sex vice propagated by the internat in a speech to the Académie des sciences morales et politiques.[13] Collège de France Professor Michel Bréal soon followed up on these charges in *Quelques mots sur l'instruction publique en France,* which was similarly inscribed under the sign of the French defeat and the uprising of the Commune. He singled out the *internat* as a metonym for all that was wrong with French secondary education, and implicitly France itself. Bréal's discussion was marked by two seemingly polarized anxieties that continued to struc-

10. Ministère de l'instruction publique, *Commission pour l'étude des améliorations à introduire dans le régime des établissements d'enseignement secondaire* (1888), 65–66.
11. Michel Foucault, *Discipline and Punish: The Birth of the Prison,* trans. Alan Sheridan (1979), 141.
12. Victor de Laprade, *L'éducation homicide: Plaidoyer pour l'enfance (nouvelle édition)* (1868), 99.
13. Henri Saint-Claire Deville, "L'internat et son influence sur l'éducation et l'instruction de la jeunesse," *Revue scientifique de la France et de l'étranger* 1 (2nd series), no. 10 (1871). For a more extended discussion of this text, see chapter 2.

Figure 1. "Poor schoolkid." *Gil Blas,* 2 October 1892. President and Fellows of Harvard College: from HOLLIS #005164279. This cartoon illustrates how the boarding school deprives young boys of the pleasures of the opposite sex.

ture attacks on the *internat* through the 1890s: the dangers of democracy and those of authoritarianism, both of which were, in his view, the two faces of the same perverse coin.

On the one hand, he suggested that the *internat* posed a threat of class contagion because scholarship students lived side by side with those from elite families. While he admitted that "equality demands" such intermixing, Bréal warned against the resulting menace, when "children from families of very different moral value" come together. "As we know," he wrote, "it is the bad fruits that attack the good ones, not intact fruits that cure those that have already been attacked by corruption."[14] In other words, for Bréal the *internat* carried a risk of a moral and implicitly sexual class contamination. On the other hand, the regime of surveillance instituted to battle against such corruption paradoxically produced its own perverse effects, namely, resistance and revolt against authority. "Always placed under the eye of the master, the pupil ends up taking him to be the enemy. . . . Between the *collégien* and the *collège*, there is a secret war, in which one redoubles his ruses at the same time that the other multiplies his precautions." Under this regime, students developed, in his view, a twisted notion of liberty. "They become used to the struggle between the law and their will and feel free for the first time when they oppose the rule." In other words, they confused freedom with transgression. Bréal thus concluded, "In the school as in the State . . . if the master must ceaselessly intervene, and order is compromised once the overseer is absent, it is worth nothing."[15] According to this analysis, the very mechanisms of discipline and surveillance that were supposed to enforce moral order only exacerbated lawlessness and immorality.

Jules Simon, who was Minister of Public Instruction in the early years of the Republic, was similarly critical of the system of the *internat*. In his view, its seemingly contradictory effects—passive debauchery or revolt—were the same ills made manifest by France's most recent debacles. The lycée ultimately produced subjects who were, in either case, lacking in will. "Ten years of this regime," he wrote, "makes men who either abandon themselves to excess, or become excessively rebellious; and there, perhaps, is the psychology of France."[16] While Simon had much praise for the tutorial system of the English public school, he did not believe that it could reasonably be instituted in France. His rather utopian proposition was to have professors' families take in small groups of pensioners in order to provide them with the healthy moral influence of home life.[17] He admitted, nonetheless, that it was unlikely that the *internat* system could be done away with "by the stroke of a pen." In the meantime, he proposed, following some of Laprade's recommendations, to add more physical education and hygiene

14. Michel Bréal, *Quelques mots sur l'instruction publique en France* (1872), 304–5.
15. Ibid., 305–6.
16. Jules Simon, *La réforme de l'enseignement secondaire*, 2nd ed. (1874), 211.
17. Ibid., 223–24.

courses to the curriculum. In his view, exercise was powerful both as a "preventive discipline" and as a means of "curing" children's vice. He claimed that "when children develop a keen appetite for exercise, with the zeal and measure of their growing force, they no longer suffer from insomnia, unhealthy reveries, or effeminate habits. Nothing is more reassuring than a *collège* where children feel a bit tired when they go to bed at night."[18]

Nearly twenty years passed between Simon's 1872 curricular modifications and the next wave of significant reforms undertaken by the Commission over which he presided in 1888. In the intervening time, the state established an entirely new system of secular secondary education for girls; the model of the *internat,* was in their case, in principle, rejected, as it was thought to be important for girls to be under the influence of their mothers and in the protection of their families.[19] In the realm of boys' secondary education, the Ministry of Public Instruction made piecemeal changes, but passed no overarching reforms until engaging the wide-scale inquiry overseen by the 1888 Commission. The ministerial circular announcing the creation of that commission stressed institutional form. "The rectors have focused their attention on these seemingly modest reforms which, nonetheless, in remedying the inevitable disadvantages of the *internat,* facilitate and ensure good study and facilitate the physical and moral development of our students."[20] In effect, the subcommissions, after studying the responses to their survey, set out to remedy the alternating tendencies of revolt and passivity encouraged by the regime of the lycée.

The subcommission on "discipline" was presided over by the rector of the Academy of Paris, Octave Gréard, who had written on the problem of the *internat* in 1880 and again in the wake of student revolts at Louis-le-Grand in 1883.[21] None other than Henri Marion, now established as titular in his position as professor of the sciences of education at the Sorbonne, was the subcommission's *rapporteur.* Other members included Ferdinand Buisson, Auguste Burdeau, Gabriel Compayré, Alfred Croiset, Ernest Lavisse, Louis Liard, and Félix Pécaut, in other words, those figures who had thus far been active in the Third Republic's educational reforms. Marion's report stressed the importance of "character" over and above of "mind." "What does it matter what a man knows," he asked, "in compari-

18. Ibid., 152. These courses were added in his ministerial circular of 27 September 1872.

19. The question was very hotly debated. According to a compromise solution, municipal authorities were responsible for establishing girls' *internats*. See *Lycées et collèges des jeunes filles: Documents, rapports et discours* (1888). And Jo Burr Margadant, *Madame le professeur: Women Educators in the Third Republic* (1990), 35–36.

20. Ministère de l'instruction publique, *Commission*, xiv.

21. See Octave Gréard, *L'esprit de discipline dans l'éducation—Mémoire présentée au Conseil académique dans la séance du 26 juin 1883* (1883); Octave Gréard, *Éducation et instruction—Enseignement secondaire*, 2nd ed., vol. 1 (1889).

son with what he wants, and what does it matter what he thinks when compared what he does?"[22]

The contradictions inherent in the regime of the *internat* provided a central focus. As Marion remarked, "Liberty can be prepared only by its exercise; the *internat*, however, by its nature, can only allow for a very limited liberty. How can we modify the military discipline upon which the lycée was first conceived, in order to make it into a school of autonomy for wills?"[23] Marion's conception of "liberal" as opposed to "authoritarian" discipline structured the approach taken toward the reform of the lycée's regime.[24] The pedagogical organization of secondary education was framed as a problem of government *tout court*. "Isn't to obey because it is impossible to do otherwise, without seizing here and there occasions for revolt, the opposite of knowing how to govern one's self? To force youth to submit to this kind of obedience is not, as everyone knows, the best way to make free men."[25] For Marion and the other members of the Commission, the regime of the lycée produced subjects ill adapted to the modern democracy that they were so interested in fostering. A journalist in *Le Temps* summarized Marion's report as follows: "The goal, according to Marion—and who doesn't think like him—is to prepare the youths of our *collèges* and lycées for the free life of the citizen, for the full and active life of the man who is really a man. It is evident that the *internat*, still so popular among us, creates special difficulties in this regard."[26]

At the same time, the Commission was well aware that it would be impossible to do away entirely with the *internat*. Instead it proposed a series of reforms in order to correct the worst effects. By limiting the number of students in each establishment, they encouraged a more intimate and personal relationship between principals and their students. They did away with the monastic rules imposing silence and reduced the existing system of punishments to a strict minimum, while encouraging more recompenses and positive forms of reinforcement. And finally, they placed a new emphasis on using course grades as a method of public sanction, recommending that they be read aloud in class and sent to students' parents. The reforms sought to create an environment in which "the rule is not feared, but loved and respected."[27] This move toward liberalization contained a crucial rejoinder. The softening of the rules inside the institution had as its corollary a policy of harsher treatment toward "incorrigible students," against whom

22. Ministère de l'instruction publique, "Enseignement secondaire," 595.
23. Ibid., 597–98.
24. See the published versions of his Sorbonne lessons on the topic: Henri Marion, "Règles fondamentales de l'enseignement libéral: La méthode active," *Revue pédagogique* 12, no. 1 (1888); Henri Marion, *L'éducation dans l'université* (1892).
25. Ministère de l'instruction publique, "Enseignement secondaire," 598.
26. "Commission enseignement secondaire," *Le Temps*, 19 November 1889.
27. Ministère de l'instruction publique, "Enseignement secondaire," 610.

the new, looser system was insufficiently "armed." "We will nonetheless not undertake to make our punishments equivalent in force to their bad instincts," wrote Marion, "against students who are obstinately lazy, crude, or rebellious, we have at our disposition no other remedy but exclusion."[28] In other words, as Marion explained in a later text, "liberal discipline presupposes children who are sensitive to delicate means, who, at bottom, are not perverse, or who are at least susceptible to becoming so, and whose early education was not too lacking."[29] Marion's vision of "liberal discipline," installed by the Ministry's 1890 reforms, depended on a more careful policing of the boundaries of institutions in order to allow for the liberalization of their interior organization.

The work of the subcommission on "discipline" dovetailed with that on "hygiene," whose recommendations Marion heartily endorsed in his report.[30] The *rapporteur* of that subcommission, Édouard Maneuvrier, had attended the École normale supérieure, and was, similar to Marion, a student of philosophy. He had recently published a book about reform titled *L'éducation de la bourgeoisie sous la République,* which denounced the "total contradiction between our political system and our pedagogical system."[31] In Maneuvrier's view, democracies needed "citizens and men," and he contended that existing secondary schooling produced neither. "How do we go about in France initiating our children to democratic life? Who would believe it? We prepare them for virile action, by destroying all spirit of initiative in them, and political liberty, by bringing them up in prisons!"[32] To make matters worse, wrote Maneuvrier, "after being reduced to a veritable incapacity to act and govern themselves, all of a sudden, on the pretext that they are *bacheliers,* we open the box and let them loose. With a considerable lack of foresight, we send them alone, without surveillance or guide, to Paris, to the most dangerous milieu in the world."[33] The vices of the system, which a journalist reviewing the report referred to tellingly as "against nature," were multiple.[34] Like critics before him, Maneuvrier charged the *internat* with inducing an "atrophy of the will," which manifested itself in seemingly contradictory ways: "a mad aspiration toward a free life"; "a disdain for all authority"; and, "the reverse side of the coin," an excessive dependence on authority. In place of a system that produced at once rebellious and passive charges, destined only for useless positions as state functionaries, Maneuvrier sought to institute one which could finally

28. Ibid., 416. And the report by the subcommission on discipline (602).
29. Marion, *L'éducation,* 239.
30. Ministère de l'instruction publique, "Enseignement secondaire," 621.
31. Édouard Maneuvrier, *L'éducation de la bourgeoisie sous la République* (1888), 21.
32. Ibid., 59.
33. Ibid., 62.
34. Henry Michel, "L'éducation de la bourgeoisie sous la République," *Le Temps,* 26 February 1889.

produce a "virile bourgeoisie."[35] This emphasis on virile virtue found its clearest expression in Maneuvrier's advocacy of physical education, which he believed to be essential for making "soldiers, colonists, and men." Indeed, he proclaimed, "The dominant idea, the supreme goal of our pedagogy, will be to produce virility in its highest and most noble expression. For, one is a man more by character than by intelligence."[36]

Maneuvrier's report on hygiene addressed the reform of the *internat* environment in great detail, from problems of lighting and heating, to ventilation and furniture. He promoted the reduction of overly long work hours, which inevitably resulted in the phenomenon of "burnout" or *surmenage*. As he had in his book, Maneuvrier highlighted the "practical lessons in courage, patience, perseverance, in a word, virility," that courses in physical education would be sure to provide.[37] And, of course, he tackled the issue of "promiscuity" in the dormitories by recommending that students be given private cubicles, albeit open on one side, in order to maximize "privacy" and implicitly limit occasions for vicious contagion, while insuring that students would not escape surveillance altogether.[38]

As this survey well demonstrates, pedagogical reformers were nearly unanimous in their denunciation of the harsh regime of the *internat*. The institution, they charged, was out of step with the moral and political ideals of the Republic, and especially with their vision of a democratic elite; it fabricated, instead, alternately passive and rebellious, that is, implicitly perverse subjects, who were both incapable of self-government and ill-adapted to social order. Their accounts notably intersected with contemporary sexological figurations of the school dormitory as the lieu par excellence where youths might "acquire" inversion. In his survey of contemporary theories of "perversion and perversity," the pseudonymous Dr. Laupts thus described how, at the very moment when "the sexual instinct appears with an intensity and sometimes even with almost a furor," the adolescent "is locked up in a gloomy and unhealthy building, in the company of other adolescents of the same sex, systematically separated from all discreet feminine influence, submitted to a veritable cerebral overload, without sufficient physical out-

---

35. Maneuvrier, *L'éducation*, 62–70, 73.

36. Ibid., 305, 67.

37. Édouard Maneuvrier, *Commission pour les études des améliorations à introduire dans le régime des établissements d'enseignement secondaire: 4e sous-commission* (1889), 16. See also Robert A. Nye, "Degeneration, Neurasthenia and the Culture of Sport in Belle Epoque France," *Journal of Contemporary History* 17, no. 1 (1982); Eugen Weber, "Pierre de Coubertin and the Introduction of Organized Sport in France," *Journal of Contemporary History* 5, no. 2 (1970); Eugen Weber, "Gymnastics and Sports in Fin-de-siècle France: Opium of the Classes," *American Historical Review* 76, no. 1 (1971). On physical culture and a new masculine corporeal ideal see, Tamar Garb, *Bodies of Modernity: Figure and Flesh in Fin-de-siècle France* (1998), 55–79.

38. Maneuvrier, *Commission*, 30. See also Ministère de l'instruction publique, "Enseignement secondaire," 621.

let" and is, hence, "all prepared to be prey to the inversion, the perversion of the sexual instinct."[39] And, while sexual scientists and medico-legal experts endeavored to draw a distinction between "acquired" and "innate" or "congenital" inversion, their writings illustrated the instability of that boundary. For as Laupts remarked at one point, "It is thus impossible to trace a rigorous limit between congenital cases, strictly speaking, and those in which sexual perversion manifests itself on the occasion of an accidental cause."[40] Contemporary sexological accounts of inversion, in other words, made explicit the implicit concerns of these school reformers regarding the potentially perverse and feminizing effects of contemporary schooling.

Several policy makers did, however, warn against the untoward effects of this avalanche of self-criticism on the part of state educational experts. Adrien Dupuy, a member of the subcommission on "discipline," cautioned that the "excessive critique" and "calumnies" that pedagogues heaped on the *internat* risked turning the public against state institutions, and toward clerical ones. What, he asked, was "a *père de famille*, whose sons are interned in lycées, to think when his sons' own teachers rant and rave in this way?"[41] Dupuy argued against reigning opinion, urging that the *internat* did not soften its charges (a risk that he notably associated with familial education). He rather claimed, "In this unjustly criticized environment, a child, unless his nature is resistant to all good influence, takes on, little by little, those virile qualities, such as candor, loyalty, energy, a spirit of justice and solidarity, that a man must display in the world."[42] Dupuy was less than successful in convincing his contemporaries of the positive, and indeed virilizing effects, of the *internat*. He was, however, prescient in his suggestion that, by vociferously denouncing the vices of the system, the reformers on the Conseil supérieur de l'instruction publique furnished adversaries of state-run education with a dangerous instrument of critique.

The Family against the State

The eminent literary critic, historian, and renowned adversary of state centralization, Hippolyte Taine, was perhaps the most prominent of these opponents of government-sponsored education. The posthumously published final volumes of his *Origines de la France contemporaine: Le régime mod-*

39. Dr. Laupts (pseudonym of Georges Saint-Paul), *Perversion et perversité sexuelles* (1896), 30. And Julien Chevalier, *De l'inversion sexuel au point de vue médico-légal* (1885), 165–66. Nye briefly comments on these concerns: Robert A. Nye, *Masculinity and Male Codes of Honor in Modern France* (1993), 95, 115.

40. Laupts, *Perversion et perversité sexuelles,* 223. On this tension in the emergence of "psychiatric reasoning" about sexuality, see Arnold I. Davidson, *The Emergence of Sexuality: Historical Epistemology and the Formation of Concepts* (2001), 27.

41. Adrien Dupuy, *L'état et l'université ou la vraie réforme de l'enseignement secondaire* (1890), 22.

42. Ibid., 61–62.

erne (1894) constituted an influential condemnation of state schooling as a mechanism of young men's moral deformation. Excluded from official academia for political reasons under the Second Empire, Taine remained an ardent critic of what he perceived as the authoritarianism of the university system until the end of his life. He was highly skeptical of centralization and rationalist abstraction whether in monarchical, imperial, or republican form. Perceived as an oppositional figure under the Empire, he soon turned his sights on the legacy of revolution and republicanism as well—in particular, after the experience of the Commune. And, although Taine refused adherence to official political parties or movements, his position as a "consecrated heretic," according to Christophe Charle, legitimated him in the eyes of an entire younger generation of reactionary critics who followed in his wake, including writers such as Maurice Barrès, Paul Bourget, and Charles Maurras.[43] In vehemently denouncing state centralization, Taine emerged as a fervent advocate of "local" interests. Important for my argument here, he articulated this anti-universalism in specifically gendered terms. In his writing on schools, he assailed the state for rending the fabric of family relations and perverting or devirilizing young men. In his view, a century of government-run schooling had disrupted the natural continuity of "filiation" and hence social reproduction *tout court.*

Like republican reformers, Taine denounced the Napoleonic organization of education for undermining "virile virtues." Hopelessly cut off from the "real world," this schooling, in his view, distorted the social, providing the very opposite of what was most necessary for a "civil and lay career," namely, a firm comprehension of sexual difference. He suggested that "after this long *internat,*" students are "amply provided with a knowledge of math and Latin; but they lack two invaluable acquisitions: they have been deprived of two indispensable experiences; upon entering society, the adolescent remains totally ignorant of its two principal actors as he will encounter them, man and woman. He has no notion, or rather one that is preconceived, arbitrary, and false."[44] The lycéen's ignorance of sexually appointed roles epitomized and produced social maladjustment.

Taine saw state schooling as an invasive "mechanism," which, driven by a "single central motor," both assaulted paternal authority and devirilized its young charges. The expansion of the Napoleonic and Jacobin "schooling machine" under the Third Republic consummated, in his view, a century-

---

43. See Christophe Charle, "La magistrature intellectuelle de Taine," in *Taine au carrefour des cultures du 19ᵉ siècle,* ed. Stéphane Michaud (1996). And Susanna Barrows, *Distorting Mirrors: Visions of the Crowd in Late-Nineteenth-Century France* (1981), 89–91; Claude Digeon, *La crise allemande de la pensée française (1870–1914)* (1959), 215–34.

44. Hippolyte Taine, *Les origines de la France moderne: Le régime moderne,* vol. 2, *Église, école* (1894), 262. Taine here rephrases Jules Vallès's dedication to his 1881 novel: "To those who, fed Greek and Latin, have died of hunger." In Jules Vallès, *Le bachelier (1881)* (1970), 46.

long effort to break down local and familial control over education.[45] Conceived as a genealogy of contemporary French institutions, his text began with an examination of Napoleon's refinement and perfection of "Jacobin" educational machinery into factories streamlined to produce loyal and pliant state functionaries. Taine's imagery of industrial production implied that state education was antithetical to traditional and implicitly natural practices of cultivation. In order to obtain a uniform output, this mechanism, in his view, treated its students like raw material, effectively abolishing all semblance of individual difference. "As it operates mechanically, by exterior force, the human material on which it acts, must be passive, composed not of diverse persons but identical units: its students are merely names and numbers."[46]

Taine took these industrial procedures to be emasculating. While perhaps indispensable for the functionary, the diploma, he claimed, was a poor arm in the quotidian battles confronted by the young graduate. The "unnatural and antisocial regime" of the lycée made feeble provision for the exigencies of a "real life" of masculine responsibilities, "the adulthood and virile duties which the grown man must exercise." Rather than acceding to their *âge d'homme* as "armed, equipped, well-trained, hardened," prepared to assume their appointed roles, the spineless subjects described by Taine emerged from the state's schools without even the most essential character traits—"the solidity of good sense, will, and nerves."[47]

The pernicious results of this mechanical reproduction became manifest once the *diplômés* were released from the heavily regimented world of the lycée. Similar to Maneuvrier, Taine argued that the masses of young men swarming the streets of Paris on graduation were constitutionally incapable of self-government. The system wrongly presumed that they would accede to adulthood instantaneously, that "the pupil becomes a man all at once . . . that his conscience, suddenly masterful, and his reason, suddenly adult, will not bend to seduction, or that he will quickly re-erect himself after a downfall." Thus prone to corporeal, financial, and sexual dissipation, the graduate fell prey to the feminized and feminizing pleasures of "the street, café, brasserie, public balls, obscene publications, passing acquaintances, and low-quality liaisons." Indeed, claimed Taine, "against all this, he has been disarmed by his prior education; instead of developing his moral force, the long and strict *internat* maintains his moral debility. He cedes to the occasion, to example: he follows the current, floating haphazardly, he lets himself go."[48] For Taine, this descent into disarray was nearly inexorable. Totally "disarmed" as upstanding moral agents, the students

---

45. Taine, *Les origines*, 283–84.
46. Ibid., 258–59. See also Vital Rambaud, "Barrès et 'le sens du relatif'," *Mesure* 4 (1990): 188–89.
47. Taine, *Les origines*, 296.
48. Ibid., 265–66.

themselves could not be held accountable for their fall into depravity. Rather, the state and its centralized education were at the origin of this pressing social problem.

What is more, weaned of family allegiance by years of schooling, the young *diplômé*, according to Taine, bore only disdain for his parents. State education stripped fathers, now mistrusted by their own progeny, of any recourse to stem the tide of their own children's deviance. "He is suspect when it comes to his children, their interests as well as his own needs; he is not a good judge; the State is more enlightened and better intentioned. As a result, the State has the right to constrain him, and from on high, it does so."[49] The peasant father deprived by Ferry's primary schooling laws of all control over his own child exemplified this predicament. The ravages perpetrated by obligatory education on farm life were a powerful metaphor for the state's destitution of the family's timeless rhythms of production and reproduction. For Taine, its unmeasured program destroyed the natural hierarchies by which the family was ordered and governed. The abstract, superfluous, and impractical content of Republican schooling bred contempt for the traditional métier of the father, destabilized traditional modes of social and sexual reproduction, and further, sowed seeds of resentment. Taine thus bemoaned the impotence of fathers to impose their own educational regime, one presumably guided by more *terre à terre* concerns. "The *père de famille* vainly attempts to limit the extent, the mental provisioning of his children to that knowledge which they will use—reading, writing, the four rules—to devote only the time required, the appropriate season—three months in winter, for two or three winters; to keep his twelve-year-old daughter home to aid her mother to care for the younger ones; to keep his ten-year-old son at his side so that he can graze the herd or prod his cattle in front of the wagon."[50] By interfering with this natural, gendered division of labor, state schooling threatened the future of the family (and implicitly population, and hence nation).

Taine emphasized how the centralized state eroded the family's status as an essential, elementary social unit. He had intended to elaborate on precisely this point in a section devoted exclusively to the "Family," which remained incomplete at the time of his death.[51] He planned to examine in greater detail how "the atomization [*émiettement*] of individuals, isolated and diminished at the hands of the overly powerful state" undermined the almost timeless institution of the family. Its decline, in turn, contributed to the rise of contemporary egotism. The concomitant "atrophy of the social instinct" was marked by individuals' dwindling desire to belong to "groups

49. Ibid., 290–91.
50. Ibid., 290.
51. The preface cites Taine's intention to treat how "Jacobin laws concerning marriage, divorce, *puissance paternelle*, and the forced public education of children" contributed to the sad state of modern family affairs. Ibid., iv.

that last longer than they do." The family was, for Taine, coextensive with sociality *tout court,* a figure for the forces, which bound the individual to corporate entities that exceeded him. It was also a natural alibi for social, and by extension, political order.[52] Thus, the "organic deficiency of cohesive faculties," effected by the mechanistic operations of the state, and especially its schools, "results in the destruction of centers of natural grouping, and hence, political instability."[53] As a vital principle that extended life beyond the individual, assuring continuity against interruptions introduced by death, the family served for Taine "to prolong and 'perpetuate the individual' in offering the 'sole remedy for death.'" Taine rued the fact that young men were no longer encouraged to "found a family, an infinitely lasting household, to create and govern." The modern state, he charged, urged its subjects to adopt short-range goals, to think only of "self-amusement and career advancement," rather than to invest in the timeless, death-defying institution of the family.[54]

Taine's *Origines* drew an explicit connection between, on the one hand, the expansion of centralized schooling and its concomitant ideology of meritocracy and social advancement, and, on the other, the destitution of the "social instincts" embodied in the reproductive family. According to this argument, the republican state deregulated the reproductive sexual desires, which were the natural alibi for the social order. After being reduced to a state of will-less atrophy by the lycée, the thirst for unattainable advancement perverted the young *diplômé*'s appetites. He sought satisfaction outside properly domestic channels and his overblown ambitions bred revolt by encouraging desires that were destined, in most cases, according to Taine, to go frustrated. The unnatural and unmeasured character of republican education was a source of at once social and mental disequilibrium.[55] This "harsh and dangerous ordeal" produced a body of disaffected individuals, unsatisfied by their preordained social roles and hence liable to reject the entire social order. Taine thus paraphrased the outlook of contemporary youth: "'Your education led us to believe, allowed us to believe that the world is made in a certain fashion; you deceived us; it is much uglier, more insipid, dirtier, sadder and more difficult . . . we curse and ridicule your entire world, and reject your purported truths which, for us, are lies—including even those elementary truths upon which you found your laws, institutions, society, philosophy, science, and art.'" Taine concluded, "This is what contemporary youth, in its tastes and opinions, its literary, artistic,

52. On Taine's organicism, see Eric Gasparini, *La pensée politique d'Hippolyte Taine* (1993). For an account of Taine's "irrationalist" tendencies, see Alan Pitt, "The Irrationalist Liberalism of Hippolyte Taine," *Historical Journal* 41, no. 4 (1998).

53. Taine, *Les origines,* ii–iii.

54. Ibid., iv–v.

55. On Taine's association between psychological imbalance and revolution, see Barrows, *Distorting Mirrors,* 73–88.

and existential confusions, has been saying to us for the past fifteen years."[56]

Like the republican reformers who sought to remake the nation's system of secondary schooling, Taine was concerned about the perverse potential of state administered education. His account of the lycée as a devirilizing machine reiterated the analyses set forth by Laprade and Bréal, Maneuvrier and Marion. Like them, he articulated a normative conception of both masculinity and femininity, together anchored in the reproductive family, with his vision of a stable social order. But, in contrast to his contemporaries on the 1888 Commission, Taine did not seek to make way for a new, democratic elite. He rather mobilized the trope of the machine-like *internat* as an emasculating and perverse institution, in order to discredit those very ideals. He sought to indict the ravages of democratic, universalist, and meritocratic leveling which unhinged young men from the social order.

As Taine's 1894 text indicates, the reforms undertaken in 1890, rather than definitively closing the "crisis" of secondary education, set the stage for what was to become a decade-long public debate. On one side were those who argued that the reforms did not go far enough and who advocated yet more radical measures, such as the alignment of primary and secondary education, the inclusion of more modern science in the curriculum, and even the abolition of the *baccalauréat*.[57] On the other, were those who sought to roll back the reforms already initiated in order to protect classical studies from further democratic dilution.[58] Fritz Ringer has devoted considerable attention to these ongoing debates. He highlights the controversy provoked by the expansion of "modern" secondary studies, the progressive increase in *baccalauréat* awards, and a swelling university population.[59] Once graduates of the "modern" track could sit for the *bac*, the program underwent what Ringer has termed a "generalist" shift. While it remained less prestigious than the classical track, its graduates began to encroach on a territory formerly reserved exclusively for traditional *bacheliers*, contributing to increased public concern both with the *déclassement* of young graduates and with the deflated value of the diploma.[60] Meanwhile, a parallel crisis befell the world of publishing in the 1890s. This domain, particularly attractive to young graduates seeking to make a place in the world, underwent a rapid retraction in the last decade of the century, giving rise to

---

56. Taine, *Les origines*, 296–97. Taine notably cites Jules Vallès here as exemplary of this phenomenon.

57. See, for example, Marcelin Berthelot, "La crise de l'enseignement secondaire," *Revue des deux mondes* 61, n. 104 (1891); Ernest Lavisse, "Réforme nécessaire," *Revue universitaire* 1, no. 1 (1892).

58. See, for example, Alfred Fouillée, *L'enseignement au point de vue national* (1891); Alfred Fouillée, *Les études classiques et la démocratie* (1898).

59. Ringer, *Fields of Knowledge*, 127.

60. Ibid., 114. And Muller, Ringer, and Simon, eds., *The Rise of the Modern Educational System*.

anarchist sympathies among young avant-garde writers progressively excluded from officially consecrated publications. "Intellectuals" of all political persuasions thus sought to rival the entrenched power of the republican establishment by asserting their own, alternate form of power in the public sphere. This effort relied in large part on both implicit and explicit critiques of the dominant political order as corrupt and corrupting.[61] These interrelated developments exacerbated fears that young men, fresh out of the lycée, were primed more for social alienation and even revolt than for national and social integration and incorporation.

The Docile Student Body

The onset of concerns about the impact of democratized education on young men also gave rise to a new literary genre, which Denis Pernot has tellingly termed the "novel of socialization." In an argument that roughly parallels my own, Pernot suggests that the construction of "youth as a problem" in both pedagogical and literary discourse emerged with the opening of a "new political era in France."[62] Numerous authors, most famously Paul Bourget and Maurice Barrès, developed this genre as a supplement and even antidote to the perceived failings of state education; it constituted, in Pernot's view, the literary field's response to the perceived crisis of youth and relied, for its "discursive strategy," on a critique of republican schools.[63]

Maurice Barrès's novel, *Les déracinés* (1897), exemplifies how these novels aimed to put youths, purportedly deformed by the new Republic's system of education, back on the track to proper socialization. This first volume of a trilogy titled *Le roman d'énergie nationale* famously depicts how state schooling perverted and devirilized the nation's youth. Playing on the conventions of the "novel of education," Barrès recounted the ascension of seven ambitious provincials to Paris. Based on his own lycée experience at the end of the 1870s, the novel retrospectively reconstructed this pivotal moment in the creation of the Republic and its schools. In Barrès's narrative, the graduates of Paul Bouteiller's course in Kantian philosophy take leave of their bucolic Lorrain intoxicated by illusions of abstract individualism. It is a foregone conclusion that their exploits will in no way resemble

61. Christophe Charle, *La crise littéraire à l'époque du naturalisme* (1979), 52–54; Venita Datta, *Birth of a National Icon: The Literary Avant-garde and the Origins of the Intellectual in France* (1999); Richard Sonn, *Anarchism and Cultural Politics in Fin-de-siècle France* (1989), 192–94.

62. Denis Pernot, *Le roman de socialisation, 1889–1914* (1998), 34–35. For related discussions of the "novel of adolescence," see John Neubauer, *The Fin-de-siècle Culture of Adolescence* (1992); Justin O'Brien, *The Novel of Adolescence in France: The Study of a Literary Theme* (1937).

63. Pernot, *Le roman*, 91.

success. This story of "negative exemplarity" set out to discredit the republican ideology of the seven protagonists' philosophy professor.[64] Barrès charged that this philosophy, by promoting individualism and destroying social and familial ties, had dismembered the French nation. In his later attacks on Dreyfusard intellectuals, Barrès similarly targeted the toxic effects of the Republic's Kantianism. Indeed, he figured the Dreyfus Affair as a symptom of the social decline already depicted in the novel, noting in an article reprinted in *Scènes et doctrines du nationalisme,* "This affair is a marvelous illustration of *Les déracinés* who were anterior to it."[65]

Written in the year before Émile Zola launched the public phase of the Affair, the novel depicted republican schools and their Kantian philosophy as sources of moral dissolution, criminality, and perversion. For Barrès, the state's universalist and rationalist doctrines had undermined the "unconscious" and "sacred" foundations of an at once stable and vital social order, most notably the individual's quasi-religious ties to family and place of origin. As his contemporaries noted, this critique clearly borrowed from Taine.[66] Like his mentor, Barrès argued that republican schooling disrupted the sexual and social order of "filiation."

The novel's opening scene accented this generational fissure by portraying the "violent" emotion provoked by the arrival of the new philosophy professor to the lycée of Nancy in 1879; the teacher, Paul Bouteiller, immediately created a revolutionary tumult among his future students.[67] The first signs of the anarchy to be sown by his thought were perceptible from the outset: "A strange seething agitated their brains, and an almost insurrectional rumbling pervaded their playground, refectory, and even their dormitories."[68] Barrès, like Bourget before him, played here on contemporary critiques of the perversity of the *internat*. Bourget had thus described the

64. Susan Rubin Suleiman, *Authoritarian Fictions: The Ideological Novel as Literary Genre* (1983), 85, 98–99.

65. Maurice Barrès, *Scènes et doctrines du nationalisme* (1902), 57.

66. René Doumic, "*Les déracinés* de M. Maurice Barrès," *Revue des deux mondes* 67, no. 139 (1897): 461. Paul Bourget, to whom *Les déracinés* is dedicated, thus commented: "All he had to do was to translate, into concrete facts the striking pages of the fifth volume of Taine's great work, which he entitled 'The School.'" Paul Bourget, *Essais de psychologie contemporaine* (1993), 169. In a journal entry from 1897, Barrès nonetheless expressed hesitancy about Bourget's characterization of him as a complete disciple of Taine, in Maurice Barrès, *Mes cahiers, 1896–1923,* ed. Guy Dupré (1994), 91. See also Claire Bompaire-Evesque, "Paris, centre de la vie politique dans 'Le roman de l'énergie nationale' de Maurice Barrès," *Cahiers de l'Association Internationale des Études Françaises* 42 (1990); Marius-François Guyard, "Barrès et la Révolution française: La leçon des *Déracinés,*" in *Barrès: Une tradition dans la modernité,* ed. André Guyaux et al. (1991); Rambaud, "Barrès."

67. The relationship between Paul Bouteiller and Barrès's professor at Nancy and eventual president of the Chamber of Deputies, Auguste Burdeau, has been well documented, see Jean François Sirinelli, "Littérature et politique: Le cas Burdeau-Bouteiller," *Revue historique* 272, no. 1 (1984).

68. Maurice Barrès, *Les déracinés (1897),* (1988), 69. Hereafter cited in text.

"loves against nature" which proliferated "between the walls of this prison" in his 1886 novel *Un crime d'amour*.[69] For Barrès, republican moral philosophy was the *cause* of the disruption, not its solution. He notably transposed contemporary concerns about sexual deviance onto philosophy, noting that this isolated population of adolescents was highly susceptible to "moral epidemics" (70).

Taking a page from Taine, Barrès described the devirilizing degradation, the passivity and rebelliousness, propagated by the *internat*. "Throughout all of France, these vast lycées which look from the outside as if they were caserns and convents, shelter a collectivity in revolt against laws, a solidarity of serfs who scheme and struggle, not free men who organize themselves according to a rule" (70). This moral deformation gave rise, according to the narrator, to perverse sexual comportments. In a passage traversed by anxieties of impotence and latent homoeroticism, Barrès intimated that the servile homogeneity of the school atmosphere disturbed conventional social relations, a confusion epitomized by the lycéens' incapacity to differentiate between proper and improper sexual objects.

> What kind of conception do they have of humanity? They lose touch with their fellow citizens and their entire family; they no longer turn to their mothers and fathers for assurance, for the security that, maintains the strength and charm of filial ties. Women are no longer, in their eyes, complete beings but only a sex. In their presence, they are incapable of thinking of anything but the seductions—at which young Frenchmen excelled in the last century—which their isolation, rendering them timid and awkward, has made them most unworthy. With their imaginations, so spoiled by such precocious curiosity, they blush at the sight of the sisters and cousins who come to pay a visit. On their tedious Thursday and Sunday promenades in tight ranks, they find distraction in 'scoring' the women they cross—and they show themselves to be quite severe. With this initial training, they stake their honor on having all the ones they meet, even those they find displeasing. (71–72)

At once impotent ("timid and awkward") and overly sexualized, the student was here subject to incestuous desires. Like same-sex perversion, incest represented a crisis in the familial organization of sexual difference produced by an underexposure to women. By dismembering the family and isolating adolescent boys, the school environment weakened "filiation," destroying bonds both between generations and between men and women. For Barrès, the family was the milieu par excellence of socialization, for which sexual differentiation and proper heterosexual desire were metonyms. The lycée's disrup-

69. Paul Bourget, *Un crime d'amour* (1898), 44–45. For a novelistic account of same-sex vice in a Catholic institution, see Jean Rodes, *Adolescents: Moeurs* (1904). Emile Zola's *Vérité* notably transposed the Dreyfus Affair onto a scandal of pedophilia in a Catholic school. Christophe Charle has suggested parallels between Bourget and Zola in their post-Affair novels. See Christophe Charle, "La lutte des classes en littérature: *L'étape* de Paul Bourget and *Vérité* d'Émile Zola," in *Les écrivains et l'affaire Dreyfus,* ed. Gérald Leroy (1983).

tion of the family carried as its consequence the ruination of normal relations between the sexes. Deprived of regular and regulated contacts with women, the student was incapable of seduction and, for this very reason, developed a degraded vision of the opposite sex. His sexual dysfunction was, for Barrès, a symptom of both the egotism *and* homogenizing universalism, the liberty and equality, theoretically propagated by republican educational philosophy.

Like Taine, Barrès enshrined filial affection and in particular, the cult of dead fathers, as the sacred principles on which an at once vital and stable social order was based. In *Les déracinés*, he suggested that the rationalist individualism propounded by republican educational philosophy undermined this font of devotion to a group that exceeded the singular self. To underscore the conflict between paternal and state authority, Barrès depicted the Kantian philosophy professor as an orphan, who bore sole allegiance to the state that raised him. A fatherless beneficiary of scholarships and elite education, Bouteiller gave himself over to the state. He was "a purely pedagogical product, foreign to our traditional local or familial customs, entirely abstract, suspended in a void" (85). An agent of artificial reproduction, he endeavored to remake his disciples in his own image; raising them above their regional particularity, he converted them to his ungrounded and u-topic vision of "*la patrie*"—the universal. Operating like "a sorcerer of old, but with a modern countenance" (92), Bouteiller cast a spell over his students, awakening new longings which lead them to go against their natures, to leave behind all that was literally familiar. "Their desire is for an unknown country, for the society closed to them, for the profession most foreign to that of their father. These all too young self-destroyers aspire to deliver themselves from their true nature, to uproot themselves" (100).

Bouteiller was a foreigner in their midst. Deprived of the ties that bind, he was easily seduced by the "exotic"—i.e., German—moral philosophy, which Barrès took to be deleterious to the French nation.[70] The outline of Barrès's later vituperations against "intellectuals" and "philosophy professors" at the apogee of the Dreyfus Affair were already visible in these opening pages. The state's fatherless "pedagogical products" were shown to destabilize the nation by propagating abstract ideals of universality just like the rootless, exotic Jews, with whom they came to be identified. Indeed, as Mary Louise Roberts and Christopher Forth have well demonstrated, "Jewishness," "republicanism," and unstable gender identity were strongly correlated in Barrès's writing.[71] He hinted at an essential collusion between "groundless" philosophical and financial speculation. In his journalism of the epoch, Barrès sought to illustrate the essential correspondence between

70. Digeon, *La crise allemande*, 403–34.
71. See Christopher E. Forth, *The Dreyfus Affair and the Crisis of French Manhood* (2004), 70–81; Mary Louise Roberts, *Disruptive Acts: The New Woman in Fin-de-siècle France* (2002), 107–30.

the "official philosophy" of the republic and the Jewish "idea" of the nation, a connection which explained, for him, why so-called "intellectuals" rallied to the Dreyfusard cause. Nearly interchangeable figures both in the novel and in his writing on the Dreyfus Affair, Kantians and Jews professed a metaphysical morality whose abstract character was, in his view, foreign to French "reality." Barrès argued that, like Bouteiller, Jews had no proper "*patrie.*" As he explained in his famous speech preaching devotion to "*la terre et les morts*": "The Jews do not have a fatherland in our sense. For us, the fatherland is our soil and ancestors; it is the land of our dead. For them, it is where they make the greatest profit. Their 'intellectuals' thus formulate their famous definition: 'The fatherland is an idea.' But what idea? That which is most useful, for example: the idea that all men are brothers, that nationality is a prejudice that should be destroyed, that military honor stinks blood, that disarmament is necessary (in order to make money alone powerful), etc."[72]

This address to the anti-Dreyfusard *Ligue de la patrie* also contained an all-out attack on "Kantian" doctrines.[73] The cunning of Barrès's argument was to twist the terms of "Kantianism" into their opposites. He framed the commitment to an abstract and transhistorical "duty" as a form of treason against French "reality." He portrayed the Kantian emphasis on individual reason as egotism, while simultaneously charging Kant's abstract universalism with the effacement of individual particularity. Barrès continues, "This Kantianism of our classes claims to regulate universal man, abstract man without taking into account individual differences. It tends to mold this year's young Lorrainians, Provençals, Bretons, and Parisians after an abstracted, ideal man, everywhere identical, while what we need are men solidly enracinated in our soil, our history, our national consciousness, and adapted to the needs of today's France."[74] He charged that "an orgy of metaphysicians," blinded to contemporary French "necessities," mistook their self-serving pronouncements for "Truth" and "Justice." Conversely, Barrès argued that "real" Truth and Justice were relative and literally rooted in the earth.[75]

72. Barrès, *Scènes,* 63. For an analogous discussion, see Datta, *Birth of a National Icon,* 92–94. The question of whether Barrès's corporeal and integral nationalism should be considered "proto-fascist," goes beyond the scope of my discussion here. For further treatment, see David Carroll, *French Literary Fascism: Nationalism, Anti-Semitism, and the Ideology of Culture* (1995); Robert Soucy, *Fascism in France: the Case of Maurice Barrès* (1972); Zeev Sternhell, *Maurice Barrès et le nationalisme français* (1972).

73. For a history of this league, of which Barrès was a founding member, see Jean-Pierre Rioux, *Nationalisme et conservatisme: La Ligue de la patrie française* (1977).

74. Barrès, *Scènes.* 82. Émile Durkheim, in his response to Ferdinand Brunetière at the height of the Affair critiqued precisely this tendency in the anti-Dreyfusards' attacks on individualism, a tendency which he explained in terms of a facile confusion between utilitarianism and Kant's supra-individual ethics. See Émile Durkheim, "Individualism and the Intellectuals," in *Émile Durkheim on Morality and Society,* ed. Robert N. Bellah (1973), 44–45.

75. Barrès, *Scènes,* 85. See also Rambaud, "Barrès," 183–96.

Against the unrealistic ideals produced by cerebral machinations, Barrès proposed an instinctive, incorporated brand of national devotion that took filial piety as its source and foundation. The sacred affective bonds of a son to his father and fatherland incarnated the national reality to which he laid claim. Opposed to the "university culture" whose abstract discussions of *l'homme* and *l'humanité* were socially atomizing and productive of "anarchic agitation," Barrès appealed to the "sentiments of veneration" which bind or "instruct and fix the heart." Privileging affect over abstract reason, he proposed a program for the constitution of a new national conscience and moral unity based on "unconscious" sentiments. He insisted, "In order to create a national consciousness, we must join a more unconscious, less voluntary element to the sovereign intellectualism whose method historians have so well illustrated to us."[76]

The unconscious wells from which Barrès proposed to draw nationalist sentiment were the very sources from which the university, in theory, severed the young *bachelier*: his family and *patrie*. The cemetery thus functioned, for Barrès, as a sacred site par excellence, combining as it did these two powerful springs of quasi-religious devotion. And, he hailed Antigone, who was, in his view, motivated by "subconscious elements in which respect, love, and fear not yet differentiated from one another, constitute the magnificent power of veneration," as exemplary of filial piety.[77] Antigone represented for Barrès the profound workings of a mystical conception of heredity.[78]

The mourning of dead fathers was central to Barrès's concept of familial and national continuity. His vision of the nation and of citizenship sought to avoid the conflict between the family and the state, affect and reason that, he argued, was produced by republican moral philosophy. In his writing, familial and patriotic devotion were combined in the figure of the ancestor. "We are the products of a collectivity, which speaks in us. May the influence of ancestors be permanent, sons energetic and erect, the nation one."[79] To illustrate this principle, he recalled a scene from a novel written

76. Barrès, *Scènes*, 85.

77. Barrès thus contrasts Antigone to Creon, who represents for him a "foreign" law, based on "superficial" intelligence rather than on the profound—because unconscious—sentiments that stir Antigone. Ibid., 11. Barrès's account of Antigone's filial piety is interesting when compared to Hegel's better-known treatment of her. For Hegel, the unconscious relation to divine law remains the province of the feminine, while the brother and husband exit this "nether world" of the household spirits in order to enter consciousness. Judith Butler has pointed to the tension in Hegel's argument between kinship and citizenship, a tension which Barrès seeks to overcome in his model of *"la terre et les morts."* See G. W. F. Hegel, *Philosophy of Right*, trans. T. M. Knox (1971), 273–78. And Judith Butler, *Antigone's Claim: Kinship between Life and Death* (2000), 30; G. W. F. Hegel, *Phenomenology of Spirit*, trans. A. V. Miller (1977), 114–15.

78. Barrès's simultaneously psychological and physiological understanding of "heredity" was strongly influenced by the racist psychological theorist, Jules Soury. On the importance of this relationship, see Sternhell, *Maurice Barrès*.

79. Barrès, *Scènes*, 89.

by Louis Ménard, in which two sons mourn their departed father. Their reminiscence reawakens, hence preserving, his wisdom and authority: " 'That is where duty lies; by thinking of him, his beneficent force lays over us, as it did in life; in this way, the dead extend their hands to the living.' "[80] "Duty" was rendered here not as an abstract idea, but as an affective relationship to a combined familial and national past. *La terre*—exemplified by the burial ground—mediated between the limited circle of the family and that of the *patrie*. The injunction to protect the memory of the father—and hence the sacred site upon which he was buried—fueled a fervor to preserve the national territory. The cemetery fallen into foreign hands represented, for Barrès, the ultimate national and familial tragedy.

Barrès's program to restore the nation's corporeal integrity sought to reinstate paternal authority and the resubmission of the son to the will of his forefathers. He decried the atomizing, individualistic desires instilled by the republican educational system and its "exotic" Kantian truths. In his view, an overwhelming faith in the power of "intelligence" entailed a sorry end, both for the nation and for the individual—one in which its figurative head was severed from the body. Barrès instead proposed a moral and political vision in which "force" was paradoxically based on abdication, national potency on the recognition of individual impotence. In reflecting on his "filiation," he wrote, "Horrified by my dependence, incapable [*impuissant*] of creating myself, I wanted to contemplate the powers that govern me face to face. I wanted to live with my masters, to participate in their force by devoting to them a reflective cult. While others analyze in order to decompose, I do so to recompose, to find my truth."[81] Such acknowledgment of heteronomy provided a sense of certainty, which in turn allowed the son to stand erect.

Revolting Figures

Les déracinés recounted the rotten potential of sons once they abandoned their fathers and fatherland for the nation's capital. On their arrival, these youths encountered the ugly underside of the transcendental illusions built up by the Republic's philosophy professors.[82] According to critics of urban modernity like Barrès, the whirlwind of Paris, centrifuge-like, produced atomization and isolation amongst the "proletariat of bacheliers." Broken down and "attenuated," they were, in his novel, "deprived of the conditions that might allow them to blossom into citizens" (179). The uprooted

80. Ibid., 90.
81. Ibid., 12.
82. On Barrès's representation of the nation's capital as an agent of moral dissolution, see Bompaire-Evesque, "Paris, centre de la vie politique"; Denis Pernot, "Paris, province pédagogique," *Romantisme* 21, no. 83 (1994).

provincials that descended on Paris after acceding to their *baccalauréat* become agents of anarchy, vehicles of social disaggregation paradoxically produced by the Republican "order" itself.

Once displaced to Paris, Bouteiller's students gather together on their new common ground—the sterile and inhospitable terrain of the student café. The noxious setting portends the inauspicious future that awaits them. Here, the narrator suggests, "one's moral hygiene is more gravely compromised than by any other vice" (135). Cramped and jostled under the gaslights, the ingénus make a valiant attempt to realize their collective aspirations, imagining themselves "as forming a powerful tree in which the forces of each, like a circulating sap, benefited all" (146). Failure and frustration soon undermined the hopes hung high on the branches of this pastoral image of fraternity. The narrator intimates that, in this debauched climate, men were softened rather than formed, reduced to docile and unproductive subjects sought out for state service. This profoundly demoralizing atmosphere was diametrically opposed to a mythic natural environment propitious to the formation of "a real brotherhood in arms." He comments that, "Even if this primitive life no longer exists, if man now no longer knows the nuances of nature, the seasons, the diverse positions of the sun, certain youths still aim, in their brave endeavors, to sacrifice themselves, to expend their vigor." They are, however, "in the minority, these daring souls! The immense herd consumes its poetry while waiting to become bureaucrats. Card-playing, chit-chatting, and consuming, these half-men or rather, soft creatures that the administration has prepared like it likes them, wait, in vile unproductivity in the café, for nothing but their nomination" (135–36). While close contact with nature produced healthy organic societies, the students' "artificial life" (146) lent itself to a sort of herd mentality. Barrès represented these dissolute and feminized subjects as at once impotent—passive and unproductive—and as avidly desiring. Unregulated by the forces of nature such as the sun and seasons, their bestial appetites knew no limits; their loss of individual boundaries carried as a consequence an inability to master bodily impulses.[83] With its effacement of distinctions and animalistic character, the appetite of this herd incarnated a desire without limit. "Swarm in which no individuals, only a species is recognizable. The gas, smoke, drunkenness, and desires cast violent, alternately red and black splotches on this heap of youth. So many different adolescents, screaming and squirming, do not lead you to think they are more than one. They form a single, federated animal, all hands held out, all mouths open to alcohol and prostitution" (147). This inchoate, avidly desiring "federative animal" was the counterimage of the "tree" whose blighted future the novel depicts. The perpetually mobile desire of this

83. On the feminized, alcoholic, and politically volatile crowd, see Barrows, *Distorting Mirrors;* Forth, *The Dreyfus Affair.* On Barrès, see Datta, *Birth of a National Icon,* 122–23.

swarm is both symptom and cause of a failed attachment to the social order.

Deprived of a stable position, the Latin Quarter inhabitants depicted in the novel resort to the *brasserie de femmes* in order to find a meager sense of belonging and the occasional comforts of the opposite sex. Barrès's description of this world of displaced persons was charged with sympathy, indicating an ambivalence toward the revolting character of student life, whose suffering and pleasure he had romanticized in texts of his youth.[84] As director of a formerly Boulangist, socialist newspaper *La Cocarde,* Barrès had allied himself with this *"prolétariat des bacheliers."*[85] Writing after his electoral defeat in 1893, he identified with the uprooted souls who were promised everything and delivered nothing. Conducting a xenophobic campaign against foreign workers, while ardently defending the *"petite patrie,"* he associated the struggles of declassed youth with his own. "We know to whom we speak; in particular, to the proletariat of *bacheliers,* to those youths whom society has given a diploma and nothing else, at the risk of turning them into an urban mass of *déclassés.* We know we are in agreement with their reflections and, in any case, with their instinct, clamoring for the resurrection of their native lands where they might be gainfully employed."[86] These figures in revolt were, for him, a powerful potential vanguard in this project of *revanche.*[87]

In *Les déracinés,* however, the proletariat of *bacheliers* is a figure of waste not a promising impetus for social and political change. The frustrated ambitions of youth give way, in the novel, to crime, not heroic revenge against the foreign invader. Barrès nonetheless reserved his harshest critique for the state educational system, which was, in his view, responsible for squandering the nation's vital energies and for decimating an inordinate number of youths in order to produce a handful of servile functionaries.[88]

---

84. Drawing from his own experience as a youth in Paris, the novel's chapter, "Un prolétariat des bacheliers et des filles," cites a text written nearly a decade before: Maurice Barrès, *Sensations de Paris—Ces messieurs—Ces dames: 52 croquis par nos meilleurs artistes* (1888), 27. On the *brasserie des filles* as a new locus of prostitution, see Alain Corbin, *Les filles de noce* (1978), 250–54.

85. For discussions of Barrès's political orientation at this moment, see C. Stewart Doty, *From Cultural Rebellion to Counterrevolution: The Politics of Maurice Barrès* (1976), 117–37; Richard Sonn, "The Early Political Career of Maurice Barrès: Anarchist, Socialist, or Protofascist?" *Clio* 21, no. 1 (1991); Sternhell, *Maurice Barrès.*

86. Maurice Barrès, "La glorification de l'énergie," *La Cocarde,* 19 December 1894.

87. Quoted in Paul Lagarde, "La maison du peuple," *La Cocarde,* 24 December 1894. On Barrès's attempt to capitalize on the "popular and primitive" psychic energies of the bohemian masses as a precursor of his "irrationalist" nationalist politics, see Jerrold Seigel, *Bohemian Paris: Culture, Politics, and the Boundaries of Bourgeois Life, 1830–1930* (1986), 287–88. On Barrès in the context of anti-immigrant sentiment, see James R. Lehning, *To Be a Citizen: The Political Culture of the Early Third Republic* (2001), 127.

88. He described the overproduction of degrees, relative to the available number of positions as responsible for the production of the *"prolétariat des bacheliers"* (185).

BRASSERIE, par Serge BASSET.

Figure 2. "Brasserie." *Gil Blas*, 29 December 1899. President and Fellows of Harvard College: from HOLLIS #005164279. A lycéen surrounded by corrupting company in a "brasserie des filles."

By inciting desires that it could not satisfy, the system, according to Barrès, produced its own destruction by sowing seeds of resentment and revolt.

One of the seven Lorrainians, Honoré Racadot, incarnated this perilous dynamic. His trajectory, from descendent of serfs to *bachelier* to criminal illustrated the hazards of republican educational philosophy. The narrative of his demise echoed contemporary debates about the impact of state-sponsored schooling, meritocracy, and secular morality on increased rates of juvenile criminality.[89] Swollen by ambition, Racadot had no sense of the practical limits on his desires; he quickly fell prey to the seductions of the capital, which "excite violent appetites" (115). The easy pleasures of his debauched lifestyle lulled him into a false sense of potency. "Of all these appetites, woman was the most imperious, even before eating and drinking. The certitude of finding one gave him a sensation of force in all his nervous centers, and more precisely, a philosophy of optimism in his brain." This is precisely what made him so menacing, for, as Barrès added, "No amount of armed force would be enough: a boy who has such audacity and who has no reasoned understanding of the relation between means and consequences, effort and obstacle, is most dangerous. The primary condition of social peace is that the poor have a sense of their impotence" (232). Perverted by delirious individualist fictions, he refused any social limits. Racadot's excessive sexual desire incarnated an anomie implicitly produced by academic abstraction.

Barrès's novel sought to reveal the tragic reality behind this academic fantasy. Skeptical of official pedagogy, the novel's own moral "authority" occupied a difficult and contradictory position, an instance of the paradox of the *roman à thèse* so well described by Susan Suleiman.[90] In order to skirt the problem posed by his own authorial legitimacy, Barrès appealed to Taine. As a character in the novel, he propounded an organic social vision, embodied by a tree, whose growth exemplified an "acceptance of life's necessities," which is to say, the limits that inevitably confine and contain individual existence (244). His philosophy provided an antidote to the skewed Kantian perspective of Bouteiller.[91]

At the same time, Taine's utopian model and its presumption of a stable and unified social order no longer seemed to apply in a France

89. Jacques Bonzon, *Le crime et l'école* (1896); Ferdinand Buisson, "La jeunesse criminelle et l'éducation: Réponse à M. G. Tarde.," *Revue pédagogique* 30, no. 4 (1897); Alfred Fouillée, "Les jeunes criminels: L'école et la presse," *Revue des deux mondes* 67, n. 139 (1897); Gabriel Tarde, "La jeunesse criminelle," *Revue pédagogique* 30, no. 3 (1897). On criminological interest in social causes of delinquency such as individualism and materialism, see Stephen A. Toth, "Desire and the Delinquent: Juvenile Crime and Deviance in Fin-de-siècle French Criminology," *History of the Human Sciences* 10, no. 4 (1997). On delinquency, see Michelle Perrot, "Dans le Paris de la Belle Epoque, les 'Apaches,' premières bandes de jeunes," in *Les ombres de l'histoire: Crime et châtiment au XIXe siècle* (2001).

90. Suleiman, *Authoritarian Fictions*, 34–35. See also Pernot, *Le roman*, 193–94.

91. For an analogous discussion of Taine's role in the novel, see Ringer, *Fields of Knowledge*, 132–33.

which the novel's narrator described as "dissociated and decerebrated [*décérébrée*]."[92] Incoherent and decomposed, France now wasted the vibrant youth that should be the source of its regeneration. Assembled in the nation's capital, they were deprived of "a common point around which to rally" (277). Encouraged in their egotism, deprived of a shared passion or faith, the youths of Barrès's novel spend their forces along unproductive channels. Meanwhile, the state and its schools continued to manufacture waste. Churning out functionaries—for whom there were an insufficient number of posts—its yield was ultimately unproductive. As atomized individuals, they were held together by no common social tie and "work only for themselves" (280). The novel suggested that these unintegrated particles had no other place to turn but against the order that made them. Likened to a polluting miasma, the refuse embodied by the *prolétariat des bacheliers* was a threat to public health. "In the mass of the nation, between the loosened blocks, there lies a great dust of individuals. It is a waste of forces. Even if this rubbish were made up of madmen, incompetents, and the ill willed, it would still be regrettable, because dangerous: in a badly swept city, when the sanitation service falters, the smallest storm creates an insalubrious mud" (281). Barrès imagined France as headless, fractured, and essentially anarchic, capable of producing only social debris and disorder.

In *Les déracinés*, Racadot's trajectory mimes in miniature the tragic fate of the "real republic." Abandoned by his supposed associates once he has wasted his resources on a failed newspaper (la *Vraie République*), Racadot was desperate and disillusioned, left with a sole conceivable issue: crime. He and his accomplice Mouchefrin choose their victim: the exotic, bejeweled Armenian, Astiné Aravian, whose mysterious airs and intoxicating perfumes had previously seduced their associate Sturel "away from the interests of French life" (172). When Astiné tries to escape their clutches, Racadot and Mouchefrin explode with fury; energized, they tear into their victim with the extreme, all-consuming ferocity that she has nonetheless provoked. "Luxurious beast, she had irritated the desires of their blood with her disdainful body." Astiné embodied all their antisocial and unproductive aspirations, concentrating the exotic, the sexual, and the material in a single figure. The menace represented by their insatiable craving is revealed in its most brutal essence. "She was," in other words, "killed by two indigents, who were also arrogant males. These two traits, when they aren't mutually exclusive, create a most dangerous species" (427). The very image of their impossible desires, Astiné simultaneously provoked in them a sense of horror and ritual hatred. An outward expression of the violence of their lust, her sacrifice was an explosive expenditure. "Bewildered with terror,

---

92. I have chosen here to translate *décérébrée* as decerebrated because the connotations of the word are important to my argument. It means, literally 'lobotomized' and figuratively to be unreflective. I want to suggest that this figure of 'headlessness' is central to Barrès's argument.

they dispensed repeated blows with excessive effort, as if she were an invincible idol and their worst enemy" (427–28).[93] Immolated in this festival of waste, Astiné is mutilated and decapitated. At once executioners and victims, Racadot and Mouchefrin are destined for a similar fate. The assassination is an eruption of the extravagant, egotistical impulses that had sapped, according to Barrès, the vital energies of France. Their crime was a momentary actualization of a France "*dissociée et décérébrée.*"

Racadot and Mouchefrin were, according to the novel, the monstrous products of the idealistic enterprise headed up by the Ministry of Public Instruction. "Unable to provide a good terrain for 'transplantation,'" it "worked in such a way as to turn them into young beasts without lairs. Removed from their natural order, perhaps humble but at least social, they turned to anarchy and mortal disorder" (480–81). Rather than "cultivating" these young subjects into model citizens, state education had sown destruction and reaped waste. Racodot and Mouchefrin were proof of its terrible failure, the menacing material reality haunting the transcendental illusion, its accursed share and excluded remainder. Indeed, at the novel's conclusion, Sturel describes them as the inevitable "sacrifice," the waste created by Bouteiller's project of raising the seven *diplômés* to his ideal. As he explained, "A potter or glassmaker loses a high percentage of pieces in the kiln, and that percentage rises whenever he tries to make a particularly beautiful piece. In our little band's effort to rise up, it was certain that there would be waste. Racadot, Mouchefrin are our ransom, the price paid for our perfection. I hate their crime, but persist in seeing them as my sacrifices" (492–93). A year later, in an article published at the height of the Dreyfus Affair, Barrès used the same metaphor to describe the "intellectuals" responsible for fomenting the contemporary crisis.[94] The disruptive Dreyfusard intellectual was, in his view, the extension and telos of the *prolétariat des bacheliers*. Filled with frustration and resentment as the excluded residue of the republican elite in formation, these intellectuals turned their wasted energies against the social order.

Debates about the fate of secondary education in the 1890s were intimately tied to competing visions of the future of France and its male citizenry. Questions of who had access to the prestigious *baccalauréat* degree and on what terms played an important role in ongoing arguments about the relationship between democracy and social hierarchy in the new Republic. In staking their positions, political progressives and conservatives

---

93. On Astiné's role in the novel, Martine Reid, "L'Orient liquidé (Barrès, *Les déracinés*)," *Romanic Review* 83, no. 3 (1992); Suleiman, *Authoritarian Fictions*, 207–10; Carroll, *French Literary Fascism*, 32–34. On representations of sadism as a product of sexual frustration and the overexcitation of appetites (especially in urban milieus), see Angus McLaren, *The Trials of Masculinity: Policing Sexual Boundaries, 1870–1930* (1997), 158–81.

94. Barrès, *Scènes*, 46.

charged that the existing system responsible for training the nation's male elite paradoxically produced demoralization. Republican pedagogical reformers expressed anxiety that the authoritarian character of the lycée would create subjects who were ill adapted to the regime, based on autonomy and meritocracy, that they sought to institute. Reactionaries, by contrast, condemned republican educational philosophy, with its apparent emphasis on reason and individualism over traditional social hierarchy, as responsible for contemporary social disorder and dissatisfaction. Progressives, who were frequently associated or allied with the state educational system, sought reform from within. Conservatives, whose symbolic capital was located outside academic institutions and in fields such as literature, assaulted secondary schooling from without, and created a counterpedagogical discourse of their own. While occupying opposing positions on the terrain of educational debate, both sides appealed to a normative construction of masculinity in order to articulate their respective pedagogical visions. Their educational and social ideals similarly invoked devirilization and sexual perversion as symptoms of the waste, unproductivity, and asociality that improper schooling might produce. The heterosexual masculinity of the citizen, and the specter of its failure, was a structuring assumption of these arguments.

4 *Life and the Mind*

Even after the 1890 reforms, debates about both the form and content of lycée and university instruction persisted. While appealing to contrasting arguments and strategies, pedagogical traditionalists and progressives insisted on the need to better adapt education to the exigencies of modern life in order to address the problem of the "intellectual proletariat." Conservatives, like the philosopher and sociologist Alfred Fouillée, argued that the diversification of programs, which elevated the "modern" track to the same level as the "classical" one, exacerbated tendencies toward *déclassement* and amplified ambitions that exceeded students' means and capacities. Fouillée advocated a "practical" and utilitarian education, which would orient its graduates toward "industry, commerce, agriculture and colonial exigencies," but which was sharply distinguished from the elite classical lycée training.[1] Those with a more reformist orientation, such as the esteemed chemist, professor at the Collège de France, and Minister of Public Instruction from 1886 to 1887, Marcelin Berthelot, also addressed the inadequation between secondary schooling and modern life, but took an opposite tack in calling for a further modernization and diversification of lycée programs. As a scientist, Berthelot was particularly critical of the programs' literary emphasis. In an article entitled "La crise de l'enseignement secondaire," published in *La revue des deux mondes* in 1891, he proclaimed that classical literary instruction "no longer responds to the ensemble of careers and fundamental needs of the modern epoch. A large number of citizens clamor for another discipline, founded on a deeper understanding of the sciences, which have become indispensable for practical life as well as

---

1. Alfred Fouillée, *Les études classiques et la démocratie* (1898), 230. For a discussion of Fouillée, see Fritz Ringer, *Fields of Knowledge: French Academic Culture in Comparative Perspective* (1992), 155–59.

for the general direction of societies."[2] The creation of a "scientific track" within lycée education represented a parallel strategy for adapting instruction to modern society. When a new inquiry into the reform of secondary education was convened at the end of the decade, the issue of establishing correspondences between "instruction" and "life" remained omnipresent.[3] The officials in charge of state schooling wanted to make sure that elite education did not become a dead letter.

While Berthelot optimistically hoped to align education and life, others wondered about the impact of schooling on the nation's vitality. Was scientific enlightenment the answer or did it create new problems? Did practical consciousness and rational calculation create more harmonious social integration or would it introduce new desires and needs that further upset social equilibrium? At their core, these concerns about the relationship between knowledge and life were always also questions about social democratization and the future of the nation. In examining how school reformers, cultural critics, and contemporary demographers addressed these issues, this chapter shows how idealized conjugality, and the reproductive heterosexual masculinity it implied, framed and fantasmatically resolved the perceived conflict between intellect and vitality.

Love Life

At the end of the decade, the Chamber of Deputies launched a new study of these questions. An 1899 Commission on Secondary Education Reform, presided over by Alexandre Ribot, produced five volumes of testimony, including 196 depositions by the nation's most prominent academics, as well as by representatives of local chambers of commerce and regional councils. The sheer number of solicited opinions testifies to the complexity of the problems and diversity of positions regarding the subjects at hand: whether or not to abolish the *baccalauréat,* the uniformity of programs, the relative value of "classical" versus "modern" literary study, and of "literary" versus "scientific" education, and, once again, the future of the *internat.* Berthelot, in his testimony, again urged that "literary culture," "more delicate, one might say, and more aesthetic," demanded only by a privileged minority of families, had become "an insufficient instrument for the development of the great majority of citizens of modern states, and of the French in particular."

2. Marcelin Berthelot, "La crise de l'enseignement secondaire," *Revue des deux mondes* 61, no. 104 (1891): 374.

3. On the 1899 Commission, see Viviane Isambert-Jamati, "Une réforme des lycées et collèges: Essai d'analyse sociologique de la réforme de 1902," *Année sociologique* 20 (1969); Viviane Isambert-Jamati, *Crises de la société, crises de l'enseignement: Sociologie de l'enseignement secondaire français* (1970), 141–76; Ringer, *Fields of Knowledge*, 141–95. John I. Brooks, *The Eclectic Legacy: Academic Philosophy and the Human Sciences in Nineteenth-century France* (1998), 135–40.

He argued that, "Upon leaving the benches of secondary instruction, the young man right away enters into the struggle for life. . . . However, the study of classical authors, the knowledge of rhetoric and other fundamental subjects of classical instruction do not sufficiently prepare for this struggle."[4] In framing the problem in terms of young men's inadaptation to modern life, Berthelot's critique closely resembled that made by Taine and Barrès. In his view, however, it was classical literary education, and not universalist philosophical abstraction, that failed to sufficiently "arm" the young man for life in the modern world.

The noted historian and professor on the Faculté des lettres in Paris, Ernest Lavisse, elected to the Académie française in 1892, also testified before the commission. He, too, argued that young *bacheliers* were insufficiently prepared for life beyond the lycée's walls. He criticized the rigid discipline of the institution from which young men were let free "into the city streets and exposed to all the abuses of a liberty of which they have no experience." Their education, furthermore, did not serve to interest them in "life." He hence criticized an excessive emphasis on "disinterested" study, exclaiming, "Don't we neglect a fundamental duty toward the country by bringing up, without making him interested in the life that he will lead, a young man, who upon leaving the lycée at the age of eighteen or nineteen years, or a short time thereafter, will be a French citizen?"[5] Lavisse sought to make better citizens by introducing subjects that were more relevant to "modern life," notably, if unsurprisingly given his own interests, geography and history.

Henry Bérenger, a young novelist and journalist who specialized in writing about education was also among those called on to testify before the commission, specifically as an expert on the "intellectual proletariat."[6] Bérenger attended the Lycée Henri IV in Paris, studied at the Sorbonne, where he obtained his university diploma and worked toward the *agrégation,* before giving up academia for life as a writer and editor (he would eventually serve as an ambassador and senator in the interwar era). No longer in the academy, Béranger denounced the existing system as a "caste education," which served to reproduce a bourgeois elite.[7] Skeptical of piecemeal efforts, Bérenger advocated for genuine democratic reforms, including the abolition of the separation between primary and secondary schooling. In his view, the proletarianization of intellectuals resulted from too little meritocracy, not too much. And, in his campaigns to extend schooling to

4. *Enquête sur l'enseignement secondaire: procès-verbaux des dépositions,* vol. 1 (1899), 9.

5. Ibid., 38–39. On Lavisse, see Ringer, *Fields of Knowledge,* 161–62, 77–80.

6. On Bérenger as spokesperson for the "intellectual proletariat," see Christophe Charle, *Naissance des "intellectuels," 1880–1900* (1990), 59–63. See also Christophe Charle, *La crise littéraire à l'époque du naturalisme* (1979); Christopher E. Forth, *The Dreyfus Affair and the Crisis of French Manhood* (2004), 70–81.

7. *Enquête,* 491.

adolescents from the popular classes, he chastised the state for not going far enough in its educational reforms, explaining, "This is the greatest social danger threatening the secular State. . . . Between eleven and twenty years of age, popular youth are socially abandoned at the moment when puberty awakens, consciousness is troubled, and the spirit is formed."[8]

Bérenger had long been preoccupied by the problem of contemporary youth. In a glowing 1892 review of *Jeunesse* by the liberal Protestant pastor and associate of Ferdinand Buisson, Charles Wagner, he highlighted how the twin forces of "Democracy" and "Science" had contributed to the current crisis. In contrast to Berthelot who figured "science" as a solution to contemporary social ills, Bérenger saw it as a force of materialism, fragmentation, and skepticism. Contemporary youth was, he suggested, characterized by "the absence of a disinterested ideal, a lack of seriousness and respect, a taste for brief and vile pleasures."[9] The solution, in both Wagner and Béranger's view, was to encourage affective attachment to objects beyond the self, such as the family, friendship, nature, woman, and *la patrie*. Bérenger highlighted the corruption of sentiment, and especially "the ease of cheap pleasures which have developed in a frightening manner" and "the taste for debauchery." He upheld "love," and a corresponding respect for woman, as a necessary corrective to the crisis, proclaiming, "The heroic and chaste sentiment of love will always be a source of the most sublime energies."[10] This is precisely the position set forth in his two novels devoted to how corrupt materialism had ruined modern love. Very much in the genre of the "novel of socialization," *L'effort* (1893) and *La proie* (1897) recount the trials of youths who attempt to make their way in the world. Peppered with references to Barrès, Bourget, and Taine, Bérenger's novels assaulted academic culture for corrupting youthful ideals and desires.

L'effort narrates the inexorable slide toward suicide of its well-educated and privileged but entirely disaffected antihero. In the preface, Bérenger declared: "Intelligence has killed intuition! It has given man a kind of impotence before life: it has broken its ancient engagement [*fiançailles*] with nature, and that love which, once, exalted towards her with heroic energy!"[11] Bérenger's references to impotence and failed engagement were not idle

8. Henry Bérenger, "De l'école au régiment: Enquête sur l'éducation des adultes," *Revue bleue* 4, no. 8 (1895): 227. Léon Bourgeois and Henri Marion responded to Bérenger's inquiry but did not adopt his radical position. See Henry Bérenger, "De l'école au regiment," *Revue bleue* 4, no. 10 (1895). See also Kathleen Alaimo, "Shaping Adolescence in the Popular Milieu: Social Policy, Reformers, and French Youth, 1870–1920," *Journal of Family History* 17, no. 4 (1992); Kathleen Alaimo, "Adolescence, Gender and Class in Educational Reform in France: The Development of *Enseignement Primaire Supérieur*, 1880–1910," *French Historical Studies* 18, no. 4 (1994).

9. Henry Bérenger, "Jeunesse (à propos d'un livre de M. le pasteur Wagner)," *Revue pédagogique* 20, no. 3 (1892): 209.

10. Ibid., 211. See also Denis Pernot, *Le roman de socialisation* (1998), 20–21.

11. Henry Bérenger, *L'effort* (1893), xv. On the novel as a critique of "science," see Gaston Dechamps, "Une croisade contre la science," *Le Temps,* 15 October 1893.

metaphors. Georges Lauzerte, the novel's central figure, had graduated from lycée and university, and begun an uninspiring career as a functionary in the Ministry of Foreign Affairs. Not yet married, he is torn between his first mistress and the woman approved by his parents, a class-appropriate *haute bourgeoise,* who is beautiful, and without an idea in her head. Unable to renounce his mistress, an aspiring actress whom he cannot marry, Georges commits suicide. Suffering from anomie, he "died because he did not know what he wanted." According to his best friend, Jean Darnay, an *agrégé* in philosophy at work on a doctoral thesis tellingly entitled "Will and Sentiment," Georges "had the vertigo of death, because he had, one after another, broken around him all the protective barriers [*les garde-fous*] which separate man from the definitive void."[12]

The degradation of married love was at the heart of the youthful malaise that, Béranger suggested in his lengthy preface, was produced by the educational system and the class privilege it perpetuated. As he maintained, "At eighteen, when one throws off the *képi,* the tunic, and ugly shoes, the oppressed and dried out soul straightens toward real life: the sap mounts with the call of the senses, but by what strange channels and what a pathological [*maladive*] spurt! Strange education of the heart, that which begins nine times out of ten at the Moulin-Rouge, the *brasseries de femmes,* or worse yet! For most, the sensibility is forever withered by the gross character of these first memories."[13] Bérenger explained that, trained in reason, male youths had lost touch with their "intuition" and "sentiment," the "conscious manifestation of the effort, which precedes thought, and dominates it." In response to the oppressive constraint of too much intelligence, calculation, and speculation (particularly in matters of the heart), Bérenger sought a return to "effort" and, by extension, "love": "To seize oneself in the consciousness of all effort in throwing oneself toward another, that is still a primitive intuition. The living synthesis of the 'I' and the 'non-I' is given in effort, and men have consecrated it with the name love. Doesn't one, in love, melt into that which is not one, and melt the others that are in one? Love is thus the most intense reality of life. Real life, is to love. Love is the essence of the soul, of every soul, of the universe. A society whose intelligence grows and where love is extinguished is a society destined to perish."[14] He called, that is, for a paradoxical reaffirmation of the masculine self in selflessness.

While the privileged Georges suffered from not knowing what he wanted, Jean Darnay was plagued by knowing what he wanted, without being able to obtain it. From a modest background (his grandfather was a peasant, his father an engineer for a railway company), he falls in love with Georges's

12. Bérenger, *L'effort,* 252.
13. Ibid., xvi–xvii.
14. Ibid., xxxi–xxii.

sister, Marthe. Their class difference made the hope of this marriage based on love a near impossibility. For both Georges and Darnay, then, the spirit of calculation and material concern had killed the spontaneous energy and good virile effort that arose out of true love. Georges was a figure of bourgeois decadence, poisoned by the very system set up to maintain class domination. Jean, on the other hand, exemplified the ideal of republican meritocracy, as yet unfulfilled. His schooling gave him access to the salons of the Lauzerte and their kind, but he remained socially marginal, a classic *déclassé* who could no longer return "home." His aspiration to marry Marthe represented his frustrating and frustrated desire. Darnay predictably denounced arranged marriage as "the worst of social lies." Indeed, he proclaimed, "Love is at the same time the most common and the most sacred fact of existence: the taste for money has perverted it for us."[15] While Georges commits suicide, Darnay briefly contemplates anarchism and eventually resigns himself to a sober and celibate existence given over to his career. The novel ends, however, with a faint glimmer of hope. Taught a painful lesson by Georges's suicide, Marthe reconsiders the possibility of marrying Darnay. In the final scene, a new day dawns.

These characters' fate demonstrated the dangers of an education that emphasized "intelligence" over "intuition," "calculation" over "love." And, while Bérenger's politics were socialist rather than reactionary, his account of the frustration and deviation of their youthful desires echoed Barrès. His later writings on the "intellectual proletariat" thus recalled the sordid student milieus of *Les déracinés*, as he described how "it is here that they contract the habits, stimulate their lusts, amass the rancor, and forge the bondage which will leave traces on their lives as adult men."[16] While he criticized Barrès's politics, Béranger launched an analogous attack on contemporary education. "As if inebriated by the grandiose abstraction of a purely scientific university, they hail the new recruits of young intellectuals, ceaselessly overflowing, claiming to see in them the elite which will regenerate France. Do they hear the noise, muted but formidable, of all those that the University disappoints, who thank it for being raised up just to fall into misery—those who one begins to speak of everywhere now as the intellectual proletariat?"[17] Béranger likewise suggested that the deficit of appropriate posts posed a veritable threat to national health, as thwarted expectations found their issue along antisocial and insalubrious channels. As he ex-

15. Ibid., 158–59.

16. Henry Bérenger, "Les prolétaires intellectuels en France," in *Les prolétaires intellectuels en France,* ed. Henry Bérenger (1901), 21–22. He here suggested that Barrès's novel might contribute to a generalized "opinion campaign" against the overproduction of *diplômés* (46–47). For his critique of *Les déracinés,* see Henry Bérenger, *La France intellectuelle* (1899), 96–99. On the parallels between Barrès and Bérenger, see Venita Datta, *Birth of a National Icon: The Literary Avant-Garde and the Origins of the Intellectual in France* (1999), 71–73, 123; Ringer, *Fields of Knowledge,* 127–40.

17. Bérenger, "Les prolétaires intellectuels," 2.

plained, "The physiological poverty diminishes the race; the psychological poverty creates a general state of revolution and anarchism; poverty plain and simple causes a growth in criminality, prostitution, and parasitism in all its forms." In his view, these social ills were the result of the deregulated desires propagated by the republic's unfulfilled promise of meritocracy. Living on limited means, this new degraded class was forced to choose between bachelorhood or a loveless marriage of financial convenience; both issues were disastrous for France's future. "The existence of the intellectual proletariat diminishes the race in two ways. Their unhealthy bodies make less healthy babies, and this inheritance aggravates the bad traits of the family. In addition, life as a couple or as a few has become too costly; marriages and even more so births fall off. For the intellectual proletariat, love is a luxury and children a ruinous folly."[18] The frustration of professional ambitions aggravated these impediments to reproductive, married love.

Like Barrès and Taine, Bérenger drew an intimate connection between the rise of the intellectual proletariat and a remarkable expansion of bureaucracy under the Third Republic. Functionaries exemplified the contemporary degradation of an overeducated and overly ambitious youth destined for disappointment. For Bérenger, then, the "intellectual proletariat and functionarism are two twin brothers."[19] The contemporary "proletarianizing" of functionaries, as Judith Wishnia has suggested, did correlate with the expansion of state education. In its first three decades, the Republic quintupled the number of state employees, drawing many of them from the primary school system put into place by Ferry. In an effort to keep costs low, the government financed this rapid expansion by keeping salaries at a minimum. What is more, functionaries were denied the right to unionize, as granted to other professions by the Waldeck-Rousseau law of 1884. They endured their fate in passive silence. Petty bureaucrats incarnated, both economically and socially, a degraded class paradoxically produced by the republican state itself.[20]

The plight of the functionary illustrated a marked discrepancy between the Republic's official commitment to moral autonomy and a humiliating— and implicitly devirilizing—reality. Béranger underscored this blatant contradiction, proclaiming, "One tells them: 'Be proud; be independent; be fair.' And then they are forced by their position to become rebels or serfs!"[21] This moral degradation was exacerbated by a physical one, both at work and at home. Cramped behind desks, deprived of proper lighting,

---

18. Ibid., 27.

19. Henry Bérenger, "La crise du fonctionnarisme en France," in *Les prolétaires intellectuelles en France*, ed. Henry Bérenger (1901), 53.

20. See Judith Wishnia, *The Proletarianizing of the Fonctionnaires: Civil Service Workers and the Labor Movement under the Third Republic* (1990), 1–12. See also Guy Thullier, *Bureaucratie et bureaucrates en France au 19ᵉ siècle*, ed. École pratique des hautes études (1980).

21. Bérenger, "Les prolétaires intellectuels," 26.

— Dis donc, mon chéri, tu m'enverras ton article sur la dépopulation ; ça m'amusera.

Dessin de G. JEANNIOT.

Figure 3. "Dearest, send me your article on depopulation. It will amuse me." *Le rire,* 11 September 1897. President and Fellows of Harvard College: from HOLLIS #008654106. This cartoon mocks the hypocrisy of a young journalist who pens articles about fertility decline and visits prostitutes.

forced to carry out monotonous tasks, the health of the "intellectual proletariat" was precarious. Given a meager salary, they and their families were
improperly clothed and fed; the vitality of their children and hence of the
nation was tainted. Debilitated and degraded, they suffered a diminished
"force of vital resistance," an impotence invariably passed on to their progeny.[22] According to Bérenger, the very agents charged with protecting public welfare weakened the health of the nation.

Like Barrès, Bérenger figured the intellectual proletariat as an inassimilable remainder, an overflow produced by surging desires for social ascension; this new class of *declassés* was a violently expended excess which
threatened to provoke mass destruction. "The intellectual proletariat," he
wrote, "is a fatal residue of the universally enflamed appetites that emanated from the French Revolution. It is the boiling lava of a volcano that
remains menacing."[23] While cautious about the deregulation and disruption
resulting from revolution, Bérenger remained a convinced republican. He
did not call into question the meritocracy of the state educational system,
but instead argued for its stricter implementation in order to limit the overproduction of mediocrity. In calling, before the Ribot Commission and in
his journalistic writings, for more state-funded scholarships, Bérenger upheld the republican educational system even as he criticized it for not going
far enough.[24] Thus, while highlighting the dissuasive potential of Barrès's
and Bourget's works, he differentiated himself from these "retrograde" critics.[25] His evaluation of the intellectual proletariat's benighted condition,
nonetheless, displayed marked parallels to their analyses of the debilitating
and devirilizing effects of state education. Like them, he alluded to a deregulation of desire created by republican schooling and drew a direct connection between the professional and sexual frustrations of this new proletariat. These diminished men were forced by their degraded position to
remain single, childless, or trapped in loveless marriages. These trends were,
at the same time, the focus of contemporary demographers' apprehensive
speculations about the effects of education and unrealized ambition on the
nation's population.

Singular Wills

In *Les déracinés,* Barrès saw proof of France's withering forces in "the observation that our reproductive powers are on the decline, that our resistance on the Eastern frontier is enfeebled, and that the German spirit
spreads everywhere on our territory and in our spirits" (281–82). Histori-

22. Ibid., 27.
23. Ibid., 42.
24. Ibid., 44.
25. Bérenger, "La crise du fonctionnarisme," 58.

ans have well documented the currency of these anxieties surrounding depopulation. According to this widespread narrative of degenerating national health, the country's feeble fertility rate was both a symptom and cause of debilitation. Concerns about the birthrate wove together internal and external politics in such a way that domestic problems—and quite literally those related to the family—were directly linked to France's ability to perpetuate itself in an international arena.[26]

Historians of the efflorescence of social reform in the first decades of the Third Republic have likewise cited the influence of this perceived degeneration on policy makers and doctors working in the related arenas of child welfare and maternal health.[27] And, as Joshua Cole has shown, natalists concerned with regulating women's bodies integrated nationalist themes into their rueful documentations of fertility decline in order to lend added force to their arguments.[28] The statistical techniques developed by demographers to evaluate France's population problem targeted women and held them accountable for France's chronically low birthrate. Despite the political and religious diversity among them, natalists could all agree that, "the problematic individual in French society was female."[29] It is thus not surprising that "feminism" as well as "a fear of the servitude of maternity; woman's aesthetic preoccupations; the excesses of individualism," figured among numerous causes of depopulation catalogued by an extra-parliamentary commission established by Prime Minister René Waldeck-Rousseau in 1902 to study the problem.[30] As Cole argues, population experts read women's refusal of their purportedly natural sexual role to be a consequence of their "individualism," their claims for rights in the "public sphere," and hence of their masculinization. Fertility decline was, in other words, symptomatic of gender trouble. It indicated that the purportedly natural laws, which were imagined to ground women's sexual difference, were unreliable. This very unreliability, in turn, legitimated the regulation and oversight of women's sexuality and ongoing limitations on their public roles. If women's egotism was symptomatic of their masculinization, how

26. Alain Becchia, "Les milieux parlementaires et la dépopulation de 1900 à 1914," *Communications (Dénatalité: L'antériorité française [1800–1914])* 44 (1986); Joshua Cole, *The Power of Large Numbers: Population, Politics, and Gender in Nineteenth-century France* (2000); Angus McLaren, *Sexuality and Social Order: The Debate over the Fertility of Women and Workers in France, 1770–1920* (1983); Robert A. Nye, *Crime, Madness, and Politics in Modern France: The Medical Concept of National Decline* (1984).

27. See Elinor A. Accampo, Rachel G. Fuchs, and Mary Lynn Stewart, eds., *Gender and the Politics of Social Reform in France, 1870–1914* (1995); Karen Offen, "Depopulation, Nationalism, and Feminism in Fin-de-siècle France," *American Historical Review* 89, no. 3 (1984); Jean E. Pedersen, *Legislating the French Family: Feminism, Theater, and Republican Politics, 1870–1920* (2003).

28. Cole, *The Power of Large Numbers*, 156, 210.

29. Ibid., 208.

30. Commission de la dépopulation, *Procès-verbaux: Sous-commission de la natalité* (1902), 2–3.

did social reformers interpret the potential excesses of men's individualism? And how did they propose to solve this problem, given that, the individuality of male citizens was at once presumed and protected?

Individualistic men, and in particular, the male bachelor, indeed, haunt the reports presented to the 1902 Commission.[31] The traits of this figure—namely, his unruly and wayward desires—recall the characters we have encountered so far in the writings of pedagogical reformers and novelists. Schooling was not incidental to the problem of male bachelorhood. In a presentation before the Académie des sciences morales et politiques in 1885, Gustave Lagneau proclaimed, "The longer the apprenticeship, the more time needed for studies, the harder it is to obtain a desired position, and the more bachelorhood is prolonged."[32] Pierre Garnier, the author of numerous popular medical works on social and sexual problems, highlighted how, paradoxically, "Those whose superior faculties, whose mind and knowledge are above average, whose gifts for study and work permit them to aspire to the highest ranks of their professions are fatally consigned to celibacy."[33] Population experts targeted the bachelor's voluntary sterility, which resulted, in their view, from a combination of protracted study, excessive ambition, hardened egotism, and financial insecurity.

Given the 1902 Commission's proactive and pragmatic orientation, it is not surprising to find that its proceedings concentrate on the volitional, rather than the natural, causes of the decline.[34] A report by Doctors Adolphe Pinard (a prominent gynecologist and infant health expert) and Charles Richet (who was to become prominent in the French eugenics movement) demonstrates this tendency well. Their study named venereal disease as the principal physiological cause of sterility in French couples. Their diagnosis and proposed treatment, however, highlighted the volitional component of infertility. "In order to remedy France's diminished birth rate, we can count only on means that will change the will of French families, that will convince them to have more children than they want to today."[35] This emphasis on the role of the "will" in the falling birthrate echoed the Commission's report on the "moral and social causes" of depopulation, presented by well-known demographer, Jacques Bertillon and

31. On the divergent tendencies between those who concentrated on how to make men more prolific and those who addressed women, see Pedersen, *Legislating the French Family*, 174–84. Karen Offen hints that Bertillon's "paternal patriotism" signaled "a crisis in virility," in Offen, "Depopulation, Nationalism, and Feminism," 669.

32. Gustave Lagneau, *Remarques démographiques sur le célibat en France* (1885), 33. See also Gustave Lagneau, *Du surmenage intellectuel et de la sédentarité dans les écoles* (1887).

33. Pierre Garnier, *Célibat et célibataires: Caractères, dangers et hygiène chez les deux sexes* (1889), 107.

34. Becchia, "Les milieux parlementaires et la dépopulation de 1900 à 1914," 202.

35. Alphonse Pinard and Charles Richet, "Rapport sur les causes physiologiques de la diminution de la natalité en France (séance 10 décembre)," in *Commission de la dépopulation: Sous-commission de la natalité* (1902), 10.

Figure 4. "Old Bachelor! 'France is declining and depopulating. I've been saying it in vain for fifteen years.'" *Assiette au beurre,* 1 April 1901. Typ 915.01.1668F, Department of Printing and Graphic Arts, Houghton Library, Harvard College Library. This cartoon ridicules the aging bachelor as a symptom of the very trend he deplores.

natalist activist André Honnorat, who had together founded the Alliance nationale pour l'accroissement de la population in 1896.

In their exposés, both Bertillon and Honnorat associated chronic marriage delay and low birthrates with individual and familial ambition. Their analyses were indebted to the theory of "social capillarity" developed by the idiosyncratic socialist demographer Arsène Dumont, who, despite a certain measure of controversy, was also elected to serve on the commission. Essentially conservative in their political and social goals, Bertillon and Honnorat nonetheless appropriated Dumont's critique of the perversity of bourgeois avarice—without going so far as to adopt the more radical aspects of his political program. They insisted along with Dumont that depopulation was not merely a problem of the physiological capacity to reproduce but also of the social obstacles, which diverted and deviated man's natural procreative desires.[36]

In his writings, Dumont suggested, in a telling modification of Jean-Jacques Rousseau, that society corrupted man's natural sexual instincts: "Man is born for sexual union and society induces him to remain for a longtime, or definitively, single."[37] Dumont's analysis of the perverse potential of "civilization" rested on a theory of normal and healthy, because natural, male desire. France's population crisis was, in his view, a direct result of the *socialization* of men's instincts. His study of average marriage age, published as part of the commission's proceedings, concentrated on male subjects, since, he argued, men were responsible for initiating marriage. He urged that measures targeting men's resistance to family life would simultaneously, if indirectly, address women.[38] In the exposé, he interrogated why young men would delay marriage, when forceful natural drives propelled them toward this end, commenting that, "It is perhaps surprising to see such a large proportion of unmarried men at an age when nature permits or even demands that they be [married]." What forces could successfully drown out the powerful call of nature? He suggested that the "voice of instinct" had been silenced by "the voice of individual and family interest."[39]

Unhindered by social obstacles, men's sexual drives, in his view, expressed themselves freely and easily in nature. "In animal species, the sexual instinct is generally not very picky in its choices. Any object will do, as long as the instinct is satisfied. In brutal, uncultured humanity, it is about the same: love is blind, its ardor clouds its foresight." Dumont was predictably ambivalent about the "blindness" of these bestial drives. He thus endorsed the refinement of instinct operated by the sentiment of "love." In this state,

36. Cole, *The Power of Large Numbers*, 204–6.
37. Arsène Dumont, "Rapport sur l'âge au mariage et son influence sur la natalité," in *Commission de la dépopulation: Sous-commission de la natalité* (1902), 15.
38. Ibid., 9.
39. Ibid., 8.

factors besides pure sexual satisfaction, namely health, grace, goodness, honor, and intelligence, contributed to men's object choice. Dumont represented this advancement as a *natural* good, which "is profitable to the race." Love enhanced and improved nature without undoing its essential aims: "Love encourages young boys and girls towards marriages of inclination which are favorable to the number as well as the physical and moral value of their posterity." Problems arose when "extrinsic" concerns—fortune, profession, relations, and social status—took precedence over the "intrinsic" qualities sought out by genuine sexual and sentimental attraction. In this unfortunate scenario, "Society and the family—i.e., corrupt civilization—work together to multiply marriages of convenience which favor individuals' egotistical interests."[40] Like Béranger, Dumont claimed that the mercenary aims of bourgeois family strategy deviated men's desires from their more natural and healthy procreative goals. Parents encouraged their sons, and sons in turn desired a lucrative career and a dowered wife rather than a vibrant and fulfilling *famille nombreuse*. Living out his youth in an unnatural state, the bachelor inevitably succumbed to the temptations of vice—prostitution, pornography, alcoholism, etc.[41] Chronic population decline coincided, in Dumont's vision, with the universalization and democratization of this unfortunate bourgeois ideal.

The perverted desire characteristic of modern democratic society was, for Dumont, an effect of "social capillarity." According to his "scientific" analysis of this phenomenon, social ambition was another kind of drive—but one that was ultimately wasteful and destructive rather than reproductive. "Fatal" and "devouring," this impulse was deadly rather than life affirming. "Seduced" by the ideal of ascension, it dissipated itself, and others, in pursuit of all-consuming goals. For Dumont, "social capillarity" was a mechanical rather than organic principle that destroyed the natural law of filiation.[42] By contrast, "In a milieu where social capillarity is not felt, where everyone limits their desire and seeks only to remain in the position in which he was born, without expecting anything better for his children, every generation turns in the circle traced by the preceding generation . . . In such cases, men no longer have a motive for depriving themselves of the pleasures of paternity; strangers to progress, they obey, like animals, nature's impulses."[43] The progressive elimination of barriers to social ascension in democratic cultures, he suggested, universalized "capillary" desires and provoked an across the board decline in family size. While Dumont saw democracy as a potential cause of young men's perversion, he proposed, like Béranger, a further expansion of social and economic rights as a solution.

40. Ibid., 15–16.
41. Ibid., 11–12.
42. Arsène Dumont, *Dépopulation et civilisation* (1890), 106, 108–9.
43. Ibid., 111.

The restoration of healthy, normal, reproductive sexuality was, in his view, contingent on an abolition of class differences. [44]

An avid critic of social hierarchy, Dumont viewed state centralization and its corollary, a rigidly ordered bureaucracy, to be incompatible with both real democracy and a healthy birthrate. The functionary exemplified, for him, the exaggerated egotism produced by social capillarity. Entirely given over to his ambitions of rising through the ranks, the bureaucrat disdained family life as so much "excess baggage," devoting himself to the pursuit of individual advancement. According to his analysis, with the democratization of education, the number of candidates aspiring to government service inevitably rose, creating more competition and even greater population decline.[45] This disdain for marriage and the pleasures of fatherhood, as we have already seen, led to a life of selfish debauchery; excessive ambition went hand in hand with an unproductive sexuality that menaced both individual and national destiny. "The increasingly corrupt individual has taste only for sensorial pleasure. He cultivates sensations, and his desire is further courted by those 'two amiable girls, debauchery and death.' Such are, in a few words, the stages of this decay: he loses interest in his country, and no longer wants to be citizen and soldier; he loses interest in his family, and no longer wants to be a father; soon he will lose interest in himself, and will cease wanting to exist."[46] For Dumont, the selfishness associated with the refusal of patriotic and familial duty was paradoxically tantamount to suicide.

A dark side thus haunted the progress initiated by the growth of democracy; society unmade itself and its members in and by its very advancement. Or, as Dumont wrote, "Democracy, by augmenting the value of the individual and the ambition to reach summits of all kinds, contributes in two ways to diminished birthrate. On the one hand, it excites passions, which rival love and paternity. On the other, it augments cerebral life; man, in becoming more capable of self-mastery, is less dominated by his natural impulses." Democracy, for Dumont, by deregulating "unconscious" nature, paradoxically produced too much desire *and* too much reason. The expansion of "consciousness" which accompanied the spread of knowledge, while promoting the development of culture, threatened to impair the perpetuation of the species. In other words, "the ruses of the unconscious lose their influence over an analytic people; or rather, the unconscious becomes conscious. Once love is no longer a blind god, once fecundity is no longer something nocturnal and shadowy but rather the result of conscious, reflective will, it inevitably diminishes."[47] In other words, democracies, which

44. Ibid., 127.
45. Ibid., 221–22. On delayed marriage age among republican elites, see Christophe Charle, *Les élites de la République, 1880–1900* (1987), 258–63.
46. Dumont, *Dépopulation et civilisation*, 328.
47. Ibid., 364–65.

make a virtue of individual enlightenment, inevitably run up against an obstacle. Professional ambition and unproductive sexuality were, for Dumont, the twin symptoms of an overly refined consciousness.

In his report to the Depopulation Commission, André Honnorat made an analogous argument. Relying in part on Dumont's findings, he explained how the "refinement" of the individual in and by culture introduced a fracture between life's two fundamental drives: "the instinct of conservation" and "the instinct of reproduction." In the self-regulating realm of nature, these two instincts remained in perfect equilibrium. "As long as individuals remain unconscious," he wrote, "the two are satisfied simultaneously, and according to nature's needs. Totally ignorant, man submits to them."[48] All ignorant beings—animals, primitives, the uneducated—demonstrated, for Honnorat, this happy balance. However, the growth of consciousness or, as he put it, "intellectuality" entailed an ever sharpening discordance between the two principles; the individual's capacity to master his own destiny developed at the expense of the species. Honnorat, similar to Dumont, identified a troublesome motor of deregulation at the very heart of "life" itself. "The whole question—the only definitive one—is whether life, in ceaselessly pushing individuals to preserve themselves from the perils that surround them, dries up its own well. In inducing them to modify their conditions, to develop as a result self-consciousness, it has incontestably created a certain discordance between their two guiding instincts whose equilibrium is their ultimate safeguard." Because now unable to maintain the necessary equilibrium, the individual required external assistance to regain his lost balance; and it is along these lines that Honnorat envisioned the work of the commission. The ideal harmony once maintained in nature is here a crucial referent. And yet, because nature was no longer capable of assuring this delicate balance, it was hopelessly inadequate. Honnorat advised recourse to exterior intervention—the influence of milieu, legislation, advantages for large families—in order to (re)develop the "family spirit that has disappeared."[49]

While skeptical of Dumont's socialist program, Bertillon likewise appealed to the principle of "social capillarity" in his report on the "moral and social causes of depopulation." He figured France, "for a longtime republican, and even longer democratic," as uniquely plagued by excessive personal ambitions.[50] Anxious to rise up the social ladder and to acquire exterior signs of wealth, the French, in his view, sacrificed "their fecundity" to singularly selfish desires. In his 1897 text written to publicize the work of the recently founded Alliance pour l'accroissement de la population, Bertillon categorically denounced these desires for social ascension by ex-

48. Commission de la dépopulation, *Procès-verbaux*, 12.
49. Ibid., 13, 11.
50. Ibid., 20.

plicitly citing "fathers' ambition for their children" as a cause of the decline in births.[51] In Bertillon's account, the functionary once again embodies a devirilized passivity that was here linked to a refusal of fatherhood. "Functionaries, more so than other Frenchmen, resign themselves to a dull and delimited, albeit tranquil and vegetative life, stripped of the pleasures and pains of paternity."[52] Selfish and unproductive both at home and at work, the functionary was essentially parasitical and implicitly opposed to those who worked in more fruitful domains, such as agriculture or industry. Natalist pamphlets thus regularly denounced the functionary's lack of "social value" and hence the "hypertrophy" of the state. As one commenter remarked, "All the country's blood has gone to its head; its limbs are frozen. . . . At least half the bourgeoisie withers in administrations, while France, who works to maintain them, is crushed under the weight of taxes."[53] The persistent references to the diminished and infertile functionary signaled wider concerns regarding the republican state's ability to cultivate vibrant and prolific citizens who were well anchored in the social order.

As is suggested by this overview, turn of the century natalist discourse relied on "nature" as a crucial reference and model. These thinkers presupposed a model of primitive instinctual auto-regulation in which the interests of the individual and the group were seen to seamlessly coincide. In their view, the unconscious individual, like the animal or primitive unwittingly served the interests of the species in and by catering to his own needs and desires. Population experts argued that the development of "consciousness" and concomitant appearance of "individuality" disrupted this natural equilibrium, introducing a fracture between the satisfaction of personal needs and those of the group. They presumed a self-regulating natural instinct, and, in particular, a vision of the healthy functioning of male sexual desire, while attempting to remedy the deleterious effects of "civilization" or society on that desire. At once naturally heterosexual and reproductive, this instinct was also fragile, unstable, given over to excess and diversion.[54] Impulses appeared here as essentially ambivalent; they were a source of a social good (reproduction) and—for this very reason—potential social disarray. In this conception of instinct, judicious reason was not opposed to unruly passion; indeed, for these natalists, "consciousness" was responsible

51. Jacques Bertillon, *Le problème de la dépopulation* (1897), 23.
52. Commission de la dépopulation, *Procès-verbaux*, 13.
53. Dr. Rommel (Alfred Duplessin), *Au pays de la revanche* (1886), 117. Written under a pseudonym, the text masquerades as a German doctor's study of French national decay. Another pseudonymous text makes similar claims: Georges Rossignol (Roger Debury), *Un pays de célibataires et de fils uniques* (1896).
54. On the invention of "instinct" as a category, see Arnold I. Davidson, *The Emergence of Sexuality: Historical Epistemology and the Formation of Concepts* (2001), 1–29; Michel Foucault, *Les anormaux: Cours au Collège de France, 1974–1975*, ed. François Ewald and Alessandro Fontana (1999), 263–65.

for sexual deregulation. Their model of men's heterosexual instinct set forth a norm that was distinguished *at once* from the excesses of rational calculation and the deviations of desire. The problem of course was how to (re)establish a healthy balance, once "unconscious" nature had been disturbed.

In the 1890s, widespread anxieties about social "waste" converged in the figure of the overeducated, underemployed "bachelor." Contemporary writings on both schooling and natality were concerned with young men's sterility, which is to say, their lack of social productivity and reproductivity. Demographers' accounts of the disruptive effects of "consciousness" on men's naturally equilibrated instincts coincided with discussions of the social deviance potentially produced by secondary schooling. Social reformers and critics intimated that an excess of "intellect," instead of moderating and mastering men's desires, could in fact pervert them. They imagined that sterile learning (whether construed as Kantianism, classical literature, or science) and the institutions that cultivated it destroyed men's social instincts, including their capacity to "love."

These concerns notably intersected with and generalized arguments made by contemporary sexologists, who increasingly sought to explain sexual deviance in terms of the perversion of an instinct, whose "normality" was at once presumed and belied by their studies. Indeed, in their efforts to understand how such deviance arose, sexual scientists cited the similarly perverting effects of contemporary society on these purportedly normal and natural instincts. Thus, in a tract devoted to *Des anomalies de l'instinct sexuel et en particulier des inversions du sens génital,* Dr. Maurice Legrain proclaimed, "Nothing is more different than love and sexuality when considered in a social state and in the state of nature. The absence of the coeducation of the sexes, the isolation of a child far from his own in a unisexual milieu . . . the stigmatization of free marriage as a moral crime, social marriage pushed to limits far from puberty for reasons of interest or convenience, all of these things and their inevitable consequences: moral imbalance, prostitution, etc., profoundly trouble the normal and regular evolution of the sexes, develop degeneracies and warp judgments."[55] Pierre Garnier's assessment was even more pointed. "Pederasty," he claimed, "is the final term or ultimate stage of the vice which leads to the celibacy of man."[56] Contemporary efforts to ground the normal and natural character of an idealized cross-sex "love" in a notion of the sexual instinct, also figured that ideal as fragile and perpetually subject to potential deviation. This framework, in turn, served

55. Dr. Maurice Legrain, *Des anomalies de l'instinct sexuel et en particulier des inversions du sens génital* (1896), 46.
56. Garnier, *Célibat et célibataires,* 397.

LES BEAUX ADOLESCENTS

Tirons un monstre encor de la masse grouillante.
L'éphèbe aux mines accueillantes
S'avance et dit, d'agréable façon :
« Je suis le roi de la famille,
Car moi, j'ai l'âme d'une fille
Dans la peau d'un joli garçon. »

1316

Figure 5. "Les beaux adolescents." *Assiette au beurre,* 4 October 1902. Typ 915.01.1668F, Department of Printing and Graphic Arts, Houghton Library, Harvard College Library. The poem accompanying this image of androgynous adolescents clearly indicates their "inversion." It states, "Me, I have the soul of a girl; In the skin of a pretty boy."

to both articulate and address the problem of how best to socialize young men.

Pedagogical, literary, and demographic debates about how best to form the male youth destined to become the nation's elite expressed a network of concerns surrounding France's political and economic modernity. Writing from diverse and at times diametrically opposed perspectives, they focused on a common problem, namely how to bind autonomous male citizens to a wider social and national order, for which marriage and "the family" were often vehicles and metonyms. In highlighting the relationship of citizens to their "filiation," the past and future of families, critics celebrated the socially adhesive and altruistic role of heterosexual and parental "love," over the atomizing, anomic, and implicitly devirilizing effects of democratization, rationalization, and materialism. According to the normative vision of heterosexual masculinity that they embraced, too much reason, too much individualism, and too much ambition could be just as destructive, and indeed, as deviant, as not enough. Those figures whose comportments failed to conform to this fragile, because so delicately balanced ideal, were considered sterile and perverse, which is to say both unwilling and incapable of becoming socially productive and reproductive. Comprising the abjected poles of the masculine social and sexual norm, the attributes of this perversity were overdetermined and seemingly contradictory, combining passivity and revolt, impotence and profligacy, calculation and irrationality, selfishness and self-loss.

The dilemma of how to create masculine citizens who were at once autonomous and socialized was considerably exacerbated by the widespread perception that the state itself was part of the problem. The very confusion about how best to resolve these questions was reflected in the 1902 secondary education reform itself. It sought, in an uneasy compromise, to reconcile competing educational visions by diversifying the courses of study leading to the *baccalauréat* in order to include tracks in modern languages and sciences. It would remain the subject of some controversy for years to come.[57] The seemingly paradoxical fact that the state's educational philosophy, institutions, and policy contributed to the devirilization of citizens and the disruption of their "filiation" highlighted the challenge involved in anchoring the male citizen in a productive and reproductive social order. It also explains why the sterile "bachelor" was such a useful rhetorical tool in the hands of those who sought to bring about reform.

57. Isambert-Jamati, *Crises de la société*, 196; Georges Weill, *Histoire de l'enseignement secondaire en France (1802–1920)* (1921), 214–26.

PART III

ÉMILE DURKHEIM AND
DESIRABLE REGULATION

> With the advance of evolution, the ties that bind the individual to his family, native soil, the traditions inherited from the past and collective group customs become attenuated. More mobile, he changes milieu more freely; he leaves his kin in order to go elsewhere, to live a more autonomous life, to formulate his own ideas and sentiments. . . . If he does not create other [ties] than those derived from resemblance, the effacement of the segmental type [of society] would be accompanied by a progressive moral decline. Man would no longer be sufficiently held in check; he would no longer sense around him the salutary pressure of society which moderates his egotism and turns him into a moral being. This is the moral value of the division of labor. As a result of it, the individual resumes consciousness of his dependence upon society; the forces that retain and contain him are derived from it.
>
> Émile Durkheim, *De la division du travail social*

In his doctoral dissertation, published in 1894 as *De la division du travail social*, Émile Durkheim outlined the inexorable decline of traditional society in the modern West. Now viewed as a sociological classic, this text offered at the time a novel, and indeed controversial, account of the historical relationship between individuals and the social order. Durkheim heralded the progressive erosion of traditional modes of social production and reproduction, and the gradual "attenuation" of the familial and territorial bonds of "filiation" celebrated by Barrès in his paean to *"la terre et les morts."* Like his colleagues in the academy, and contemporary social critics more generally, Durkheim was profoundly concerned with the potential ill effects of this transformation, in particular, with the "pathological" or deviant phenomena to which it might give rise. He did not, however, see these pathologies as the inevitable, irremediable *telos* of "civilization." Indeed, he viewed the social evolution from "primitive" to "modern" social forms as responsible for the liberation of an implicitly male individual from the dictates of homogenizing "communal consciousness." He argued that this development freed sons from the oppressive constraints of religious and paternal authority. At the same time, he announced the advent of new kinds of social bonds, ones that were no longer based on the "resemblance" or commonality of familial and regional ties, but rather on difference and relations of mutual complementarity. This model of complementary differences, and the "organic solidarity" they were supposed to produce, structured his normative vision of how to integrate male individuals into the modern social order. It also informed his understanding of the social virtues of married love. Durkheim's thought thus provides an exceptionally lucid account of how conjugality, as a socially necessary institution, at once emancipated sons from patriarchal authority and effectively regulated their sexual passions. Modern marriage was, in his view, neither purely natural nor transhistorical, but culturally contingent, the result of a gradual social evolution. This culturalist aspect of Durkheim's thought demarcated him from his contemporaries—philosophers and pedagogical reformers, cultural critics, and demographers—despite the clear correspondences and echoes in their concerns.

Durkheim's personal trajectory to some extent epitomized the *déracinement* and disavowal of paternal authority excoriated by Barrès. He was, like the philosophy professor Boutellier in *Les déracinés,* "a pure product of the parliamentary republic." Born in 1858 in Epinal, Alsace, an enclave of traditional Judaism, to a family in which sons were expected to become rabbis, Durkheim cast off his weighty heritage.[1] Without reducing his thought to mere biographical anecdote, the fact that both his father and grandfather were rabbis clearly informed Durkheim's tendency to confound familial or paternal and religious authority. In his dissertation, he figured ancient Hebrew biblical law to be the very incarnation of the repressive legislation characteristic of "primitive" or mechanical solidarity.[2]

Choosing the path of state education rather than the rabbinical seminary, Durkheim left his *sol natal* to pursue studies in Paris at the Lycée Louis-le-

1. On Durkheim's relationship to his religious heritage, see Pierre Birnbaum, "French Sociologists between Reason and Faith: The Impact of the Dreyfus Affair," *Jewish Social Studies* 2, no. 1 (1995); Venita Datta, *Birth of a National Icon: The Literary Avant-Garde and the Origins of the Intellectual in France* (1999), 109–11; Alexandre Derczansky, "Note sur la judéité de Durkheim," *Archives de Sciences sociales des religions* 69, no. 1 (1990); Jean-Claude Filloux, "Il ne faut pas oublier que je suis fils de rabbin," *Revue française de sociologie* 17, no. 2 (1976); Louis M. Greenberg, "Bergson and Durkheim as Sons and Assimilators," *French Historical Studies* 9, no. 4 (1976); Bernard Lacroix, *Durkheim et le politique* (1981); W. S. F. Pickering, "The Enigma of Durkheim's Jewishness," in *Debating Durkheim*, ed. W. S. F. Pickering and H. Martin (1994); Jerrold Seigel, "Autonomy and Personality in Durkheim: An Essay on Content and Method," *Journal of the History of Ideas* 48, no. 3 (1987); Ivan Strenski, *Durkheim and the Jews of France* (1997).

2. See his discussion of Talmudic law: Émile Durkheim, *De la division du travail social,* 11th ed. (1986), 283. And see Émile Durkheim, *Le suicide* (1930), 160.

Grand and the École normale supérieure. After passing the *agrégation* in philosophy in 1882, he taught in the provincial lycées of Puy, Sens, Saint-Quentin, and Troyes, and received a year-long grant to study social science in Germany. In 1887, he was appointed to teach the new sequence of required courses in pedagogy and social science at the Faculty of Letters in Bordeaux, becoming titular in 1895. This position was designed along the same lines as the chair in the Sciences of Education at the Faculty of Letters in Paris, first assumed by Henri Marion, and subsequently by Ferdinand Buisson. Durkheim was well primed to take up the post at the Sorbonne in 1902. Given this formation and professional trajectory, Durkheim was deeply implicated in the pedagogical project of secular republican moral and social reform. He also played an instrumental role in the reorientation of its assumptions about the nature of morality and the relationship between individuals and the social order.

Since the French Revolution, and indeed, before it, the question of the relationship between the "individual" and "society" was a subject of ongoing philosophical and political reflection and rearticulation. In his earliest writings on the history of "social science" in France, Durkheim commented upon and positioned himself in relationship to this "tradition." He suggested how figures such as Jean-Jacques Rousseau and the revolutionaries of 1789, by turning their sights on "society" as a source of inequality and oppression, made social bonds between individuals into a political and moral problem. In his *Discourse on the Origin of Inequality*, for example, Rousseau had figured social relations as a source of dependence, which inevitably gave rise to inequality. This dependence could, according to his later writings, only be held in check by the social contract. The Revolutionaries, meanwhile, in their efforts to do away with the social privileges upon which Old Regime society was based, famously abolished the corporate order—on the night of 4 August 1789, in the Declaration of the Rights of Man and Citizen, and with the Le Chapelier law of 1791. In the new nation, society was comprised of theoretically equal male individuals, stripped of the particularities and privileges produced by intermediary bodies or corporations.[3] In the wake of these radical transformations, the status of the "social," which is to say the modalities and norms regulating the relations between individuals, emerged as an ongoing problem in the nineteenth-century. Indeed, in Durkheim's view, "from the day when the revolutionary tempest had passed, the notion of sociology [*science sociale*] was formed as if by magic."[4]

In his effort to demonstrate an indigenous tradition of French social thought, Durkheim cited Henri de Saint-Simon and Auguste Comte as his

3. Pierre Rosanvallon, *Le modèle politique français: La société civile contre le jacobinisme à nos jours* (2004), 25–54; William H. Sewell, *Work and Revolution in France: The Language of Labor from the Old Regime to 1848* (1980), 62–91.

4. Émile Durkheim, "Sociology in France in the Nineteenth Century," in *Émile Durkheim: On Morality and Society*, ed. Robert N. Bellah (1973), 6.

principal predecessors. Their respective projects of creating a science of society as a way to address the perceived ills of the post-Revolutionary order were, of course, among numerous and varied attempts to at once diagnose and remedy the atomization and disarticulation of new regime society. They developed their "social physiology" and social science in order to counter the perceived disorganization of the present, and to create a more harmonious and productive order in the future. Alongside them, reactionaries such as Joseph de Maistre and Louis de Bonald, liberals such as Benjamin Constant, social Catholics such as Félicité de Lamennais, and socialists such as Charles Fourier and Pierre Leroux explored the nature and necessity of social attachment and association.[5] And, under the Second Empire, political and social thinkers, liberals and republicans alike, in their writings and associational life, sought new ways of mediating between "the individual" and "the State."[6]

Once the Third Republic, committed in principle to individual liberty and equality, had been definitively established in 1877, the question of the social bond re-emerged as a pressing philosophical and political problem. As Durkheim himself commented, "The country found itself faced with the same question as at the beginning of the century."[7] This new context gave rise to novel efforts to understand and imagine how individuals might be articulated to the social order. More specifically, it marked the advent of "sociological" thinking as a new academic discipline and a significant reconceptualization of associative and affective bonds, as we have seen in Marion's discussion of "solidarity," for the moral and political formation of citizens.

Durkheim, like Marion, was trained in the spiritualist and neo-Kantian philosophical tradition that remained prominent in contemporary writings on morality and pedagogy. He, at the same time, drew significant inspiration from Auguste Comte, whose positivist philosophy was sharply critical of the "metaphysical" presuppositions about individual selfhood implicit in Victor Cousin's eclecticism.[8] Durkheim's early writings were hence marked by his engagement with thinkers such as Comte and Alfred Espinas, who had begun to reimagine the relationship between society and the individuals which comprised it. In the process, Durkheim sought to articulate an idea of morality as rooted in a specific social milieu, rather than as transcendental. And he, in turn, critiqued abstract conceptions of "the individual" as isolated and egoistic, conceptions which he traced back to Rousseau and the

5. Rosanvallon, *Le modèle,* 157–76.
6. Sudhir Hazareesingh, *From Subject to Citizen: The Second Empire and the Emergence of Modern French Democracy* (1998); Philip Nord, *The Republican Moment: Struggles for Democracy in Nineteenth-century France* (1995).
7. Durkheim, "Sociology in France in the Nineteenth Century," 12. See also Rosanvallon, *Le modèle,* 265–75.
8. Jan Goldstein, *The Post-Revolutionary Self: Politics and Psyche in France, 1750–1850* (2005), 305–8.

Revolution and which, in his view, structured Kantian moral philosophy and utilitarian economic thinking alike. Rather than viewing society as "a machine of war against individuals," he insisted, instead, on how individuals are attached to and constituted by the social order in which they live.[9] The next two chapters show how his writings on the evolution domestic forms and concomitant emergence of "the individual" both contributed to and reflected this overarching moral vision.

Numerous studies devoted to the emergence of sociology as an academic discipline in France have highlighted how the professional and epistemological aims of Durkheim and his school coincided with the political exigencies of the Republic, as they crystallized around the time of the Dreyfus Affair. In order to address both nationalist and socialist currents of political opposition, and the material and moral strains associated with the growth of a modern industrial nation, turn-of-the-century politicians and social reformers increasingly appealed to a normative vision of "society" as the foundation of an at once equitable and stable political and moral order. They articulated new principles of civic equality and legal right in order to define social responsibility as an obligation. This reformulation of the terms of citizenship, which is to say the complex of rights and responsibilities conferred on those individuals who comprised the polity, was perhaps best exemplified by turn-of-the-century discussions of "solidarity" as an immanent law of modern social life. In the words of Léon Bourgeois, one of the earliest and most prominent of the doctrine's proponents, "It is not a matter of defining the rights that society has over men, but of the rights and responsibilities that the fact of association creates between men as real beings, and the only possible subjects of right and responsibility."[10] Contemporary policy-makers, pedagogues, and philanthropists appealed to this philosophy of social peace in formulating reform legislation (for workers' accident insurance, a shortened work week, assistance to the elderly and infirm) and in promoting mutuality and assistance in civil society as well (through mutual aid societies, voluntary associations, and the like). In the process, they set forth a conception of the individual as bound up with and indeed dependent upon the social order.[11] Like Durkheim, they figured "society," not as a force of oppression, but as a condition of individual freedom.

9. Émile Durkheim, "The Principles of 1789 and Sociology," in *Émile Durkheim: On Morality and Society,* ed. Robert N. Bellah (1973), 39–40.

10. Léon Bourgeois, *Solidarité,* 2nd ed. (1897), 90.

11. On solidarist philosophy: J. E. S. Hayward, "Solidarity: The Social History of an Idea in Nineteenth-century France," *International Review of Social History* 4, no. 2 (1959); J. E. S. Hayward, "The Official Social Philosophy of the French Third Republic: Léon Bourgeois and Solidarism," *International Review of Social History* 6, no. 1 (1961); Kristin A. Sheradin, "Reforming the Republic: Solidarism and the Making of the French Welfare State, 1871–1914" (Ph.D. diss., University of Rochester, 2000). For Solidarism's broader political, social, and intellectual contexts, see Datta, *Birth of a National Icon,* Jacques Donzelot, *L'Invention du social: Essai sur le déclin des passions politiques* (1994); Sanford Elwitt, *The Third Republic Defended: Bourgeois Reform in France, 1880–1914* (1986); François Ewald, "A Concept of

Solidarism also extended republican efforts to elaborate a secular moral and social philosophy. And it was, for this reason, a privileged subject of discussion among prominent members of the educational establishment, who understood it as a way to overcome the social and political rifts produced by the Dreyfus Affair. Alfred Croiset, the dean of the Paris Faculty of Letters, thus wrote in his introduction to a collection of speeches on the topic, "Solidarity has nothing metaphysical or confessional about it. It is based on the positive fact that men on this earth are obliged by nature to live in close association, and it attempts to make this association as felicitous as possible, using all the means that our intelligence and heart can furnish. All beliefs, all philosophical opinions can accommodate themselves to the idea of solidarity."[12] Because men needed instruction in these principles, solidarism placed education within the purview of its reformist efforts. For as Léon Bourgeois explained in a speech on the subject, "it is up to education, not law" to "elevate men to the notion of social duty."[13]

Durkheim's work clearly circulated in this political and intellectual milieu.[14] As a professional academic, Durkheim did not often engage directly with questions of public policy or the legislative mechanics of social reform. According to his own understanding of the organic solidarity produced by a "division of social labor," direct political concerns fell outside his vocation as a member of the nation's intellectual elite. As he proclaimed in a short article on the subject, "Above all our action must be exerted through books,

Social Law," in *Dilemmas of Law in the Welfare State,* ed. Gunther Teubner (1985); François Ewald, *L'état providence* (1986); Rachel Fuchs, "France in Comparative Perspective," in *Gender and the Politics of Social Reform in France, 1870–1914,* cd. Elinor A. Accampo et al. (1995); Janet A. Horne, *A Social Laboratory for Modern France* (2000); James T. Kloppenberg, *Uncertain Victory: Social Democracy and Progressivism in European and American Thought, 1870–1920* (1986), 298–415; Philip Nord, "The Welfare State in France, 1870–1914," *French Historical Studies* 18, no. 3 (1994); Pierre Rosanvallon, *L'état en France de 1789 à nos jours* (1990), 171–74; Debora Silverman, *Art Nouveau and the Fin-de-siècle in France: Politics, Psychology, and Style* (1989), 49–51.

12. Léon Bourgeois and Alfred Croiset, *Essai d'une philosophie de la Solidarité: Conférences et discussions (1901–1902),* ed. École des hautes études sociales (1902), xiii–xiv.

13. Ibid., 97. Also see Émile Durkheim, "Rôle des universités dans l'éducation sociale du pays," in *Congrès international de l'éducation sociale* (1901), 128–38, 366–74.

14. For discussions of Durkheim's relationship to this political and intellectual context, see John I. Brooks, *The Eclectic Legacy: Academic Philosophy and the Human Sciences in Nineteenth-century France* (1998); Terry Nichols Clark, *Prophets and Patrons: The French University and the Emergence of the Social Sciences* (1973), 162–95; Robert Alun Jones, *The Development of Durkheim's Social Realism* (1999); Victor Karady, "The Durkheimians in Academe: A Reconsideration," in *The Sociological Domain: The Durkheimians and the Founding of French Sociology,* ed. Philippe Besnard (1983); Victor Karady, "Durkheim et les débuts de l'ethnologie universitaire," *Actes de la recherche en sciences sociales* 74 (1988); Dominick LaCapra, *Émile Durkheim: Sociologist and Philosopher* (1972), 67–73; Laurence Loeffel, *La question du fondement de la morale laïque sous la IIIe République (1870–1914)* (2000), 127–92; William Logue, *From Philosophy to Sociology: The Evolution of French Liberalism, 1870–1914* (1983); Steven Lukes, *Émile Durkheim: His Life and Work* (1972), 350–54; Laurent Mucchielli, *La découverte du social: Naissance de la sociologie en France (1870–1914)* (1998), 80–112.

seminars, and popular education. It is our function to help our contemporaries know themselves in their ideas and in their feelings, far more than to govern them."[15] This devotion to at once explaining and promoting a renewed vision of social morality by his writing and teaching animated Durkheim's work and constituted his engagement with contemporary efforts to reimagine the norms of democratic society. In this way, he clearly partook of the wider endeavor in which his contemporaries were engaged.

In the next two chapters I explore, specifically, how Durkheim's work articulated and theorized a conception of the male citizen as a social subject. I illustrate how social subjectivity was presumed to be masculine in Durkheim's thought and how he imagined masculine citizens to be both produced and contained by a conjugal social matrix.[16] I outline how Durkheim addressed contemporary concerns about social pathology and deviance—the potential excesses of men's individualism and social alienation, the simultaneous dangers of their economic and sexual deregulation—in novel ways that consolidated modern masculinity by inscribing married heterosexuality, not as a transhistorical moral or natural fact, but as an at once obligatory, desirable, and quasi-sacred social norm. This model of conjugality, I suggest, was a crucial component of his account and understanding of men's social citizenship.

Durkheim's thought is remarkable and famous for its effort to "explain the social by the social." This commitment is clearly evidenced in his account of men's sexual desire as a distinctly social, rather than simply natural, problem, and in his figuration of conjugality as its uniquely modern solution. His understanding of women, and more specifically, of the nature of their sexual desire was much more problematic. In calling attention to their troublesome place in his writings on marriage and the family, we see how, while Durkheim notably broke with nature as a framework for social explanation, his very account of that break nonetheless relied on presumptions about nature. Indeed, his understanding of how male individuals were ideally completed in and by the social order was conceptually dependent on a set of assumptions about the heterosexual character of desire, the nature of the "primitive," and the place of "women" in the modern social order. An exploration of these conceptual paradoxes in Durkheim's thought brings the stakes and aims of his sociological project and its relationship to contemporary concerns surrounding the socialization of male citizens into sharp focus.

15. Émile Durkheim, "The Intellectual Elite and Democracy," in *Émile Durkheim on Morality and Society*, ed. Robert N. Bellah (1973), 59. See also George Weisz, *The Emergence of Modern Universities in France, 1863–1914* (1983), 271–314.
16. On the gendering of the "social" and the reconfiguration of citizenship in the early Third Republic, see Joan W. Scott, *Only Paradoxes to Offer: Feminism and the "Rights of Man" in France, 1789–1940* (1996), 90–124.

5   *The Limits of Desire*

Durkheim is well known for his diagnosis of the "pathologies" of modern social life, and especially for his analysis of the egotism and anomie that, he argued, plagued contemporary civilization. He was not, however, a prophet of modern doom. An enlightenment faith in the healing powers of science, and especially of social science, in contrast to cultural pessimism, motivated his concern with the "pathological" social effects of modernity. His interest in the potential excesses of individual desire was inspired by an effort to discern the contours of a healthy social norm.

Unlike many of his contemporaries, Durkheim embraced the mobility, migration, and "*déracinement*" that were characteristic of modernity. He celebrated the novelty, diversity, and mutability of urban life as a veritable leaven of social progress and similarly viewed transplantation, not as an inevitable source of young men's perversion, but as an occasion for their liberation from repressive tradition.[1] His efforts to reimagine the organization of politics and civil society on the basis of national, as opposed to local corporations, similarly hailed de-territorialization as a necessary source of diversity and innovation.[2] According to Durkheim's account of social evolution, the progress of "civilization" and concomitant rise of individuality did not inexorably lead to alienation and social fragmentation. Rather than coming at the expense of social cohesion, individuation ideally increased subjects' dependence on others. Men's social dependency was, he claimed, normal. Durkheim's individual was thus defined, not by wholeness and self-sufficiency, but by lack and desire. His vision of what it took to be a "whole man," as a result, did not oppose autonomy and solidarity, but rather fig-

1. See, for example, Émile Durkheim, *De la division du travail social,* 11th ed. (1986), 281–82.
2. Ibid., xix–xx.

ured them as historically and morally coterminous. In this chapter, I show how marriage operated in Durkheim's writings as both an illustration and condition of men's social "wholeness." Conjugality, I argue, secured the citizen's masculinity at the same time that it inscribed him as implicitly lacking. Married heterosexuality was, in other words, a condition and caution of the citizen's health and happiness, despite the fact that the benefits of marriage were less than evident for the citizen's spouse.

Bachelorhood, Suicide, and Modern Social Pathology

As we saw in part 2, young men's unwillingness and inability to embrace marriage and paternity were, at this time, potent symbols of the morbid effects of unbridled egotism in modern society. Durkheim reflected on these phenomena early on in his career in an article titled "Suicide et natalité" published in the *Revue philosophique* in 1888. In this short text, he developed an account of suicide rates as indicators of social malaise, a theory that he elaborated at greater length a decade later in *Suicide*. Drawing a statistical correlation between low levels of population growth and elevated suicide rates, Durkheim sought to isolate the common factor between them. By figuring suicide as a gauge of relative levels of happiness, he concluded that individuals tended to suffer greater distress when they limited their fertility. Indeed, according to his analysis, bachelors and childless husbands were more likely to commit suicide than the *père de famille*. Fertility decline was not, he argued, a result of egotistical individuals' rejection of a larger social good for the sake of their own pleasure. It was rather a symptom of the decline of family sentiments, a decline that also contributed to individual unhappiness.

This analysis of France's waning fertility responded directly to Jacques Bertillon's discussion of rampant, selfish materialism as the cause of the nation's falling birthrate. Calling into question the demographer's utilitarian premises, Durkheim inverted the logic of Bertillon's argument which, as we saw in chapter 4, figured ambition and the appetite for material gain as responsible for the waning strength of the family. Instead he claimed that the contemporary decline of family sentiment had opened the door to both more materialism and lower fertility. Building on this analysis, he answered the arguments made by demographers such as Bertillon, urging that, "material well-being would never have gained such importance in popular morality if the joys of collective life had not lost theirs." Durkheim thus concluded that, "if suicides increase when fertility declines, it is because the two phenomena result from a regression of domestic sentiments."[3]

3. Émile Durkheim, "Suicide et natalité: Étude de statistique morale," *Revue philosophique de la France et de l'étranger* 26, no. 11 (1888): 462.

For Durkheim, collective feelings were essential to individual well-being. Personal satisfaction was, in his view, enhanced by society, and not hopelessly opposed to it. Mobilizing a rhetoric of vitalistic energies, his analysis of domestic sentiments demonstrated how "the social" amplified the individual's "forces."[4] Durkheim's repeated references to "courage," "force," and the "struggle for life" intimate that "the individual" with whom he was concerned was male. In the well-knit family, he argued, "the individual is part of a compact mass with which he is connected [*solidaire*] and which multiplies his forces: his power of resistance is thus increased. He is better outfitted for struggle the less isolated he is. However, when the family is sparse, poor, thin, the individuals, who are less close to one another, allow spaces to open up where this cold wind of egotism, which freezes hearts and defeat courage, blows."[5] "Egotism" does not here emanate from the "individuals" themselves; it is rather a structural effect that weakens the individual rather than lending him greater "courage." The family, in sum, enhanced and strengthened men. By exploiting the slippery category of "the individual," which was unmarked yet implicitly masculine, Durkheim avoided the question of how the close-knit family impacted women.

Similar to his contemporaries, Durkheim was concerned that the alienated male individual tended to waste and dissipate himself, expending his energy, and in the extreme case of suicide, extinguishing it entirely. Durkheim did not, however, propose a return to the traditional family as the solution to the twin problems of sexual and economic deregulation. Like many of his fellow republicans, Durkheim criticized the patriarchal family as obsolete, as no longer able to assume the total social function it had held in the past. The family was, nonetheless, central to his analysis of modern social pathology. And he, in turn, explained how the modern conjugal family, as opposed to the traditional, patriarchal one, was a vital institution of social and sexual regulation.

Morality, Pedagogy, and the Conjugal Family

Durkheim did not see a return to the traditional patriarchal family as a viable solution to the resolutely modern dilemmas created by urbanization, economic expansion, migration, secularization, and democratization. He instead argued that a new domestic form had emerged—"conjugal society"—which was better adapted to these now irreversible developments. An essentially "companionate" conception of marriage, conjugality served a

4. On this organicism, see Rémi Lenoir, *Généalogie de la morale familiale* (2003), 196; Robert A. Nye, "Heredity, Pathology, and Psychoneurosis in Durkheim's Early Work," in *Émile Durkheim: Critical Assessments*, ed. Peter Hamilton (1990).

5. Durkheim, "Suicide et natalité," 463.

delimited, yet crucial function in Durkheim's overall moral and social vision. Sociologist Georges Davy said as much in an essay devoted to his mentor's conception of kinship. "The family," he wrote, "is a foyer of morality, energy, and gentleness, a school of duty, love, and work, in other words, a school of life, which could not lose its role."[6]

According to Durkheim's evolutionary understanding of the history of familial forms, the primitive family comprised at once religious, political, and domestic functions, and hence organized and regulated the totality of social life. This was no longer the case in the modern West. He contended that, in the present and future, new kinds of secondary bodies would assume the economic, religious, and political roles once proper to the family. "Conjugal society" nonetheless retained an important social function by protecting male individuals from the twin forces of egotism and anomie. Without it, as the article on suicide and fertility intimated, male individuals were quite literally at a loss. Durkheim notably insisted on the importance of domestic life for *men's* moral well-being, not women's. His argument relied on the presumption that women were always already located in the family. And, he did not seek to explain why domesticity was ultimately beneficial for women, even when he was presented with evidence to the contrary. In order to sustain his vision of the conjugal family as beneficial to *both* individuals and society, Durkheim occluded women's apparent domestic suffering. This lapse in his thinking reveals the gendered and sexual assumptions on which his theory of the family was based.

In 1887, after concluding his own *"beau mariage"* to Louise Dreyfus, Durkheim assumed a new post at the Faculty of Letters at Bordeaux, where he taught pedagogy, moral philosophy, and practical training for the *agrégation*.[7] In addition to this standard fare, he began a weekly public lecture series in "social science," which provided him with an ideal forum in which to chart the entry of sociology into French academic life.[8] Beyond encouraging the development of the discipline as a nascent science of morality, these lectures articulated practical moral ends. His introductory lecture to the new course, delivered in the fall of 1887 underscored that sociology was best suited to address the moral crisis, the socially "dispersive tendency" which, he suggested, plagued contemporary society. In the rousing conclusion to this lecture, he proclaimed, "Society must regain consciousness of its

---

6. Georges Davy, "La famille et la parenté d'après Durkheim," in *Sociologues d'hier et d'aujourd'hui* (1950), 119.

7. On Durkheim's marriage, see Christophe Charle, "Le beau mariage d'Émile Durkheim," *Actes de la recherche en sciences sociales*, no. 55 (1984). On his appointment to Bordeaux, see Terry Nichols Clark, *Prophets and Patrons: The French University and the Emergence of the Social Sciences* (1973), 163; Victor Karady, "The Durkheimians in Academe: A Reconsideration," in *The Sociological Domain: The Durkheimians and the Founding of French Sociology*, ed. Philippe Besnard (1983); Steven Lukes, *Émile Durkheim: His Life and Work* (1972), 99–108.

8. Lukes, *Émile Durkheim*, 137–38.

organic unity. . . . Well! Messieurs, I believe that sociology, more than any other science, is in a position to restore these ideas. It will make the individual understand what society is, how it completes him and how he is insignificant [*peu de chose*] when reduced to his own forces." By inverting the valences of "independence" and "dependence," Durkheim suggested that isolation "reduced" individual forces, while social solidarity enhanced them. As he explained, "there is nothing diminishing about being in solidarity with and depending on an other, about not belonging entirely to oneself."[9]

After spending a year outlining the basic principles of sociological investigation, Durkheim narrowed the focus of his course. Beginning in 1888, he devoted his lecture series to the sociology of the family, which traced an evolution from the "primitive" to the modern, "conjugal" form. Durkheim's progressive narrative was structured by a theoretical distinction between primitive societies held together by bonds of resemblance and modern ones in which social ties are based on the differences created by a division of labor.[10] This opposition borrowed from the work of contemporary English and German sociologists—Herbert Spencer, Ferdinand Tönnies, and Albert Schaeffle—yet significantly inverted their basic presumptions. In depicting primitive society as *mechanical* and modern society as *organic,* Durkheim enacted an at once semantic and conceptual reversal of Spencer's account of "industrial society" and Tönnies depiction of modern *Gesellschaft.*[11] He hence dismissed widespread assumptions that egotism and alienation were intrinsic to modernity, by claiming that social ties between individuals should *normally* be strengthened by the differences produced by the modern division of labor. Durkheim's account of the evolution of the family played an important role in his efforts to substantiate this claim.

Given the centrality of the family to contemporary theories of social evolution, it is unsurprising that Durkheim took domestic institutions as a point of departure in elaborating his vision of sociology as a science of morality.[12] While motivated, as we have seen, by a vision of the morally restorative role of his new discipline, Durkheim sought to approach the highly contentious and polemical subject of the history and typology of fa-

9. Émile Durkheim, "Cours de science sociale: Leçon d'ouverture," *Revue internationale de l'enseignement* 8, no. 1 (1888): 48.

10. The majority of these lectures have been lost. The synthetic work published by Davy remains an indispensable guide in retracing the broad strokes of Durkheim's arguments. See Georges Davy, "La famille et la parenté d'après Durkheim."

11. See, for example, Durkheim, "Cours de science sociale"; Émile Durkheim, "Communauté et société selon Tönnies (1889)," in *Textes 1,* ed. Victor Karady (1973); Émile Durkheim, "Organisation et vie du corps social selon Schaeffle (1888)," in *Textes 2,* ed. Victor Karady (1973). And his critique of Spencer in Durkheim, *De la division,* 169–76.

12. See Mary Ann Lamanna, *Émile Durkheim on the Family* (2002), 39–61. And more broadly, Adam Kuper, *The Invention of Primitive Society: Transformations of an Illusion* (1988), 1–122.

milial forms with "perfect serenity." He wanted to avoid "pessimistic" accounts, like those of Ferdinand Le Play, which rued the decline of the traditional patriarchal family. At the same time, he warned against the subjective bias of "optimistic" ones, which deplored the supposed immorality of primitive society and celebrated the purported "superiority" of modern civilization. He was, in these early writings, skeptical of travelogues and missionary reports, frequently flawed, in his view, by an absence of objective criteria, as viable sources for genuine social scientific inquiry. Thus, while he praised contemporaries, such as anthropologist Charles Letourneau (who made extensive use of these kinds of sources) for their erudition, he dismissed their work as essentially lacking in systematic analysis. Hierarchized value judgments of "superiority" and "inferiority," Durkheim argued, had no place in scientific endeavor. And, he thus concluded his introductory lecture on the family, "Today's family is neither more nor less perfect than that of yesteryear: it is different, because circumstances are different. It is more complex because the milieu in which it exists is more complex."[13] These claims to scientific objectivity, did not, however, proscribe the sociologist from making pronouncements about the, albeit contingent and adaptive, norms of domestic morality, in the past, present, or future.

In the subsequent lectures that he delivered on the topic in 1888–89, and from 1890–92, Durkheim retraced the historical evolution of the family into its modern conjugal form. His account followed successive stages, each characterized by increasing differentiation and individuation: an initial communal and clan-based phase, an intermediary patriarchal and paternal stage, and a final conjugal one. In keeping with his understanding of "primitive," "mechanical solidarity," Durkheim portrayed the communal family as an aggregate mass. Within this organization, domestic, religious, political, and economic responsibilities were all confounded; the family's social function was not differentiated, and neither were its members.[14] Drawing on Lewis Henry Morgan's ethnographic accounts of Native Americans in his *Ancient Society* and Lorimer Fison and A. W. Howitt's descriptions of Australian aboriginal society in *Kamilaroi and Kurnai*, Durkheim described the "ideal type" of this society in *De la division du travail social*: "One must consider it to be an absolutely homogeneous mass whose parts are indistinguishable from one another." Notably, in these societies, "adults of both sexes are one another's equals."[15] This uniform, primitive "horde" was, he argued, succeeded by the "segmentary" politico-familial organization of

13. Émile Durkheim, "Introduction à la sociologie de la famille (1888)," in *Textes 3*, ed. Victor Karady (1973), 24–25.
14. Émile Durkheim, "La famille conjugale (1892)," in *Textes 3*, ed. Victor Karady (1973), 41. This text was posthumously published by Durkheim's nephew, Marcel Mauss, in 1921. See also Davy, "La famille," 91–92; Lamanna, *Émile Durkheim*, 47–48.
15. Durkheim, *De la division*, 149–50.

"clans," which introduced a measure of division into the originary "proto-plasm." As in the case of the communal family, solidarity within clan-based societies was again founded on resemblance; it was derived "from simili-tude, because society is formed by similar segments and these, in turn, con-tain homogeneous elements."[16]

The patriarchal family represented a further modification of this initial order. Here, the circle of relations was reduced; the head of the household was "liberated" from the other members who remained, more or less, in a position of equality vis-à-vis the "father."[17] Patriarchal authority, exempli-fied by the Roman *patria potestas*, unified the family in and through rela-tions of subordination. For Durkheim, this patriarchal structure was "monarchical."[18] A "Germanic" or "paternal" phase of familial organiza-tion, represented a softening of absolute patriarchal authority. It introduced both a more egalitarian treatment of maternal and paternal kinship lines, and more freedom for sons, who could now emancipate themselves from paternal authority in order to found their own families, independent of the father's household.[19] The modern Western form of "conjugal society" de-veloped out of this more attenuated structure of parental authority.

Durkheim described the distinctly modern structure, the "conjugal fam-ily," in the concluding lecture of his course on the family delivered in 1892. Here he distinguished this most recent evolutionary phase from the pre-existing ones by the ever-increasing differentiation and individuation of the domestic unit's members to the extent that "each has his own individuality, his own sphere of activity."[20] In keeping with his vision of "organic" soli-darity, the ties binding this family together depended on a network of dif-ferential relations, not on a common investment in the group's heritage and inheritance. As a result, in the conjugal society, "individual personalities" developed, "each member takes on a distinct physiognomy, a personal manner of feeling and thinking."[21] This is *not* to say that the conjugal fam-ily represented, for Durkheim, a detached realm of private sentiment and individual expression, unconnected to wider social concerns or those of the state.

Durkheim, in fact, argued, both in his lecture on the conjugal family and in *De la division du travail social* that the state's growing penetration of do-mestic life was the impetus behind recent changes in family structure. As he explained, "The conjugal family would never have emerged out of the pa-triarchal or paternal family, or a mixture between the two, without the in-

16. Ibid., 152. Durkheim suggests "the Negroes of Africa," the Ancient Hebrews, and the Kabyle of Algeria were characterized by this clan-based society.

17. Durkheim, "La famille conjugale (1892)," 42.

18. Davy, "La famille," 112–15. See also Émile Durkheim, "Origines du testament romain (1910)," in *Textes 3*, ed. Victor Karady (1973).

19. Davy, "La famille," 115–16.

20. Durkheim, "La famille conjugale (1892)," 37.

21. Ibid., 42.

tervention of this new factor: the State."[22] Durkheim cited the state's increasing limitations on the terms and extent of paternal rights as evidence of this shift. He noted the postrevolutionary creation of the *conseils de familles* to regulate family disputes and the 1889 law allowing for the state divestiture of paternal authority as significant instances of the French state's growing intervention in and regulation of family affairs.[23] Increasingly traversed by the government's rules and representatives, the family was no longer, Durkheim argued, a realm at once modeled upon and yet discrete from that of the state; he understood, in other words, that the modern state, rather than establishing the family as a separate "private" sphere, actually penetrated and sanctioned its relations.

In addition to signaling the state's new limitations on fathers' rights vis-à-vis their children, Durkheim described notable mutations in the relationship between husband and wife. The conjugal couple's new moral and legal status was a historical corollary to the decline of paternal authority. As fathers' control over kinship relations declined, marriage took on an increasing role as "the sole condition of kinship." And, in a society no longer ruled by the law of the father, state regulations become integral to the delineation and enforcement of domestic morality. Matrimony reaches the "apogee of its development" with conjugality—its bonds became "nearly indissoluble" and monogamy "nearly complete." The state's new role, exemplified by its oversight of civil marriage, was, he argued, part and parcel of the process by which marriage became "consolidated" and "coherent."[24]

Given his insistence on the increasing role of the state in domestic life, Durkheim refused to see modern marriage as a private contract between discrete individuals.[25] In *De la division du travail*, he explicitly invoked marriage in order to critique voluntarist conceptions of the contract as a "spontaneous agreement of individual interests," which subtended the liberal social theory of figures like Spencer.[26] Durkheim instead claimed that the state sanctioning of modern marriage demonstrated how "not everything in the contract is contractual."[27] In a notable reversal of Spencer's liberal presumptions, Durkheim argued that such "social controls" on marital and domestic obligations would "only continue to increase," and further, that these controls were both necessary and desirable. "The regulatory organs of soci-

22. Ibid., 38. See also Lenoir, *Généalogie*. 224–26.

23. Durkheim, "La famille conjugale (1892)," 38. For a discussion of the history of the *conseils de familles*, see Suzanne Desan, *The Family on Trial in Revolutionary France* (2004). For the 1889 law on the destitution of paternal authority, see Véronique Antomarchi, *Politique et famille sous la Troisième République, 1870–1914* (2000), 51–58; Sylvia Schafer, *Children in Moral Danger and the Problem of Government in Third Republic France* (1997).

24. Durkheim, "La famille conjugale (1892)," 46.

25. Durkheim, *De la division*, 184–85. See also Émile Durkheim, "Évolution juridique en France à l'époque monarchique (1904)," in *Textes 3*, ed. Victor Karady (1973).

26. Durkheim, *De la division*, 180.

27. Ibid., 189.

ety need to intervene," he explained, "in order to exercise a moderating, and in certain cases, a stimulating action on its manner of functioning."[28] In its modern, conjugal form, Durkheim contended, marriage "completely ceases to be a personal contract and becomes a public act."[29] He hence described common law marriages or *"unions libres,"* which escaped official consecration, as socially disruptive and threatening to the state's moral authority.[30]

Now held together by emotional bonds rather than economic ones, the new affective conjugal family coincided, for Durkheim, with the abolition of hereditary privilege and concomitant rise of meritocracy. This liberation of "personal worth" from the influence of heredity, in his view, enhanced individual differentiation, rather than effacing it.[31] Durkheim overtly championed this movement toward greater economic justice and its related valorization of individual merit in *De la division du travail social,* where he argued that both biological and financial "heredity" were obstacles to the normal progress of the "division of labor" in modern society. In his view, inherited family professions or *"vocations natives"* acted as agents of social stagnation, which stifled the blossoming of the (male) individual. "They chain us to our race, just as the collective consciousness chains us to our group, and hinder the liberty of our movements."[32] Durkheim contended that, while occupations might be "distributed according to race" in primitive and "inferior" societies (his examples included ancient Abyssinia, African tribes, and India "still today"), this principle no longer applied in the modern West.[33]

For Durkheim, the modern individual was a self-made man, a product of his own efforts and talents and not reducible to his filiation. As he explained, "We tend to believe that the individual is mostly a son of his own works and even to ignore the ties binding him to his race—upon which he still depends; this, at the very least, according to the widespread opinions and complaints of psychologists of heredity."[34] In contradistinction to the "psychologists of heredity," such as Théodule Ribot, or figures like Barrès, Durkheim applauded this emancipation—a liberation that clearly spoke to his own departure from well-entrenched family and religious traditions.[35] In

28. Ibid., 188. For Spencer's analysis and critique of increasing state-intervention into the realm of the family, see Herbert Spencer, *The Principles of Sociology: Domestic Institutions (1885),* 3rd ed., vol. 3 (1910), 717–24.
29. Durkheim, "La famille conjugale (1892)," 46.
30. Ibid., 48.
31. Ibid., 44.
32. Durkheim, *De la division,* 291–92.
33. Ibid., 295.
34. Ibid., 296. He would appear here to be referring to Théodule Ribot, on whose text, *L'hérédité psychologique* he nonetheless drew in order to construct his argument. Durkheim thus both used Ribot's arguments about primitive societies and refuted his claims about the persistence of hereditary considerations for modern man.
35. See Laurent Mucchielli, *La découverte du social: naissance de la sociologie en France (1870–1914)* (1998), 163–64. On Ribot, see John I. Brooks, *The Eclectic Legacy: Academic Philosophy and the Human Sciences in Nineteenth-century France* (1998), 67–96.

what amounted to a curiously biological account of the declining importance of biology, Durkheim suggested that "the more activities become specialized, the more they escape from hereditary influence."[36] He concluded that social milieu now played a greater role in a son's choice of profession than heredity. While they might inherit "general capacities," children were no longer born with "particular aptitudes." These capacities, in turn, "befit a host of different specializations and guarantee their success."[37] For example, a son might just as well become a sociologist as a rabbi.

The decline of family tradition—epitomized by changes in patterns of inheritance—could, however, prove to be too libratory. Deprived of all connection to the past and future, to an entity such as the "domestic being," the modern individual tended to drift along without ballast. Durkheim thus sought out new social institutions, and most notably, the professional group, to replace the moral function once served by the family.[38] As supplementary forms of kinship, corporations complemented the now more delimited marriage, whose emergence Durkheim documented in his lecture on the conjugal family and in *De la division du travail social*. Indeed, in his 1902 preface to that work, Durkheim would comment, "The corporation thus emerges as a substitute for the family in the exercise of a function that used to be domestic, but could no longer remain so."[39] Hence, while Durkheim celebrated young men's liberation from the oppressive weight of family tradition, he also warned against the untoward effects of this emancipation, if left unregulated by new social norms. He saw a return to conventional family values as socially and historically impossible. His normative ideal of modern society instead set forth an understanding of the "conjugal family" and professional groups as complementary "social organs," which would each contribute to the moral regulation of men, and hence their health and happiness as well as that of the social order.

Nature, Culture, and the Division of Sexual Labor

Initially written as a doctoral dissertation, *De la division du travail social* resonated with and reflected on contemporary debates in political and moral philosophy. As both a product and promoter of the Third Republic's educational ideology, Durkheim participated in current discussions of how to articulate individual autonomy with moral and social solidarity.[40] In shifting his

36. Durkheim, *De la division*, 299.
37. Ibid., 303.
38. Durkheim, "La famille conjugale (1892)," 47.
39. "Préface de la séconde édition," Durkheim, *De la division*, xx. See also M. J. Hawkins, "Durkheim on Occupational Corporations: An Exegesis and Interpretation," *Journal of the History of Ideas* 55, no. 3 (1994).
40. See Jean Baubérot, "Note sur Durkheim et la laïcité," *Archives des sciences sociales des religions* 69, no. 1 (1990); Jean-Claude Chamboredon, "Émile Durkheim: Le social, objet de science: Du moral au politique?" *Critique* 40, no. 445–46 (1984): 480–82; Jean-Claude Filloux, *Durkheim et l'éducation* (1994); François-A. Isambert, "Durkheim: Une science de la

inquiry from the domain of philosophical reflection to that of sociological investigation, Durkheim sought new answers to the questions that philosophers and pedagogues such as Ferdinand Buisson and Henri Marion had been posing for more than a decade. His thesis committee, which counted Marion and neo-Kantian philosopher Émile Boutroux among its members, met this daring departure from standard philosophy with ambivalence and skepticism.[41] In contrast to Kant and contemporary Kantians, Durkheim situated morality not in the realm of universal Reason but in the sphere of the "social." At issue for Durkheim was less the individual's conformity to the moral principles dictated by Reason than the subject's dependence on a wider social order. His reworking of basic Kantian categories resulted in a significantly transformed model of the subject. In contrast to the more abstract formulations of his predecessors, Durkheim's individual was an eminently social being "constituted in a way that does not ruin the collectivity with which it is solidary; it remains adapted to the collectivity, even while it detaches itself. It is in no way antisocial, because it is a social product."[42]

Durkheim's account of conjugality distilled this social vision. It is hence significant that, in his original introduction to *De la division du travail social,* he directly engaged Kant's conception of the human person as articulated in and by his description of marriage. More specifically, he suggested that Kant's vision of the moral self could not explain how or why individuals might give themselves up to wider social ends, a self-sacrifice exemplified, in Durkheim's view, by marriage. As he explained, "real charity, that which consists in a gift of self, necessarily implies that I subordinate my person to a larger end." Because such acts entailed a self-humiliation, Kant viewed them as immoral. By contrast, for Durkheim, life was full of these actions, including, most notably, marriage. He thus argued that "nothing is more lamentable than to see the way in which Kant derives the constitutive rules of marriage. In his eyes, this act of sacrifice, by which the spouse consents to be the instrument of pleasure for the other spouse, is, in itself, immoral and only loses this character because it is bought back by the analogous and reciprocal sacrifice of the second by the first." Durkheim responded with emphatic skepticism that "it is this trade in personalities that puts everything in order and re-establishes a moral equilibrium!"[43]

---

morale pour une morale laïque," *Archives des sciences sociales des religions* 69 (1990): 129–46; Dominick LaCapra, *Émile Durkheim: Sociologist and Philosopher* (1972), 27–82; Laurence Loeffel, *La question du fondement de la morale laïque sous la IIIe République (1870–1914)* (2000), 167–92; Lukes, *Émile Durkheim,* 355–60; George Weisz, "The Republican Ideology and the Social Sciences: The Durkheimians and the History of Social Economy at the Sorbonne," in *The Sociological Domain: The Durkheimians and the Founding of French Sociology,* ed. Philippe Besnard (1983).

41. Lukes, *Émile Durkheim,* 296–301.

42. Durkheim, *De la division,* 264.

43. Émile Durkheim, "La définition du fait moral," in *Textes 2,* ed. Victor Karady (1975), 259–60. For Kant's views of marriage, see Immanuel Kant, *The Metaphysics of Morals,* trans. Mary Gregor (1996), 61–64; Isabel V. Hull, *Sexuality, State, and Civil Society in Germany, 1700–1815* (1996), 301–13; Anthony J. La Vopa, "Thinking about Marriage: Kant's Liberal-

While for Kant marriage was a bargain to buy back the imperfections of man's animal nature, it exemplified, for Durkheim a social good, an instantiation of the moral value of social bonds.

As we saw in part 1, contemporary philosophers, while they endeavored to "soften" Kant's moral doctrine, nonetheless took the individual as their point of departure. Henri Marion, for example, appealed to marriage in order to tautologically explain how individuals were seduced or attracted by the moral norm that conjugality itself represented. Marriage operated in his thought as a synecdoche for the reconciliation between an individual will and social norms, independence and attachment, affect and reason, etc. Durkheim, by contrast, understood the individual to be an effect of modern society and its division of social labor. Marriage did not, in his view, reconcile otherwise autonomous individuals to an external social norm. It actually exemplified the new social bonds to which, he argued, individual differentiation normally gave rise. His vision of marriage as a partnership founded on gender difference and mutual attraction in turn illustrated the idealized operations of the division of labor *tout court*.

In order to show how the individual depended on the social order, Durkheim drew on contemporary analyses of "the division of labor" as a principle of evolution in the writings of philosopher Alfred Espinas and zoologist Edmond Perrier. Espinas, who was the dean of the Faculty of Letters at Bordeaux, had been instrumental in securing Durkheim his post. As many authors have noted, there were clear parallels between their respective projects.[44] In his controversial book, *Des sociétés animales: Un essai de psychologie comparée* (1877), Espinas traced the organic laws, which, he argued, served to regulate social structures.[45] His account of animal associations, from coral colonies to beehives and bird families, erected the cooperation between differentiated "organs"—whether corporeal or social—as a fundamental vital principle. Espinas used this analysis of the biological laws of social evolution in order to show how individual liberty coincided with the social order, rather than existing in conflict with it.[46] In his work on "animal colonies," Edmond Perrier similarly argued that the functional division of labor was necessary to the survival of all highly developed organisms. He elaborated on how, in sophisticated "colonies," strong bonds of "solidarity" developed between differentiated but mutually depen-

---

ism and the Peculiar Morality of Conjugal Union," *Journal of Modern History* 77, no. 1 (2005).

44. Brooks, *The Eclectic Legacy*, 194–95; William Logue, *From Philosophy to Sociology: The Evolution of French Liberalism, 1870–1914* (1983), 110–11.

45. Alfred Espinas, *Des sociétés animales: Étude de psychologie comparée* (1877). On the controversy surrounding it, see Alfred Espinas, "Etre ou ne pas être ou du postulat de la sociologie," *Revue philosophique de la France et de l'étranger* 26, no. 5 (1901); Mucchielli, *La découverte*, 86.

46. Logue, *From Philosophy*, 108.

dent organs—in effect, between organs that were mutually dependent precisely because differentiated and vice-versa.[47] According to both Espinas and Perrier, the processes of differentiation that led to the emergence of specialized "organs," resulted in an increasing dependence between the individuated parts of a larger whole.

Durkheim did not directly extrapolate the laws of social evolution from those of biological development. He did, however, draw analogies between the two processes.[48] And, like Espinas, he figured progressive transformations in family structure as a key to discovering the rudimentary principles of social evolution. Recapitulating the logic of Espinas and Perrier's arguments, he argued that specialization, which lent individuals their singularity, also produced singular wants or needs. In his view, subjects became whole or fulfilled only in their relations with those others who were capable of supplementing their lacks. "As gifted as we might be," wrote Durkheim, "we always lack something and the best amongst us have a sense of our insufficiency. This is why we seek among our friends the qualities we are lacking; in uniting ourselves with them, we participate in their nature and feel less incomplete."[49] Solidarity, in other words, completed and perfected the individual.

For Durkheim, the division of labor, by supplementing individual inadequacies, had, in complex societies, a largely moral rather than purely economic function.[50] Durkheim's text, as Dominick LaCapra has suggested, does not clearly demonstrate *how* the division of labor actually produces social bonds.[51] His moral claim was based on a presupposition that, in social life "difference, like resemblance, can be a cause of mutual attraction."[52] Durkheim notably depicted the bonds created by difference or complementarity as both stronger and more complex than those based on resemblance, which were, in his view, characteristic of "mechanical" or "primitive," societies. Drawing on contemporary phrenological studies by Gustave LeBon and anthropological claims by Theodor Waitz, Durkheim argued that "primitives" were largely undifferentiated from one another and hence characterized by their profound physical and mental similarity. In "civilized" societies, where individuals are increasingly differentiated, social bonds were founded on mutuality or complementarity.[53]

"Conjugal solidarity" provided Durkheim with a poignant illustration of the affective, moral ties purportedly created by this division of labor. Durkheim figured marriage as "yet another striking example" of organic

---

47. Edmond Perrier, *Les colonies animales et la formation des organismes* (1881), 705.
48. Durkheim, *De la division*, 167–69.
49. Ibid., 18–19.
50. Ibid., 19, 363–65.
51. LaCapra refers to this as a "missing link." LaCapra, *Émile Durkheim*, 127.
52. Durkheim, *De la division*, 18.
53. Ibid., 103–8.

solidarity, as if it were one instance among many. However, aside from his vague invocation of the complementary structure of friendship, it was his *only* concrete example.[54] While professional groups were theoretically based on an analogous moral principle, his discussion of them remained largely conjectural. Meanwhile the apparent self-evidence of the affective bonds between husband and wife in "civilized" society allowed Durkheim to assert that differentiation produced social solidarity. In other words, his account of how the historical evolution of a "division of sexual labor" had produced conjugal solidarity demonstrated the moral value and function of the division of labor *tout court*. The presumed mutual attraction between men and women helped him to ground, or at the very least, to illustrate, his overarching claim for the mutual attraction between opposites.

As we have seen, Durkheim did not collapse natural and social divisions of labor. As a result, he did not base marital solidarity on men and women's physiological differences or even on their "eminently ephemeral" sexual relations. He instead appealed to a more "spiritualized" notion of passion that nonetheless assumed heterosexual desire to be self-evident. He claimed that what lends "sexual attraction" its "specific character and produces its particular energy, is not the resemblance but the difference between the natures it unites." Thus, "it is because men and women differ from each other that they seek one another out with passion." As product and proof of heterosexual passion, modern conjugal solidarity bolstered Durkheim's wider claims about the moral and social function of the division of labor. He insisted on the affective quality of encounters between mutually attractive opposites. "The image of the person who completes us," as a "natural complement," was, in his view, integrated into the lacking self, becoming "an integral part of our consciousness." It is for this reason, he wrote, that "we love the company of the one it represents."[55]

The historical emergence of conjugal solidarity was a case in miniature of a larger movement from "primitive" indifferentiation to "complex" social specialization and individuation. As Durkheim recounted the story, once upon a time, men and women resembled one another both physically and mentally; their difference was "limited exclusively to their reproductive functions." Relying on a number of racialist anthropological sources, he argued that androgyny was the norm among primitive humans. He claimed ontogeny's repetition of phylogeny as material proof of this primitive indifferentiation, writing, "If one admits that individual development reproduces and summarizes that of the species, one has the right to conjecture that the same homogeneity could be found at the beginning of human evolution—to see the feminine form as an approximate image of what was

---

54. Ibid., 19. Jerrold Seigel notes but does not comment on this. See Seigel, "Autonomy and Personality in Durkheim: An Essay on Content and Method," *Journal of the History of Ideas* 48, no. 3 (1987): 500.
55. Durkheim, *De la division*, 25.

originally the singular type from which the masculine variety has slowly but surely distinguished itself." He further appealed to the "mathematical precision" with which LeBon had demonstrated the similarities in "primitive" men and women's brain sizes. This physical resemblance was, in his view, borne out by an essential functional similarity. Not known for their "*gentleness*," primitive women were in fact valiant warriors. At this stage in the history of the family, "there was no such thing as marriage." Instead, "sexual relations were created and dissolved at will, without any juridical obligation binding the two partners." As Durkheim had already suggested in his lectures on the sociology of the family, "the state of marriage in those societies in which the sexes are only weakly differentiated testifies to the fact that conjugal solidarity itself was very weak."[56] Durkheim's account of the evolution of marriage thus contrasted "primitive" androgyny and homogeneity to "civilized" sexual differentiation and complementarity.

Conjugal solidarity only developed once the sexual division of labor was extended to functions well beyond reproduction, that is, once men and women developed distinct social roles. "It was long ago that woman withdrew from war and public affairs, that her life became entirely concentrated in the interior of the family. Since then, her role has only become more specialized." Women's progressive retreat into the private sphere produced a "dissociation of the two main psychic functions"—"one of the sexes has taken over affective functions and the other, intellectual functions." Returning to Le Bon's physiological evidence, Durkheim argued that these psychic differences "are rendered materially perceptible by the morphological differences that they have produced."[57] He thus presented men and women's corporeal difference as material evidence of an essentially social transformation.

Conjugal solidarity gave figurative form to Durkheim's claims about the affective ties elicited by the division of social labor. In his narrative of the progressive solidification of marriage bonds, the emergence of "the individual" out of a primitive state of implicitly devirilized homogeny occurred through gender differentiation. This evolution fostered the emergence of specialized subjects who were at once more distinctive and yet also, unto themselves, fundamentally lacking. Notably, "masculinity"—or the clear delineation of a masculine social role—was a result of this progress toward complex social organisms. Masculinity was hence defined by its lack of femininity. This mutual want differentiated men and women more clearly and fueled their desire to be completed in and by each other. According to Durkheim's account, the "sexual division of labor" in modern society produced a shared need and dependence between men and women that transformed what had been merely transitory sexual desire into durable affective

56. Ibid., 20, 22.
57. Ibid., 23–24.

bonds of solidarity. Durkheim's analysis shored up the "masculinity" of those male subjects that he also figured as lacking precisely by explaining their dependence on the social order in terms of their heterosexuality. Married love or "conjugal solidarity" was, in other words, the matrix of the "civilized" male individual.[58]

While he drew biological analogies, Durkheim did not understand the social division of labor to be an extension of physiological processes. Taking his distance from Espinas and Perrier, he drew a critical distinction between the division of physiological labor (i.e., the distinctions between different bodily organs) and that of social labor. While animals were perpetually tied to an organic or natural order, human social progress initiated an upward spiral of "spiritualization" by which men were gradually freed from material or biological constraints. In the case of animals, "the organism assimilates social fact . . . transforming them into biological facts." In their case, "social life takes material form." By contrast, "in humanity, especially in superior societies, social causes are substituted for organic ones. The organism becomes spiritualized."[59] This process of "spiritualization" and concomitant decline of "inheritance," was also responsible, in Durkheim's view, for the emergence of "civilized" societies out of more primitive ones. As his story of the evolution of marriage demonstrates, Durkheim's theory of the "spirtualization" of "human nature" relied on presuppositions about both "animal nature" and primitive society in order to understand and account for this transformation.

Man's liberation from the forces of nature—and foremost among them the weight of "inheritance"—produced a need for an alternate set of "spiritualized" social rules. Thus, with the rise of human society, a civic order ideally replaced the natural one. While society also played a regulatory function, it was, in Durkheim's view, *sui generis,* altogether new and different, and not simply an extension of the natural laws which applied in the biological realm. In his account of the emergence of this new social order, Durkheim both drew on and significantly revised Rousseau's narrative of the passage from nature to culture.[60] In his lecture course devoted to the author of *The Social Contract,* first delivered in Bordeaux, he formalized an account of this transition as a kind of *Aufhebung,* that is, as a simultaneous negation and preservation of the physical order in and by the social. "In this way, the characteristic attributes of the state of nature need to transform themselves, while being all the same maintained." He thus explained that,

58. For an analogous argument, see Joan W. Scott, *Only Paradoxes to Offer: Feminism and the "Rights of Man" in France, 1789–1940* (1996), 9–10, 96–97.

59. Durkheim, *De la division,* 336–38. For a later formulation of this dualism, see Émile Durkheim, "Le problème religieux et la dualité de la nature humaine (1913)," in *Textes 2,* ed. Victor Karady (1973).

60. For an extended analysis, see Robert Alun Jones, "Durkheim, Realism, and Rousseau," *Journal of the History of the Behavioral Sciences* 32, no. 4 (1996); Robert Alun Jones, *The Development of Durkheim's Social Realism* (1999), 268–301.

"civic man, while profoundly different than natural man, needs to sustain the same relation with society as natural man with physical nature."[61] For Durkheim, man's liberation from nature was not a liberation *tout court.*

"Human nature," Durkheim contended, now depended on the moral limits provided by social life. Conjugal marriage, and the gender and sexual norms that it implied, were an exemplary instance of this *social,* as opposed to natural, regulation. For Durkheim then, when and where these regulatory social norms were lacking, or in a "pathological" state of disarray, the consequences for human nature were indeed hazardous, as his early article on the correlation between suicide and the falling birth rate had well demonstrated. In subsequent works, and especially in that devoted to suicide, Durkheim explained how conjugal society provided a necessary regulatory framework for men's now "spiritualized" sexual desires. He upheld this position, despite the fact that the institution of marriage, while theoretically founded on social and sexual complementarity, had notably unsettling effects on women.

Suicide and Conjugality

Like many of his contemporaries, Durkheim sought to attach young male citizens, now purportedly freed from their hereditary ties to their fathers and fatherland, to a wider social order. He similarly figured the regulation of men's desires as central to any effort to adequately address this modern problem. These pressing concerns animated his efforts to understand and remedy what he saw as a significant symptom of social maladaption, namely suicide. According to his normative social vision, professional associations could ideally regulate economic, and to some extent, political needs and interests.[62] Conjugal society, or, to be more specific, the conjugal couple, meanwhile, served as the primary site of men's *sexual* regulation. Durkheim, in other words, took sexual desire to be a distinct and distinctly social problem. The marital couple was thus a necessary complement to the occupational corporation, as Durkheim's treatment of matrimony in his study of contemporary suicide made quite clear.[63]

By giving both concrete form and content to his sociological method, *Suicide* helped Durkheim to establish and legitimate sociology as a new academic discipline. It enhanced and extended his earlier, piecemeal accounts of how suicide rates were indicators of social malaise with detailed statistical analysis and a formal typology. A showcase for his sociological method,

61. Émile Durkheim, *Montesquieu et Rousseau: Précurseurs de la sociologie* (1953), 149.
62. For a specific treatment of the question, see Hawkins, "Durkheim on Occupational Corporations."
63. See also the lecture notes republished as Émile Durkheim, *Leçons de sociologie: Physique du moeurs et du droit* (1950). And the 1902 preface in Durkheim, *De la division.*

the work figured suicide as an explicitly "social" rather than "individual" illness. In order to carve out a conceptual space for his new discipline, Durkheim sought to distance himself from several dominant strains of contemporary thought—degeneracy theory, racialist anthropology, and Gabriel Tarde's psychology of "imitation."

In an intellectual and political context in which reactionary and anti-Semitic opponents of the Republic increasingly appealed to racialist discourse, Durkheim's rebuttal to theories of hereditary and racial degeneracy amounted to a scientific defense of republican meritocracy and secularism. In keeping with the line of thought already traced out in *De la division du travail social,* Durkheim disputed the efficacy and relevance of biological approaches to social problems. He thus refused to treat suicide as a symptom of madness and overtly dismissed vague racial typologies as useful indicators of complex social phenomena.[64] His effort to dispute biological or hereditary explanations of social phenomena nonetheless relied on an understanding of the relationship between natural human needs and their "spiritualized" or collective complement.

Durkheim argued that individual, corporeal needs had no social component. He claimed that social needs or "spiritualized" desires, which bore no relation to and could even contradict material well-being, only arose with advent of social life or "civilization." As he explained, "civilized man who has become an adult . . . has a host of ideas, sentiments, and practices which bear no relation to organic necessities" (226). The emergence of new spiritual desires irrevocably altered human nature to such an extent that the individual could suffer from social deprivation just as he might from material want. Once stripped of collective ends and limits, the individual might lose his will to live and give himself up to suicide. Durkheim claimed, as he had in his earlier article relating low birth rates to suicide, that excessive individualism generated not greater personal happiness, but profound despair. In *Suicide,* he argued that the disintegration of any community, whether religious, political, or familial, could provoke suicidal anguish.

Basing his study on detailed statistical analysis, Durkheim upheld family life as an important factor in the prevention of suicide. His demonstration took the statistically higher rates of suicide among *célibataires* (single men and women) established by demographer Louis Adolphe Bertillon, father of Jacques Bertillon, as a point of departure. Domestic life, he contended, protected individuals from the existential despair and egotism which chronically plagued bachelors and drove them in greater numbers to suicide. In order to prove this correlation, Durkheim disputed claims, set forth by anthropologist Charles Letourneau, that marital preservation was merely an epiphenomenon of healthy inheritance, that, in other words, men and women who marry are likely to be healthy. The holder of the chair in the

64. Émile Durkheim, *Le suicide* (1930), 33, 57. Hereafter cited in text.

"history of civilizations" at the École d'anthropologie de Paris and author of *L'évolution du mariage et de la famille*, Letourneau adhered to the principles of racialist and materialist ethnology propounded by other members of the École such as Paul Broca.[65] Durkheim set out to dismantle Letourneau's organicist evolutionary theory by demonstrating that "marital selection" did not function uniformly. He showed that relative rates of "marital preservation" reflected not the hereditary predisposition of individuals who marry but the culturally contingent effects of domestic life.

Durkheim discredited Letourneau's analysis by pointing to the divergent effects of marriage on men and women. While organicist in its focus on hereditary traits, Letourneau's theory did not differentiate between men and women. By contrast, Durkheim separated out his statistical data along gender lines in order to show that women in France tended to "gain less" from marriage than men, while in a control case provided by the Duchy of Oldenbourg, they "gained more" than their husbands. He concluded that "the family is, in the two countries, constituted in such a way that it acts differently on the two sexes" (191). This difference was, in the French case, illustrated by a patently adverse impact of marriage on wives (in certain cases, single women killed themselves less frequently than married women). Durkheim thus contended that "the hypothesis of matrimonial selection does not apply at all to the feminine sex. Nothing allows us to think that a woman called to marriage possesses a privileged constitution, which protects her, to some extent, from suicide." Durkheim was so invested in overturning Letourneau's theory that he appeared to be strikingly unperturbed by his radical discovery of the "depressive" effects of marriage on women. He insisted, instead, on how, given its failure in the case of women, "marital selection" had "as little foundation where men are concerned" (201). Durkheim's demonstration of marriage as a social, rather than "natural," institution was based on an assessment of its differential effects on men and women, a difference which his statistical analysis presumed from the outset.[66]

Durkheim did, however, seek to explain why marriage did not have a uniformly positive effect on women. In order to do so, he appealed to the mind/body dualism that subtended his theory of suicide more generally. He lent this dualism a gendered cast by, unsurprisingly, locating women on the side of corporeality. That is, while he figured men as double, and hence split

---

65. For a discussion of Letourneau and the École more generally, see Claude Blanckaert, "La crise de l'anthropométrie: Des arts anthropotechniques aux dérives militantes," in *Les usages de l'anthropologie: Discours et pratiques en France (1860–1940)*, ed. Claude Blanckaert (2001); Clark, *Prophets*, 116–21; Mucchielli, *La découverte*, 48–58.

66. For discussions of how statistical analysis both presupposes and produces gender difference as scientifically significant. See Joan W. Scott, "A Statistical Representation of Work: La statistique de l'industrie de Paris," in *Gender and the Politics of History* (1988). And Joshua Cole, *The Power of Large Numbers: Population, Politics, and Gender in Nineteenth-century France* (2000).

between their bodily and spiritual or social sides, he suggested that women were closer to children, old people, primitives, and animals. He argued that because women were regulated almost exclusively by physical need, their social needs were exceedingly rudimentary.[67] In one remarkably reductive statement, he commented, "Woman lives more outside of, is penetrated less by communal life than man: she needs society less because she is less impregnated by sociability. She has few needs in this sense, and she is easily pleased. With a few devotional practices and a few animals to take care of, the old maid has a full life" (231). Durkheim here provided a characteristically tautological "social" explanation of women's exclusion from social life. Women remained closer to the organic, in his view, because they were isolated from "public life" and led a largely "private" existence. Women's needs, in other words, were less socialized than men's.

Durkheim curiously offers this as an explanation of women's relative immunity from the beneficial effects of marriage, a social institution from which they were clearly *not* excluded. Indeed, in his discussion of "altruistic" suicide, which he saw as characteristic of "primitive" and undifferentiated societies, he argued that the suicide of wives in the wake of their husbands' death (i.e., *sati* in India) illustrated an excessive integration into the life of the community (235). He obfuscates this apparent contradiction, however, by appealing to the ridiculous figure of the spinster. But hadn't Durkheim argued since the outset of his career that marriage and domestic life were essentially social, *not* "natural" forms? Given the centrality of women to precisely *these* institutions, how could he claim that they were not "impregnated" by sociability? The reasoning which underwrote this seemingly contradictory claim is revealed in Durkheim's subsequent discussion of the other dominant form of contemporary suicide, that resulting from limitlessness or "anomie." He here argued that because women's sexual desires were naturally regulated, they, in contrast to men, did not need marriage as moral limit on their passions.

Durkheim's account of anomie was founded on his theory of human desire. Again taking man's dualistic nature as a point of departure, he distinguished between the limited, physical character of "animal" needs and the infinite character of human ones. In animals, he claimed, want and need balanced out automatically. "When the void dug in its resources by living is filled, the animal is satisfied and demands no more." Not so with men, because "their needs do not depend . . . upon the body" (272). Indeed, "what characterizes man is that the limit to which he is subject is not physical, but

67. Durkheim's association of women with nature and men with culture has been widely noted; see Philippe Besnard, "Durkheim et les femmes ou *Le suicide* inachevé," *Revue française de sociologie* 14 (1973): 30–33; Mike Gane, "Durkheim: Woman as Outsider," in *The Radical Sociology of Durkheim and Mauss*, ed. Mike Gane (1992); Lamanna, *Émile Durkheim*; Jennifer M. Lehmann, *Durkheim and Women* (1994); R. A. Sydie, "Sex and the Sociological Fathers," *Canadian Review of Sociology and Anthropology* 31, no. 2 (1994): 122.

moral, which is to say social" (279). Having broken with nature's auto-matic equilibrium, the individuated subject was incapable of regulating his own desires. Only the external, moral force of the social order could limit these new, "spiritualized" passions. As he explained: "The awakening of consciousness ruptured the state of equilibrium in which the animal slum-bered; only consciousness can furnish the means to reestablish it" (275).

Similar to the social critics discussed in part 2, Durkheim signaled a con-temporary crisis in authoritative limits on individuals' social and economic ambitions and desires. His treatment of "anomic suicide" drew a similar parallel between all-consuming social ambitions and the deregulation of sexual desire. Individual desires, because unconstrained, remained ever in-satiable and the torment produced by this dissatisfaction led to anomic sui-cide. The rapid and unabated progress of modern industrial economies had, in his view, produced an anomic crisis by ceaselessly fanning the flames of social and material longing. "From the top to the bottom of the social scale, desires [*les convoitises*] are aroused without knowing where they might de-finitively rest. . . . One thirsts for new things, unknown pleasures, unnamed sensations, which lose their flavor as soon as they are known" (285). With no fixed limit, ambitions were characterized by an analogous voracity. "Overexcited ambitions always exceed achieved results; nothing informs them that they need go no further" (281). Those who, in this modern in-dustrial order "have nothing but the void above them are almost obliged to lose themselves in it, if there is no force which holds them back" (287). Durkheim projected a radical reorientation of professional groups in order to provide new moral limits on the boundless and undisciplined economic and social longings which traditional ties to father and fatherland no longer held in check. The conjugal couple would, meanwhile, provide the neces-sary moral constraints on men's unregulated *sexual* desires.

The presumed dualism of human nature once again structured his analy-sis. With the "spiritualizing" effects of civilization, men's sexual instinct had developed an intellectual as well as physical character; it was hence par-tially "liberated from the body." Thus, "what man seeks in women is not only the satisfaction of reproductive [*génésique*] desire." He suggested that men's sexual desires exceeded such bodily needs. The body alone did not regulate men's sexual desire, which "no longer has the regular and auto-matic periodicity of animals." Men now relied on exterior, social rules to govern their otherwise infinite sexual penchants. "Because there is nothing in the body to contain them, they must be held back by society. This is the function of marriage. It regulates all this life of the passions, and monoga-mous marriage more strictly than any other. For, in obliging men to attach themselves to one woman—always the same—it assigns his need to love a rigorously defined object and closes his horizon" (303–4). In other words, men's spiritualized sexual desires needed social constraints in order to be adequately sated. Without this salutary limitation, men sought satisfaction everywhere without ever being able to find it—as in the case of the hardened bachelor who, as we saw in part 2, embodied pathological, because unrestrained sexual desire. By mobilizing statistics on single men's suicides, Durkheim made the connection between bachelorhood and morbidity quite explicit. "From the moment that one is stopped by nothing, it is impossible to stop oneself. Beyond those pleasures already experienced, one imagines and wants others; if one has just about traveled the possible, one dreams of the impossible; one thirsts for the nonexistent. . . . The uncertainty of the future, joined with [the subject's] own indetermination, condemns him to a perpetual mobility. What results is a troubled, agitated, and unhappy state, which necessarily increases the chances of suicide" (304–5). For Durkheim, in other words, indeterminate sexual desire was, for men, literally deadly.

Durkheim grounded his discussion of sexual deregulation on a statistical correlation between divorce rates and suicide that had been established by Jacques Bertillon. As a pronounced advocate of divorce reform, Bertillon sought a complete liberalization of the restrictions on marital separation that had been reinstated in the Civil code after divorce was abolished in 1816. He hoped that the elimination of unhappy marriages would allow divorcés to found new, happier—and hence more prolific—foyers. According to a theory that could be seen as a corollary of Letourneau's account of "marital selection," he suggested that those spouses most liable to provoke domestic conflict were most likely mentally ill and hence also more vulnerable to committing suicide.[68] In other words, Bertillon attributed suicide to hereditary defects, not social pathology. He meanwhile presented himself as a valiant defender of those hapless victims (usually figured as abused wives) who were forced to remain with mentally imbalanced husbands. He ultimately found a valuable ally in Senator Alfred Naquet, who was instrumental in the passage of the 1884 law, which legalized fault-based divorce claims.[69]

Durkheim, by contrast, worried about divorce's negative effects on domestic morality. He once again interrogated the demographer's findings and contested Bertillon's attribution of both suicide and divorce rates to "psychopathic defects." Durkheim, instead, urged that, "the cause of this remarkable relation is not in the organic predisposition of subjects but in the

68. Francis Ronsin, "Une aventure de jeunesse de sociologie: Les relations entre le divorce et le suicide," *Revue d'histoire moderne et contemporaine* 42, no. 2 (1995): 297.
69. On the history of the Naquet bill and of divorce more generally, see Antomarchi, *Politique et famille*, 27–50; Antony Copley, *Sexual Moralities in France, 1780–1980: New Ideas on the Family, Divorce, and Homosexuality* (1989), 108–34; Theresa McBride, "Divorce and the Republican Family," in *Gender and the Politics of Social Reform in France, 1870–1914*, ed. Elinor A. Accampo et al. (1995); Jean E. Pedersen, *Legislating the French Family: Feminism, Theater, and Republican Politics, 1870–1920* (2003), 13–74; Francis Ronsin, *Les divorciaires: Affrontements politiques et conceptions du mariage dans la France du 19ᵉ siècle* (1991).

intrinsic nature of divorce" (293). Bertillon's analysis of hereditary defects, in theory, applied equally to both men and women. By pointing to national and gender variations in suicide rates, Durkheim contested Bertillon's biological determinism, much as he had done with Letourneau. Durkheim held that where divorce was infrequent (particularly in Catholic states and Switzerland's Catholic cantons), married men displayed a greater immunity to suicide than bachelors of the same age. The inverse was true for women. By contrast, in Protestant states and Swiss cantons, wives had a greater "rate of preservation" than single women, while married men were less well protected. Durkheim concluded that the facility of divorce in Protestant areas undermined the salubrious limits imposed by marriage on men's sexual desire. In other words, the nature of divorce law, not hereditary defects, provoked the correlation between divorce and suicide rates.

Statistical evidence of women's difference from men once again functioned as a diacritical tool in Durkheim's analysis. He used the divergent statistics in order to demonstrate how divorce had specifically anomic, and not merely "egotistic," effects on matrimony. Women and men, he argued, could be expected to suffer equally from divorce's role in the disintegration of family sentiment. According to his statistics, "however, it is exactly the inverse" (298). Because the relative facility of divorce had sharply divergent effects on men and women, suicides could not be attributed to "family constitution" alone. Durkheim hence surmised that, at least in men's case, they were the result of sexual anomie. Husbands, he contended, became increasingly susceptible to this form of anomie, when the statutory limits placed on their sexual desires by marriage were eroded by the ease of divorce. Divorce, in other words, diminished the institution of marriage, at least as far as men were concerned. "The limit that it placed on desire is no longer as fixed; because it is easily shaken and displaced, it no longer contains passions as forcefully; they hence tend to spill over it" (306). How then did Durkheim explain wives' seeming immunity to the deleterious effects of this deregulation? Why, indeed, did women apparently benefit from a more flexible rule?

The answer, according to Durkheim, lay in the different—because less "spiritual" or "intellectual"—character of their desire. "The woman's sexual needs have a less mental character because, in general, her mental life is less developed. They have a more immediate relation with the exigencies of her organism, which they largely obey and hardly exceed; they find in it an effective break. Because woman is a more instinctive being than man, she need only follow her instincts in order to find peace and calm. Such a restrictive social regulation as marriage, and above all, monogamous marriage is not necessary for her" (306). Women were, in his view, more "instinctual" and "animalistic"—essentially less "social"—than men. This observation led Durkheim to a rather startling provisional conclusion—

namely, that women did not have much to gain from marriage. At moments, he seemed to critique the effects of excessive marital regulation on women, remarking that men and women's interests were essentially antagonistic: "one needs constraint and the other, liberty." He further noted that marital restrictions were more "attenuated" for men, referring presumably to their frequent recourse to adultery and prostitution (306). In marriage, he perceptively concluded, it is women not men who make the greater sacrifice. "We thus arrive at a conclusion that is quite removed from conventional ideas of marriage and its role. It is assumed that it was instituted in order to protect the wife against masculine capriciousness. Monogamy, in particular, is often presented as a sacrifice of men's polygamous instincts in order to better women's condition in marriage. In reality, whatever the historical causes that determined the imposition of this restriction, it largely benefits him. The liberty, which he renounced, could only be for him a source of torment. Not having the same reasons to abandon such liberty, one might say that, in submitting herself to the same rule, it is she who makes the sacrifice" (310–11). Marriage thus contributed to men's health and happiness by regulating their desires. For women, on the other hand, it was a thoroughly unprofitable transaction; the excessive constraint of matrimony was for them a pure loss.

In his discussion of the "practical consequences" of these findings, Durkheim made recommendations about how the position of women might be improved. He did so, however, in order to shore up the institution of marriage, which, in his view, could not "accommodate two beings at the same time when one is an almost entirely social product while the other has remained largely as nature made [her]." Durkheim here notably construed the difference between woman's nature and men's culture as a source of antagonism, not attraction. In order to save marriage from this apparent conflict (and this, not the "liberation" of women appears to be his primary goal), he recommended that women be allotted a more substantial social role, "which, while specially fitting for her, would be more active and important than that of today." Durkheim proposed that women's, heretofore natural, difference could be put to cultural use without being effaced. Indeed, following his theory of the division of social labor, he suggested that the sexes might become even more different. "The feminine sex will never return to being like the masculine; on the contrary, one might foresee her becoming yet more differentiated. Only, these differences would be more socially utilized than in the past." For example, he thought that women might devote themselves to aesthetic concerns, while leaving utilitarian matters to men. Meanwhile, marriage would be strengthened. "The two sexes would, in this way, become closer, while at the same time further differentiating themselves. They would be equally socialized, but in different ways" (443). While purportedly granting women an equally social existence,

Durkheim's understanding of their future role remained founded upon a residually naturalized conception of sexual difference. In a book review published some years later in the *Année sociologique,* he reiterated this position, writing, "It remains quite true that women should seek equality in those functions that conform to their own nature."[70]

Durkheim's attempts to demonstrate the fundamentally social and in turn socially necessary character of conjugality were hence paradoxically dependent upon and indeed, productive of this naturalized notion of women's difference from men. His figuration of women and specifically of the character of their sexual desire as "naturally" regulated was not or not merely a lingering prejudice.[71] His novel effort to prove the social, as opposed to merely natural, character of *men*'s sexual desires and of conjugality as an institution that was ideally suited to their regulation relied upon this conception of women as largely instinctual. As a result, his understanding of the social value of marriage for men did not entirely break with a set of assumptions about nature, despite his clear philosophical and disciplinary commitment to doing so. In Durkheim's effort to "resolve" this problem, to explain that is, how women might become more socialized, while remaining fundamentally different, we see that he was not unaware of this contradiction. This attempted resolution did not, however, address a core difficulty, namely, the status of women as subjects of desire, and hence why marriage might be socially desirable for them.[72] Because he was so invested in conjugality as a regulatory institution that was essential both for the health of the social body and for the male individuals whose happiness depended on it, he remained resistant to revising these assumptions, even when, as Jean Pedersen has suggested, he was faced with overt feminist critiques of his position.[73] His interventions in contemporary debates about the extent and limits of divorce reform demonstrate well this commitment to marriage as a socially necessary institution.

70. In this review, Durkheim notably criticizes Anna Lampérière for assigning women exclusively to the private sphere; he suggests that while this role might well be fitting for married women it could not account for single women or widows without children. He even questions whether it is entirely appropriate for wives. See Émile Durkheim, "Review of Anna Lampérière, *Le rôle social de la femme,*" in *Journal sociologique,* ed. Jean Duvignaud (1969).

71. On this question, see Besnard, "Durkheim et les femmes"; Howard I. Kushner, "Suicide, Gender, and Fear of Modernity in Nineteenth-century Medical and Social Thought," *Journal of Social History* 26, no. 2 (1992); Lehmann, *Durkheim and Women;* Jean E. Pedersen, "Sexual Politics in Comte and Durkheim: Feminism, History, and the French Sociological Tradition," *Signs* 27, no. 1 (2001); Janet Hinson Shope, "Separate but Equal: Durkheim's Response to the Woman Question," *Sociological Inquiry* 64, no. 1 (1994); Edward A. Tiryakian, "Sexual Anomie, Social Structure, Societal Change," *Social Forces* 59, no. 4 (1981).

72. For an account of shifting contemporary conceptions of elite women as subjects of desire in marriage and outside of it, see Michèle Plott, "The Rules of the Game: Respectability, Sexuality, and the *Femme Mondaine* in Late-Nineteenth-century Paris," *French Historical Studies* 25, no. 3 (2002).

73. Pedersen, "Sexual Politics."

Marital Preservation and the Preservation of Marriage

Durkheim's overwhelming investment in preserving marriage was explicitly articulated in his responses to the public campaign for "divorce by mutual consent" initiated by the left-leaning literary figures, Paul and Victor Margueritte in 1900. The issue of no-fault divorce was not new. Alfred Naquet's initial version of his proposed bill had included a mutual consent clause, but the article was eventually eliminated in order to assure the legislation's passage in 1884.[74] Durkheim's argument, published in the *Revue bleue* in 1906, focused on the "interest of the matrimonial institution in itself," but also made claims regarding the interest of individuals. He was notably suspicious of the contractualist model of matrimony that was implicit in the campaign in favor of mutual consent. He suggested that the reform "under the pretext of remedying individual suffering, would constitute, in itself, a grave social illness, which would in turn harm the individual."[75]

In order to strengthen his claim to be defending both individual and social interest, Durkheim eliminated the troublesome statistical evidence regarding the effects of marriage on women's rates of suicide. By revising and recalculating his numerical data, Durkheim arrived at a surprising new conclusion, namely, that woman "is a little excluded from the moral effects of marriage."[76] He, however, maintained his account of men's vulnerability to sexual anomie, contending that "it remains evident that marriage exercises, especially on the male sex, a moralizing influence from which individuals benefit. . . . This is because marriage, by imposing a rule on the passions, gives man a moral basis [*assiette morale*] which enhances his force of resistance. In assigning his desires a definite and, in principle, invariable object, he is prevented from exasperating himself with ever renewed, ever changing pursuits—which immediately afterwards lose their interest and leave behind only fatigue and disenchantment."[77] The strictures of marriage made men stronger, while the dissipation of single life reduced their vital energies. And, because men were incapable of self-regulation, they needed the supra-individual authority of the state to enforce these rules, as well as, of course, a woman to serve as that "invariable object." For Durkheim, then, only judges, not private individuals should be granted the power to dissolve marriage bonds.

74. Ronsin, *Les divorciaires*, 235–66.
75. Émile Durkheim, "Le divorce par consentement mutuel (1906)," in *Textes 2*, ed. Victor Karady (1975), 182.
76. Ibid., 188. Critical accounts of this manipulation include Besnard, "Durkheim et les femmes," 58–60; Lehmann, *Durkheim and Women*, 78–79; Pedersen, "Sexual Politics."
77. Durkheim, "Le divorce par consentement mutuel (1906)," 188–90. This invocation of "principle," rather than the fact, seems to suggest, once again, that Durkheim imagined that marriage bonds were somewhat flexible for men. On this point, see Anne-Marie Sohn, "The Golden Age of Male Adultery: The Third Republic," *Journal of Social History* 28, no. 3 (1995).

Thus, while marriage might violate men's passions, these limits, in Durkheim's view, were a condition of their happiness and satisfaction. He suggested that "man cannot be happy, he cannot satisfy his desires normally unless they are regulated, contained, moderated, and disciplined."[78] "Normal" sexual fulfillment was thus, in his view, a product of the external, social limits placed upon individual desire. Moral order and men's happiness conveniently coincided here, making the normative regulation of desire in itself desirable for man and society alike. In contrast to many of his contemporaries, then, Durkheim placed the problem of men's desire and its satisfaction, *not* the reproductive health of the French family, at the center of his defense of marriage.

Durkheim articulated this position most clearly in a debate on divorce conducted by the Union pour la vérité in 1909. In introducing the topic, Paul Desjardins, a professor at the École normale supérieure de jeunes filles at Sèvres and the founder of the group, summarized the differend around which the discussion was organized. "Is marriage," he asked, "an act of social life, in which society as a whole has a right to intervene, or is it a purely private contract, of interest to the two parties and left up to their will?"[79] In the midst of this diverse gathering of jurists, feminists, and academics, Durkheim reiterated his critique of a voluntarist conception of marriage and his commitment to fault-based divorce. Feminist Jeanne Chambon, legal scholar Henry Berthélemy, and jurist A. Fabry upheld a contractual model of marriage as an accord between two individuals. Durkheim, by contrast, argued against this contractualist conception of the conjugal bond, explaining that marriage "first and foremost, disciplines sexual life," and that "matrimonial regulation, and above all monogamous regulation, imposes a break on sexual appetites." A further relaxation of divorce law was hazardous, in his view, because when men become "more free to satisfy all their caprices, life becomes less tolerable." He admitted that, "woman is not afflicted by the weakening of the matrimonial institution." He no longer appealed to women's nature in order to explain this difference, but to the fact that women's "sexual instinct is already contained and moderated, even outside of marriage, by moeurs and opinion." This more explicitly "social" rather than natural explanation nonetheless continued to figure women's desire as always already regulated. But this caveat did not prevent him from concluding that "matrimonial regulation is salutary for the individual."[80] Given Durkheim's contention that marriage did not impact women's health, the "individual" whose life was preserved by matrimonial regulation was clearly male. The marital preservation of men's health nonetheless demanded women's participation. Durkheim's defense of matrimony thus ap-

78. Ibid., 193.
79. "Mariage et divorce," *Libres entretiens* 5, no. 1 (1909): 246.
80. Ibid., 278–80. Also in Émile Durkheim, "Débat sur le mariage et le divorce (1909)," in *Textes* 2, ed. Victor Karady (1975), 212–13. See also Pedersen, "Sexual Politics."

pealed to a purportedly gender-neutral individual, who was in fact male, in order to shore up an institution that, according to his own argument, essentially benefited men. Men's health, which Durkheim equated with that of the social order as a whole, was justification enough for this otherwise unnecessary regulation of women.

For Durkheim, the modern male individual was, fundamentally, a subject of desire. Motivated by a thirst for new pleasures and new experiences, he was, in keeping with his civilization, perpetually on the move. Durkheim's social vision took the distinctly modern character of these desires as a point of departure. Desire within limits was, as we have seen, a source of both social progress and social cohesion. Beyond these limits, however, it became a source of "pathological" social disorder and men's individual unhappiness. This regulatory dilemma was foundational to Durkheim's thought and can be seen, in a sense, as its implicit motor.

This chapter has explored one aspect of Durkheim's effort to address this regulatory problem. Conjugal marriage, I argue, played a crucial role in his idealized vision of modern social order. According to his evolutionary account, conjugality was neither natural, nor transhistorical. Its emergence demonstrated the distinctly social, as opposed to simply natural or reproductive, value of heterosexual attraction. Founded on the force of this presumed attraction, modern marriage exemplified, for him, how the normative limitation of men's desires was a condition of their individual happiness and a source of social solidarity. Durkheim claimed that because men's sexual desires were no longer "naturally" regulated, nor constrained by the homogenizing forces of communal consciousness, they were potentially boundless. They required, in his view, an external limit which only marriage could provide. Healthy masculinity was, according to this account, both avidly desiring and socially bounded. Durkheim's effort to demonstrate the modern moral and social value of conjugality, at the same time, produced a conceptual paradox. For, the model of sexual difference and heterosexual desire that explained the social value of modern marriage for men, could not, in fact, account for how that institution was desirable for women. Their status as subjects of desire, which is to say, as "individuals" who needed social regulation, was unclear. Durkheim's vision of the modern social order thus reveals with great clarity how normative masculinity depended on the organization of men's desire by marriage. It also reveals that, from the perspective of women, this model of social organization was less than ideal.

6 *The Sacralization of Heterosexuality*

Turn-of-the-century moral and political philosophy developed a social conception of citizenship that was based not on the abstract and isolated individual, but on the situated subject who was born into a differential network of social relations. Solidarists in their effort to imagine a new moral and legal framework of social justice thus proclaimed that "isolated man does not exist."[1] Their often eclectic doctrine was loosely organized around arguments that the subject's a priori dependence on and indebtedness to the social order underwrote both the citizen's responsibility to society and that of society to the citizen. The fact of social association was, according to solidarists, also an ethical imperative. Because, in their view, "isolated man" did not exist, the formal and informal principles of social responsibility upheld by solidarism did not represent a limitation on the citizen's liberty. In the words of Léon Bourgeois, this law should hence not be seen "as a necessity arbitrarily imposed from the exterior, but as a law of interior organization which is indispensable for life; no longer a servitude, it is a means of liberation."[2] The self-limitation required to live according to society's rules, was conceived, not as a restriction on life, but as its extension and goal.

Similar to many of the other figures who wrote and reflected on contemporary questions of right and responsibility, Durkheim articulated a social theory of morality that contributed to the solidarist project broadly conceived. More specifically, in foregrounding how individuals depended on and were hence responsible to the social order, Durkheim's sociology, like solidarism more generally, recast republican citizenship in new terms. The citizen, according to this moral and social vision, was not an autonomous individual, but a socially dependent subject. As we saw in the last chapter,

---

1. Léon Bourgeois, *Solidarité*, 2nd ed. (1897), 136.
2. Ibid., 63. And, part 3, n. 9, above.

this social dependency did not undermine the citizen's masculinity, because the masculinity instituted by married heterosexuality was imagined as an effect of that dependency. Durkheim's conception of the moral and social value of conjugality actually guaranteed the citizen's masculinity as an attribute of his social difference. In other words, because Durkheim presumed gender difference and heterosexual attraction as constitutive of the modern social order, his articulation of men's social particularity confirmed their status as masculine. In this chapter, I explore how Durkheim's theorization of the modern male individual as a subject of heterosexual desire undergirded his theory of morality and how, in turn, that vision affirmed the normative value of conjugality as, I suggest, a quasi-sacred social principle.

Duty, Desire, and the Sacred

Solidarists frequently appealed to the moral feelings created in and by social relationships in order to extrapolate normative values from the fact of association. Philosopher Alfred Fouillée, for example, viewed sexual relations between men and women as proof of the sympathetic structure of social organization. Building on the conception of altruism developed by Auguste Comte and Émile Littré, he invoked sexual reproduction in order to claim that the principles of love, association, and union, rather than conflict or the "struggle for life," were the basis of the social order. In a text devoted to the "sociological elements of morality," Fouillée contended that the organic necessity of reproduction placed sympathy rather than competition at the core of social life. "Fecundity," he wrote, "is a force of collective expansion which is attached to 'love' rather than 'hunger,' to generation rather than nutrition, to sympathetic union not war."[3]

Durkheim, while similarly interested in the moral value of conjugality, was quite critical of such vague, naturalist pronouncements. As Durkheim explained in a review of Fouillée's text, "What contributes to the persistence of this simplistic attitude is the existence of certain very general sentiments, which appear to be congenital to the nature of man, and which seem to suffice in order to account for fundamental duties. For example, in order to explain domestic morality or conjugal morality, one invokes filial piety, fraternal love, sexual jealousy, all sentiments which are considered to be inherent to the human heart. It is hard to see how such general tendencies can explain anything but very general duties." In contrast to Fouillée and many of his contemporaries, Durkheim was interested in accounting for morality not as a set of abstract and general pronouncements, but as "precise and

3. Alfred Fouillée, *Les éléments sociologiques de la morale,* 2nd ed. (1905), 183. Fouillée had, in an earlier text, laid out the gendered and racialist presuppositions on which his argument was based: Alfred Fouillée, *Tempérament et caractère selon les individus, les sexes et les races* (1895).

particular obligations, which bear the imprint of the time and social type in which they are observed."[4] Appeals to the natural basis of social sentiments were, in Durkheim's view, hopelessly inadequate to any genuinely sociological account of morality.

Other philosophers, while similarly skeptical of naturalist claims, nonetheless imagined sympathetic sentiment as a crucial complement to more abstract moral aims of justice. Émile Boutroux, the eminent philosopher at the University of Paris, for example, explicitly invoked the family as a source of general moral sentiments. "It is not the idea of abstract justice alone, it is rather a sentiment of piety and familial solidarity, which brings us to sanctify [*bénir*] our ancestors as benefactors and parents . . . it is the same sentiment of human sympathy, turned toward our contemporary companions in existence, which makes it our duty to show our sons the recognition that we deliver to our fathers."[5] For Boutroux, solidarity was based on an idea of filiation, a displacement of responsibility toward one's ancestors onto the social body as a whole. As his references to piety and sanctification suggest, this feeling, while not attached to a specific religious doctrine, was imagined in quasi-sacred terms. But what were these sentiments and how, exactly, did they come to embrace the moral ideal of solidarity, which appeared as both their source and aim? Could vague invocations of familial sentiment and sympathy account for how morality operated in practice? Durkheim, ever since he wrote *De la division du travail social,* was inclined to think not.

In the original introduction to that work, Durkheim highlighted the inadequacy of philosophical abstraction. In his view, philosophical accounts of morality, while they might discuss "general duties," could not account for "more specific rules, like those that prohibit marriage between close kin, or *unions libres,* or those that establish inheritance rights, or which impose guardianship on the kin of an orphan. The more specific and concrete moral maxims are, the more difficult it becomes to perceive the link between them and such abstract concepts."[6] Only sociology, he argued, could explain and in turn promote morality, not just in theory, but in practice as well. And, the sociology of the family would remain one of the principal ways in which Durkheim sought to illustrate that claim.

Durkheim's writings on morality were thus in perpetual dialogue with those of his predecessors and contemporaries who remained more firmly anchored in the domain of metaphysics. As a result of both his intellectual

4. Émile Durkheim, "Review of Fouillée, *Les éléments sociologiques de la morale* (1905–1906)," in *Journal sociologique*, ed. Jean Duvignaud (1969), 574–75.

5. Émile Boutroux, "Rôle de l'idée de solidarité," in Léon Bourgeois and Alfred Croiset, *Essai d'une philosophie de la solidarité: Conférences et discussions (1901–1902),* ed. École des hautes études sociales (1902), 279–80.

6. Émile Durkheim, "La définition du fait moral," in *Textes 2,* ed. Victor Karady (1975), 262.

formation and the politics of establishing sociology as a semi-autonomous discipline, Durkheim maintained close ties to his colleagues in the field of philosophy. He and members of his school continued to publish in "philosophical" journals such as the *Revue de métaphysique et de morale* and regularly attended the meetings of their scholarly societies. While engaging in a critique of philosophy's metaphysical presuppositions, Durkheim continued to look to the discipline for intellectual legitimation, even as he sought to rework the foundations of republican ethics. Durkheim's project is hence best understood not as a radical break with philosophy but as its continuation by other means.[7]

In developing his critique of philosophy in *De la division du travail social*, Durkheim argued that, with the diversification and specialization of science, philosophy could no longer maintain its position as a sovereign, unifying discipline. Like the uniform "conscience collective" that had declined with the rise of a "division of labor," the abstract syntheses of metaphysics, he argued, were rendered obsolete by the development of more specialized sciences.[8] As Jean-Louis Fabiani has suggested, sociology gave philosophy "a chance to survive" once the academy itself became structured by a division of labor. Rendered increasingly precarious by the efflorescence of the new knowledge and disciplines described by Durkheim, philosophers were, according to Louis Pinto, obliged to take the new theoretical possibilities offered by sociology into account.[9] This was especially true in contemporary discussions of moral and social pedagogy. And once he had been named to the chair in the Sciences of Education at the Sorbonne in 1902, Durkheim was an undisputed expert in this field.

Durkheim's lectures on "moral education," delivered as part of his regular course offerings at the Sorbonne, set forth how the empirical knowledge provided by the new discipline acquired persuasive normative force. They describe how sociological evidence of the benefits of social and moral norms, in, for example, statistics on suicide, could explain why individuals should willingly embrace those norms. Durkheim thus surmised, "We can understand very well that it is in our natures to be limited by forces which are exterior to us; and, consequently, freely accept this limitation because it is natural and good, without it being any less real. Only, because our con-

7. On this point, see Daniela S. Barberis, "The First *Année sociologique* and Neo-Kantian Philosophy in France" (Ph.D. diss., University of Chicago, 2001); John I. Brooks, *The Eclectic Legacy: Academic Philosophy and the Human Sciences in Nineteenth-century France* (1998); Jean-Louis Fabiani, "Métaphysique, morale, sociologie: Durkheim et le retour à la philosophie," *Revue de Métaphysique et de Morale*, no. 1–2 (1993); Victor Karady, "The Durkheimians in Academe: A Reconsideration," in *The Sociological Domain: The Durkheimians and the Founding of French Sociology*, ed. Philippe Besnard (1983); Dominick LaCapra, *Émile Durkheim: Sociologist and Philosopher* (1972).

8. Émile Durkheim, *De la division du travail social*, 11th ed. (1986), 324–56.

9. Fabiani, "Métaphysique, morale, sociololgie," 189; Louis Pinto, "Le détail et la nuance: la sociologie vue par les philosophes dans la *Revue de Métaphysique et de Morale*, 1893–1899," *Revue de Métaphysique et de Morale*, no. 1–2 (1993).

sent is enlightened, it ceases to be a humiliation and a servitude."[10] This pedagogical claim explained how sociology, as an empirical science, also served a prescriptive function. By proving that individual pleasure depended on moral norms, it could generate a desire for those norms. Durkheim's science could, in other words, performatively produce, through the dissemination of its findings, adherence to the normative moral order that it described. In this sense, sociology both explained and promulgated modern secular morality.

As his understanding of anomie in *Suicide* and subsequent writing on marriage and morality made clear, moral limits, unlike organic ones, did not exist, for Durkheim, within the body or even within an individual subject; they were external imperatives. In his view, social rules authoritatively *countered* individual nature. As he explained in *L'éducation morale*, if morality "simply demanded that we behave according to our natures, it would not need to speak in the imperative." The "vast system of interdictions" which constituted morality, "actually forms around every man an ideal barrier at the foot of which the flood of human passions comes to die, without being able to go further." Without this "ideal barrier" in place individuals were condemned to the "perpetual torment" of anomie and, as we have seen, more liable to commit suicide. In these lectures, Durkheim once again appealed to conjugal morality as an agent of sexual regulation in order to illustrate this claim. He thus continued, "If, for example, the rules of conjugal morality lose their authority, if the duties which spouses owe one another are less respected, and if the passions and appetites that this aspect of morality contain and regulate, were to unleash and deregulate themselves, exasperating themselves in this very deregulation, becoming impossible [*impuissantes*] to satisfy because liberated from all limit, they would bring about a disenchantment, which would be visibly translated by suicide statistics."[11] At least, that is, in the suicide statistics of men.

In Durkheim's view, desires needed regulation in order to be satisfied. The obligatory or "imperative"character of moral laws, was hence not "an accidental aspect of the moral law," a result of man's animal imperfection, as it appeared to be in the Kantian moral philosophy in which he had been trained.[12] Durkheim, rather, contended that, "the nature of man cannot be itself unless it is disciplined." This discipline was necessary, in his view, not because such inclinations were "evil" or undeserving of satisfaction, but "because otherwise they would never obtain their proper [*juste*] satisfaction."[13] Moral rules, in other words, made satisfaction possible. "Liberty,"

10. Émile Durkheim, *L'éducation morale* (1963), 99.
11. Ibid., 36–37.
12. Ibid., 93. See also his critique of a conception of ethics as "an inferior and perverted morality"—exemplified by Charles Renouvier—in Durkheim, "La définition du fait moral," 262–63.
13. Durkheim, *L'éducation morale*, 44.

which Durkheim associated with this happiness, was hence a product of the *presence,* not the absence, of regulation. For this reason, "the rule should not be simply accepted with docile resignation; it deserves to be loved."[14] The individual loves the moral limit as the very source and origin of his own potential pleasure; it is, in other words, both obeyed and *desired.*

Durkheim further elaborated on the ethics of pleasure in a speech delivered to the neo-Kantian Société française de philosophie in 1906. In this lecture, he distinguished his moral vision from both Kantian and Utilitarian schemas, by asserting the necessary coincidence between "obligation" and "desirability" in moral action. He reiterated his critique of Kant, insisting that "to pursue an end which leaves us cold, which does not strike us as *good* and which does not touch our sensibility, is a psychologically impossible thing. In addition to having an obligatory character, the moral end must be desired and desirable." This desire was, according to Durkheim, of a special sort, one whose satisfaction required effort and even an element of "violence" to the self. Despite the seeming contradiction, he urged, "One could show that pleasure and desirability penetrate even obligation; we find a certain charm in completing the moral act commanded by the rule—by the very fact that we are commanded. We experience a *sui generis* pleasure in doing our duty, because it is a duty. . . . Eudemonism is, like its opposite, everywhere in the moral life."[15] The pleasure that Durkheim described was intimately linked to the sense of obligation and duty, not contrary to it. He did not, however, reduce duty to desire, as did the utilitarians. For he claimed, "One can never derive obligation from the desirable, because the character of obligation is to a certain extent, to do violence to desire."[16] By finding pleasure in obligation, the subject ultimately desires this violation of ordinary desire. This was, of course, what Durkheim argued in *L'éducation morale* and *Suicide,* when he proposed that man's happiness was contingent upon the moderation and even forceful limitation of his otherwise unlimited desires.

Kant similarly presumed that moral compliance entailed displeasure—to the extent that it implied a "constraint for the sensibly affected subject." Actual "love" for dutiful action existed, in Kant's view, however, only as a regulatory ideal, which sensibly affected humans could only approach asymptotically. Kant described the relationship of the subject to moral law as follows: "For, in the case of what we esteem highly but yet dread (because of consciousness of our weakness), through increased facility in satisfying it, the most reverential dread changes dread into liking and respect into love; at least this would be the consummate perfection of a disposition devoted to the law, if it were possible for a creature to attain it."[17] For Kant,

14. Ibid., 47.
15. Émile Durkheim, *Sociologie et philosophie* (1996), 63–64.
16. Ibid., 67.
17. Immanuel Kant, *Critique of Practical Reason,* trans. Mary Gregor (1997), 72.

then, this combination of love and dread, or rather, the transformation of dread into love was an impossible ideal.

Durkheim, by contrast, situated a dynamic between respect and desire at the heart of moral action. This seemingly contradictory impulse was, for him, not a theoretical ideal, but the essential reality of moral life. His account of the "sacred" as that which inspires both fear and attraction, at once respect and desire, explained this relation. Like morality, he explained, "the sacred object inspires within us, if not fear, a respect, which holds us apart and at a distance; and, at the same time, it is a loved and desired object; we tend to approach ourselves, to aspire to it. Here is a dual sentiment, which seems contradictory, but nonetheless exists in reality."[18] The historically close relationship between religious principles and moral laws in most human societies demonstrated, in his view, that morality was a sacred object par excellence. In providing a rational and scientific (i.e., sociological) explanation of this dynamic between respect for and attraction to moral laws, Durkheim sought to preserve morality's "sacred" character, even while cleaving it from religion proper. This account of the dual character of the moral law was however remarkably abstract, and indeed, quite philosophical. In order to understand the terrain upon which he developed this account of the "sacred" character of morality, we need to turn to his more explicitly sociological work, in particular, that on religion and the family.

Familial Origins

We have seen that vague notions of "social sentiment" could not, in Durkheim's view, explain specific moral rules like those, for example, that "prohibit marriage between close kin." Only sociology, he suggested, could do that work, a point that Durkheim explicitly developed in a study on "the origins of the prohibition on incest." He published this article in 1898, as the inaugural entry in the inaugural issue of his school's new showcase journal, the *Année sociologique*.[19] By intervening in a heated set of contemporary debates about the origins of exogamic marriage and social organization, the project of Durkheim's study was at once methodological and moral. His genealogical investigation of the incest taboo exemplified the

18. Durkheim, *Sociologie et philosophie*, 68.
19. Émile Durkheim, "La prohibition de l'inceste et ses origines," *Année sociologique* 1 (1898). Reprinted in Émile Durkheim, "La prohibition de l'inceste et ses origines," in *Journal sociologique*, ed. Jean Duvignaud (1969). This text has received surprisingly little scholarly attention. Notable exceptions include Adam Kuper, "Durkheim's Theory of Primitive Kinship," *British Journal of Sociology* 36, no. 2 (1985); Mary Ann Lamanna, *Émile Durkheim on the Family* (2002). On the *Année sociologique*, see Barberis, "The First *Année sociologique*"; Philippe Besnard, "The *Année sociologique* Team," in *The Sociological Domain: The Durkheimians and the Founding of French Sociology*, ed. Philippe Besnard (1983); Terry Nichols Clark, *Prophets and Patrons: The French University and the Emergence of the Social Sciences* (1973), 181–90.

model of sociological inquiry mapped out several years before in *Les règles de la méthode sociologique,* where he made a case for rigorously separating the "efficient causes" which produce social phenomena from the social functions they eventually come to fulfill.[20] As is suggested by the article's title, this is exactly what he endeavored to do in his analysis of the incest taboo; he distinguished between the contingent "origins" of the taboo in "primitive" totemistic belief and its subsequent social function as an institution charged with the regulation of kinship and sexual relations. His analysis worked in two directions at once in order to dispute, on the one hand, "materialist" theories, which derived the taboo from natural or instinctual repugnance, and, on the other, "spiritualist" ones, which explained the prohibition as the realization of a transhistorical moral idea. Inverting both theories, he suggested that arguments about biological aversion and "moral" repudiation of incest were the secondary effects, rather than primary causes, of the taboo. They were, in other words, products of the law rather than its initial ground. While casting doubt on contemporary theories, which mistook effect for cause, Durkheim postulated that the taboo originated in primitive religious belief. He hence sought, not to provide a new, stronger *originary* ground, but rather to distinguish the subsequent, social effects of the law from its basis in primitive beliefs.

Durkheim simultaneously derived his own "moral" from the history of the incest taboo, one in keeping with the social vision articulated in texts such as *Suicide* and his lectures on moral education. The perpetuation of the prohibition, which was, in his view, neither natural nor inevitable, illustrated how collective, social constraints on purportedly "natural" individual desires produced positive social effects, from which individuals ultimately benefited as well. The regulation of sexual desire by a sacralized (because religiously sanctioned) heterosexuality, instantiated by the taboo, made these at once social and individual benefits manifest. The ban on incest, in other words, did not ratify a pre-existing natural or self-evident moral order; it rather instituted and organized that order, and the gender and sexual relations it implied, as a socially desirable norm.

The moral project implicit in Durkheim's article coincided with a professional strategy to legitimate his school and method. By intervening in debates about the history of human marriage, Durkheim entered an internationally burgeoning field of anthropological and social inquiry. Part and parcel of nineteenth-century colonial endeavors, ethnographic studies of "primitive" moeurs were a growth industry that offered up a wealth of new data to social scientific exploration. These studies were clearly of interest to secular moralists, since the history of human kinship relations, as Friedrich

20. Émile Durkheim, *Les règles de la méthode sociologique,* 18th ed. (1973), 95. See also his discussion of the taboo in Émile Durkheim, "The Principles of 1789 and Sociology," in *Émile Durkheim: On Morality and Society,* ed. Robert N. Bellah (1973), 36.

Engels remarked in his preface to *The Origins of the Family, Property, and the State,* had been recently liberated from the grip of religious orthodoxy by the combined efforts of Swiss jurist Jacob Bachofen's *Die Mutterrecht* in 1861, British anthropologist John Ferguson McLennan's book on *Primitive Marriage* in 1865, and American ethnographer Louis Morgan's *On Systems of Consanguinity* in 1870.[21] These authors resolutely broke with biblical narratives in order to trace the development of exogamy and monogamy out of a primitive state of sexual promiscuity. Charles Darwin likewise entered the fray in 1871 with his publication of the *Descent of Man,* which outlined the role of natural selection in human sexual relations. Herbert Spencer similarly addressed the "super-organic" evolution of domestic institutions in the first volume of his *Principles of Sociology.* These anthropological accounts of the history of human marriage and kinship played a central role in how the discipline came to imagine the "primitive."[22] As Victor Karady has suggested, Durkheim's nascent school gained academic legitimacy by contributing to this newly thriving international field, a move that roughly coincided with the elaboration of their project in the *Année sociologique.* The benefits that they accrued were multiple: access to a wealth of new sources which had proliferated in the wake of the second wave of imperial expansion, possibilities of academic recognition beyond the borders of France, and within France itself, a relatively open space, beyond entrenched academic disciplines, in which to elaborate novel methods and doctrines.[23]

Durkheim's account of the origins of the incest taboo was clearly marked by this strategy. His text at once built on and took distance from a set of primarily foreign and largely Anglo-Saxon interlocutors, including McLennan, Morgan, and Spencer as well as the Darwinian inspired Finnish anthropologist, Edward Westermarck. Durkheim privileged historicist accounts of the origins of marriage and the family over organicist ones, which relied on concepts of nature or instinct. In a lengthy review of Westermarck's *The History of Human Marriage,* published in the *Revue philosophique* in 1895, he overtly rejected materialist efforts to derive the institution of marriage from sexual instinct. In critiquing Westermarck, Durkheim praised the landmark works by Bachofen, Morgan, and McLennan, for having opened "for speculation and in practice a wide field of research." While skeptical of these authors' conclusions, he, like Engels, lauded them for unsettling contemporary presuppositions about marriage

21. Frederick Engels, *The Origin of the Family, Private Property, and the State* (1975), 74.

22. Adam Kuper, *The Invention of Primitive Society: Transformations of an Illusion* (1988), 1–122. On incest, see Adam Kuper, "Incest, Cousin Marriage, and the Origin of the Human Sciences in Nineteenth-century England," *Past and Present* 174, no. 1 (2002).

23. Karady, "The Durkheimians"; Victor Karady, "Durkheim et les débuts de l'ethnologie universitaire," *Actes de la recherche en sciences sociales* 74 (1988); W. Paul Vogt, "The Uses of Studying Primitives: A Note on the Durkheimians, 1890–1940," *History and Theory* 15, no. 1 (1976).

and the family, and hence for denaturalizing domesticity. He suggested that, prior to their studies, one would never have suspected that the organization of the family "could have been thoroughly different than it is now."[24] Durkheim's own work on the origins of the family and, in particular, of the prohibition on incest, was committed to precisely this sort of denaturalization.

Bachofen, Morgan, and McLennan all argued that exogamous and monogamous marriage had evolved out of a primitive state of promiscuity. Westermarck, by contrast, appealed to Darwin's conception of primitive sexual jealousy in order to disprove their theories and to affirm the conjugal couple as the at once originary and natural form in which sexual instincts had been and could be best satisfied. Westermarck made similarly naturalizing claims regarding the prohibition on incest, which he thought reflected an "instinctive aversion" to sexual intercourse between kin. In other words, he wrote, "The family foyer is protected from the stain of incest, neither by law, nor by custom, nor by education, but by an instinct which, in normal circumstances, makes sexual love between closest kin a psychic impossibility."[25] Westermarck hypothesized that because unions between family members were disadvantageous for the species, sexual attraction between consanguines "under normal circumstances" simply did not exist.

As part of his strategy to found and legitimate the new discipline of sociology, Durkheim contested the kind of biological determinism upheld by Westermarck's account. As we have seen, the origins of eminently social institutions such as the family and marriage provided a crucial terrain on which he waged this at once methodological and ideological battle. Durkheim's sociology was concerned with sexual relations only to the extent that they were subject to "imperative rules whose violation is forbidden by the surrounding society, clan, tribe, city, etc."[26] Arguments like Westermarck's which sought the origins of social rules and norms in instinct remained arrested in tautology, and in Durkheim's view, ultimately explained nothing. As he urged in his text on the prohibition, "It is like saying that men condemn incest because it seems to them to be condemnable."[27]

As an interdiction that appeared to be grounded simultaneously in biological instinct and transhistorical moral principle, the prohibition on incest provided a challenging test for Durkheim's sociological interpretation of morality, and especially of family morality. In carrying out this analysis, Durkheim figured kinship as an inherently social, rather than biological re-

---

24. Émile Durkheim, "Origine du mariage dans l'espèce humaine d'après Westermarck (1895)," in *Textes 3*, ed. Victor Karady (1973), 91.
25. Édouard Westermarck, *Origine du mariage dans l'espèce humaine*, trans. Henry de Varigny (1895), 305.
26. Durkheim, "Origine du mariage," 80.
27. Durkheim, "La prohibition," 71.

lation. To make his case, he turned to ethnographic studies, such as those by Scottish theologian and anthropologist, W. Robertson Smith, and his student, James Frazer, who, following McLennan, had linked "primitive" totemistic religion to exogamy. Smith, for example, argued that totemistic principles, rather than direct parental lineage, determined "blood relations" between ancient Arab tribesmen. Because based on mythical beliefs of a shared ancestry (i.e., the totem), rather than biology, their organization of kinship represented a network of social not physiological ties.[28] This definition of kinship and corresponding practices of exogamy in totemistic societies demonstrated, for Durkheim, the pre-eminently social character of the family. He highlighted, in turn, how certain exogamous societies permitted marriages, which could be considered incestuous from a strictly biological standpoint. And, in disputing the physiological basis to which authors like Morgan and John Lubbock laid claim, he explained that it was impossible to "link a sentiment which depends so much on a fact as eminently social as totemism to the individual's congenital disposition."[29] Exogamy was, in his view, a distinctly social and not at all natural or necessary phenomenon.

In order to displace the organicist arguments of his contemporaries, Durkheim sought to uncover and explain the taboo's *religious* origins, namely, by linking exogamy to ritual fears of contact which resulted from the "the religious character with which one of the sexes [i.e., woman] is imprinted."[30] As evidence, Durkheim catalogued examples of primitive bans on contact between men and women, interdictions of which the incest taboo could be seen as a subcategory. Drawing on findings collected by James Frazer and Frazer's student Ernest Crawley, as well as a number of passages from Leviticus, Durkheim described the "religious horror" surrounding certain forms of commerce between the sexes. Crawley had compiled extensive evidence of the prevalence of primitive "sexual taboos," which he published as an extended article in the *Journal of the Anthropological Institute* in 1895 and later collected in a two-volume book devoted to primitive marriage, *The Mystic Rose*. In these writings, he argued that religious prohibitions originated in men's primal fear of women, whose difference and inferiority he both presumed and proved by accumulating examples of the universal social and symbolic forms of exclusion to which they were subject. Religious prohibitions on contact between the sexes orig-

28. See W. Robertson Smith, *Kinship and Marriage in Early Arabia* (1885). See also Robert Alun Jones, "Robertson Smith, Durkheim, and Sacrifice: An Historical Context for *The Elementary Forms of Religious Life*," in *Émile Durkheim: Critical Assessments*, ed. Peter Hamilton (1990); Kuper, "Durkheim's Theory."

29. Durkheim, "La prohibition," 72. For Morgan and Lubbock's arguments, see John Lubbock, *The Origin of Civilization and the Primitive Condition of Man: Mental and Social Condition of Savages* (1882); Lewis Henry Morgan, *Ancient Society; or, Researches in the Lines of Human Progress from Savagery, through Barbarism to Civilization* (1877).

30. Durkheim, "La prohibition," 74.

inated, in his view, in men's fear of women as contagious sources of "weakness and cowardice."[31] This understanding of femininity as contagiously devirilizing expressed itself most clearly, according to Crawley, in taboos on contact with women during their "periodic crises," that is, those moments when their natural sexual difference took on an apparent and apparently disease-ridden guise.[32] Religious fears accentuated an estrangement produced by women's essential physiological difference from men. As he explained in *The Mystic Rose,* such taboos "thus enforced more strongly such separation as is due to nature."[33] Religion simply extended and exaggerated a prior, natural difference between men and women.

By mining many of Crawley's examples of primitive sexual prohibitions, Durkheim drew a direct correlation between these taboos and women's sexual crises, namely menstruation. Durkheim, however, reversed the terms of Crawley's argument. Women, he suggested, were perceived as dangerous not because they were feminine—for, this tautology explained nothing—but because they were bloody and because their blood was endowed with a sacred character.[34] In Crawley's analysis, religious proscriptions on sexual contact followed a "hygienic" logic; they protected individual men from being contaminated and debilitated by femininity, as if femininity itself were a disease. Durkheim, by contrast, refused to interpret sexual taboos as rules of public health.[35] Taboos on sexual contact between men and women, he claimed, rather resulted from a system of primitive totemistic belief, which invested clan women's blood with religious significance.

Durkheim appealed to Robertson Smith's work on the ancient Semites in order argue that primitives figured blood as sacred, because it created, constituted, and represented the unity of their clans. Blood provided a material instantiation or support for a diffuse idea of collective unity. Using Smith's example of the "blood-covenant" by which foreigners were adopted into the ancient Arab tribes, he argued that this "common blood" did not represent family in the strict sense of consanguinity.[36] As an incarnation of collective unity, the blood of clan members implicated the life of the community as a whole. The sacred character of this vital fluid explained the origin of "sex taboos" and, in particular, religious proscriptions against women, because, according to Durkheim, "woman is, in a chronic manner, a theater

31. Ernest Crawley, "Sexual Taboos: A Study in the Relations of the Sexes," *Journal of the Anthropological Institute of Great Britain and Ireland* 24 (1895): 229.

32. Ibid., 222.

33. Ernest Crawley, *The Mystic Rose: A Study of Primitive Marriage and of Primitive Thought in Its Bearing on Marriage (1902),* 2nd ed., vol. 1 (1927), 86.

34. Crawley had, in fact, brought up this possibility only to dismiss it: Crawley, "Sexual Taboos," 220.

35. For a further critique of this hygienic premise, see Émile Durkheim, "Mariage et sexualité primitifs selon Crawley (1903)," in *Textes 3,* ed. Victor Karady (1973), 74.

36. See, for example, W. Robertson Smith, *Lectures on the Religion of the Semites* (1889), 255.

of bloody manifestations. The sentiments awakened by blood are carried over to her; we know with what facility the taboo propagates itself. Women are thus also, in a chronic manner, taboo for the other members of the clan."[37] Durkheim's argument, to the extent that it figured women as a "chronic theater of bloody manifestations" rested on a physiological claim about women's difference. This brute physical fact, however, while it accounted for *how* women became taboo, did not, in his view, explain the taboo's origin, as it had for Crawley. For, according to Durkheim, what made (certain) women dangerous was, in fact, not their difference, but their "sameness," in other words, the fact that they shared the "common blood" of the totem. In placing a ban on women who shared the blood of the clan, the prohibition on incest, in fact, privileged difference over sameness. The sexual difference that was instituted in and by sexual taboos, and the incest taboo in particular, was for Durkheim a cultural artifact; it could only have had, in his view, a religious, which is to say, social origin.

In order to claim that sexual taboos, and, in particular, prohibitions on incest were eminently social institutions, which produced new modalities of desire, Durkheim nonetheless invoked a naturalized conception of heterosexual attraction or "instinct." Like many of the theorists of kinship relations that preceded and followed him, Durkheim foreclosed same-sex desire from the outset; this foreclosure, in turn, operated as the founding presupposition of his account of the taboo.[38] This repudiation of relations between members of the same sex was reiterated in and by the creation of a ban on relations between members of the same family. As an exemplary moral (as opposed to natural) rule, the prohibition on incest, as theorized by Durkheim, simultaneously instituted gender difference and the social organization of heterosexuality as constitutive of sociality itself. His theory, rather than simply ratifying a pre-existing state of nature, sought to explain the eminently *social* character of this arrangement. We have already seen how Durkheim privileged the social value of difference in his account of the shift from primitive bonds of "mechanical" solidarity, based on relations of sameness, to "organic" ones, based on the mutual attraction between opposites. An analogous logic underlies his account of the institution and perpetuation of the prohibition on incest.

Durkheim conceptualized morality as a system of externally imposed, supra-individual rules which limit individual desires. Sexual taboos, as social rules which disrupted purportedly "natural" heterosexual instincts, appeared, according to Durkheim, to do just that. "Most of all, when one thinks of the force of the instinct which pushes men and women together and incites them to approach one another, it becomes evident that their sur-

37. Durkheim, "La prohibition," 82.
38. For analyses of this foreclosure, see Judith Butler, *Gender Trouble: Feminism and the Subversion of Identity* (1990), 72–77; Gayle Rubin, "The Traffic in Women: Notes on the 'Political Economy' of Sex," in *Feminism and History*, ed. Joan Scott (1996).

prising antagonism must result from a cause which, far from simply extending natural tendencies, does violence to them."[39] Durkheim thus granted heterosexual attraction an originary, instinctual status. He did *not*, however, directly derive the social organization of exogamous marriage from this natural heterosexual desire. He rather argued that the institution of exogamy in and by the incest taboo constituted a break from nature. The impetus to disrupt a natural condition of generalized heterosexual desire with kinship rules could not, in his view, have been immanent to nature; it necessarily came from elsewhere—namely, religion. The practices of marriage to which these rules gave rise thus reinstituted heterosexuality and the simultaneous production and regulation of sexual difference that it implies *not* as a natural law, but as a sacred social principle.[40]

According to a rather surprising line of argument, Durkheim suggested that the eventual separation between sexual partners and family members created by the incest taboo was neither natural nor necessary. "Their dissociation must have been imposed by a particularly powerful external force. In other words, the moral incompatibility in the name of which we now prohibit incest is, itself, a consequence of this prohibition, which must have initially existed for an entirely different reason."[41] Durkheim explained the "moral incompatibility" which was produced by the institution of exogamy as follows: once sexual relations (which he presumed to be exclusively cross-sex, and never same-sex) were banished from the realm of kinship, they developed as a domain of liberty, as a space purportedly given over to the free play of desire. "Thus, owing to exogamy, sensuality—all the instincts and individual desires connected to the relations between the sexes— was liberated from the yoke of the family, which would have contained and more or less stifled it; it constituted itself separately."[42] This investment of heterosexual relations by the passions appeared, for Durkheim, as a happy effect of the incest taboo. With time, the distance between sex and the family never ceased to widen. Once it functioned as the basis for the moral organization of society, this distinction could not be undone, even after the decline of totemism, without jeopardizing the entire social order. Subsequent religions—down to the present day—perpetuated an already existing state of affairs by continuing to banish sex from the family, which is to say,

---

39. Durkheim, "Mariage et sexualité," 97.

40. Lévi-Strauss in his critique of Durkheim's purely "culturalist" and historical account of the origins of the taboo underplays the naturalist presumption of heterosexual desire which structured this interpretation. The presumption of heterosexuality as a natural universal is something their analyses ultimately share. See Claude Lévi-Strauss, *The Elementary Structures of Kinship* (1970), 21–25. For a discussion of the heterosexual presumption that has structured the history of anthropological considerations of kinship, see John Borneman, "Until Death Do Us Part: Marriage/Death in Anthropological Discourse," *American Ethnologist* 23, no. 2 (1996). On heterosexuality as the matrix of sexual difference, rather than its logical extension, see Butler, *Gender Trouble*.

41. Durkheim, "La prohibition," 96.

42. Ibid., 97.

passion from morality. Indeed, Durkheim asks at the end of his article, "Isn't our morality that of the categorical imperative?"[43] He here intimated that his genealogy of the incest taboo revealed the "social" origins of the morality enshrined in Kant's transcendental maxim.

Without promoting the "primitive" beliefs on which he imagined sexual taboos to have been based initially, Durkheim described what he saw as their positive (i.e., both constructive and desirable) historical effects. He figured the primitive prohibitions to have produced a socialized form of sexual desire, a kind of passion, which his article inscribes as exclusively and necessarily heterosexual. In his conclusion, Durkheim signaled how, in contemporary relations between the sexes, "without understanding why, we still obey these antique prejudices, so long stripped of all reason to exist." While its original rationale had long since faded away, the separation between men and women remained very much in place. The heterosexual passion, which, Durkheim argued, emerged as an effect of the prohibition, now functioned as its legitimating ground. This is particularly evident in his concluding lyrical invocation of romantic love between men and women. "This mystery, which we, rightly or wrongly, like to surround women, this unknown that each sex is for the other—and which constitutes the principal charm of their commerce; this very special curiosity which is one of the most powerful stimulants to love's scheming [*la brigue amoureuse*]; all the ideas and practices which have become one of life's distractions [*délassements*] would hardly be maintained if men's and women's lives mixed too much."[44] Despite its foundation in obscure, "primitive" conceptions of menstrual blood, the "mystery" of difference remained a persistent "charm" in the amorous relations between the sexes. Too much mingling, too much similarity between them would, in Durkheim's view, destroy this charm. The pleasures of romantic love hence required the "mystery" of a difference, which, for Durkheim, *was* sexual difference. Desire between individuals who resemble one another too closely was rendered here as unimaginable. For this reason, he intimated, women should not try to become like men. This privileging of the "mystery" of sexual difference simultaneously repudiated same-sex desire. Durkheim did not overtly rely on nature in order to justify the social organization of heterosexuality. He instead claimed the desirability of socially instituted sexual difference as the principal ground and reason for its perpetuation. Durkheim felt no need to justify its persistence with an appeal to a "natural" origin.

Durkheim provided a thoroughly sociological analysis of the incest taboo's emergence and of its subsequent social and moral effects. He rejected contemporary accounts of its origins that appealed to either nature or transcendental moral ideas. In the process, he reinscribed heterosexuality,

43. Ibid., 98.
44. Ibid., 99.

not as a natural law nor as an abstract moral principle, but as socially desirable norm. His lyrical defense of the moral and social order that developed in the wake of the prohibition on incest figured the production and regulation of sexual difference by exogamous marriage as a simultaneously social and individual good.[45] As the matrix of romantic passion between men and women, the prohibition on incest provided Durkheim with a model of social law that was underwritten not by an originary principle but by its own desirable effects. Durkheim's depiction of relations between men and women as a locus of charm and mystery, whose magic would be lost if their sexual difference were effaced, upheld married heterosexuality as a sacred social principle.

Sex, Science, and the Sacred

Informed by such studies of primitive society and religion, Durkheim's later writings increasingly used the concept of "the sacred" in order to understand and explain how moral norms inspired both desire and respect. For example, in the wake of his pro-Dreyfusard engagement, exemplified by his famous response to Ferdinand Brunetière, "Individualism and the Intellectuals," Durkheim upheld "personhood" as a socially constituted sacred value.[46] In a lecture titled "La Détermination du fait moral" at the February 1906 meeting of the Société française de philosophie, Durkheim, in fact, described the "human person" as the very embodiment of "the sacred" in modern society, as an object, that is, of *both* quasi-religious respect and sympathetic attraction. "On the one hand, s/he inspires a religious sentiment in the other that holds one at a distance. Any infringement upon the domain in which a person like us moves appears as a sacrilege. S/he is surrounded by a halo of sanctity. . . . But at the same time, s/he is the eminent object of our sympathy."[47] Durkheim's figuration of the individual here was not explicitly gendered. His conception of the person as sacred did, however, inscribe this dynamic of respect and attraction as a foundational principle of modern ethics. And, because his vision of heterosexual relations exemplified an analogous dynamic, they too were endowed, according to

45. On how theories of kinship based on the incest taboo reinscribe conventional ideas about sexual difference and heterosexuality, see Judith Butler, *Antigone's Claim: Kinship between Life and Death* (2000), 72–77; Judith Butler, *Undoing Gender* (2004), 102–30, 152–60. For an analysis that problematically reproduces the association of incest and homosexuality as socially "unproductive," see Françoise Héritier, *Two Sisters and Their Mother,* trans. Jeanine Herman (2002).

46. See Durkheim's well-known response to Ferdinand Brunetière at the height of the Dreyfus Affair: Émile Durkheim, "Individualism and the Intellectuals," in *Émile Durkheim on Morality and Society,* ed. Robert N. Bellah (1973), 51–52. On the Dreyfus Affair and the figuration of the individual as sacred and even Christ-like, see Christopher E. Forth, *The Dreyfus Affair and the Crisis of French Manhood* (2004), 67–102.

47. Durkheim, *Sociologie et philosophie,* 68.

Durkheim, with an inherently sacred, which is to say, moral quality. The intimate association between his notion of the human person and his account of the moral character of conjugal relations was made explicit five years later, at yet another meeting of the Société française de philosophie.[48]

Held in February 1911, the meeting introduced a debate over "sexual education." The invited presenter was Dr. Jacques Amedée Doléris, a well-known gynecologist, hygienist, and natalist advocate, who worked at the maternity hospital Boucicaut in Paris. At this meeting, Doléris summarized a report on "Sex Education by the Family, Science, and Morality" that he had recently delivered at the Third International Congress of School Hygiene. The issues up for discussion recalled those entertained at the society's 1906 meeting: the foundations of morality, the bases of moral self-mastery, and the relation between religious and secular ethics. Doléris confronted his audience, comprised of both neo-Kantian philosophers and Catholic moralists, with an altogether different logic: medical rationality. At stake in this discussion was the question of whether hygienic concerns could serve as an adequate ground for modern sexual morality.

At once pro-natalist and anticlerical, Doléris insisted that only medical science could provide a sufficient and solid basis for instruction in sexual matters. "Education by science," he proclaimed, "appears to me to be the only possible and legitimate kind."[49] As we will see in the next chapter, his program was not unique; it was a typical expression of the attitudes of hygienist doctors—generally employed at major Parisian hospitals—who, at the turn of the century, engaged in campaigns to fight the spread of venereal disease while increasing the health and number of French births. Of particular interest for our current discussion was the apparent conflict in this debate between two, ultimately different approaches to the problem of contemporary sexual regulation: Durkheim's social science and Doléris's hygienic one.

The hygienists' sexual education courses aimed to make men more sexually responsible and women more aware of the dangers they ran at the hands of men. According to these doctors, families could not be trusted to sufficiently inform their children—either girls or boys—about the dangers and pleasures of sex. It fell on society to assume the burden. While conservative Catholic physicians remained closely aligned with family-advocates who fought against these measures, public health experts petitioned for the inclusion of programs of sexual education in the army and in schools. In the controversies that ensued, hygienists criticized "irrational" religious moral-

---

48. For a similar observation, see Jean-Claude Filloux, "Personne et sacré chez Durkheim," *Archives des sciences sociales des religions* 69 (1990).

49. J.-H. Doléris, "L'éducation sexuelle," *Bulletin de la Société française de philosophie* 11 (28 February 1911): 30. For a more global discussion of the debate, see Jean E. Pedersen, "Something Mysterious: Sex Education, Victorian Morality, and Durkheim's Comparative Sociology," *Journal of the History of the Behavioral Sciences* 34, no. 2 (1998).

ity as a menace to public health, and hence to society. They argued that by shrouding sex in a mysterious and ignorant silence, clerical attitudes aided and abetted the propagation of unwanted pregnancies (and hence abortions) and the menace of venereal peril. Sex education courses like those proposed by Doléris sought to teach men about the dangers of syphilis in order to make them more "moral." They complemented efforts by infant health experts to introduce rational and hygienic practices and instruction in hospital maternities.[50] In a presentation on rising abortion statistics before the Société française de prophylaxie sanitaire et morale in 1906, Doléris drew an explicit parallel between these projects. In addition to encouraging women to give birth in maternity wards, rather than at home, he proclaimed, "I also believe in the necessity of social reforms . . . in the moralization of men."[51]

But how did Doléris understand the relationship between hygiene and morality? In his exposé on sex education, he argued that efforts to regulate men's sexual instincts with moral abstractions, whether religious or philosophical, ultimately ended in failure. In "affirming man's metaphysical duties," he claimed, they "always forget the nonetheless simple fact that the sexual functions exercise a real, indisputable, material attraction on man." Total continence was hence, for Doléris, "a dangerous and inhuman dream." The stated goal of sex education should instead be, according to the hygienist, "the regularization, the normal organization of the sexual function." While upholding "the education of the will" as an important component of such schooling, the morality that Doléris defended was based on the hard and fast facts of science, clearly "shown in the light of day," not "confused" and "enveloped" like that of philosophers or clerics.[52] But was such "enlightenment," provided by the science of hygiene, sufficient?

Doléris assumed that, in light of proper scientific instruction, sexual functions could achieve a normal equilibrium, a balance unjustly and dangerously obscured by old, hypocritical moralities. At the same time, he intimated that even the best lessons in hygienic science, could not always guarantee that men's sexual instinct would become normal, which is to say, self-regulating. Doléris admitted that children with "imbalanced natures" might be perverted by these proposed lessons in natural science. In such cases, albeit few and far between, he advocated, instead, "a solid moral education."[53] He did not clarify the principles upon which this education was to be based—but one might assume that he was referring to those obsolete abstractions whose efficacy he also called into question.

50. See Françoise Thebaud, *Quand nos grand-mères donnaient la vie: La maternité en France dans l'entre-deux-guerres* (1986).
51. Société française de prophylaxie sanitaire et morale, *Bulletin de la Société française de prophylaxie sanitaire et morale* 6 (1906): 235.
52. Doléris, "L'éducation sexuelle," 42.
53. Ibid., 31.

In his contributions to the debate, Durkheim predictably focused on this very problem. He stated: "From hygiene, Dr. Doléris passes on to morality; it is here that I have much more difficulty in following him. In effect, he seems to admit that one can legislate morality in the name of hygiene, while judging strange the pretension to legislate hygiene in the name of morality." Durkheim, as we saw in his article on the incest taboo, drew a sharp distinction between hygiene and morality. He hence argued that, "they are two absolutely distinct social functions." The real challenge, according to Durkheim, "is to know why continence is a duty and how the reasons behind this duty can be shown to the young man." He interrogated whether an education concentrating on the health risks of extramarital sexual activity could effectively "make the young man understand that marriage is legally justified and that extramarital sexual commerce is immoral."[54] Durkheim refused to reduce human sexuality to a biological function. At issue was the very "nature" of sex itself. "In reality, if, as M. Doléris seems to be asking, we speak of the sexual act as an ordinary physical act, we denature it. . . . The contradictory, mysterious, exceptional character that public conscience grants it is part of its nature. How can we conserve this if we speak of it without veil, without any sort of precaution? And what moralizing effects could we achieve, if we lead youths to see sexual commerce only as a manifestation of a biological function, comparable to digestion and circulation."[55] Durkheim refused to collapse sexual hygiene and sexual morality. In contrast to Doléris, he suggested that bringing sexuality out into the light of day by discussing it "without veil," would "denature" it rather than reveal its true essence. As his lyrical language intimates, Durkheim once again figured sexual relations as eminently sacred. In restricting sex to its mechanical components, Doléris stripped it of higher significance. While Durkheim conceded that some rudimentary education in sexual hygiene might well serve a positive social function, he concluded that Doléris was misguided in his belief that such teaching could be substituted for genuine moral instruction.

In his response, Doléris sought to claim the scientific high ground by charging Durkheim with obscurantism. For Doléris, the "mysterious" aspects to which Durkheim referred were symptomatic of the "reigning prejudices" standing in the way of a truly rational sexual education.[56] In their successive attempts to delegitimate one another, Durkheim and Doléris were, of course, fighting over professional territory. Their conflict was hence symptomatic of the very "divisions of labor" which Durkheim had celebrated in his other works. However, this debate over sexual education did not produce cooperation or consensus. It remained a border skirmish between competing visions of science and its purported social and moral ends.

54. Ibid., 33.
55. Ibid., 35.
56. Ibid., 37. Pedersen notes the implicit anti-Semitism of Doléris's charge, Pedersen, "Something Mysterious," 142.

Durkheim claimed that his approach took reason a step further by moving beyond Doléris's brute materialism. In his view, a properly rational *moral* education needed to account for the complex and contradictory, which is to say "sacred," sentiments evoked by the sex act, rather than its mere biological bases. In keeping with his vision of the sacred as always double and seemingly contradictory, Durkheim presented "sexual commerce" as essentially ambivalent. He urged that "the best way to strike the spirit of the young man is to make him understand the reasons behind the singular, troublesome character of the sex act."[57] He sought, in other words, to provide a rational explanation of the act's ambivalence. In order to do so, he appealed to his notion of the human person as "sacred," as an object of both respect and attraction, subject to both ritual interdiction and yet always also desirable. "If modesty exists, the sex act is the immodest act par excellence; it violates modesty, negating it; and because modesty is a virtue the act has, in that alone, an immoral character. But, on the other hand, there is no act which ties human beings more closely together; it has an associative, and as a result, an incomparably moral power."[58]

As he so often did in his elucidation of moral facts, Durkheim began with Kant. He reiterated the philosopher's account of how the sex act debased the human person. "Kant already sensed that there was something in sexual commerce which offends moral sentiment; he says that for one individual to use another for pleasure is contrary to human dignity." Translating Kant into his own terminology, Durkheim explained, "To touch a sacred thing without using the proper, respectful precautions prescribed by ritual, is to profane it; it is to commit sacrilege."[59] As with any sacred object, he suggested, the human person must be approached with ritual respect. For Kant, marriage made sexual activity "acceptable," but it did not endow sex with a wider moral function.[60] By contrast, for Durkheim, marriage indeed countered the debasing character of the sex act, but, beyond that, represented an inherently social—and hence, for him—moral good. The sex act, as a model of communion endowed with "associative power," assumed this distinctly moral character. "At the same time, it itself contains something to efface and buy back this constitutional immorality. In effect, this profanation produces, on the other hand, the most intimate communion that can exist between two beings. As a result of this communion, the two people who unify

---

57. Doléris, "L'éducation sexuelle," 46.

58. Ibid., 34–35.

59. Ibid., 46. Durkheim is once again referring to Kant's famous account of marriage in Immanuel Kant, *The Metaphysics of Morals,* trans. Mary Gregor (1996), 62.

60. Isabel V. Hull, *Sexuality, State, and Civil Society in Germany, 1700–1815* (1996), 301–11; Anthony J. La Vopa, "Thinking about Marriage: Kant's Liberalism and the Peculiar Morality of Conjugal Union," *Journal of Modern History* 77, no. 1 (2005). See also Eric O. Clarke, *Virtuous Vice: Homoeroticism and the Public Sphere* (2000), 101–25. On heterosexual presumption in ideas about human dignity, see Carolyn J. Dean, *The Frail Social Body: Pornography, Homosexuality, and Other Fantasies in Interwar France* (2000).

become one; the limits which initially circumscribed each of them are displaced and pushed further; a new person is born which contains the two
others. The profanation disappears when this fusion is chronic, when the
new unity constituted in this way becomes durable—for now there are no
longer two separate and distinct persons present, but only one."[61] The sex
act, when regulated and reproduced within the framework of marriage was
hence a figure of and for sociality. Implicitly based on a heterosexual model
of gender complementarity, conjugal sex, according to Durkheim, produced
a new moral being, a "new person," which transcended the discrete and
separated individual. This union constituted and confirmed the social value
of the married couple, while relegating all other sexual relations to the
realm of "profanation."

Durkheim's representation of "conjugality" as a form of solidarity in the
debate on sexual education thus echoes his analysis in *La division du travail
social,* where, it will be recalled, heterosexual passion functioned as a metaphor for sociality. Durkheim, in contrast to Kant, represented the union
with the other as both desired and desirable. He suggested that if this
sought-after union fails to remain "chronic" and "durable," the deal turns
bad. If the "new person" born of the act is not, in turn, respected, the relation becomes one of pure loss. "If the individuals, after having unified, separate from one another again, if each of them, after having given himself to
the other, resumes his independence, the profanation remains both total
and without compensation."[62] This was, of course, one of the dangers, in
Durkheim's view, of divorce by mutual consent. In the moral economy of
conjugal sex, the "pay off" is not, or at least, not just in the physical pleasure. It depends on the obligations to the other founded in and by the
union, and given juridical sanction by marriage. The sex act, without this
properly social component, is a waste—both for the self and the other. As
the place where desire and obligation coincide, marriage was, for him, an
instantiation par excellence of the moral character of the social. This is precisely what made it a sacred institution.

Durkheim's account of sexual regulation exemplified the dynamics at
work in his social account of morality more generally. His writings on the
incest taboo and sexual education upheld conjugality as a sacred social
principle, as an eminently moral rather than simply natural ideal. Married
heterosexuality quite literally embodied and animated the desirable discipline or loveable regulation that he imagined to be the motor of morality.
This conjugal ideal relied on and reproduced sexual difference and a heterosexual organization of desire. By conferring a "sacred" social value on
sexual difference and the desire which it was imagined to inspire, conjugal-

61. Doléris, "L'éducation sexuelle," 46–47.
62. Ibid., 47.

ity represented how freedom and regulation were, for men, productively reconciled. In embracing marriage, male citizens were both socialized and autonomous, which is to say "masculine." As a result, the refusal of conjugality, epitomized by the anomic bachelor and the divorcé, entailed social, and even literal death, and, its corollary, failed masculinity.

This construction of conjugality as a moral ideal, in addition to confirming men's masculinity through their desire for and dependence on women, had as its corollary the gendered complementarity of the social body itself. For some of Durkheim's contemporaries this companionate logic, to the extent that it described women as at once equal and different from men, made a limited conception of women's suffrage imaginable. This was the case, for example, for Ferdinand Buisson. In 1911, the same year as the debate on sexual education between Doléris and Durkheim, Buisson, now a deputy from the Seine, presided over the Chamber's Committee on Universal Suffrage. The text of his carefully documented report, published under the title *Le vote des femmes,* advocated women's right to vote in municipal elections. In making his case, Buisson notably wondered, citing Marcel Prévost, why twenty-one-year-old bachelors "who think only of amusing themselves" should have suffrage, while thirty-five-year-old widowed mothers did not.[63] His argument was not, however, founded on the claim that women were the *same* as men. Indeed, quite the opposite. For, he claimed, "Equality does not imply identity. Two valuables that cost the same price can be very different. It is not necessary for woman to be the same as man to be his equal."[64] In defense of their suffrage, Buisson invoked the sexually specific role that feminists had played in public life by bringing "comfort, introducing a little more justice, and prevention," into "moeurs, the life of the family, the factory, and the school." He hence concluded, "presumably, it will be the same everywhere that woman exercises some action in public life: it is nature itself which assigns her this role."[65] Women's purportedly "natural" difference had an explicitly social and moral function.

In order to justify the reform philosophically, Buisson cited a "bisexual" notion of national sovereignty, enunciated in a 1902 text, by Charles Turgeon, titled *Le féminisme français.* According to Turgeon, "There is no way to pretend that sovereignty is essentially masculine. Its nature is double: it is, one might say, male and female. In other words, sovereignty does not stem, either from men, or from women, but all members of the nation. It is bisexual. This being so, one conclusion imposes itself: everyone is sovereign, everyone is an elector."[66] Turgeon, who was an economist and jurist, indeed

63. Ferdinand Buisson, *Le vote des femmes* (1911), 308.
64. Ibid., 311.
65. Ibid., 322. See also Joan W. Scott, *Only Paradoxes to Offer: Feminism and the "Rights of Man" in France, 1789–1940* (1996), 110.
66. Buisson, *Le vote des femmes,* 317. For Turgeon's discussion, see Charles Turgeon, *Le féminisme français: L'émancipation politique et familiale de la femme* (1902), 35. On Turgeon's opposition to individualist or "integral" feminism, and the coincidence between solidarism and "maternalist" feminism, see, Karen Offen, "Depopulation, Nationalism, and Fem-

affirmed women's right to vote. But he was also opposed to many strains of feminism, especially those associated with socialism and anarchism. The greatest social danger posed by feminists, according to him, lay not in demands for suffrage, but in "anti-matrimonialism." Like Durkheim, Turgeon rued the disruptive effects of divorce on social order. In his view, "the law which re-established divorce represents a conquest of individualism over the social spirit." He thus warned, "A prideful, avid, and undisciplined individualism undermines and dissolves us. There is our secret and shameful illness."[67] For Turgeon, as for Durkheim, marriage was a necessary moral and social limit on this excess.

The social conception of citizenship that underwrote both Turgeon's "bisexual" notion of sovereignty and his idealization of marriage, inscribed heterosexual masculinity and femininity as characteristics of the national political and social order. Masculinity here did not disavow men's particularity in the name of individual abstraction; it was, instead, constituted and contained by marriage. His idea of popular sovereignty, in turn, reflected this complementary social vision. In their efforts to preserve the "sacred" character of conjugality from the forces of individualist and anomic desire, figures like Durkheim and Turgeon questioned the pathological and unregulated effects of divorce. Meanwhile, hygienists, like Doléris, devoted themselves to detecting a different "secret and shameful illness" that plagued society. They too aimed to protect the health of the heterosexual social body and engaged in their own project of imagining and regulating the male citizen.

---

inism in Fin-de-siècle France," *American Historical Studies* 89, no. 3 (1984). For an account of how an analogous logic of the couple, while not initially operative in the theorization of women's political parity, came to structure certain arguments for its implementation in recent debates in France, see Joan W. Scott, *Parité! Sexual Equality and the Crisis of French Universalism* (2005).

67. Turgeon, *Le féminisme français,* 238.

PART IV

PRESERVING MEN

> Experience and reason during the springtime of life, in the prime
> years of youth! What mockery! Truly, would it not be more realistic
> to observe that it is at this age that syphilis is acquired the most un-
> consciously in the world, in total ignorance, or, at least, without the
> least worry about the dangers incurred? Above all, would it not be
> more charitable to try, by whatever means, to protect these young be-
> ings, almost children, precisely because they are incapable of protect-
> ing themselves?
>
> —Dr. Alfred Fournier, *Danger social de la syphilis*

In his report to the First International Conference for the Prophylaxis of
Syphilis and Venereal Disease in 1899, the leading French syphilis doctor of
his day, Alfred Fournier, proclaimed that syphilis was not just an individual
illness, but also a veritable "social danger." Society, he hence argued, had a
right to defend itself against it.[1] As professor of Cutaneous and Syphilitic
Diseases at the Hôpital Saint-Louis in Paris since 1879, Fournier had been
sounding this alarm for some time. He had already reported to the French
Academy of Medicine on the gravity of the danger in 1887. By the turn of
the century, the question of what public means should be used to fight
against venereal contagion had become a matter of significant national and
international debate. On the program at the 1899 conference in Brussels
was the question of "whether society has the right, and even obligation, to
defend itself against syphilis with measures of public prophylaxis."[2] "Public
prophylaxis," in the jargon of hygienists such as Fournier meant, in reality,
the medical and police regulation of prostitution. The legal and hygienic rationale for such sanitary surveillance of prostitutes, well secured in France
throughout the nineteenth century, had been significantly weakened by

---

1. Alfred Fournier, "Danger social de la syphilis," in *Compte rendu des séances*, ed. Conférence internationale pour la prophylaxie de la syphilis et des maladies vénériennes (1899).
   2. Ibid., 36.

185

abolitionist arguments, which grew out of the campaign against the Contagious Disease Acts in Britain and continued on an international scale after their abolition in 1886.[3] While hygienists such as Fournier remained committed to regulation, they sought to undo its association with arbitrary and immoral police power. They aimed to rearticulate it as a rational public health practice.

In 1901, Alfred Fournier founded the Société française de prophylaxie sanitaire et morale (SFPSM), an organization recognized as serving the public good under the 1901 law on associations. It devoted itself to educating the public on the extent of the social danger of syphilis, while also elaborating neo-regulationist policy proposals that countered the efforts of contemporary abolitionists to get rid of regulation altogether. In a classic article devoted to the "venereal peril" in the Belle Epoque, Alain Corbin has convincingly argued that the work of Fournier and his associates was largely successful.[4] The SFPSM notably helped to save regulation, despite the fact that the *bloc des Gauches* administrations that took power in the wake of the Dreyfus Affair were largely sympathetic to the arguments in favor of individual rights set forth by the abolitionist cause. By provoking widespread public anxiety of venereal disease, Fournier and his associates, as Corbin has noted, promoted married heterosexuality. Their seemingly contradictory program sought to dissuade male youths from engaging in pre- and extramarital sexual behavior, while also defending the need to reinforce and

3. The literature on the regulation of prostitution, representations of prostitutes, and the history of venereal disease in France is extensive: Andrew R. Aisenberg, "Syphilis and Prostitution: A Regulatory Couplet in Nineteenth-century France," in *Sex, Sin, and Suffering: Venereal Disease and European Society since 1870,* ed. Roger Davidson et al. (2001); Jean-Marc Berlière, *La police des moeurs sous la Troisième République* (1992); Charles Bernheimer, *Figures of Ill Repute: Representing Prostitution in Nineteenth-century France* (1989); Alain Corbin, "Le péril vénérien au début du siècle: Prophylaxie sanitaire et prophylaxie morale," *Recherches* 11, no. 29 (1977); Alain Corbin, *Les filles de noce* (1978); Jill Harsin, *Policing Prostitution in Nineteenth-century Paris* (1985); Jann Matlock, *Scenes of Seduction: Prostitution, Hysteria, and Reading Difference in Nineteenth-century France* (1994); Julia Miller, "The 'Romance of Regulation': The Movement against State-regulated Prostitution in France, 1871–1948" (Ph.D. diss., New York University, 2000); A.-J.-B. Parent-Duchâtelet, *La prostitution à Paris au 19ᵉ siècle: Texte présenté et annoté par Alain Corbin* (1981); Claude Quétel, *History of Syphilis,* trans. Judith Braddock et al. (1990). Important histories of prostitution and its regulation elsewhere include Ann Taylor Allen, "Feminism, Venereal Disease, and the State in Germany, 1890–1918," *Journal of the History of Sexuality* 4, no. 1 (1993); Laurie Bernstein, *Sonia's Daughters: Prostitutes and Their Regulation in Imperial Russia* (1995); Allan M. Brandt, *No Magic Bullet: A Social History of Venereal Disease in the United States since 1880* (1987); Roger Davidson and Lesley A. Hall, *Sex, Sin, and Suffering: Venereal Disease and European Society since 1870* (2001); Laura Engelstein, *The Keys to Happiness: Sex and the Search for Modernity in Fin-de-siècle Russia* (1992); Mary Gibson, *Prostitution and the State in Italy, 1860–1915,* 2nd ed. (2000); Donna J. Guy, *Sex and Danger in Buenos Aires: Prostitution, Family, and Nation in Argentina* (1991); Gail Hershatter, *Dangerous Pleasures: Prostitution and Modernity in Twentieth-century Shanghai* (1997); Philippa Levine, *Prostitution, Race, and Politics: Policing Venereal Disease in the British Empire* (2003); Judith Walkowitz, *Prostitution and Victorian Society: Women, Class, and the State* (1982).

4. Corbin, "Le péril vénérien."

rationalize the sanitary regulation of women who were prostitutes. The venereal horrors recounted in their advice pamphlets and in their conferences or displayed in the wax museum of the Hôpital Saint-Louis aimed to provoke sanitary fear among those adolescents purportedly threatened by the temptations of prostitution and other pleasures of the street.

Corbin presents this discursive explosion as a notable counterpoint to Michel Foucault's critique of the "repressive hypothesis" in volume 1 of *The History of Sexuality*. While signaling its garrulous character, manifested by the proliferation of tracts, journals, conferences, and commissions devoted to the cause, Corbin suggests that the effects of the crusade were essentially repressive. It constituted a "dissuasive" strategy, which principally targeted male youth. In contrast to the *scientia sexualis* described by Foucault, it was concerned not with unearthing the hidden truth of pleasure, but rather with its repression. Corbin thus writes, "as banal as it might seem, the excessive fear of la '*vérole*,' formidable obstacle erected against pleasure, ultimately took up where sin left off; and this is what fed the syphilophobia that was so widespread."[5] In underscoring the "dissuasive" character of the SFPSM's literature, however, Corbin presumes that the sexuality targeted by syphilis experts was a coherent entity, a self-evident force to be repressed or blocked.[6] His argument ultimately begs the question of how writings on the venereal peril defined the contours of the male sexuality it sought to discipline. By contrast, in the following chapters, I examine the "productive" character of sexual hygiene. I explore how, in their advice pamphlets and lectures, as well as in their formulation and implementation of hygienic policy, syphilis experts produced understandings of male sexuality and its socialization, rather than simply "repressing" it. Their project, I argue, was based on assumptions about the differences between minority and majority, men and women, savage and civilized. In examining these assumptions, we see how they reconciled their promulgation of marriage and reproduction as a moral and social ideal for the adult citizen, with an ongoing commitment to the regulation of prostitutes, and, as we shall see, certain men. Their policy proposals, in other words, drew significant distinctions between subjects, even as they promoted hygiene as a universal social good. They were, indeed, premised on the medical, and hence, social necessity of those very distinctions.

Medicalized discourses on venereal disease participated in and contributed to contemporary analyses of how best to moralize and socialize men within the secularized framework of republican politics that I have

5. Ibid., 282.
6. Foucault, of course, did not argue that "prohibition is a ruse," but rather that "it is a ruse to make prohibition into the basic and constitutive element from which one would be able to write a history of what has been said concerning sex starting from the modern epoch." Michel Foucault, *The History of Sexuality, Volume I: An Introduction,* trans. Robert Hurley (1980), 12.

been tracing throughout this book. Discussions of men's sexuality, I have been arguing, both expressed and addressed the wider social and political problem of how men, as autonomous, rights-bearing citizens, were related and responsible to society. Sexuality operated, in other words, as a powerful site through which individuals could be articulated to the social order, and not simply as a force to be "repressed." Conceived of as both an individual illness and as a social danger, venereal disease symbolized the connection between the individual and the social body. Debates about prophylaxis, as a result, both revealed and sought to resolve perceived tensions between the rights of male individuals and those of "society." One of the ways in which syphilis experts navigated this problematic was to address themselves to male subjects who were moral and legal "minors," that is, to subjects who had not or not yet acceded to full rights as citizens. In the first decade and a half of their activities, doctors directed their attention to adolescents, soldiers, and colonial subjects. They designed educational propaganda which alerted these populations to the menace of the disease and to the necessity of seeking medical cures in the case of contamination. With the mass mobilization of the World War I, and its attendant medical and moral upheaval, many of the tactics, both pedagogical and practical, developed by venereal hygienists in delimited contexts underwent considerable expansion. And, in the wake of the war's hecatombs, sexual hygiene emerged as a moral principle which lent new meaning to citizenship and the masculine rights and responsibilities it conferred.

While the reform of prostitution clearly constituted an important backdrop for the projects mounted by these hygienic experts, I do not here focus on the history of prostitution per se. I highlight instead how hygienists, regulationists, and abolitionists alike posed the problem of men's sexuality and *its* regulation in new ways. Like the writers discussed in past chapters, they were preoccupied with how social norms and especially those surrounding sexuality, could best be instituted and upheld in a republican context in which pedagogy rather than outright legal repression was the privileged technique of socialization. Similar to Durkheim, they appealed to scientific authority in order to legitimate their claims to institute and explain social and sexual norms. In basing their arguments on hygienic rather than social science, however, they ultimately shifted the terms in which men's sexual regulation was articulated.

7   *Venereal Consciousness and Society*

The Société française de prophylaxie sanitaire et morale (SFPSM)'s programs of administrative and educational reform aimed to defend "society" from the venereal peril through the application of scientific knowledge and hygienic principles. In adopting a social approach to illness, venereal disease experts developed a variable and differentiated strategy in order to battle these maladies. Hygiene, and sexual hygiene in particular, was a flexible science that, while addressing a universal good, inscribed and reproduced differences—between men and women, adults and minors, citizens and subjects—in order to best cure the ills of the nation's population. A gendered system of legal right, in which men had protections that women were frequently denied, shaped their efforts to prevent and treat syphilis. The hygienists' strategies were, at the same time, structured by presumptions about the variable relationship between sexual desire and "consciousness" in men, women, and adolescents. The troubling character of sexual awareness and sexual knowledge was, in fact, at the core of these doctors' speculations and recommendations in the realms of pedagogy, law, and administration.

As men of science, venereal disease experts purported to have a monopoly on "consciousness." They conceived of syphilis and its supposed "carrier," prostitution, as ubiquitous and yet strangely hidden. It was, in turn, their duty to reveal the truth of these dangerous repositories of "ignorance." How could they do this and to whom could they speak? In this chapter, I argue that their epistemology of venereal disease had differential effects. Determinations of who could know about it, and how it could be known, structured their varied approaches to disease prevention and cure. The problematic relationship between sex and knowledge, I argue, animated many of their debates: about the legal right to medical secrecy; the logic of regulation; the sexual education of young men; and the possibility of penalizing disease transmission. In foregrounding questions about sexual knowledge, these doctors imagined subjects as alternately capable or incapable of consciousness. Their policy proposals both reflected and reproduced these presumptions.

The Terrain of Regulation

A majority of the founding members of the SFPSM were influential doctors at major Parisian hospitals, including the prison-hospital for prostitutes in Paris, Saint-Lazare, where two of the league's vice-presidents, Toussaint Barthélemy and Louis Le Pileur, held their posts. Roughly 75 percent of the initial 368 members were doctors, dentists, or pharmacists. Many, like Fournier himself, belonged to the Academy of Medicine. Other notable members were luminaries in the fields of law and administration, as well as politics, such as the Police Prefect of Paris, Louis Lépine and Senator Réné Bérenger, who had long been active promoters of the public regulation of unseemly urban vice.[1] As Alain Corbin has clearly demonstrated, the professional concerns of the SFPSM members, and particularly their close ties to public administration, informed their perspectives on how to preserve men and, in turn, society, from the "venereal peril." Unsurprisingly, a referendum on the principle of regulation, submitted to the SFPSM's 863 members in 1904, returned 410 votes in favor of the "medical surveillance of prostitution," 51 votes against, and 10 abstentions.[2]

As the numerous histories of prostitution in France have shown, the problem of regulating prostitution was not in itself new. Established in Paris under the Consulate by the *arrêt* of 12 Messidor an VIII (1 July 1800), the regulation of prostitution functioned in France, from the 1830s onward, according to a system outlined and streamlined by the Parisian public health expert (also well known for his studies of the city's sewers), A.-J.-H. Parent-Duchâtelet. Within the framework of regulation, women were forced to undergo regular medical examinations for venereal disease in order to legally work as prostitutes. They were obliged to register with the local prefecture of police and could operate either out of an organized bordello (*maison close*), or alternately, as independent agents or *filles en carte*. Women who were arrested as suspected prostitutes could be examined, registered, and imprisoned for treatment without legal review. Despite its tenuous legal basis, regulation as both a social institution and system of public health prevention remained relatively uncontested for nearly half a century.

1. For a list of the SFPSM's founding members, see the *Bulletin de la Société française de la prophylaxie sanitaire et morale* 1 (May 1901): 213–24. Hereafter abbreviated as BSFPSM. And Alain Corbin, "Le péril vénérien au début du siècle: Prophylaxie sanitaire et prophylaxie morale," *Recherches* 11, no. 29 (1977): 256–57.
2. BSFPSM 4 (December 1904): 543.

At the beginning of the Third Republic, however, the widespread tolerance toward what essentially constituted a state-sanctioned public vice became increasingly subject to contestation and vocal critique. The heightened
investment in the state as an agent of moralization brought to the fore the
apparent contradictions of a system which made public officials (namely,
mayors, the police, and the doctors who worked at dispensaries and lock-
hospitals) responsible for preserving a healthy *corps* of prostitutes for the
pleasure and distraction of male citizens. As Émile Zola's *Nana* demonstrated, the proliferation of prostitution was associated in the eyes of many
republicans with the decadence and moral dissipation of the Second Empire. In addition, the vocal and militant British abolitionist movement
founded by Josephine Butler in her crusade against the passage of the Contagious Diseases Acts served as a model for the numerous moral purity
leagues founded in the last decades of the century. Critics increasingly
showed up the inadequacies and patent failures—both moral and sanitary—of regulation. Those physicians who argued in favor of maintaining
official sanitary controls on prostitution rather than banning it outright
were obliged to develop a coherent and cogent response to these charges.[3]
Abolitionists argued that so-called public prophylaxis was a double evil.
In their view, it both promoted men's immorality and violated the republican commitment to individual rights by subjecting women to the arbitrary
power of the vice police or *police des moeurs*. Activists associated with the
cause further contended that, given the contemporary proliferation of clandestine, which is to say, unregulated prostitution, police surveillance was no
longer effective as a hygienic measure. It rather gave immoral men a dangerously false sense of security, while also leaving them free to contaminate
their innocent wives and children. Abolitionists such as feminist Ghenia
Avril de Saint-Croix and Paris Municipal Councilmen Yves Guyot and
Louis Fiaux sought to do away with the "old regime" of regulation by instituting gender-neutral laws that would criminalize public solicitation by
either men or women. From the perspective of the French abolitionists, who
were more secular in orientation than their British counterparts, venereal
disease was first and foremost a matter of men's as well as women's individual responsibility. They contended that a sexual hygiene policy based on
principles of liberty would be more effective than one based on arbitrary
police force. In the words of Fiaux, who, like Fournier, was present at the
1899 international conference in Brussels, "The new medical organization
will, through liberty, cure more of the sick, than the old did by force."[4]

---

3. On the history of regulation and abolitionism in France, see pt. 4, n. 3, above.
4. Louis Fiaux, *L'organisation actuelle de la surveillance médicale de la prostitution est-elle
susceptible d'amélioration* (1899), 121. See also Yves Guyot, *La préfecture de police* (1879);
Yves Guyot, *La prostitution* (1882); Yves Guyot, *La police* (1884). As well as the debates in the

Positioned against such claims, Fournier's account of the social danger of syphilis at the 1899 Brussels conference sought to remake the case for regulation on new grounds. He did so, in part, by showing that those who were most at risk for contracting syphilis, namely male youths, were incapable of self-regulation. They were, in other words, moral and legal minors, who lacked the necessary "experience and reason" to protect themselves. By manipulating his statistics on rates of contagion in his Paris practice, Fournier claimed that youths between the ages of twenty and twenty-three were the highest risk category. In his view, "these are the first years of youth. These are the first years of inexperience, they are (at least for men) *les années folles*. In any case, they in no way correspond, in my conception, to what we might call the age of reason."[5] According to this logic, irresponsible and "unconscious" male youths needed to be protected against the venereal peril by the regulation of prostitution—for their own good, as well as for the good of their future wives and children, which is to say, "society" and "the race."

In answer to the abolitionists' claims regarding the discriminatory operations of the *police des moeurs,* Fournier argued that the regulation of prostitution actually protected innocent women and children. The *régime des moeurs* was, of course, based on the presumption that women who were prostitutes were incapable of self-regulation, and hence undeserving of basic legal protections of their individual rights. Administrative surveillance was symptomatic of women's civic and political disability more generally, and became, for this reason, a prime target for many turn-of-the-century feminists. As Avril de Sainte-Croix proclaimed, "For the majority of men, we do not exist from a civil point of view. Unable to place our ballot in the electoral urns, injustices committed against us have only relative importance."[6] Fournier's vision of "public prophylaxis," indeed, presumed the prostitute's civil irresponsibility. It notably also proclaimed the moral minority of male youth; for, as we have seen, their "unconsciousness" was a linchpin in his defense of the sanitary regulation of prostitutes.

The document announcing the "Goals and Aspirations" of the SFPSM, cited the specific increase in the incidence of syphilis among *men* (13 to 16 out of 100 in Paris) as clear evidence of the inadequacy of current measures of prophylaxis. Beyond menacing these male individuals, venereal disease also endangered "the family, the child, the species, and the nation." The

Bulletin official de la ligue des droits de l'homme 2 (January 1902). And Dr. Ernest Gaucher's report in BSFPSM 2 (May 1902): 219–24.

5. Alfred Fournier, "Danger social de la syphilis," in *Compte rendu des séances,* ed. Conférence internationale pour la prophylaxie de la syphilis et des maladies vénériennes (1899), 40.

6. Ghenia Avril de Sainte-Croix, *Une morale pour les deux sexes* (1900), 15. See also Jill Harsin, *Policing Prostitution in Nineteenth-century Paris* (1985), xix–xx, 324–26.

declaration lamented the "persistence among us" of the "French malady," its capacity "to foil" all efforts taken to combat it. Venereal disease was figured as a kind of flood, in which existing measures were but "insufficient dikes against the ever rising tide of contaminations."[7] The statement, scrupulously avoided attributions of individual responsibility. The fight against syphilis was, instead, a collective battle to be carried out on the part of the social body.

Acting in the name of public service, the SFPSM sought to address a "crowd" of questions, chief among them "the repression of venereal infections and of their great carrier, prostitution." Prostitution was, in their view, contiguous with disease itself, a medically discernible object, a carrier of contagion, which required regulation. Like the feminized "foyer" or insalubrious home in the discourses of the new hygiene experts analyzed by Andrew Aisenberg, prostitution was an entity whose polluting potential was a public health risk to be treated with the aid of medical science. A composite, abstract category given legitimacy by its seeming clinical status, it—like the unwholesome home—conveniently circumvented questions of individual rights and agency.[8] The "sanitary prophylaxis" named in the SFPSM's title, largely targeted this fantasmatic and essentially feminine entity. Men, in their accounts, were victims, not agents of disease, who, because of legal protections on their privacy, could not be subject to hygienic surveillance. By contrast, according to the logic of regulation, women who chose to become prostitutes renounced, by virtue of this decision, the right to normal legal protections, which is to say, judicial review or the doctrine of medical secrecy enshrined in the penal code.

As Raymond Villey's history of medical secrecy in France has shown, venereal disease, and syphilis in particular, was a frequent test case for the extent and limits of the legal enforcement of professional confidentiality established by article 378 of the Napoleonic Penal Code. Writing into law a tenet already well-entrenched in the eighteenth century code of medical ethics and founded upon the Hippocratic Oath, the article was initially composed in order to protect the rights of individual privacy and, in turn, public order. The "public interest" cited by the Conseil d'État in 1810 was less concerned with public hygiene per se than with the integrity of families. By the end of the nineteenth century, according to Villey, jurisprudence regarding medical secrets became much more stringent. While an 1828 deci-

7. BSFPSM 1 (May 1901): 7.
8. For this compelling discussion of the foyer, see Andrew R. Aisenberg, *Contagion: Disease, Government, and the "Social Question" in Nineteenth-century France* (1999), 113–38; Ann-Louise Shapiro, *Housing the Poor of Paris, 1850–1902* (1985). And Andrew R. Aisenberg, "Syphilis and Prostitution: A Regulatory Couplet in Nineteenth-century France," in *Sex, Sin, and Suffering: Venereal Disease and European Society since 1870,* ed. Roger Davidson et al. (2001).

sion by the Cour de cassation had left considerable leeway to individual doctors, an 1885 case made the principle of secrecy "absolute."[9]

By the 1890s, the president of the Society of Legal Medicine and dean of the Paris Faculty of Medicine, Paul Brouardel, called for an inflexible application of the article. "It is in society's interest," he wrote, "that each of its members, even those who are loathsome, be able to demand medical aid, and be sure that he deposits his secret in the breast of a man who will never, under the least pretext, betray his confidence."[10] Brouardel categorically rejected the doctor's right, for example, to inform the fiancée's father (let alone the fiancée herself!) of a future husband's syphilitic condition. In his view, beyond the protection of the individual, "the safeguarding of society" depended on this "medical dogma."[11] Brouardel's text illustrated the anxieties provoked in the medical profession by recent changes in the arena of public health regulation. His absolutist statements need to be taken within a context in which he, as president of the Comité consultatif d'hygiène publique from 1884 to 1904, helped to usher in the obligatory declaration of epidemic diseases as an amendment to an 1892 law regulating the medical profession. In his work as a public hygienist, Brouardel played an important role in reconceiving the relationship between health regulation and private liberty.[12] And yet, even this convinced public hygienist assumed a strict interpretation of professional secrecy in cases concerning syphilis. Defined as "transmissible" and not "epidemic," venereal diseases were notably excluded, along with tuberculosis, from the list of diseases requiring declaration.[13] Public hygienists upheld *men's* right to privacy in these cases as necessary for the health of the social body. As Georges Thibierge, a physician at the Hôpital Broca in Paris, explained, "Professional secrecy, which seems to be designed only to protect the individual interests of syphilitics, is in reality, a safeguard for society, because it removes an obstacle that would prevent numerous syphilitics from seeking treatment."[14] Indeed, even the most radical critics of absolute medical secrecy shied away from legally requiring "prenuptial certificates" of venereal health.[15]

9. Raymond Villey, *Histoire du secret médical* (1986), 59–63, 87–88. See also Paul Brouardel, *Le secret médical*, 2nd ed. (1893), 15; Gustave Lagneau, "Du secret médical relativement aux maladies vénériennes," *Extrait du Bulletin de la Société de médecine légale*, no. 12 (juillet 1869): 5; Lion Murard and Patrick Zylberman, *Hygiène dans la République* (1996), 304.

10. Brouardel, *Le secret médical*, 6.

11. Ibid., 44.

12. On Brouardel: Aisenberg, *Contagion*, 89–94; Murard and Zylberman, *Hygiène*, 198–208, 312–14. On private practitioners' resistance to obligatory declaration, see Aisenberg, *Contagion*, 132–36; Pierre Guillaume, *Le rôle social du médecin depuis deux siècles, 1800–1945* (1996), 96–101; Martha L. Hildreth, *Doctors, Bureaucrats, and Public Health in France, 1888–1902* (1986), 136–42; Shapiro, *Housing the Poor of Paris, 1850–1902*, 149–57.

13. Murard and Zylberman, *Hygiène*, 644 n. 13.

14. Georges Thibierge, *Syphilis et déontologie* (1903), 6.

15. See Henri Cazalis, *La science et le mariage: Étude médicale* (1900); J. Th. Dupuy, *Le dogme du secret médical (essai de réfutation): Étude de médecine légale, d'hygiène sociale et de*

For syphilis experts, the principle of medical secrecy was, where men were concerned, a social good essential to the protection of public health. Regulationists argued, however, that women who were prostitutes did not deserve this protection, because they could not be counted on to seek treatment. They meanwhile defended, again in the name of society, a husband's right and, indeed, "moral duty" to deceive his wife about his syphilitic condition.[16] By appealing to a higher "social" good, regulationists trumped abolitionists' efforts to argue that medical surveillance and forced hospitalization violated women's individual rights, including the protections of medical confidentiality. Notably, when the Ligue des droits de l'homme debated the question of regulation in 1902, it upheld that prostitution, as an "unhealthy profession," should be subject to "measures of surveillance, destined to guarantee the interests of the collectivity, the first of which is public health."[17] Thus, when abolitionists, and especially abolitionist feminists, sought to claim privacy as an "individual right," the basis of that protection shifted from absolute principle to flexible hygienic norm. The social good of public health was, in other words, an adaptable notion that could underwrite variable administrative policies. Regulationists used it both to legitimate the ongoing surveillance of prostitution *and* to defend adult men's rights to privacy. Their educational propaganda aimed at male youth similarly spoke in the name of societal defense.

For Our Sons

The SFPSM initially dedicated itself to developing propaganda directed at the two male populations that, in their view, were particularly susceptible to contamination: students and soldiers. They focused, that is, on male adolescents and youths who, while on the verge of majority, remained legal and moral minors, not yet endowed with their full rights as citizens.[18] We have already seen how "unconscious" and "irresponsible" youth figured promi-

morale professionelle (1903); Charles Valentino, *Le secret professionel en médecine: sa valeur sociale* (1903). For the SFPSM debate "Les Garanties sanitaires du mariage," see BSFPSM 3 (June–July 1903). The debate shifted after the First World War; see Anne Carol, *Histoire de l'eugénisme en France: Les médecins et la procréation, 19ᵉ–20ᵉ siècle* (1996); William H. Schneider, *Quantity and Quality: The Search for Biological Regeneration in Twentieth-century France* (1990).

16. Alfred Fournier, *Syphilis et mariage: Leçons professées à l'Hôpital Saint-Louis* (1880), 180–89. And Jill Harsin, "Syphilis, Wives, and Physicians: Medical Ethics and the Family in Late Nineteenth-century France," *French Historical Studies* 16, no. 1 (1989).

17. *Bulletin official de la Ligue des droits de l'homme* 2 (January 1902): 116.

18. On the similar orientation of the German league, see Andreas Hill, " 'May the Doctor Advise Extramarital Intercourse?': Medical Debates on Sexual Abstinence in Germany, c. 1900," in *Sexual Knowledge, Sexual Science*, ed. Roy Porter et al. (1994), 290–91. And Ann Taylor Allen, "Feminism, Venereal Disease, and the State in Germany, 1890–1918," *Journal of the History of Sexuality* 4, no. 1 (1993).

nently in Fournier's 1899 account of the "social danger of syphilis." And, in its early debates and proposals, the SFPSM addressed contemporary concerns surrounding the socialization of young men who, like Barrès's *déracinés* and Durkheim's bachelors, were no longer constrained by familial authority but not yet ready (or willing) to assume the responsibilities of marriage. Their efforts, like those we have encountered in past chapters, revealed an ambivalence about the family's role in children's (sexual) moralization. In order to justify their intervention into the domestic realm, syphilis experts questioned the efficacy of parental instruction, while speaking in the name of the family itself.

The SFPSM framed their project in universal terms. They suggested that *all* men—and hence, all families—risked venereal infection. In order to mobilize public recognition and support, they insisted on the widespread extent of the menace—even and especially for bourgeois families. Indiscriminate in its selection, syphilis, they claimed, did not have a terrain of predilection. In contrast to tuberculosis, they argued, venereal diseases did not target weak constitutions or unsanitary milieus.[19] In a discussion of prophylactic education in schools, Dr. Toussaint Barthélemy, physician at St. Lazare, the prison-hospital for prostitutes and Secretary-General of the SFPSM, asserted that, "this infection is not influenced, in its nature and barely in its form, by sex, age, social position, and not at all by religion, philosophy, or political opinion." Doctors such as Barthélemy grounded the universality of their mission and message in the egalitarian comportment of the disease itself. They argued that those who appeared to be best protected—by their health, class, and morality—remained prone. Even students of "religious establishments" furnished a "nonnegligible number of victims."[20]

The doctors of the SFPSM appealed to medical expertise in order to justify their interventions. While he questioned "neither the value, nor the utility" of "purely theoretical and moral advice," Barthélemy contended that such counsel alone was an "unreliable rampart" against "natural instincts." Because the peril coincided with men's natural drives, syphilis prevention was a physiological matter proper to the domain of medicine. And, since syphilis was "particularly destructive to the prosperity of households," public health required the intercession of the medical expert for the good of the family and its progeny.[21] The best way for doctors to come to the rescue of male youth, then, was through educational propaganda.

In one of the SFPSM's earliest meetings, Fournier delivered a report on whether "upper-level students should be alerted to the dangers of venereal infections."[22] Given his statistics on the high rates of contamination among

19. On tuberculosis and hygiene: David S. Barnes, *The Making of a Social Disease: Tuberculosis in Nineteenth-century France* (1995), 112–37.
20. BSFPSM 1 (July 1901): 73.
21. Ibid., 73–74.
22. BSFPSM, 1 (June 1901): 42–57.

youths prior to their twentieth birthday, Fournier argued that this education was imperative. The leading syphilis expert of his day, Fournier worked both in a public capacity as head of the syphilis and skin disease clinic at the Hôpital Saint-Louis and as a private physician for a largely bourgeois clientele, whose interests he was surely interested in protecting. In defending public intervention into the intimate affairs of families, Fournier posed as a father and as an ally of fathers. He generously proposed that medical experts like himself might be able to "help out in this safeguarding effort," "to give a parallel support in the good fight" led by parents in this difficult struggle.[23]

Doctors, he suggested, could also replace absent fathers, for example, for students who were "cloistered in *internats*." He asserted the primacy of "paternal instruction," while figuring medical advice as a surrogate, *faute de mieux*. Yet Fournier also claimed that the "scientific lecture" had "a greater impact, was more useful than all the warnings and recommendations which come from the family home." While the student might appear to listen to his father with respect, he would undoubtedly remain "barely affected by paternal sermons, which he will judge to be excessive, exaggerated, stodgy, 'old hat,' to use the current expression." By contrast, an "impersonal and collective instruction," from a "stranger's mouth," a doctor or professor, "speaking in the name of science" and with the aid of "scientific documents," would ultimately have a far greater impact.[24] Clerical defenders of "individual" or "religious" instruction, such as the Abbé Fonssagrives, were notably wary of Fournier's proposed program.[25]

In order to defend this usurpation of parental authority in the name of preserving the family, Fournier signaled the domestic foyer's de facto permeability to external corrupting forces. He played on contemporary concerns surrounding the proliferation of pornography, its greater availability and visibility, as a further argument in favor of the salutary aims of a science-based sex education.[26] Fournier claimed that pornography was like an insidious disease, which threatened the integrity of the happy and healthy home by submitting children's sexuality to a precocious publicity.

23. Ibid., 47.
24. Ibid., 53. See also Dr. P. LeGendre, "Le rôle du médecin scolaire," in *Premier congrès d'hygiène scolaire et de pédagogie physiologique*, ed. Ligue des médecins et des familles pour l'hygiène scolaire (1903), 33.
25. See Joseph (Abbé) Fonssagrives, *Conseils aux parents et aux maîtres sur l'éducation de la pureté* (1902). He presented his views to the SFPSM during the session devoted to "Prophylaxie dans la classe ouvrière," BSFPSM 4 (January 1904): 29.
26. Fournier presented his project as coincident with that of leagues, such as the Société de protestation contre la licence des rues, founded in 1894 and presided by Senateur Réné Bérenger, who was also vice-president of the SFPSM. On the relation between syphilis and pornography see, for example, Réné Blondeau, "Etalages immoraux," BSFPSM 3 (April 1903): 166–72. On pornography, see Carolyn J. Dean, *The Frail Social Body: Pornography, Homosexuality, and Other Fantasies in Interwar France* (2000); Annie Storra-Lemarre, *L'enfer de la Troisième République: Censeurs et pornographes (1881–1914)* (1990).

Hinting at the indecent works "hidden beneath students' desks," Fournier saw the school as an equivocal site of both perverse and edifying instruction. The risk associated with such prior corruption justified his project as a necessary corrective and helped him to draw a significant distinction between the morally upstanding intent and effect of science and the corrosive potential of deviant knowledge circulating undercover. Sex education would not "excite unhealthy curiosities" or "awaken premature sensuous appetites," claimed Fournier, precisely because adolescents were, unfortunately, already in the know. He was eager to dispense with the charge that this proposed lesson would add insult to injury, that it would amount to nothing better than "a licentious, libidinous, pornographic, or even just bawdy and titillating instruction." On the contrary, urged Fournier, it would be based exclusively on "science, hygiene, self-respect and good morals."[27]

With the enthusiastic endorsement of the SFPSM, Fournier composed a brochure based on these principles. His *Pour nos fils quand ils auront 17 ans: Quelques conseils d'un médecin* was posed as a model lecture to high school youth. Of all the brochures authored by the SFPSM, Fournier's was the most widely cited and recognized; it was a template of the genre for decades to come.[28] It is, as a result, illuminating to examine this text in some detail. The tract opened with a description of the dangers associated with the male youth's nascent sexuality. Fournier notably read puberty as a "dawning" of "a number of signs which are the privileges [*apanages*] of an approaching virility," that is, as an indicator of a sort of "right" associated with male adulthood, a status that the seventeen-year-old had not yet achieved. The genital organs "have acquired their grown size; a new function has constituted itself; in parallel, special appetites, needs never before known awaken"—so many signs that "the child has lived and the man has just been born." The sexual orientation of this new desire was assumed to be clear, as Fournier indicated that "woman ha[d] been born" for them. As "a great law of nature," this desire was, for Fournier, inevitable and irrepressible. Indeed, he warned, "do not defend yourself from it, do not accuse or excuse yourself."[29] Heterosexual attraction was normal, while its outright repression, he suggested, might have untoward consequences. The "dangers" which he brought to light were not intrinsic to this seemingly unproblematic natural desire; they were rather external, and largely embodied by prostitution and other temptations of the street.

In making his case, Fournier distinguished his perspective from that of "a moralist, a philosopher, a religious educator," in other words, from other

---

27. BSFPSM 1 (June 1901): 50–51.
28. See, for example, BSFPSM 22 (July 1922): 125–26.
29. The text was published as a supplement in the July issue: BSFPSM 1 (July 1901): i–ii.

LE COURS DE SYPHILIGRAPHIE

L'ÉLÈVE. — Mais non, monsieur, je vous assure que ce n'est pas ça! Moi, je l'ai!!!

Les Avariés

Figure 6. "Course in syphilography." *Assiette au beurre,* 18 March 1905. Typ 915.01.1668F, Department of Printing and Graphic Arts, Houghton Library, Harvard College Library. In this cartoon, a student with two syphilitic cankers on his cheek corrects his professor's lesson on the disease, while his classmates pore over a pornographic picture.

contemporary experts on youthful sexual awakening. Speaking as a doctor, he did not condemn outright the "easily taken step" from "desiring a woman to possessing one." He rather testified to the frequency of this *passage à l'acte*. "One crosses this line with so much impunity and it is then up to medicine to gather the wounded and mend the disasters."[30] In contradistinction to the imagined philosopher or religious moralist, Fournier described the unfortunate consequences of disease as a catastrophe and injury, not as punishment for a fault. Fournier did figure syphilis as a "triple social danger"—to wives, children, and the species—and he outlined how husbands could menace their wives and family. And yet he suggested that the husband's responsibility was not present to itself. For, he explained, "syphilis only presents its bill (if you will excuse the expression) when the once carefree young man has transformed himself into a husband, and father . . . it is most often the husband who pays the debt of the boy."[31] Fournier meanwhile addressed his youthful audience, not as guilty perpetrators, but as vulnerable victims of a ubiquitous "feminine provocation" which targeted them as "easily exploitable prey." This menace was, according to Fournier, omnipresent and brazenly displayed on every street corner both night and day, constantly threatening to corrupt the adolescents' sexual instincts. In this description, nearly all women were suspect. For the *insoumise* was everywhere and yet difficult to detect; she hid her true character behind a seemingly legitimate cover—as a "*pseudo-ouvrière*," actress, shopgirl in a boutique, "set up for a totally different industry."[32]

Regulated prostitutes, despite the supposed guarantees offered by the current system of surveillance were equally menacing. Fournier thus criticized the government for failing to act quickly and decisively to integrate public health reforms proposed by doctors like himself. In the name of public health, Fournier also heaped scorn on abolitionism, "born of English prudery of mystical Protestantism" as no less of a threat to public safety. More in keeping with national character, his proposals were purportedly based on reason-based French science, and not on disease as a divine punishment of "the luxurious flesh." This was, of course, a tendentious and strategic depiction of French abolitionism, which, in fact, made legal, rights-based arguments alongside moral ones. Abolitionists such as Avril de St. Croix indeed insisted that, "we are not dreamers, blind pietists, we are simply people who want liberty and justice for all."[33] Fournier nonetheless urged, "Let's count on the good sense of the French to resist such doctrines, whose

30. Ibid., ii.
31. Ibid., xvii–xviii.
32. Ibid., xxi.
33. Statement cited in Commission extraparlementaire du régime des moeurs, *Procès verbaux des séances* (1909), 62. See also Alain Corbin, *Les filles de noce* (1978); Julia Miller, "The 'Romance of Regulation': The Movement against State-regulated Prostitution in France, 1871–1948" (Ph.D. diss., New York University, 2000).

only result would be the rapid expansion of the venereal peril."[34] Fournier wanted to cleave health from a religious or metaphysical moral vision, in order to configure hygiene as its own ethical imperative and end.

Fournier did recommend sexual continence or "individual prophylaxis" to these students. He did not, however, valorize such self-monitoring as a model of reasoned self-discipline or as a noble combat of the will against unruly sexual instincts. Continence was necessary in order to preserve adolescents, less from a danger lurking within themselves (for, as we have seen, he conceived of heterosexual desire as natural and normal), than from the *external* risks to which they remained ever vulnerable. He wrote, "Let's start by protecting ourselves; this is more worthwhile and sure than to rely on someone else's vigilance to safeguard us." Importantly then, Fournier figured premarital chastity not as a model of moral autonomy, nor, following Durkheim, as a social protection against the excesses of infinite individual desires, but as a pragmatic response to a social threat of disease. While focused on individual comportment, this self-monitoring was not a minimum requirement for entering into a public sphere governed by reason but rather a safeguard against a sociality conceived in terms of an implicitly feminine and feminizing contagious risk. It was a consequence of sociality, not its precondition. Fournier, while cautioning adolescents against external risk, presented their heterosexual desires as unproblematic. This was also true of his account of their duty to seek treatment in case they fell victim to disease.

Fournier had a distinct professional investment in describing syphilis contamination as both blameless and curable. The legitimacy and success of his profession depended on a representation of syphilis as a disease like any other. Before the German researcher Paul Ehrlich's discovery of arsenic as an effective cure in 1909, the only known and medically sanctioned treatment was mercury. The unpleasantness of this prolonged and extremely painful cure, in combination with the social stigma attached to the disease, fueled a sizeable demand for quack treatments. While technically outlawed by the Chevandier law of 30 November 1892 regulating the legal exercise of the medical profession, charlatans remained the bête noire of the specialists, who lobbied for the repression of the louche advertisements crowding the walls of public urinals and who decried their notices in the back pages of popular journals.[35]

Fournier thus rhetorically asked, "What if, one day, your senses lead you to betray your will, and misfortune strikes you, what should you do?"[36]

34. BSFPSM 1 (July 1901): xxiii.
35. BSFPSM 2 (April 1902): 132–35. The Paris prefecture initially refused the SFPSM request in 1904, arguing that the postings, not in themselves "obscene," were protected by the freedom of the press; it ultimately accepted the measure in 1905. See Thierry Lefebvre, "Syphilis et automédication au tournant du siècle," *Revue de l'histoire de la pharmacie*, no. 306 (1995). For examples of the journal advertisements, see publications such as *Le Rire* and *Gil Blas*. On the 1892 law, see Hildreth, *Doctors*, 164–204.
36. BSFPSM1 (July 1901): xxiii.

Avoiding a language of culpability, Fournier represented the will as "betrayed" by the senses and not as, in itself, responsible for the failure. The disease here is an accident, which befalls an unlucky subject. The appropriate response, he urged, was avowal, not shameful silence. Fournier was, in fact, more critical of dissimulation than of the sexual act responsible for the contraction of the disease in the first place. "The bad, the very bad [response], is silence and dissimulation." In order to encourage his audience to speak up in the case of contamination, he warned against the dangers entailed in thinking of syphilis "as a shameful disease . . . whose nature is to remain secret." Fournier instead advised his youthful listeners to divulge the truth of their condition to a proper medical authority. He concluded, "The good move is, and can only be, avowal."[37]

Fournier's tract, which was widely approved by the SFPSM members, clearly catalogued the dangerous effects of syphilis in order to encourage its audience to avoid precocious sexual experiences. But it did so in a way that normalized, naturalized, and universalized heterosexual desire as definitive of manhood. Fournier avoided an overtly punitive account of male sexual desire. He rather criticized the operation of "silence" and shame as dangerous, because uncontrolled and uncontrollable in their effects. In this sense, Fournier can be read as a critic of "repression," which does not mean that his advice pamphlet argued for sexual liberation. It did, however, set forth a distinctly heterosexual model of male sexual desire as in itself normal and healthy *and* for precisely this reason constantly at risk.

A similar attitude toward men's sexual desire was reflected in prolific playwright Eugène Brieux's 1901 social drama, inspired by and dedicated to Fournier, *Les avariés*.[38] Brieux's play tells the story of Georges, who, while having contracted syphilis as a result of a youthful indiscretion, proceeds with a "*beau marriage*," against his doctor's counsel. Disaster predictably ensues. His irresponsibility results in the contamination of his innocent wife, their child, and the child's wet nurse. When informed of the tragedy, Georges's father-in-law, a deputy of the Sarthe, passes into a murderous rage, which the reasonable doctor attempts to calm. Georges, the doctor argues, is to be pitied rather than condemned. Given the frequency of youthful "misadventure," claimed the doctor, his illness had to be seen as a result of bad luck, and not exceptional fault. To make his point, the doctor introduces the deputy to several of his clients, including a father whose "poor son was seduced by one of those women as he was leaving his school." The

37. Ibid., xxiv.
38. Eugène Brieux, *Théâtre complet de Brieux*, vol. 6, *Les avariés; Les hannetons: La petite amie* (1923). For a more extensive discussion of the play, see Claude Quétel, *History of Syphilis*, trans. Judith Braddock et al. (1990), 152–58. On Brieux and social drama more generally, see Jean E. Pedersen, *Legislating the French Family: Feminism, Theater, and Republican Politics, 1870–1920* (2003).

case provides the doctor with an occasion to discourse about the virtues of sex education for youth.

The *real* fault, according to the doctor, lies in the perception of syphilis as a disease, which dare not speak its name. "We must cease treating syphilis as a mysterious ill, whose name one must not pronounce," proclaims the doctor. The skeptical deputy responds, "We cannot very well unveil it to children, in our institutions of schooling. . . . It would be imprudent to awaken curiosity." The doctor promptly disabuses him of this prejudice, convincing him of the patent dangers of keeping the glories of reproductive heterosexuality in the dark. Left to their own devices, these curiosities, which cannot be "smothered," will be satisfied "as they can be, villainously, basely." There is nothing "immoral," urges the doctor, "in the act which perpetuates life by means of love." The true problem, then, is the "gigantic and rigorous conspiracy of silence that is organized around it."[39] Syphilis was, for Brieux's fictional physician, a metonym for the sickness and danger of sexuality when it is kept in the dark, its vulnerability to corruption when it remains in a shadowy zone of non-knowledge and shame. By revealing its truth as healthy and reproductive, the doctor suggests, sexuality will be cleaved from the perverse and perverting forces of mystery, darkness, and disease.

The solution, in his view, is to represent sexuality in the sacred and divine light of science. "The spirit of the young man must be elevated, by protecting [*soustrayant*] these facts from mystery and jokes; pride in the creative power which makes each one of us equal to a god must be awakened in him; he must be made to understand that he is a kind of temple in which the future of the race is elaborated and taught that he must transmit this heritage, of which he is the guardian, this precious heritage which all the tears, misery, and suffering of an interminable line of ancestors has painfully built."[40] The doctor's account of this sacred heritage distinctly recalls Barrès's paean to his "filiation," to the son's mystical devotion to his ancestors, incarnated by "la terre et les morts," and to solidarists' account of social existence as a form of indebtedness to predecessors.[41] Here, however, the son does not just submit himself to his ancestral fathers, but also to the "godlike" power of fatherhood within himself. Reproductive heterosexuality is a source of pride, effectively cleaved from shameful mystery and ridicule. This glorious, reproductive masculinity relies on the revelation of the danger of syphilis as its perverse and devirilized opposite. The production and dissemination of knowledge about syphilis here helped to concretize and define the contours of healthy masculine sexuality.

Impervious to its edifying message, theater censors initially kept Brieux's

---

39. Brieux, *Théâtre*, 90–91.
40. Ibid., 91.
41. See chapters 3 and 6, above.

204 | *Preserving Men*

play in the dark, citing its purported indecency. It was only made public in Paris in 1905 at the Théâtre Antoine, after the SFPSM had been hard at work in its campaign to raise awareness of the dangers of syphilis. In the same year, the long-standing reformer of university education, Louis Liard, who had become vice-rector of the Academy of Paris in 1902, called on the SFPSM to lecture on the venereal peril at the École normale supérieure. Ernest Lavisse, the director of the elite school beginning in 1904, seconded Liard's suggestion. The physician of the École and member of the SFPSM, Dr. Vaquez, had the "honor" of assuming this important responsibility. In Lavisse's estimation, it was the first time that venereal disease had been openly spoken about at the École. And indeed, according to the report in the SFPSM's Bulletin, the purpose of Vaquez's lecture was to promote further efforts to spread the word. The physician urged his audience of future lycée and university professors that "We must no longer have the excuse of ignorance, an ignorance that has been desired up until this day as a result of a false and guilty modesty, when, on the contrary, for the greatest good of humanity, we must not hesitate to reveal the truth, in all its sadness and its hope. For, if the truth is sometimes frightening, science is there to attenuate the ill and cure its victims."[42] Once again, the silence and ignorance associated with "false modesty" were condemned as "guilty," and hence as hazardous for both individual and national health. The "truth" and its ally "science" were, by contrast, sources of salvation. It would appear that the SFPSM successfully relayed its message. Starting in August 1905, a unit on venereal disease was included in the new program for training primary school teachers at the *Écoles normales primaires.*[43]

Civil Responsibility

The social value of health education was an object of consensus among abolitionists and neo-regulationists alike. In their reform proposals presented, for example, to the *Ligue des droits de l'homme,* abolitionists repeatedly endorsed "the real social interest in drawing the public's attention, and especially that of youth, to the dangers that prostitution poses to both sexes and the disastrous consequences of venereal diseases."[44] While seeking to end the administrative regulation of prostitution, they, like the majority of SFPSM members, endorsed sex education, especially for young men, as a part of their efforts to make men sexually responsible. For abolitionist doctor Louis Fiaux, scientific instruction devoted to the risks and dangers of venereal disease would complement the legal prosecution of "intersexual

42. BSFPSM 5 (July 1905): 340.
43. See Fournier's announcement of the reform, BSFPSM 5 (1905): 389–90. And Georges Maurice Debove and Dr. A.-F. Plicque, *Hygiène,* ed. Félix Martel (1906).
44. *Bulletin official de la Ligue des droits de l'homme* 2 (January 1902): 47.

contamination," which he proposed as a replacement for regulation. By giving young men prior warning, argued Fiaux, "they will all understand, from this point on, that the contaminator is responsible for his guilty act."[45] While Fiaux did not condemn sexual profligacy outright, he did make a case for the criminality of "voluntary" contamination, which he denounced as "a shameful, bad, and antisocial action, which must be publicly scorned and punished."[46] Sexual responsibility would hence be founded on a knowledge of the social dangers of syphilis.

Such penalization of willful or negligent transmission of syphilis was also a prominent topic of discussion at the 1902 International Conference on Prophylaxis, held once again in Brussels. Articles criminalizing contamination had been integrated into the Danish penal code in 1866, were adopted in Norway in 1902, and were under debate in Germany.[47] The SFPSM in turn took up the subject in the months following the 1902 conference. The matter, according to Senator René Bérenger, was one of national pride. "Will France," he asked his colleagues, "allow herself to be surpassed by all the European legislation before addressing such serious interests?"[48] Bérenger, a public morality advocate who authored legislation against "*les outrages aux bonnes moeurs*" and fought to establish the *recherche de paternité*, outlined the legal bases for civil and penal responsibility for venereal disease transmission. The principle of civil responsibility was already present in the Civil Code, whose articles 1382 and 1383 covered the infliction of harm and indemnification of negligence.[49] The matter of penal responsibility for disease was, however, more complicated and, in the view of most jurists, would require an amendment to the existing penal code.

Bérenger was well aware of the difficulties raised by this proposed reform, as it pit public health against private right. As he stated in his report, "To authorize the denunciation and pursuit of facts which are of such an intimate and mysterious nature would open private life, turn over the most secret acts to investigation, risk bringing alarm and disturbance into the very heart of the family, there sowing seeds of disunion, hence provoking scandals from which morality will have nothing to gain. It would further authorize bodily examinations, and open the way for all manner of abuses of blackmail. The legislator has sometimes recoiled in the face of such reason-

---

45. Louis Fiaux, *Enseignement populaire de la moralité sexuelle* (1908), 40.
46. Ibid., 8.
47. See Édouard Jeanselme, "Maladies vénériennes," in *Traité d'hygiène: Étiologie et prophylaxie des maladies transmissibles par la peau et les muqueuses externes,* ed. A. Chantemesse et al. (1911), 668–69.
48. BSFPSM 3 (January 1903): 33.
49. They state, respectively: Art. 1382: "Every action of man whatsoever which occasions injury to another, binds him through whose fault it happened to reparation thereof." Art. 1383: "Every one is responsible for the damage of which he is the cause, not only by his own act, but also by his negligence or by his imprudence." In André Cavaillon, *L'armement antivénérien en France: Préface de Prof. Pinard* (1928), 48.

ing." The question, for Bérenger, was whether "the interest of public health, the vigor of the race, and power and rank of the nation in the world" could justify such a clear violation of sexual privacy.[50] A majority of the SFPSM's members were disposed to thinking that it did.

Bérenger was quite zealous in his defense of this principle. He argued that all individuals who transmitted syphilis were de facto criminally responsible, whether or not the infliction of harm was intentional or even conscious. In answer to reservations raised by some of the jurists present, such as V. Mercier, an attorney of the Cour de cassation, Bérenger insisted: "It is vain to seek out a distinction between a willfully sought transmission and one in which contamination is merely a result of imprudence. If the intention to do harm in the latter case is less direct, it nonetheless exists by virtue of the fact that the agent is perfectly aware of the danger that he poses in voluntarily and knowingly completing the act which is its cause."[51] In contrast to the adolescents discussed by Fournier, the unscrupulous men and women targeted by this proposed amendment were figured not as unknowing victims, but as conscious and willful, and hence responsible for infection. Sexual consent was here a metonym for fully intentional action, whether or not that comprised a specific intent to contaminate another person. Youthful sexual indiscretions were, in Fournier's presentation, a sign of the moral irresponsibility of adolescents. Here, by contrast, sexual activity was interpreted as always already conscious and, hence, as intentional. If male youths were victims of their unconsciousness, the targets of this amendment were responsible for their lack of conscience. Bérenger thus argued that "even if contaminations are most frequently unconscious, the author of the contamination doubtlessly has no illusions regarding the almost fatal danger of a sexual encounter. In such cases, the unscrupulous man and the professional prostitute, led by egotism, sensuality, or the desire for lucre, continue to renew relations, while they are fully aware of the contagious character of their infection."[52] Bérenger's case for criminalization relied on this semantic slippage between the purported intentionality of sex acts and criminal intent.

Bérenger urged that new legal measures were necessary, given the public interest at stake. Supporters of the criminalization of transmission multiplied their pleas in favor of protecting public health. Henri Hayem stated, "The system which seems best to me is to always consider syphilitic contamination to be a crime; I believe that the importance of its social conse-

50. BSFPSM 2 (June 1902): 266, 268.
51. BSFPSM 2 (December 1902): 432.
52. Réné Bérenger, "Y a-t-il lieu de créer une responsabilité civile pénale en matière de transmission de la syphilis et des affections vénériennes?" BSFPSM 2 (June 1902): 263. For a detailed discussion of Bérenger, see Annie Storra-Lemarre, La République des faibles: Les origines intellectuelles du droit républicain, 1870–1914 (2005), 55–64.

quences authorizes the legislator to inscribe such an exacting principle in the penal code."[53] Fournier similarly stressed the health issues at stake. "It is a question of preventing those who are dangerous from spreading their horrifying disease all around them with carelessness and impunity; the law is made against those who do not want to listen to any opinion and who are obstinate in playing with the health, life, and happiness of another."[54]

Bérenger foregrounded the purportedly "feminist" intent of the law, namely, the protections it would afford women who risked being infected by careless and negligent men. The strict regulationist Le Pileur argued in favor of Bérenger's proposal along similar lines. Because men could not be forced into treatment, Le Pileur argued, the newly defined crime would remedy the injustices in the current system of prophylaxis. Unlike the abolitionist Fiaux, who hoped to eliminate regulation by instituting a gender-neutral law, Le Pileur saw the amendment as a complement to the sanitary surveillance of women rather than as its replacement. He contrasted voluntary and knowing transmission in men's case to the supposed ignorance of women (i.e., prostitutes). "Parity seems to me to be re-established as much as is possible, because we will give the almost always unconscious propagator, that is to say the woman, mandatory treatment, and we will punish the man who, whatever he says, is always a voluntary transmitter and hence guilty; I would even say a criminal."[55] The illusion of "parity" provided by the criminalization of transmission in Le Pileur's formulation reinforced a distinction between the "unconsciousness" of prostitutes, their incapacity for self-government that the practice of regulation presumed, and the principle of adult men's moral and legal responsibility. While constructing mandatory treatment and criminal prosecution as comparable, Le Pileur actually reinforced the logic underlying men and women's differential treatment.[56]

But could "intentional" sexual activity be collapsed into "criminal intent"? The jurist Mercier was skeptical. He urged that while perhaps voluntary, the sex acts in question did not constitute a "will to do harm"; in his view, "the act is intentional, but not in this manner." The guilty party had "the intention of satisfying either his sensuality or [her] desire for money. He commits a grave and weighty fault, a criminal imprudence. But it is impossible for me to perceive in this fact a voluntary transmission in the sense of penal law."[57] Mercier did, however, uphold the viability of civil cases for irresponsible transmission. Extrapolating from previous trials concerning contaminated wet nurses, Mercier advocated civil penal-

53. BSFPSM 3 (January 1903): 23.
54. Ibid., 40.
55. BSFPSM 3 (February 1903): 108.
56. On the legal treatment of women as purportedly lacking reason, especially in "crimes of passion": Ann-Louise Shapiro, *Breaking the Codes: Female Criminality in Fin-de-siècle Paris* (1996). See also Edward Berenson, *The Trial of Madame Caillaux* (1992); Ruth Harris, *Murders and Madness: Medicine, Law, and Society in the Fin-de-siècle* (1989).
57. BSFPSM 2 (December 1902): 435.

ties—indemnification in accordance with articles 1382 and 1383 of the Civil Code—rather than criminal ones. The prosecution of such cases would not require any amendments to the code. Based solely on the fact of injury caused to another, the principle of civic responsibility did not require proof of intentionality. Article 1383, in particular, stated that individuals were civilly responsible for an injury caused not only by an "action [*son fait*]," "but also out of negligence or imprudence." These articles had already been applied in a number of cases regarding the responsibility of parents, the State, and doctors, in the contamination of wet nurses by infected infants. Members of the SFPSM wholeheartedly supported the application of these articles to cases of sexual transmission.

During the very months devoted by the SFPSM to these discussions of individual legal responsibility for the transmission of syphilis, the Parisian lawyer Louis Schmoll helped to mount a case against a certain bachelor A. In this civil trial, the accused was charged with contaminating a minor C., apparently seduced, infected, and abandoned—with child on the way.[58] C.'s case was based on a series of letters and a medical certificate attesting to her virginity prior to the liaison with A. The correspondence showed that A., when informed of C.'s malady in June 1901, expressed "neither surprise nor indignation." From the months of July through December, he continued their relationship and "lived conjugally with her." He promptly abandoned her upon being informed of her pregnancy, apparently on account of alternate marriage plans. The charge of contamination thus carried behind it an implicit accusation of paternity. However, while coming under increasing attack, the Civil Code's ban on the *recherche de paternité* remained in place in 1903.[59] The court found in favor of the victim on the count of contamination alone, ordering A. to pay damages amounting to 12,000 francs. The scenario of seduction and abandonment doubtlessly lent C. a great deal of sympathy.[60] A., however, was ostensibly not on trial for this reason. The sole charge under consideration was his negligence in transmitting syphilis.

The 29 January 1903 verdict pronounced by the civil tribunal of the Seine was to some extent a landmark. Cases regarding the syphilitic contamination of wet nurses had been prosecuted since 1867, but this was the first time that a court granted indemnification in a case involving the "direct contamination from one person to another" (i.e., via sexual relations rather than a diseased infant). The Paris appellate court confirmed the lower

58. Tribunal Civil de la Seine, "Syphilis," *Gazette des Tribunaux* 78, no. 23426 (1903). And Cours d'appel et tribunaux, "Paris, 12 janvier 1904: Responsabilité, Maladie contagieuse," *Dalloz jurisprudence générale* (1904): 157–58. Schmoll presented the tribunal's verdict during the concluding discussions on the *délit*: BSFPSM 3 (February 1903): 111–14.

59. On the *recherche de paternité*, see Véronique Antomarchi, *Politique et famille sous la Troisième République, 1870–1914* (2000); Rachel Fuchs, "Seduction, Paternity, and the Law in Fin-de-siècle France," *Journal of Modern History* 72, no. 4 (2000); Pedersen, *Legislating the French Family*.

60. On how such melodramatic scripts favored wronged women, see Shapiro, *Breaking the Codes*, 136–78.

court's judgment in 1904.[61] The legal justification of A.'s conviction was analogous to that applied to parents who had put infected infants out to nurse. Wet nursing had, notably, been the subject of one of the Third Republic's initial pieces of social hygienic legislation, Senator Théophile Roussel's 1874 Loi sur la protection des enfants du premier âge. The law required parents to register with the municipal authorities and subjected wet nurses' homes to inspection by the sanitary police—not unlike that required for prostitutes.[62] The law established a framework for considering negligence as a public health risk. In this case, the concept of hygienic imprudence was applied to situations beyond that of wet-nursing.

The court denied A.'s claim that "the communication of any disease, whether venereal or otherwise, cannot be considered as an intentional fault." Following the logic inscribed in article 1383, they instead found that "the transmission of a contagious disease constitutes a fault, even when it does not take place intentionally, and is caused by the imprudence or negligence of the person who is infected." In his defense, A. argued that he was being unjustly criminalized for his sexual behavior, while that of the plaintiff had been forgiven. He sought to undermine C.'s character (and hence right to reparation) by asserting that her demand "should not be valid because it was caused by the minor's immoral act." The court refused the charge, responding that her demand "was not based on the immoral act that she committed." Hygiene, they claimed, and *not* sexual morality, was at issue. The reparations would compensate the "odious fault committed by the defendant who was not afraid to transmit the terrible disease with which he was infected to a sixteen-year-old child, for whom, it appears, he was the first lover."[63] The rhetoric employed in the decision ("odious fault," "terrible disease," "sixteen year-old child") clearly indicates a moral indictment. And the sum of 12,000 francs was a severe punishment indeed. Given the circumstances of seduction and abandonment involved in the case, it is probable that the court sought to censure A. for his egregious conduct. But it was the principle of hygienic imprudence that made it possible to charge him with responsibility for his sexual act.

The fault of negligent transmission was applied in other cases regarding sexual partners—even when two consenting adults were involved. A year later, in Rouen, a civil tribunal awarded a dame P., infected by her long-time partner F., the same sum of 12,000 francs. As in the previous instance, letters exchanged between the couple provided the bulk of the plaintiff's evi-

61. Cours d'appel et tribunaux, "Paris, 12 janvier 1904: Responsabilité, Maladie contagieuse," 157–59.
62. On this connection, see Sylvia Schafer, *Children in Moral Danger and the Problem of Government in Third Republic France* (1997), 61–64. See also George D. Sussman, *Selling Mothers' Milk: The Wet-Nursing Business in France, 1715–1914* (1982). The SFPSM devoted extensive discussions to the topic and eventually recommended that fathers be submitted to sanitary surveillance before putting their children out to wet nurse: BSFPSM 5 (December 1905): 480–81. The measure was met with significant resistance: BSFPSM 6 (January 1906): 60–69. See also Jeanselme, "Maladies vénériennes," 671–77.
63. Tribunal Civil de la Seine, "Syphilis," 106.

dence. In order to mount a successful case, P. was obliged to prove, in the court's words, "that the plaintiff had relations which could lead to contamination with her adversary and that, at the moment at which these relations took place, the latter was infected and knew or could have known himself to be liable to transmit the contagion." P. was in possession of correspondence in which F. admitted to suffering from a certain disease and to undergoing repeated and harrowing treatments. Once informed of his lover's contamination, F. alluded, in his letters, to his probable guilt. Based upon the weight of this evidence, the court decided in P.'s favor. "The propagation of the disease, presupposing the conscious participation of the infected agent in the act destined to transmit it, and from which he could have abstained, appears, in the eyes of the law, as the consequence of a sufficient intent to harm to render him responsible."[64] F.'s responsibility was determined by the voluntary character of his act, his "conscious participation." In other words, the intentionality of the sexual act was equated with a will to inflict harm.

These cases show how social hygienic principles could open the way to legal instruction into adult men's private sexual conduct. Yet they also reveal why, despite their legal viability, such trials, in fact, remained few and far between. Most notably, it was up to the contaminated party (i.e., the woman) to initiate the procedure. Involving *unions libres* and not married couples (for married women instead pursued divorce proceedings), these women were obliged to submit their sexual pasts to public scrutiny in order to prove their charges. They were held to strict rules of evidence and had to furnish concrete proof, especially in the form of letters, that their former partners were aware that they had the disease. Because of rules regarding medical secrecy, they could not force doctors to testify. Male bachelors who risked being brought to trial benefited from the social pressures operating against women who might publicly expose themselves in this way. What is more, if the plaintiff failed to prove her case, she would be responsible for the costs of the trial and would even risk a countersuit.[65] While theoretically establishing, in the words of Le Pileur, a measure of "parity" between men and women by making men legally responsible for their negligent sexual behavior, these cases demonstrate the practical, social limits on this liberal principle of civil responsibility. By advocating for the *délit* of transmission, the SFPSM figured adult men as ideally capable, and indeed, legally required to be sexually self-knowing and hence responsible. In practice, however, legal sanctions were rarely applied to men's sexual indiscretions.

The venereal disease experts of the SFPSM conceived of syphilis and prostitution as repositories of dangerous ignorance from which society

64. Cours d'appel et tribunaux, "Rouen, 25 novembre 1905: Responsabilité, maladie contagieuse," *Dalloz jurisprudence générale* (1906): 55–56.
65. Jeanselme, "Maladies vénériennes," 667.

needed to be protected. Their own legitimacy, their right, that is, to speak in the name of an unconscious and at risk social body, depended on this invocation of disease as an expression of ignorance. The "unconsciousness" of the social body in the face of this peril appeared in a number of different guises, marked, in each case by assumptions about both gender and class: innocent bourgeois wives contaminated by irresponsible husbands, unknowing adolescents seduced by "the pleasures of the street," young girls seduced by careless bachelors. The SFPSM's pedagogical strategy focused on the adolescent because he could be imagined as at once ignorant and yet also capable of consciousness and agency; he was situated on the border between the ignorant social body, deserving of protection and solicitude, and the adult male citizen, whose individual rights were premised on a capacity for self-control. The social body as a whole stood to gain from this project of sexual enlightenment.

While arguing over the legitimacy of police surveillance of prostitution, abolitionists and regulationists agreed that young men could learn to be sexually responsible. Their pedagogical endeavor was premised on an imagined distinction between the unknowing adolescent and the ideally knowing adult man. Male minors, they contended, were not so much irresponsible as "unconscious," or, at least, they were irresponsible because they were ignorant. Doctors and jurists, meanwhile, imagined adult men as capable of exercising requisite caution and self-control. This claim founded both their defense of men's right to medical secrecy and their advocacy of civil responsibility. Only secrecy, they urged, would guarantee that men would avow their disease and seek proper, rather than illicit, treatment. Because it allowed for the public scrutiny of men's sexual privacy, the prosecution of men as civilly responsible for disease transmission appeared to work in the opposite direction. But it, too, assumed adult men's "consciousness." Adult men were legally accountable, precisely because they were presumed to be responsible individuals. For the reasons suggested above, men were rarely prosecuted in practice. The SFPSM's advocacy of the principle of civil responsibility upheld the crucial distinction between men's minority and majority on which their reformist efforts were based. In revealing the dangers of syphilis to unknowing male youth, they proposed to found a healthy reproductive masculinity, cleaved from the perversities of ignorance. The ideally responsible adult man provided their pedagogical project with a guiding norm that, frequently, was observed in the breach.

8   Hygienic Citizens

If male adolescents could be considered sexually irresponsible and adult men as sexually responsible, in theory, if not in practice, "soldiers" occupied an intermediate realm between "adult" and "minor." While technically adult in terms of age, the soldier was a legal minor, liberated from his family, but still in tutelage to the state; he was barred from voting, and subject to limitations on his individual rights, including that to marry, while serving under the national flag.[1] Conscripts were, in the words of one retired army doctor, "intellectually and socially minor; and as such, need to be protected."[2] Recently emancipated from their families, these young men were eager to test their newly found freedom. As Dr. Brissaud, a hospital physician in Paris and member of the SFPSM, explained, "In fact, the incorporation date is also that of the true emancipation of youth. They leave their homes and families in order to begin, the very next day, a new existence whose necessary discipline only exalts their appetite for independence during their moments of leisure. Of all the ways in which this independence claims to affirm itself, the one which seems to respond to the natural exigencies of the [sexual] function is and will always be the 'choice method.' "[3] Brissaud suggested that this explosion of sexual activity among soldiers was a perverse expression of soldiers' limited liberty. It was thus tied to a wider set of questions regarding the rigor of military discipline and its potentially adverse consequences.

Similar to adolescents, soldiers were liminal subjects who posed an analogous, although not identical, regulatory dilemma. Military officers and

---

1. On restrictions on political rights, see Jean Paul Charnay, *Société militaire et suffrage politique en France depuis 1789* (1964); David B. Ralston, *The Army of the Republic: The Place of the Military in the Political Evolution of France, 1871–1914* (1967), 64–65.
2. BSFPSM 2 (March 1902): 102.
3. BSFPSM 1 (May 1901): 30.

doctors, as Brissaud's comment intimates, conceived of soldiers' heterosexual desire as simultaneously normal and problematic. The health and discipline of the army depended on the proper management of these supposedly normal, but potentially unruly desires. The very structure of military life, however, made this disciplinary task difficult. For, in the eyes of hygienists and moralists alike, the army exacerbated this sexual predicament by uprooting young men, taking them away from their families and villages, and isolating them in a community of other young men. Philosopher Alfred Fouillée thus commented on the soldier's ambivalent character in a work evaluating France from "a moral point of view." In his estimation, "A crowd of youths returns today from their regiments more debauched and drunk, with a taste for city life and disdain for the country. They have a greater spirit of independence and indiscipline, and universal incredulity. Physically, they bring back all sorts of diseases which end up weighing on entire generations. They have passed their youth in a relative laziness or doing unproductive labor, often mechanical and without initiative." He thus concluded, "It is not enough to organize universal military service to morally transform a people."[4] In the past, the potentially degrading effects of military life were concentrated and contained by the professional army. With universal conscription, soldiers' demoralization affected (and in the case of venereal disease, infected) the social body as a whole.

This chapter explores both how venereal disease experts and military hygienists posed conscripts' sexual desires as a problem and how, with a variety of seemingly contradictory strategies, they endeavored to address the apparent conflict between army life and sexual health. In particular, I explore how, because of their status as minors, soldiers could be and were subject to hygienic and disciplinary measures that were unthinkable in the case of either civilians or, in many cases, officers. The army thus provided a kind of experimental space, where new pedagogical and hygienic tactics were explored and implemented. If this held true for the metropolitan army, it was even more so for the colonial army and especially for its indigenous troops. The legal status of colonial soldiers and spaces allowed military hygienists even more room to explore the limits of their hygienic imaginations. The mass mobilization of the Great War, I suggest, operated a similar expansion. In the wake of the war, venereal disease experts extended the framework of these at once pedagogical and practical prophylactic strategies beyond the military, to society as a whole. In sketching out this narrative, I trace the emergence of a citizen whose moral and social duty was defined in explicitly hygienic terms. Hygiene here meant not just individual health, but the present and future of the nation. Moralists and hygienists alike defined the rights and responsibilities of this "hygienic citizen" as an

4. Alfred Fouillée, *La France au point de vue moral* (1900), 293.

injunction to marriage and reproduction. They hence took care to guarantee that citizen's health.[5]

Military Preservation

With the passage of the 1872 law instituting obligatory individual service, the effects of conscription on the nation's youth emerged as a widespread source of concern. Politicians and public figures upheld military service as an exemplary school of virility, a veritable crucible of republican citizenship, but also criticized it as a potential source of demoralization. This questioning escalated as the number of soldiers serving under the national flag increased after the passage of the 1889 military conscription bill, which generalized three-year service and reduced (without entirely eliminating) the exceptions that remained present in the 1872 law. And, while the 1889 law brought about an overall reduction in the number of years each conscript served, medical experts continued to discuss the potentially deleterious effects of service on the nation's youth.[6] In 1890, Gustave Lagneau, in a paper presented before the Académie des sciences morales et politiques, went so far as to figure the army as a veritable cause of degeneration and depopulation. "Obligatory military celibacy," he wrote, "is too often followed by a voluntary bachelorhood which is more or less prolonged; it causes not only prostitution and its morbid dangers, and illegitimate births, which, given the high mortality rate of illegitimate children, little profits population growth, but, in postponing marriage, seems to make it less fecund."[7] These anxieties about the moral and hygienic effects of military service persisted. And, especially in the wake of the Dreyfus Affair, politicians and social critics focused new energies on the army as an object and agent of moral reform.

Military medicine had, of course, long been concerned about venereal disease.[8] The infamous British Contagious Disease Acts were enacted as a measure of military hygiene in port and garrison towns; their extension to virtually the entire British Empire was made in the name of protecting soldiers, even if that was not the only logic subtending this policy of regulated

5. The idea of the "hygienic citizen" might be seen to correspond to Pierre Rosanvallon's account of the "hygienic state." See Pierre Rosanvallon, *L'état en France de 1789 à nos jours* (1990), 128–34.

6. On soldiers and conscription, see Odile Roynette, *"Bons pour le service": L'expérience de la caserne en France à la fin du XIXᵉ siècle* (2000); Eugen Weber, *Peasants into Frenchmen: The Modernization of Rural France, 1870–1914* (1976), 292–302. On the 1889 bill, see Annie Crépin, *La conscription en débat: Le triple apprentissage de la nation, de la citoyenneté, de la République: 1789–1889* (1998); Ralston, *The Army of the Republic.*

7. Gustave Lagneau, *Remarques démographiques sur le célibat en France* (1885), 44.

8. Philippe Avon, "Contribution à l'histoire des maladies vénériennes dans l'armée française—Prophylaxie et traitement" (Docteur en médecine, 1968); Louis Fiaux, *L'armée et la police des moeurs: La biologie sexuelle du soldat* (1917).

prostitution.[9] In France, the military placed pressure on garrison towns to establish houses of prostitution, and quickly exported its system of sanitary surveillance to imperial holdings; regulated brothels were, for example, set up in Algeria nearly immediately after its colonization.[10] In America, the urgency of keeping soldiers "fit to fight," made the army a primary locale for the discussion and enactment of new tactics of venereal prophylaxis.[11] In France and elsewhere, the health and welfare of the army was a privileged front in the battle against the venereal peril; the preservation of soldiers' health epitomized how national strength depended on effective measures of prevention and cure.

In order to justify their adherence to the doctrine of regulated prostitution, French military doctors made frequent reference to the extremely high rates of contamination in the army in Britain, where, since the abolition of the Contagious Diseases Acts, prostitution was unregulated.[12] Given France's increasing military competition with Germany, its ongoing imperial ambitions, and pervasive anxieties about population decline and waning national strength, hygienists insisted that there was still room for improvement. Beyond advocating a rigorous policy of surveillance, army doctors regularly reported the names of prostitutes who were purportedly responsible for infecting soldiers to local authorities. Because the military did not officially oversee the policing of prostitution, it began to concentrate directly on the sexual hygiene of soldiers. The reforms proposed by military physicians aimed to expand and regularize the inspection, education, and treatment of venereal disease among conscripts. Official policy toward venereal prophylaxis was shaped by contemporary ideas about the role of the nation's army; it sought to balance conceptions of the military as, on the one hand, an agent of national defense and, on the other, a crucible of republican citizenship. Coming in the wake of the Dreyfus Affair and subsequent efforts to republicanize and democratize the army, the proper equilibrium between these two exigencies was a highly charged question.

Military doctors were generally supportive of efforts to moralize soldiers. At the same time, as Médecin-principal Moty proclaimed in one meeting of the SFPSM, "Neither noble sentiments, nor elevated moral principles can

9. See Mark Harrison, "The British Army and the Problem of Venereal Disease in France and Egypt during the First World War," *Medical History* 39 (1995); Philippa Levine, *Prostitution, Race, and Politics: Policing Venereal Disease in the British Empire* (2003); Judith Walkowitz, *Prostitution and Victorian Society: Women, Class, and the State* (1982).

10. See Fiaux, *L'armée*; B. Joyeux, *Le péril vénérien et la prostitution à Hanoi* (1930); Christelle Taraud, *La prostitution coloniale* (2003).

11. Allan M. Brandt, *No Magic Bullet: A Social History of Venereal Disease in the United States since 1880* (1987).

12. See, for example, the report to the Academy of Medicine in 1895: O. Commenge, *Les maladies vénériennes dans les armées anglaise, française et russe* (1895). And a report to the Commission d'études des questions relatives à la prophylaxie de la syphilis et des maladies vénériennes by M. le médecin inspecteur Dieu, *Rapport sur l'evolution et la prophylaxie des maladies vénériennes dans l'armée française*, ed. Ministère de l'intérieur et des cultes (1903), 6.

overcome the law which imposes on every human being the weight of a sex; despite the most persistent efforts, the will, in battle with inexorable nature, often breaks at the very moment when a fall is most dangerous."[13] In other words, if moral instruction was indeed necessary, so was practical education, given that such failures of the will were inevitable. In his 1901 report, the retired Médecin-Major Charles Burlureaux argued that, in the army, "inexperience" and not "misbehavior" was the primary cause of the high rates of syphilis infection, an ignorance that was exacerbated by soldiers' misapprehension of the seriousness of the disease.[14] For Burlureaux, hygiene instruction served an explicitly productive and regulatory function by combating soldiers' reluctance to disclose their infections. He denounced the public and promiscuous character of the routine health check-ups performed on conscripts, arguing that individualized health inspections would encourage patients to come to their medical visits "without fearing that their troubles would be divulged, knowing that their secret would be kept as much as possible."[15] Education, when combined with guarantees on secrecy, would produce avowal and bring hidden cases to light. In keeping with this logic, Burlureaux urged that punishment for infection (such as deprivation of leave) would be counterproductive, but also that knowing dissimulation should be duly reprimanded. Once educated, soldiers would no longer be able to feign ignorance.

Burlureaux's recommendations were met with praise on the part of medical authorities in the military, such as Paul Chauvel, the Directeur du service de santé du gouvernement militaire de Paris, and Dr. Vallin, a Médecin-inspecteur in the army. They, too, stressed the need to reform the current mode of routine health exams. Vallin denounced the existing procedures as both ineffective and degrading. "It is at once illusory and inconvenient; it represents the most intolerable violation of medical secrecy, and one cannot protest enough against such ways of proceeding."[16] By reinforcing medical secrecy, these doctors sought to provoke confession and to enhance the effectiveness of medical surveillance in the army.

A debate on the subject of medical secrecy in the Société de médecine militaire française made abundantly clear that the military physician had an ambivalent ethical relationship to his patient, torn between his responsibility to the individual soldier and his duty to the nation. As First-class Médecin-Major J. Simonin's report on the question made clear, military doctors believed absolute secrecy within the communal and disciplinary

13. BSFPSM 1 (November 1901): 162.
14. BSFPSM 1 (October 1901): 105.
15. Ibid., 110. On the advantages of these reforms, see Fiaux, *L'armée*, 184–85.
16. Vallin described the procedure as follows: "Because it had to go fast, this is how it was done in the past and sometimes even now. The men stand at the foot of their beds, in their room, sometimes an entire squadron around in a circle; sometimes the examination takes place before they take their showers; the man opens his pants, uncovers the glans, presses the urethra, the doctor takes a look and passes to the next." BSFPSM 1 (October 1901): 138.

Figure 7. "Mars and Venus." *Le Rire,* 16 January 1904. President and Fellows of Harvard College: from HOLLIS #008654106. This cartoon ridicules contemporary concerns about rates of syphilis in the army; the images illustrate a speech given by Senator Alcide Treille. It reads: "Sirs, there are subjects that one must approach as discreetly as possible. But there are also certain sores that are spread throughout the medical statistics of the army. In the service to Venus that soldiers sometimes carry out, one receives injuries of a diverse sort. . . . We observe, nonetheless with satisfaction that, for twenty years, the number of these infections have not stopped declining. They remain however quite numerous. The army of Algeria and Tunisia hold the prize, the bad prize. But the entirety of the 19th corps is still below that of an elite corps that I hesitate to mention here today: the republican guard of Paris. These guards, employed in the surveillance of bals-musettes and sidewalk hetaires, allow themselves to be seduced. This costs them dearly, as one out of ten men is injured. Firemen come right afterwards. It is not extraordinary that they should get their fingers a bit burnt. They are nonetheless affected in the proportion of 50 p. 1,000, while in the republican guard it is 102.4 p. 1,000. Well, Minister, I believe that it would be good for all these youths that we teach them to look twice before according their confidence." For the official transcript, see *Journal Officiel: Sénat; Débats* (23 December 1903): 390.

context of the army to be impossible.[17] The decision to enhance medical secrecy in the military was, as a result, conceived of not as a matter of individual right, but as a tactic of venereal hygiene.

The "private" medical exam was a strategy designed to produce soldiers'
voluntary compliance with the army's stepped-up efforts to fight the spread
of syphilis. Military doctors defended medical secrecy, not as a principle of
individual right, but as an effective method of social preservation. They argued that, when coupled with educational efforts designed to dispel conceptions of venereal disease as "shameful," secrecy would give soldiers the
"confidence and courage to reveal, at the outset, a venereal infection to the
doctor, to seek out treatment and cure."[18] The double strategy was theoretically somewhat contradictory. For, why would soldiers need to keep their
disease private if there was nothing shameful about their condition? On a
practical level, however, these two approaches aimed to encourage avowal
and facilitate treatment. They also dovetailed well with contemporary efforts to reform and "republicanize" the army in the wake of the Dreyfus
Affair.

The military's centralized and hierarchical structure facilitated reformist
measures, at least on paper. Pragmatic exigencies lessened the weight of
moral objections to the implementation of practical prophylactic policy. So,
while the SFPSM's efforts to institute sexual hygiene courses in high schools
met with scattered and at best lukewarm success, its proposals were immediately undertaken in the army. The doctors' recommendations for lectures
and the distribution of detailed hygiene tracts, "truly individual and private" health exams, and more confidential health records, were dispatched
to the Minister of War in December 1901.[19] These suggestions were extremely timely. President Waldeck-Rousseau, head of the government of
"défense républicaine," had initiated a significant post–Dreyfus Affair re-
structuring of the army by appointing the adamantly anticlerical republican
General André as minister of war in June 1900.

Once in power, André assumed the task of "republicanizing" the army.
In a series of reforms, which reflected the solidarist ideology of the day, he
sought to make the army into a school of social responsibility. Influenced by
the writings of Hubert Lyautey, he upheld a vision of the "social role of the
officer" and, between 1901 and 1904, instituted lectures for soldiers on a
range of subjects—hygiene, history, agriculture, civics and morals—in an
effort to "prepare the citizen-soldier for social life." The army, in André's
vision, needed to approach, in spirit, the system of schooling instituted by

17. Société de médecine militaire française, *Bulletin bi-mensuel* 2 (April 1908): 244. Hereafter cited as BSMMF. See also Francis Convers, "Le secret médical dans les lois modernes récentes: Le secret médical dans l'armée" (1913); L. Plisson, *Le secret médical dans l'armée*
(1908).

18. Comment by M. Dejouany, médecin-major de 2e classe, Vincennes, in BSMMF 2
(March 1908): 168.

19. BSFPSM 1 (December 1901): 190–91.

Jules Ferry. The resulting educational efforts were combined with measures to ameliorate soldiers' living conditions and to lend the army a greater role in social integration. For example, in order to fight alcoholism and prostitution and to provide soldiers with wholesome forms of distraction and entertainment, barracks were outfitted with reading and game rooms. Established with the help of the *Ligue de l'enseignement,* newly founded "*foyers du soldat*" gave recruits a "home away from home."[20]

Given this context, it is easy to understand the new Ministry's favorable response to the SFPSM's proposed reforms which, as we have seen, emphasized education and voluntary compliance as crucial strategies in the fight against syphilis. A circular published by the Minister of War on 7 April 1902 cited the work of the association and adopted its suggestions in their entirety. It called for: the education of officers, noncommissioned officers, and soldiers; "individual" monthly health exams in which men were to be examined "separately and in isolation"; "discreet" health exams in order to shield NCOs from their subordinates; a special register for venereal disease cases which would protect against indiscretion; a ban on all punitive measures, save those reserved for cases of dissimulation. Coercive measures vis-à-vis suspected prostitutes were also maintained. Soldiers were in the meantime given regular warnings about known "foyers of contamination."[21] These hygienic measures remained standard procedure, at least on paper, even after the *l'affaire des fiches* scandal revealed General André's unorthodox efforts to place "republican" officers in leadership positions. Framed in a republican language of "education" and "individual rights," the new sanitary tactics, recommended by the SFPSM and adopted by the army, illustrated the regulatory function of this "individualization." The complex and productive dynamic between "enlightenment" and "secrecy" enacted by this reform served explicitly disciplinary ends.

Civilian Liberties

The SFPSM unanimously supported these reforms of army venereal hygiene procedures. They soon passed to the next, closely related item on their

20. For a discussion of the reforms, see Raoul Girardet, *La société militaire de 1815 à nos jours* (1998), 193–221; André J. Lambelet, "A Reluctant Reconciliation: Army Officers, Conscription, and Democratic Citizenship in the French Third Republic, 1870–1940" (Ph.D. diss., University of California, Berkeley, 2001), 90–154; Douglas Porch, *The March to the Marne: The French Army, 1871–1914* (1981), 124–26; William Serman, *Les officiers français dans la nation, 1848–1914* (1982), 78–84. On Lyautey's critique of blind military discipline and his "socializing" vision of the army, see Paul Rabinow, *French Modern: Norms and Forms of the Social Environment* (1989), 104–25. On the "*maisons du soldat*," see Dr. Granjux: "Prophylaxie morale de la syphilis dans l'armée," BSFPSM 2 (December 1902): 7–16; "Prophylaxie de la syphilis dans l'armée, 1910–1911," BSFPSM 11 (April 1911): 76–85; "Prophylaxie des maladies vénériennes dans l'armée," BSFPSM 17 (April 1917): 1–3. See also Fiaux, *L'armée,* 194–96.

21. Circular reproduced in Dieu, *Rapport sur l'evolution et la prophylaxie des maladies vénériennes dans l'armée française.*

agenda—"the venereal peril in the navy." The discussions provoked by the retired navy doctor Paul Petit's report on the subject were far more contentious than those surrounding the army reforms. In his recommendations to the SFPSM, Petit crossed a boundary that had been left intact by army doctors—that between soldiers or sailors and civilians. His proposal to extend mandatory health examinations to adult male naval workers effectively assimilated citizens to sailors, who, as we have seen, remained "minor" in relation to the law. The heated debate that ensued weighed the sanctity of adult men's individual rights against potential limitations on those rights, given the national health concerns at stake. In constructing their arguments for and against the forcible examination and treatment of civilian workers, both sides purported to defend the welfare of families, that is, the women and children who risked infection at the hands of men. Hygienists in both camps thus cast civilian men's individual rights, not as fixed principles, but as contingent on a social good embodied by the health of the family.

Petit's proposal was in part motivated by the fact that the navy had already adopted significant measures to fight the spread of venereal disease. Starting in 1888, sailors had to pass medical examinations prior to obtaining permission to go ashore. If the ship's doctor detected any trace of infection, the sailor was ordered either to remain aboard or was immediately hospitalized for treatment. According to Petit, the forced confinement of sick marines was not intended as "punitive." Rather, he urged, "they are, in everyone's eyes . . . not guilty, but sick men who deserve pity and counsel."[22] Instruction supplemented this exacting medical surveillance. Living quarters featured prominent posters which warned sailors of the dangers of disease and provided detailed practical advice on how to avoid them—signs to look out for on a prostitute's body, condoms, pomades, washing, etc.[23] In Petit's view, the navy already provided adequate prophylaxis for its recruits. Any effort to further reduce rates of contamination would have to concentrate elsewhere—on the regulation of prostitution and, most notably for our present discussion, on the male civilian population in port towns.

Petit's analysis relied on the findings of another navy expert, R. Legrand, who had conducted a study of the rates of infection among civilian naval workers in cities such as Toulon and Rochefort. Legrand decried the injustice heaped upon sailors, who, while subjected to rigorous hygienic discipline, continued to be scapegoated as agents of infection. By contrast, he claimed, "the civilian is entirely free to contract venereal infections whenever and as many times as he wants." While the infected sailor was immediately consigned to treatment, "the civilian male is never inspected; he propagates [the disease] in a constant stream." Condemning this inequity,

---

22. BSFPSM 2 (February 1902): 57.
23. See ibid., 81–89, where Petit provides numerous examples of these posters.

Legrand lamented, "Our legislation gives total liberty to the most active agent of propagation: the young civilian male. It reserves all of its rigor for the woman and the military man."[24] In drawing this analogy between the regulation of prostitutes and that of sailors, Legrand's rhetoric constructed the civilian worker as a male equivalent to the *insoumise*. The only logical solution, in his view, was to extend medical surveillance to the civilians who built and maintained the navy fleet. Because these workers were granted access to medical care in the navy's hospitals, Legrand and Petit argued, the state could require infected workers to undergo hospitalization and treatment.[25]

Petit's proposal elicited considerable consternation among the SFPSM's members. Opponents denounced forcible treatment as a clear violation of individual rights. Louis Vincent argued that while civilian naval workers received certain privileges from their state employment, access to medical care and retirement pensions among them, they remained "unmilitarized" and hence in full possession of their rights as citizens. As such they were free to choose their own doctors and could not, legally, be forced into treatment.[26] The playwright Eugène Brieux was one of Petit's most vocal critics. While praising his noble intentions, Brieux claimed that Petit had "lost sight of the respect owed to individual liberty." As if this defense of individual rights were in itself insufficient, he intimated that the forced hospitalization, by violating civilian workers' right to medical secrecy, also threatened the integrity of the family—and hence society as a whole. He appealed to the "social interest" of confidentiality, claiming that the worker's home life would be wrecked by his detention; husband and wife would separate and the family would be dispersed.[27] The image of the worker as married with children was crucial to the critics' argumentative strategy. Médecin-inspecteur Chauvel thought it inconceivable to submit married civilians to venereal disease inspection.[28] Dr. Brissaud, similarly exclaimed: "I cannot conceive how one could dare to restrain, to lock up, *pères de famille*, civilian men assimilated to naval troops, under the simple pretext that they have the right to be treated by naval doctors. That is some right!"[29] In order to lend greater force to their arguments in favor of individual liberty, Petit's opponents regularly harnessed their defense to the figure of the *père de famille*; individual right was based on the familial, which is to say, the social interests at stake.

Proponents of the sanitary surveillance of naval workers responded directly to their critics' claims to protect the family. Dr. J. Ferrier contended

24. Ibid., 71.
25. For the article of Petit's proposal concerning civilian workers, see ibid., 74.
26. BSFPSM 2 (April 1902): 148–49.
27. Ibid., 150–52,
28. BSFPSM 2 (March 1902): 110–11.
29. BSFPSM 2 (April 1902): 157.

that their arguments were irrelevant because the majority of civilian marine workers were unmarried.[30] Le Pileur, a staunch supporter of the regulations (he was, it will be recalled, a doctor at the prison-hospital Saint-Lazare), largely approved of Petit's proposal. He suggested that if the employees were paid during their internment, there was no reason to hesitate. Indeed, he leapt at the occasion to demonstrate parity in the sanitary regulation of men and women, exclaiming, "I would vote for the proposition with both of my hands, as much out of concern for prophylaxis as to respond to legitimate calls for equal treatment between the two sexes."[31] He, in turn, presented sanitary surveillance as ultimately beneficial to the family—as necessary in order to protect the same "innocent" wives and children whose cause Brieux also defended.[32]

Advocates like Le Pileur sought to turn the pro-family argument against their critics. They appealed to the civilian workers' marital status as one more point in favor of wider regulation. The retired naval doctor Pourveau contended that, "this man who possesses a legitimate wife and who is nonetheless syphilitic is more dangerous than the male bachelor."[33] Le Pileur's colleague at Saint-Lazare, Toussaint Barthélemy, argued in defense of innocent women and children along similar lines. "M. Brieux is very interested in married and sick workers, even those who are contagious. Why does he not worry about wives and children? They are not the ones who went drinking, who ran around; they are not the ones who spent the week's money partying; their happiness, health, and existence are nonetheless threatened by the father's syphilis."[34] Curiously, in condemning these working-class civilian men as profligate agents of contamination, the regulation-minded doctors followed a line of argument frequently employed by abolitionists. Critics of regulation denounced the injustice and inequity of the *régime des moeurs,* which, in the words of Ernest Gaucher, "arbitrarily locks up sick women, leaving men free to spread their contagion all around."[35] The regulationists, however, sought to extend rather than to dismantle the system of sanitary regulation, as Pourveau's comments suggest. "If our compatriots love liberty, they love equality just as much. And I am surprised that in foregrounding the principle of individual liberty, one accepts that individual sanitary inspection be applied to sailors while judging it to be regrettable and humiliating for arsenal workers."[36] The regulation-minded doctors who sought to make medical inspections for civilian naval

30. Ibid., 159.
31. Ibid., 148.
32. Ibid., 152.
33. Ibid., 153.
34. Ibid., 162.
35. BSFPSM 2 (May 1902): 221. See also Louis Fiaux, *Enseignement populaire de la moralité sexuelle* (1908), 38. And Commission extraparlementaire du régime des moeurs, *Procès verbaux des séances* (1909), 87–88, 119–21.
36. BSFPSM 2 (April 1902): 152–53.

workers mandatory set the principle of "equality" against that of "liberty." In order to parry charges that hygienic regulation infringed upon the individual liberties of married civilian men, they figured the husband as a potential menace to his own family. They proposed to limit the rights of these potentially abusive (because contagious) working-class fathers in the name of the family (i.e., women and children) itself.

In the debate over the sanitary regulation of civilian workers, both sides posed as protectors of the family. The extent and limits of individual right, for which men's sexual privacy was here a metonym, was, in both cases, framed in terms of the health of the family. For regulationists, the military exemplified the primacy of communal exigencies over individual men's sphere of activity. They denounced both the injustice and health risk of applying the medical examinations only to military recruits, to the exclusion of other naval workers. However, as one of their critics, Dr. Brissaud, urged in his concluding argument, these claims obscured the major difference between civilians and marines. "Someone remarked some time ago that there is only one difference between sailors and port workers. The latter have the right to vote, while the others do not. Do you consider those who vote to be like soldiers, which is to say like minors under tutelage?"[37] Indeed, one of the jurists present at the meeting declared that the "contract" invoked by the doctors stood little chance of being upheld in court.[38] When finally submitted to a vote among the members present, Petit's measure was adopted. Obtaining only twenty-six out of forty votes, it was a long way from the unanimous approval accorded Fournier's sex education and Burlureaux's army reforms. And, when the Minister of the Navy issued a circular on the subject updating procedures of venereal prophylaxis in 1902, it contained no reference to civilian naval workers.

Colonial Experiments

As Dr. Petit mentioned in his report to the SFPSM, navy sailors had been submitted to a strict regime of examination, education, and treatment since 1888. The reason for these precocious measures went beyond the increased risks of contamination associated with the tight living quarters aboard navy ships. Sailors were seen to be at particular risk because, in circulating between exotic ports of call, they were exposed to "natives," who, according to many doctors, were thought to suffer from "endemic syphilis."[39] The naval ministry was responsible for troops sent to the colonies, before the

37. Ibid., 166.
38. Comments of Albert Paisant, président du tribunal de Senlis (ibid., 166–67).
39. Édouard Jeanselme, "Maladies vénériennes," in *Traité d'hygiène: Étiologie et prophylaxie des maladies transmissibles par la peau et les muqueuses externes*, ed. A. Chantemesse et al. (1911), 686.

creation, on 7 July 1900, of the "colonial army," which was granted a new and separate status and assigned to the responsibility of the Ministry of the Colonies.

Given its interest in the health and welfare of the military, the SFPSM soon undertook a study of "the venereal peril in the colonies," and the specific public health issues affecting the troops that served there. In his report on the question in April 1902, Dr. Burlureaux differentiated between the three major populations at risk: the troops, the *colons,* and the natives. He urged that, "while everyone is in solidarity when it comes to the venereal peril, the measures required vary according to whether we are concerned with either a category of victims to treat or healthy individuals who must be preserved."[40] The exigencies of public hygiene called for a differentiated approach to disease prevention and cure. The fact of "solidarity" was entirely consistent with this division of hygienic labor. Different tactics applied to and hence created distinctions between soldiers, *colons,* and natives.[41] In the colonies, as in the metropole, hygiene was a flexible principle that at once constructed and reproduced sexual, racial, and class differences between subjects.

The regulation of prostitution was one of the ways in which such differential tactics were instituted. As Christelle Taraud has noted in her study of "colonial prostitution" in North Africa, regulation, which is to say a system of dispensaries and the principles of police surveillance, was put into place when French troops arrived in Algeria in 1830. Similar measures were established in Tunisia and eventually Morocco, when France created protectorates in those territories. Decrees in Indochina set up analogous procedures. Resident-general Paul Bert introduced sanitary surveillance of prostitution in Tonkin in 1886, within a year of its becoming a protectorate, first in Haiphong and subsequently in Hanoi.[42] General Joseph Galliéni would do the same in Madagascar in 1897. Indeed, Galliéni's work there, for the members of the SFPSM, provided a model of how to treat a native population that was imagined to be congenitally diseased and degenerate.[43]

40. BSFPSM 2 (April 1902): 183.

41. See Ann Laura Stoler, *Race and the Education of Desire: Foucault's History of Sexuality and the Colonial Order of Things* (1995); Ann Laura Stoler, *Carnal Knowledge and Imperial Power: Race and the Intimate in Colonial Rule* (2002). And Levine, *Prostitution, Race, and Politics.*

42. Joyeux, *Le péril vénérien et la prostitution à Hanoi,* 164–67; Taraud, *La prostitution coloniale,* 20–21. On debates about the regulation of prostitution in the colonies more generally, Julia Miller, "The 'Romance of Regulation': The Movement against State-regulated Prostitution in France, 1871–1948" (Ph.D. diss., New York University, 2000), 369–409.

43. On the associations between native degeneracy, disease, and perversion in Indochina, see Frank Proschan, "Eunuch Mandarins, *Soldats mamzelles,* Effeminate Boys, and Graceless Women: French Colonial Constructions of Vietnamese Genders," *GLQ* 8, no. 4 (2002); Frank Proschan, "'Syphilis, Opiomania, and Pederasty': Colonial Construction of Vietnamese (and French) Social Diseases," *Journal of the History of Sexuality* 11, no. 4 (2002).

Military statistics on rates of venereal disease among European colonial troops were, according to most authors, alarming. In his synthetic work on the topic, Édouard Jeanselme described that, while the number of cases of all venereal diseases combined for soldiers in the colonial army stood at 87 out of 1000 in 1899, the number for "white troops" serving in the colonies was as high as 199.79 out of 1000.[44] Native troops were found to have a lower incidence of disease, an apparent immunity which was variously attributed to their habits of dissimulation and their ability to escape surveillance. The statistics regarding indigenous troops contrasted starkly with the claims doctors made elsewhere about the rates of syphilis in the native population as a whole, a seeming contradiction that was never raised in the doctors' reports. Meanwhile, the exposure of European soldiers to exotic locales and diseased native populations with "uncivilized" moeurs was often cited as the principle cause of their rates of infection. The difficulty of controlling clandestine prostitution and of administering treatment to soldiers in the *brousse* exacerbated, according to military physicians, the situation of colonial troops.[45]

The measures proposed by the members of the SFPSM to address this threat were analogous to those undertaken in the metropolitan army and navy—regular health inspections, especially at embarkation and debarkation, confinement of the sick, "soldiers' homes," lectures, and brochures.[46] Doctors also emphasized the need to extend treatment measures to the native population as part and parcel of France's imperial project. In his report, Dr. Burlureaux commented, "Special instructions should be given to the Governors of the Colonies for them to facilitate by all means possible the struggle against the venereal peril: 1.—among the European and native troops serving in the colonies; 2.—especially among the native populations, who constitute one of the foyers in which our soldiers are contaminated. Empowered by these instructions, and without having to attend to any interest other than the general interest, the Governors will be able to have a powerful and decisive impact which will quickly be translated into a notable attenuation of venereal ills."[47] Indeed, from the perspective of these doctors, the colonies were an experimental space in which they could test their hygienic visions with little or no resistance on the part of "particular" interests. For, as Burlureaux noted, "In each colony, in fact, the governor has total power; and from the synergy of efforts between administrators and doctors, great effects will result."[48] In the colonies, they could develop

44. Jeanselme, "Maladies vénériennes," 689.
45. BSFPSM 3 (March 1903): 146. See also Fiaux, *L'armée*, 164–76; Jeanselme, "Maladies vénériennes," 692–93; Ernest-Jean-François Pichon, "Les maladies vénériennes aux colonies—Leur prophylaxie dans l'armée coloniale" (Docteur en médicine, 1905).
46. BSFPSM 3 (May 1903): 252.
47. BSFPSM 2 (April 1902): 187.
48. Ibid., 183. For a discussion of the colonial space as a kind of "social laboratory," see Rabinow, *French Modern*.

CIVILISATION ET SYPHILISATION

1863

Coloutzon

Figure 8. "Civilization and Syphilization." *Assiette au beurre,* 9 May 1903. Typ 915.01.1668F, Department of Printing and Graphic Arts, Houghton Library, Harvard College Library. In this mockery of the "civilizing mission," a degenerate sailor is figured as the source rather than the victim of "syphilization."

a prophylactic vision untrammeled by the legal restrictions, protections on the individual rights of citizens, and administrative decentralization that constrained their work in the metropole. As Petit argued in his report on the question, "We seem to have admitted in our society [the SFPSM], even in the case of abolitionists, that the navy sailor and soldier, are to be considered as minor, and as such, to be protected. I hope that the shadow of Schoelcher will pardon me, but it seems that it is at the very least as true for most of our brothers of color!"[49] If soldiers were already considered as minors, then these racialized, and implicitly infantilized, natives were even more so. The hygienic policy imagined and recommended by the SFPSM doctors was premised on and legitimated by this assumption of the childlike status of the native population. In conceiving how to direct hygiene policy toward these subjects, they took their lead from that most imaginative of colonial governors, Galliéni.[50]

Syphilis doctors viewed the development of hygiene policy in French imperial holdings as part and parcel of the work of colonization. Dr. Jeanselme thus urged, "Syphilis when untreated bastardizes the race; it diminishes births and increases deaths. It contributes, in part . . . to the decline of population growth. And, in vast areas of our colonial empire the workforce is notably insufficient; this lack of men, in a climate which does not permit white men to do manual work, is certainly one of the most serious obstacles to the progress of colonization. Economic interest, alongside moral obligation, imposes the duty on the administration to improve this state of things."[51] These were the very incentives which led Galliéni to initiate, in the wake of his "pacification" of Madagascar, an all-encompassing strategy for treating syphilis among the native populations of the island. Beginning in 1898, he introduced measures to encourage native population growth. The regulation of prostitution was part of a wider effort to halt the spread of the venereal diseases, which, he argued, caused high rates of infant death and native women's sterility. Related tactics included the regularization of marriages, taxes on bachelors, the exemption of fathers of five children or more from military service, the creation of an annual festival of children, and even, encouraging native women to mate with Europeans in order to produce heartier offspring. Galliéni's health and family policy in Madagascar was designed to prevent the spread of diseases such as syphilis, malaria, and plague as well as to encourage the growth of the indigenous population.[52]

49. BSFPSM 3 (March 1903): 155. Victor Schoelcher helped to abolish slavery in 1848.
50. On Galliéni as an "experimental" administrator, see Rabinow, *French Modern*, 142–62.
51. Jeanselme, "Maladies vénériennes," 694.
52. Yves-Georges Paillard, "Les recherches démographiques sur Madagascar au début de l'époque coloniale et les documents de 'l'AMI,'" *Cahiers d'études africaines* 27, no. 1–2 (1987). 22–23. See also J. O. de Madagascar et Dependences (JOMD), 23 June 1898, 2017–2021.

Galliéni's creation, in 1901, of a system of free medical assistance for natives and of a specialized school to train native medical assistants, was intended to further these efforts. As the Governor-general made clear in his
directives, this extension of public assistance in order to develop the "Malgache race" was at once a "duty of humanity" and an economic exigency
needed to "remedy the serious obstacle to projects and enterprises of colonization in Madagascar, which is to say, the low population density in relation to the extent of territory to be exploited [*mise en valeur*]."[53] Because of
the "freedom of moeurs" that was purportedly rampant among natives,
Galliéni created a venereal hospital to treat both prostitutes and regular
members of the population, including men, outside of Tananarive. He also
established a maternity hospital for pregnant women who suffered from
syphilis and gonorrhea in order to prevent miscarriages. Finally, he initiated
efforts to disseminate information about the threat of disease to the native
population by creating brochures written in Malgache. These brochures,
which were to be distributed in the dispensaries and in weekly lectures to be
given by native medical assistants, included texts on "the hygiene of pregnant women" and the "ravages of syphilis." This system of dispensaries and
hospitals that distributed free treatment, medication, and hygienic instruction, constituted, for Galliéni, "veritable centers of influence, where natives
have begun to see the advantages of European civilization."[54]

Doctors of the SFPSM regularly cited the innovative work of Galliéni in
Madagascar as exemplary. While skeptical of their ability to quickly change
the purportedly "free" sexual moeurs of native populations, these physicians were convinced that they could appeal to the indigene's "primitive"
sense of self-interest. Indeed, they argued that the dissemination of venereal
propaganda might be facilitated by the natives' apparent lack of sexual
morality, or "shame." In his report, Paul Petit stated, "In order to instruct
our colored brothers about venereal diseases, you will not need to teach
them, as you want so strongly to do in France, that they are not at all
shameful diseases. On this point they are well in advance of us." This lack
of shame did pose a different problem, namely carelessness. Petit thus insisted, "In order to trouble this serenity, it requires an effort to address directly the interest in self-conservation of the individual, the family, the tribe.
And it is this that Gen. Galliéni has so well understood in Madagascar, and
his instructions, in this matter, can be taken as a model."[55] The presumed
shamelessness of native populations legitimated efforts at medical propaganda and treatment. Burlureaux claimed in his report that "savages are
less resistant to progress when it comes to their health than many men we
call civilized."[56] The SFPSM's recommendations on how to treat venereal

53. JOMD, 20 March 1901, 5535.
54. Ibid., 5540
55. BSFPSM 3 (March 1903): 154.
56. BSFPSM 2 (April 1902): 184.

diseases in the colonies appealed to the programs introduced by Galliéni in Madagascar. They urged that, "For the natives, the use of dispensaries must be generalized; the measures already undertaken by Galliéni in Madagascar should be applied everywhere, while adapting them to each region: free consultations, distribution of medicine, hospitalization of venereal patients in special hospitals. Instructions on venereal disease in special conferences to people of the country or with the aid of newspaper articles and small brochures in the native language."[57]

The question of protecting individual privacy appeared nowhere in these doctors' discussions of how to treat indigenous subjects. They, for example, depicted "Arab" men's resistance to medical examination and treatment as a form of prejudice or pathology, not as a matter of individual right. While doctors with experience in North Africa often noted native indifference and lack of shame about syphilis, they also cited Arab men's "excessive modesty" [*pudibonderie*] as an obstacle to their investigations.[58] This combination of indifference and excessive modesty meant that natives were less than likely to seek out medical treatment during the first stages of the disease.[59] Doctors described the difficulties they encountered in obtaining detailed information as a problem of "mentality." Doctors Levy-Bing and Gerbay wrote in a report on their experience treating "the Arab" recruited into the army, "Above all he lies, either out of disdain or lack of confidence in the medicine of 'the Roumis,' out of fear of pain, or because it is his principle to deny all sexual acts. He also lies without any apparent reason, in order to lie, because instinctive dissimulation is part of his character."[60]

Excessive modesty was further associated with the presumed prevalence of "pederasty" among Arab men. Dr. Broc, who worked in Tunis, noted, "Despite their 'special moeurs,' anal sores seem rare, but this rarity is more apparent than real, because Arabs feel a certain repugnance in showing doctors their genitals or anal region, as a result of Koranic law, which also prohibits, it seems, pederasty, but without great success."[61] Doctors viewed Arab men's resistance to intimate examination by physicians as an exten-

57. BSFPSM 3 (May 1903): 253.

58. J. Brault, "Les maladies cutanées et vénériennes chez les indigènes musulmans d'Algérie—Deuxième partie: Les maladies vénériennes," *Revue générale des sciences pures et appliquées* 15, no. 20 (1904): 938.

59. Dr. Montpellier, "La syphilis secondaire chez les indigènes musulmans de l'Afrique du nord," *Annales des maladies vénériennes* 12 (December 1917): 737.

60. Dr. Levy-Bing and Dr. Gerbay, "La syphilis, et en particulier ses manifestations nerveuses, chez les arabes aux armées," *Annales des maladies vénériennes* 12 (August 1917): 450.

61. René Broc, "La syphlis chez les indigènes musulmans de Tunis," *Annales des maladies vénériennes* 4 (December 1906): 485. For a discussion of this association, see Robert Aldrich, "Homosexuality in the French Colonies," in *Homosexuality in French History and Culture*, ed. Jeffrey Merrick et al. (2001), 205. See also Rudi Bleys, *The Geography of Perversion: Male-to-Male Sexual Behavior Outside the West and the Ethnographic Imagination, 1750–1918* (1995).

sion of their sexual and religious pathology, not as a legitimate desire for individual privacy. In their report on Moroccan troops deployed in France during World War I, Doctors Carle and Bourcart suggested that "this particular modesty can be explained if a relation with a man is the cause of the accident." When a relation with a woman was the cause, they claimed, "it seems that this mentality is religious in origin."[62] Syphilis experts, including those employed by the military, never mentioned sex acts between men as a possible mode of transmission between Europeans. Indeed, SFPSM doctors did not broach the topic of homosexuality, with the notable exception of a lecture given by Dr. Jude on the disciplinary "Bataillons d'Afrique."[63] By contrast, discussions of Arabs systematically referred to the prevalence of their perversion.[64] Doctors, in turn, constructed native subjects as simultaneously shameless and as pathologically modest, at once brazen and dissimulating, and hence as unworthy of the protections on individual privacy that remained a structuring presumption of their approaches to adult European men.

If the venereal peril in the colonies was a source of, in Dr. Burlureaux's words, "solidarity" between the colonizer and colonized, it was for that very reason, also a means of reinforcing distinctions. Colonial hygiene policy was explicitly based on ideas about native cultural, sexual, and racial differences. In delineating and legitimating approaches to native venereal hygiene, doctors regularly described indigenous populations as alternately shameless and pathologically modest, as congenitally diseased and sexually perverse, as, in sum, markedly removed from European sexual norms. Their resistance to medical treatment was similarly viewed from this perspective, namely, as a symptom of pathological obstacles in a terrain that was otherwise open to hygienic experimentation.

Military "Préservatifs"

The decade before the outbreak of the Great War was marked by a number of significant scientific innovations relative to the identification, prevention, and treatment of syphilis. In 1905 two German scientists isolated the

62. Dr. Carle and Dr. Bourcart, "Quelques considérations sur l'évolution de la syphilis chez les marocains," *Annales des maladies vénériennes* 12 (April 1917): 194–95.

63. Dr. René Jude, "Nécessité de l'isolement pendant la nuit de tout soldat subissant une peine, même de courte durée," BSFPSM 14 (1914): 8–15. These battalions had a long-standing reputation for same-sex activity. See Julien Chevalier, *Une maladie de la personnalité: L'inversion sexuelle* (1893), 209; Alexandre Lacassagne, *Dictionnaire encyclopédique des sciences médicales,* ed. Raige-Delorme et al., vol. 22 (1865–1889), 245. See also Aldrich, "Homosexuality in the French Colonies," 206–9.

64. Brault, "Les maladies cutanées et vénériennes," 935; Georges Lacapère, "Caractères généraux et évolution du chancre syphilitique chez l'Arabe: Travail du dispensaire prophylactique de Fez (Maroc)," *Annales des maladies vénériennes* 13 (1918): 90; Georges Lacapère, *La syphilis arabe (Maroc, Algérie, Tunisie)* (1923), 25–26; Georges Lacapère and Dr. Decrop, "La syphilis dans les pays arabes. Les modes de contage; Aperçu statistique," *Annales des maladies vénériennes* 12 (December 1917): 658–59.

virus—the spirochete Treponema pallidium—which causes the disease. Close upon the heels of this discovery, in 1906, another German bacteriologist, August von Wassermann, developed a blood test supposedly based on the detection of specific antibodies produced to fight the infection. This test was of questionable accuracy and serologists and public health experts worked hard in the years following its discovery to legitimate the procedure. The nearly simultaneous development of new, more effective although still quite toxic, treatments combining compounds of mercury and arsenic in 1909 by the German scientist Paul Ehrlich facilitated the institutionalization of the Wassermann test. The new diagnostic and cure reinforced each other's legitimacy and helped to open the way for the creation of public health clinics devoted to eliminating the venereal peril. French scientists contributed to this flurry of activity with the elaboration of prophylactic disinfectants designed to reduce men's risk of contamination after dubious sexual encounters. Based on the findings of two disciples of Pasteur, Elie Metchnikoff and Émile Roux, preservative pomades composed of calomel and later, the permanganate of potash, were supposed to reduce the unfortunate consequences of such exposure. The fate of this latter innovation, given its rather ambivalent moral implications, was considerably more embattled than that reserved for the other recent discoveries.[65]

For the reasons that I have been tracing throughout this chapter, the army was an ideal terrain for the experimentation and implantation of these new medical technologies. As we have seen, soldiers occupied a singular and liminal civil status. Between the student and the *père de famille,* the army conscript was no longer under the direct tutelage of his family and, most frequently, not yet a father himself. Almost adult, his rights nonetheless remained circumscribed by the military's communal and hierarchical exigencies. Post-Dreyfus Affair efforts to "republicanize" the army led to an extension of its educational role. With the universal conscription established in 1889, it represented an ideal instrument for the promotion of moral and social integration. Paradoxically, as military doctors frequently noted, the very conditions of military life exacerbated antisocial behaviors, in particular, drinking and recourse to prostitution. The army thus held out an ideal opportunity to morally form men, while simultaneously menacing to "deform" them. These concerns about the risks entailed by conscription were manifested, for example, in debates about the length of military service, which was reduced to two years in 1905. SFPSM doctors notably hailed this reform both as a way to reduce rates of contamination and to promote marriage and reproduction.[66] Military policy regarding sex education and syphilis prevention reflected this very dilemma, vacillating between morally

65. For accounts of these developments, see Brandt, *No Magic Bullet;* Ilana Löwy, "Les 'faits scientifiques' et leur public: L'histoire de la détection de la syphilis," *Revue de synthèse* 1, no. 1 (1995); Claude Quétel, *History of Syphilis,* trans. Judith Braddock et al. (1990).

66. See F. Moty, "Prophylaxie des maladies vénériennes et de la syphilis en particulier dans l'armée," BSFPSM 5 (February 1905): 116.

edifying lectures on the virtues of chastity and the implementation of practical hygienic procedures designed to prevent, identify, and treat venereal
disease.

Founded in late 1906, the Société de médecine militaire française
(SMMF) introduced, as one of its initial topics of discussion, "La prophylaxie de la syphilis dans l'armée." While criticizing municipal authorities for
excessive laxity, the SMMF members generally agreed that the regulation of
prostitution remained an essential strategy for keeping rates of syphilis infection in the army down. They praised the military doctor's new role as educator and confidant among the troops and the importance of medical secrecy for the detection and treatment of venereal disease. In a word, they
expressed a certain consensus surrounding the prophylactic measures
adopted by the army in 1902. The preservative pomade developed by Roux
and Metchnikoff added a new dimension to their debate. In his report, Second class Médecin-major Lafeuille, recommended that the new procedure
be integrated into the hygienic education for soldiers already established in
1902.[67] Advocates of "moral prophylaxis" expressed notable hesitation.
For Dr. Burlureaux, the sexually explicit instructions jeopardized the doctor's mission of moral uplift.[68] "In giving this kind of advice," another
member wondered, "does the doctor cover his authority with a certain pre-
conception: that continence is impossible for soldiers, that it is unnatural,
that it is harmful?"[69] In his conclusions, Lafeuille responded at length to
these moral misgivings. "I do not want to subtract anything from this valuable argument; but, we must not, however, delude ourselves that all we
have to do to obtain abstinence is to recommend it; and this consideration
seems to me to impose on us the duty to advise, with necessary restrictions,
the use of these preventive measures." Indeed, Lafeuille cautioned against
an overly moralizing approach to soldiers' sexual conduct; he suggested
that medical efforts to use the terror of disease as a method of inducing
chastity were counterproductive, ultimately stripping the doctor of the "authority to reassure the sick, to encourage them to submit to a prolonged
treatment with the hope of cure."[70] In his view, this more pragmatic approach ultimately upheld the moral and professional integrity of physicians
more effectively than did abstract appeals to moral prophylaxis alone.[71]

The military hierarchy in the end concurred with Lafeuille's position. A
23 September 1907 War Ministry circular "relative to the prophylaxis of

67. BSMMF 1 (February 1907): 76–78.
68. BSMMF 1 (April 1907): 321.
69. BSMMF 1 (July 1907): 496.
70. Ibid., 501.
71. On analogous debates in other national contexts: Brandt, *No Magic Bullet;* David
Evans, "Tackling the 'Hideous Scourge': The Creation of the Venereal Disease Treatment Centers in Early Twentieth-century Britain," *Social History of Medicine* 5, no. 3 (1992); Harrison,
"The British Army"; S. M. Tomkins, "Palmitate or Permanganate: The Venereal Prophylaxis
Debate in Britain, 1916–1926," *Medical History* 37 (1993).

venereal diseases," established disinfection centers in all army garrisons. The circular cited the Roux and Metchnikoff pomade and, in a language that drew a metaphorical connection between military force and public health, praised disinfection as a "new weapon" in the fight against the venereal peril. The directive clearly privileged practical prophylaxis over purely moral education. To the extent that disease prevention was aligned with social interest, it became a moral imperative of its own. The circular stated that "individual morality has never really gained anything from ignorance or dissimulation. One accomplishes a social duty by averting young soldiers to the dangers that threaten them and by furnishing them with the means to avoid, as much as possible, the consequences, when they are exposed." Reinforcing the measures already in place since 1902, military doctors were now responsible for lecturing conscripts and NCO's "on venereal disease, the conditions of their development, the dangers they pose to the individual and to the species, their treatment even, and above all their prevention." It added that they should not hesitate to enter into "certain details," drawn from "the most recent scientific discoveries." The bulk of the circular was devoted to the mechanics of establishing the new disinfection posts, to be accessible at all hours, in the infirmary. A second circular, published on 16 November 1907, gave further precisions as to the technical requirements of the new services, the proper chemicals to use in the concoction of the preservative pomade, their average cost, etc.[72] In contrast to the American army, which introduced similar procedures in 1912, the use of prophylactic stations was not obligatory and it appears that this absence of sanction, a principle that was inscribed in the 1902 circular, ultimately meant that these installations did not operate to great effect.[73]

The "practical" orientation of military hygiene did not prevent members of the SFPSM from upholding chastity as a noble moral ideal, as a 1911 debate on the subject well demonstrated. Motivated in part by national pride, they strongly reacted against the findings of certain German sexologists and syphilis experts invited to speak before the German Society for the Prevention of Venereal Disease on the topic of "Sexual Abstinence and Its Effects on Health." Doctors at the Dresden conference expressed increasing concerns about chastity as a potential health risk and source of perversions such as impotence, onanism, and homosexuality.[74] In a show of national unity, the French league unanimously rejected the German findings.[75] The

72. The texts of the circulars were included in handbooks of military hygiene. See, for example, *Hygiène des hommes de troupe*, (1909), 101–10.

73. On the American system: Brandt, *No Magic Bullet*, 65, 110–15.

74. For a discussion of this debate in the German context, see Andreas Hill, " 'May the Doctor Advise Extramarital Intercourse?': Medical Debates on Sexual Abstinence in Germany, c. 1900," in *Sexual Knowledge, Sexual Science*, ed. Roy Porter et al. (1994).

75. As Vernon Rosario and Robert Nye have shown, sexological debates at the turn of the century were influenced by Franco-German hostility. See Robert A. Nye, "The History of Sexuality in Context: National Sexological Traditions," *Science in Context* 4, no. 2 (1991); Ver-

new president of the SFPSM, Dr. Félix Balzer, a doctor, like his predecessor, at the Hôpital Saint-Louis, summarized their collective opinion on the matter. "We all agree, regarding both the man and the woman. We do not believe that continence has any serious drawbacks for health and we also believe that it is still one of the best ways to avoid venereal disease. This is, I believe, the general conclusion that emerged from everything that has been said about men and women's abstinence."[76] Prior to the war then, members of the SFPSM upheld "moralization," and in particular, conferences on the healthy effects of abstinence, alongside an ongoing commitment to the regulation of prostitution, and recourse to practical hygienic measures in the army.

The advent of the war strained syphilis doctors' commitment to "moralization," which stood in delicate balance with their pragmatic commitment to both the regulation of prostitution and "individual" prophylaxis. In the wake of the social and sexual upheavals provoked by the war, rates of syphilis contamination surged. Estimates ran as high as 200,000 new cases in the army alone in the first two years of the conflict.[77] This spike in venereal contagion did not become a significant object of debate and policy until 1916 when a commission convoked by the Academy of Medicine reported on the extent of the crisis. The doctors on the commission, many of whom were also members of the SFPSM, generally concurred that, in the words of Ernest Gaucher, "the mental disturbance caused by the war has, to some extent, overturned conventional moral ideas." In his speech, Gaucher noted that "those men who, up until now, observed conjugal fidelity, are suddenly separated from their families; and, knowing that they are continually exposed to the threat of death, forget their peace-time prudence. Venereal contagion results from the easy and suspicious encounters that men, in civilian life, would carefully avoid." And women, abandoned on the home front, similarly "let themselves go." "Ordinary women" [*des femmes quelconques*] were now responsible for contaminating men, alongside prostitutes of either the clandestine or regulated kind.[78] This wartime disruption of men and women's moral armature called for exceptional measures.

In the war, the distinction between prostitutes and "ordinary women" had all but eroded, and the new mass of men who were mobilized for service could no longer be counted on to govern themselves with "prudence." The initial response to this situation was a radical deployment of police ef-

non A. Rosario, "Pointy Penises, Fashion Crimes, and Hysterical Mollies: The Pederasts' Inversions," in *Homosexuality in Modern France,* ed. Jeffrey Merrick and Bryant T. Ragan Jr. (1996).

76. BSFPSM 12 (February 1912): 64.

77. Lion Murard and Patrick Zylberman, *Hygiène dans la République* (1996), 573. See also Jean-Yves Le Naour, *Misères et tourments de la chair durant la Grande Guerre: Les moeurs sexuelles des Français, 1914–1918* (2002), 125–55.

78. E. Gaucher, "Les maladies vénériennes pendant la guerre à l'hôpital militaire Villemin et dans ses annexes," *Annales des maladies vénériennes* 11, no. 4 (April 1916).

forts to crackdown on unregulated prostitution. Women were arrested in record numbers.[79] While this situation of *"relâchement moral"* made attempts to control the spread of disease by the regulation of prostitution alone rather futile, regulationism remained in place, and was indeed strengthened by the perceived crisis. Even Ernest Gaucher, who had been a staunch abolitionist before the war, conceded to sanitary surveillance as a wartime exigency. Especially by 1916, military health officials realized that more pragmatic hygienic measures were needed. Given the clear need to maintain France's fighting force (already thought to be numerically inferior to that of the Germans), doctors reconsidered the efficacy of "moral prophylaxis" in the context of the sexual turbulence created by the war.

The wartime reflections of SFPSM president Balzer are here exemplary. As we have seen, he upheld "moral prophylaxis" and schooling in sexual abstinence as a viable ideal in 1911. By contrast, in 1915 he wrote, "The gradual effect of moral prophylaxis does not really allow us to count much on it. The good advice and written instruction that one can give to soldiers does not sufficiently influence too many of them." Of questionable efficacy as a mode of syphilis prevention, the ideal of sexual continence seemed to carry an additional menace. While Balzer conceded that abstinence did not necessarily endanger individual health, he added that, "sometimes these periods of forced abstinence can be followed by violent reactions in which one loses all the benefits of continence."[80] He suggested that constraint could lead to uncontrolled, because violent, sexual excess. Regulated prostitution had to be left in place in order to prevent the exacerbation of such perversity.

While hesitant to abandon moral prophylaxis altogether, Balzer questioned whether such ideals were applicable in wartime. He used the German army as an example of the dangers of overbearing, repressive discipline. In a notable reversal of the 1911 argument, he presented Germany as the country in which the ideal of sexual continence had received the widest diffusion before the outbreak of war. The adverse and antisocial effects of moral stringency were, in his view, manifested by the comportment of the Reich's army in the opening stages of the conflict. "One does not know what kinds of criminal excesses the army lent itself to in throwing itself on Belgium and one is astonished that this could take place in an army which, when it comes to service, has a reputation for discipline and obedience. The

79. Murard and Zylberman, *Hygiène*, 573. For a more global treatment: Susan R. Grayzel, "Mothers, Marraines, and Prostitutes: Morale and Morality in First World War France," *International History Review* 19, no. 1 (1997); Le Naour, *Misères et tourments;* Michelle K. Rhoades, " 'No Safe Women': Prostitution, Masculinity, and Disease in France during the Great War" (Ph.D. diss., University of Iowa, 2001). On the war as a disruption of conventional gender relations: Mary Louise Roberts, *Civilization without Sexes: Reconstructing Gender in Postwar France, 1917–1927* (1994).

80. Félix Balzer, "Prophylaxie et traitement des maladies vénériennes en temps de guerre," *Presse médicale*, no. 49 (14 October 1915): 401.

unleashing of this brutal rut among the soldiers would simply have led them toward the prostitution which offered itself to them, but the sexual atrocities committed can be explained by causes which make us understand that moral prophylaxis is, from the beginning, destined to fail."[81] According to Balzar's analysis, the rigors of German discipline had produced violent excesses, which, as many authors have shown, were frequently rendered as forms of sexual perversion.[82] Meanwhile, in France, recruits had been thrown into a state of emotional tumult, both by "youthfulness and the excitations of war." Balzer concluded that, "all the measures that one might take to prevent sexual encounters during wartime are destined to miss their target at some moment during the hostilities." Soldiers' sexual conduct thus had to be addressed with pragmatism not repression—both through sanitary regulation of prostitution and an analogous regulation of the troops themselves. Balzer thus added, "*The medical surveillance of men in the regiment is the true corollary of prostitutes' medical visits;* we must make an effort to put it into practice with all else that that entails. Once a man is in danger of infection, and above all once he has been infected, he must remain under the doctor's control."[83] Dr. E. Bodin, mobilized as a médecin-chef of an army ambulance, came to similar conclusions. "The history of past centuries, the wise observation of the present teach us that it is not in preaching chastity that we will reduce venereal disease." Since excessive moralism produced dissimulation and made syphilis more difficult to treat (and hence control), he asked, "how many contaminations could have been avoided if certain patients did not draw back, out of false modesty, from a consultation which is likely to cure them or to explain the contagious nature of their outbreaks."[84]

In order to meet these needs, clinics dedicated to the treatment of venereal disease were created in the army on 30 April 1915. With the appointment of Justin Godart as sous-secrétaire d'état au Service de santé militaire on 18 July 1915, military and civilian health policy were united under a single directive instance, allowing for a better coordination of public health efforts. With, in the words of Lion Murard and Patrick Zylberman, this "militarization of hygiene," the infrastructure of civilian as well as military public health underwent rapid development.[85] Starting on 6 March 1916,

81. Ibid.
82. On associations between German military discipline and sexual perversion: Audoin-Rouzeau, *L'enfant de l'ennemi (1914–1918)* (1995); Carolyn J. Dean, *The Frail Social Body: Pornography, Homosexuality, and Other Fantasies in Interwar France* (2000), 112–15; Ruth Harris, " 'The Child of the Barbarian': Rape, Race and Nationalism in France during the First World War," *Past and Present* 141 (1993); Le Naour, *Misères et tourments*, 34–40.
83. Balzer, "Prophylaxie et traitement des maladies vénériennes en temps de guerre," 401–2 (emphasis in the original).
84. E. Bodin, "Prophylaxie et traitement de la syphilis aux armées," *Paris médical* 6 (1916): 434–35.
85. For a discussion of this transition, see Murard and Zylberman, *Hygiène*, 539–44.

the doctors responsible for overseeing the army's clinics were charged with organizing "*services annexes*" in order to extend consultations to civilian populations. The circular urged for a "close collaboration that military doctors must bring to civilian authorities in order to assure, in the best conditions, the functioning of *services annexes* for civilian venereal patients of both sexes."[86] As Dr. Gaucher proclaimed in his 1916 report to the Academy of Medicine, "Our commission has examined venereal diseases both in the army and in the civilian population, since, today, the civilian population is but an extension [*dépendance*] of the army."[87] The Academy ultimately recommended increasing the surveillance of both prostitutes and soldiers, as well as the expansion of venereal services to the civilian population at large. They also urged that colonial workers and soldiers be subject to particularly close examination, both before and after their arrival in France.

Justin Godart adopted these measures in his circular 251 Ci/7, of 25 September 1916.[88] The circular maintained a commitment to instructing troops about the "dangers of venereal disease and how to avoid them," while at the same time insisting that "venereal infections are not shameful diseases." It also established stepped up procedures for soldiers' medical examinations, which would now take place twice monthly as well as before and after their leaves.[89] The circular further made provisions for regulating the health of militarized personnel at work in munitions factories, heightened surveillance of colonial troops and workers, who as we have seen, were assumed to suffer from "congenital syphilis," and an extension of clinical services to the civilian population.

Colonial workers were the object of particular solicitude. A follow-up circular, 399 Ci/7, dated 10 January 1917, urged that "it has been observed that colonial workers and foreigners of diverse provenance (Algeria, Tunisia, Morocco, Indochina, China, etc.) employed in different work centers frequently arrive affected by venereal infections, and especially serious and highly contagious incidents of syphilis. . . . Facts of this order constitute a serious danger for the metropole which must be immediately addressed." In addition to being closely inspected on arrival, Godart urged that they be subject to monthly or bi-monthly examination during their

86. Cited in Sous-secrétariat du Service de santé militaire, Circular 251 Ci/7, 25 September 1916, Countway Library of Medicine. See also Dr. Pautrier, "Sur l'organisation générale des hôpitaux militaires de vénériens et des services-annexes," *Annales de dermatologie et de syphilographie* 6 (1916–1917): 233–56. Médecin-Major Gougerot, " 'Services annexes'—Les perfectionnements indispensables: nécessité d'une loi," *Annales des maladies vénériennes* 13 (November 1918): 650–91. For an overview of developments, see Georges Thibierge, *La syphilis et l'armée* (1917).

87. *Bulletin de l'Académie de médecine* 75 (6 June 1916): 681.

88. Sous-secrétariat du Service de santé militaire, Circular 251 Ci/7, 25 September 1916, Countway Library of Medicine. For the Academy recommendations, see *Bulletin de l'Académie de médecine* 75 (6 June 1916): 681.

89. See also Sous-secrétariat du Service de santé militaire, Circular 399 Ci/7, 10 January 1917, Countway Library of Medicine.

tenure.[90] According to Médecin-Major Gougerot, this surveillance of "native contingents" was one of the principle responsibilities of his regional military venereal and dermatology center.[91] Doctors imagined that colonial troops and workers carried foreign strains of disease and further that they were insensitive to moral instruction; their presence on metropolitan soil thus justified increased efforts to regulate prostitution. For, as one doctor noted, "What good does it do to carry out this excellent instruction in the barracks, if, in front of the door, we let the streetwalker circulate? . . . What is more, how can we expect that such teaching can reach the spirit of a Negro from the Sudan or even that of a more cultivated Muslim, whose moral shape is, thanks to the Koran, notably different?"[92] These public health experts used arguments about the proliferation of feminine vice and the moral debility and difference of colonial subjects to extend the sanitary regulation of prostitutes, soldiers, and when possible, civilian workers, both male and female.

In contrast to colonial workers and soldiers, civilian workers, according to the existing military directives, could not be forced to undergo examinations. Gougerot nonetheless urged that they should be subject to surveillance by indirect means. In keeping with Circular 516 Ci/7, dated 25 May 1917, he recommended that doctors charged with examining workers for workplace accidents use the occasion to verify that they were not suffering from any skin irruptions that might indicate venereal infection.[93] Indeed, Gougerot advised doctors to examine patients for signs of venereal disease, even when patients—both men and women—sought medical consultation for entirely different reasons.[94] The services annexes were intended to serve this civilian population by offering more discreet and anonymous treatment than did the notorious "special hospitals" reserved for venereal patients to a public who could not afford to consult private doctors. And, in the wake of the war, with significant government help, these outpatient clinics underwent a massive expansion.[95]

90. Ibid.

91. Gougerot, "Une année de fonctionnement d'un centre dermato-vénéreologique," *Annales des maladies vénériennes* 13 (May 1918): 257–306.

92. Charles Soulier, "Voeu en faveur d'une loi sur la repression du racolage et contre la contamination vénérienne," *Annales des maladies vénériennes* 12 (April 1917): 369. On racist attitudes and sexual anxiety toward colonial contingents both during the war and in the interwar period, see Le Naour, *Misères et tourments,* 260–72; Miller, "'Romance of Regulation,'" 409–42; Tyler Stovall, "The Color Line behind the Lines: Racial Violence in France during the Great War," *American Historical Review* 103, no. 3 (1998); Tyler Stovall, "Love, Labor, and Race: Colonial Men and White Women in France during the Great War," in *French Civilization and Its Discontents,* ed. Tyler Stovall et al. (2003).

93. Sous-secrétariat du Service de santé militaire, Circular 516 Ci/7, 25 May 1917, Countway Library of Medicine.

94. Gougerot, "Services annexes," 682–83. On the extent of contagion of mobilized workers and the risk to their wives: Thibierge, *La syphilis et l'armée,* 19, 23.

95. Public money put toward the effort rose from 1,200,000 francs in 1920 to 5,200,000 in 1925, reaching a high point of 42,465,000 in 1932. (The funds were subsequently cut back

In the postwar period, government funding increased for both anti-venereal propaganda and outpatient care. The SFPSM devoted itself to elaborating educational strategies which often took the hecatomb of the war as a point of departure. Gougerot, in proclaiming venereal diseases a "national danger to be combated," urged that, "syphilis has killed 1,500,000 Frenchmen in ten years, as many as the war in four."[96] Many SFPSM members sat on the Commission for the Prophylaxis of Venereal Diseases, which was created by Justin Godart in 1916 and continued to operate under the auspices of the Ministry of Hygiene after the war.[97] Hygienists called for a multifaceted and variable approach to prevention that would apply differently to individuals from different milieus.[98] In his overview of the "anti-venereal struggle in France," the inspector-general of administrative services in the Ministry of the Interior, Dr. Paul Faivre, suggested that, "If the treatment of the sick is the most certain way to stop the spread of venereal diseases, it is important to point out that there are others, which, it must be noted, are, however great, only relatively effective, in that their effect is far from identical for all individuals, and not even consistent in one individual." These methods included "moral prophylaxis," "prophylactic instruction," and "corporeal prophylaxis." Faivre remarked on the seeming contradiction between "moral prophylaxis" and recourse to prophylactic procedures, such as pomades and "préservatifs" or condoms.[99] His response was, however, clear. "Whether we want or not, the religious and moral argument, if it conserves its intrinsic value, cannot be, in all cases, usefully deployed. And isn't morality itself highly interested in the ability of individuals to keep themselves healthy in order to found a household and propagate the race."[100]

This flexible logic was well articulated in a "Manual of Prophylactic Education," edited by Doctors Just Sicard de Plauzoles and Auguste Queyrat, both members of the SFPSM and of the Commission for the Prophylaxis of Venereal Diseases. Intended as a pedagogical resource, the manual assembled brief texts by both "moralists" and hygienists, placing Ferdinand Buisson alongside SFPSM doctors such as Alphonse Pinard. It presented the "moral" and "medical" perspectives on prophylaxis as mutually reinforc-

due to the onset of economic depression.) According to the Ministry of Public Health's statistics, the number of individual consultations at the specially designed venereal disease clinics rose from 349,857 in 1920 to 4,300,659 in 1936. See the "Introduction au compte rendu statistique de l'activité antivénérienne pour l'année 1936," published by the Service de prophylaxie des maladies vénériennes of the Ministère de la santé publique in *La prophylaxie antivénérien* 10 (1938): 247–67.

96. BSFPSM 20 (May 1920): 82.

97. BSFPSM 22 (July 1922): 140–41.

98. See, for example, the list drawn up by the "Commission on the organization of a Congress for prophylactic, moral, and sanitary education," in BSFPSM 20 (May 1920): 105–6.

99. Paul Faivre, "Exposé d'ensemble de l'organisation de la lutte antivénérienne en France," *Revue d'hygiène* 44 (1922): 289.

100. Ibid., 291.

ing rather than as contradictory. Men's health had moral value precisely because it implicated the good of humanity as a whole. Any strategy, as long as it preserved that health was, in their view, worthwhile.

Ferdinand Buisson, for example, presented the "struggle against debauchery" in terms of a singular imperative: "*esto Vir.*" This command derived from a humanist idea, "Dare to declare that you want to enjoy, that enjoyment is your reason for being, that you want neither rule nor limit. No, you will perceive, that you are not alone in the world, that others have the same rights as you and that the same respect is due them." To violate such principles, in Buisson's view, was to "put yourself above morality, which is to put yourself below humanity."[101] Masculinity, according to Buisson, was constituted by a self-limitation that contained a constant risk of self-loss (i.e., debauchery). This imperative to self-control was based, however, not only on the threat of self-degradation, but on the fact that harm might be done to others as well. This idea of "humanity" both constituted and cautioned virility, and the married, reproductive, heterosexuality it implied.

More medically oriented writers parlayed this philosophical idea of humanity into a hygienic logic. For example, Adolphe Pinard, the prominent infant health specialist and SFPSM member, invoked social solidarity, which is to say, the dependence of the individual on the social body, as a hygienic truth. In an article entitled "It Is the Duty of Every Citizen to Found a Healthy Family," he proclaimed: "I repeat after Henri Marion that the individual is nothing by himself, and he feels this even more so, the more he is worth." Drawing inspiration from Marion's conception of moral solidarity, Pinard suggested that individual value was paradoxically founded on a recognition that the lone individual is nothing. This solidarity of individuals with the social body had concrete implications for his conception of citizen's rights. While he praised the consecration of individual right in the *Declaration of the Rights of Man and Citizen,* he also pointed up its limitations. These rights, he claimed, did not adequately secure the destiny "of the Species, which is to say, the persistence of humanity." The "species," for Pinard, importantly included women and children as well. This conception of right based on the welfare of "humanity" placed necessary restrictions and demands on men's individual rights. But they did so in a way that affirmed the citizen's masculinity in and through this limitation. For, as Pinard explained, "Every citizen, adult and vigorous, must reproduce and reproduce well, which is to say, found a healthy family." In his view, bachelors were only "half-citizens." He claimed that, in uniting himself with a woman for the purposes of reproduction, "the man feels a sentiment of responsibility which does not exist for the bachelor."[102] Citizenship thus enjoined marriage and procreation, not as a right, but as a duty. The citizen

101. Auguste Queyrat and Just Sicard de Plauzoles, eds., *Manuel d'éducation prophylactique contre les maladies vénériennes* (1922), 125.

102. Ibid., 127–28. On fatherhood and citizenship in the interwar and Vichy, see Kristen Stromberg Childers, *Fathers, Families, and the State in France, 1914–1945* (2003). And for the

was necessarily heterosexual and reproductive, as well as implicitly racialized. Normative masculinity, according to this ideal, served the cause of "humanity" as a whole.

Sicard and Queyrat's *Manual* also included articles on concrete prophylactic concerns. It contained sample pamphlets, tracts, and ministerial directives regarding the dangers of prostitution and practical measures of "individual hygiene." Rather than existing in contradiction to the moralization set forth in the other articles, these entries extended and elaborated the very principles that subtended them, namely, that men's sexual health and hygiene were in and of themselves morally valuable. As Léon Bernard, a professor of hygiene, remarked, "One has to confess that one cannot hope that these lessons will have perfect results; they must be complemented by more practically prophylactic teaching, which indicate the scientific procedures which will permit those young men who don't know how to impose abstinence on themselves, to shield themselves from danger."[103] Or, as another physician explained this flexible approach to battling the venereal peril, "We all bow down, out of respect and veneration before the sacred laws of morality, but we contend that doctors have a duty to teach men, not only about the venereal danger, but also how to protect themselves when they cede to the natural solicitations of their instinct. Doctors perform the highest service to the race, in maintaining its health and maybe also its youth."[104] As both the condition and aim of reproduction, racial and national hygiene was, in other words, a moral good in itself.

The hygienic citizen was not, or not exclusively, a subject who controlled himself. The limitations that framed his (sexual) existence were always also social restrictions, which arose from the need to preserve and perpetuate "humanity." This reproductive and hygienic imperative entailed theoretical restrictions on the citizen's individual rights and freedom in the name of protecting, as Pinard urged, "women and children." Because that limitation acted in the name of the monogamous reproductive family, however, it confirmed, rather than undermined, the citizen's normative masculinity. Doctors' affirmation of the moral imperative to treat men who fell prey to venereal disease, and to counsel those at risk on how to avoid it, only apparently contradicted this ideal. For, their defense of pragmatic prophylaxis, of preventing and treating venereal disease, was also made in the name of reproductive heterosexuality.

After the war, sexual hygienists' prophylactic project no longer relied on the theoretical distinction between the unconscious adolescent and the conscious adult, or between "minor" soldier and civilian male. While the adult

imperial context, see Elizabeth Thompson, *Colonial Citizens: Republican Rights, Paternal Privilege, and Gender in French Syria and Lebanon* (2000).

103. Queyrat and Sicard de Plauzoles, eds., *Manuel d'éducation,* 16.
104. Response of Dr. Eugene Briau to Faivre, "Exposé d'ensemble," 494–95.

male citizen's capacity and duty to control himself remained the normative ideal, the need to preserve those who strayed from this ideal simultaneously justified an expansion of health education and health services to the population at large. The moral ideal of conjugal masculinity and hygienic practice were, in this way, mutually reinforcing; they both took as their foundational principle the urgency of preserving "the race" through reproductive heterosexuality. As a flexible framework for articulating the relationship between individuals and the social body, hygiene could accommodate diverse and seemingly competing ideas and practices as part of an apparently unified moral vision: the preservation of national and racial health in the name of "humanity" itself.

Epilogue

The problem of how to balance the individual rights of citizens with their wider civic or social obligations is a central and persistent tension in liberal democracies. My study of the early Third Republic has examined a specific moment in this larger history in order to show how normative conceptions of gender and sexuality occupied a prominent place in the definition and determination of what it meant to be a proper citizen. Under that regime of universal male suffrage, the citizen's masculinity was at once presumed and problematic, because always subject to potential deviation. In constituting the regulation of male sexual desire as a problem, French policy makers and pedagogues, social scientists and social critics, both articulated and ideally resolved the constitutive tension between the citizen's presumptive autonomy and his social attachment. Conjugality emerged as one important way in which male citizens could be anchored in an implicitly gendered social order. This valorization of sexual complementarity, I have argued, contributed to a conception of citizenship that both guaranteed the citizen's masculinity and constituted social attachment as a civic obligation. Heterosexuality, as a quasi-sacred norm, in other words, bound together the members of the secular Republic. Presumptions of the social value of sexual mutuality, I contend, animated republican pedagogical projects and served to reconcile or "marry" their emancipatory vision with regulatory aims. These investments in heterosexuality articulated conventional gender roles and helped to fashion models of a productive and harmonious political and social order. At the same time they constituted gender and sexual deviance as forms of asociality. Citizenship, as I described it here, was thus both a legal and a normative construction.

In reconstructing this history, I have sought to show how a gendered construction of sexual desire was deeply implicated in wider concerns about the development of democracy, the progress of civilization, and social cohesion.

I thus examine sexuality, neither as an intimate quality of "private" selves nor as a repository of cultural images or representations, but as a locus of historically specific and variable problems. It is my aim to demonstrate the centrality of such historical work for our understanding of how social and civic inclusion and exclusion have been constituted in the past. This work can, I hope, also open a critical perspective onto how gender and sexuality structure the norms of French citizenship, as they are articulated and imagined today.

In recent years, political discourse in France has focused considerable public attention on the fragility and fate of a "republican model," its ability, that is, to integrate citizens from increasingly diverse backgrounds into the polity. The school, as the principal institution responsible for the formation of the nation's citizens, has been at the center of these debates, nowhere more clearly than in the inquiries and discussions which led up to the passage of a new law on *laïcité* on 15 March 2004, which bans "ostensible" religious signs, and most notably, girls' headscarves from public schools. The pedagogical legacy of the Third Republic has been a touchstone for politicians and public figures alike, as frequent references to the writings of Jules Ferry and Ferdinand Buisson in commentaries on the law well demonstrate. The "free, secular, and obligatory" primary schooling of old repeatedly appears as a model of social integration, despite the presuppositions about gender, class, and in the colonial context, race, that, as we have seen, structured its operation.

In affirming and articulating the republican mission of the school, these contemporary debates have focused on the meaning of citizenship, not only as a legal category, but also as a normative construction. As the official commission convoked to study the question, headed by Bernard Stasi, stated in its report, "the mission of the school is essential in the Republic. It transmits knowledge, forms minds to be critical, assures autonomy, openness to cultural diversity, and the growth of the person, the formation of citizens as much as future profession. Such a mission supposes clearly fixed common rules."[1] The school, in other words, continues to be a place in which the nation's future citizens learn to reconcile right and obligation, autonomy and attachment, difference and universalism. According to its most recent advocates, the principle of secularism or *laïcité* remains central to this complex pedagogical task. By describing it as under threat, public discussions of the "law on the veil," sought to shore up the social, cultural, and, I would suggest, sexual norms of French citizenship. The logic and rhetoric of crisis have lent legitimacy to this urgent call for "clearly fixed common rules."

1. Commission de réflexion sur l'application du principe de laïcité dans la République, *Rapport au président de la République* (2003 [cited 2005]); available from http://www.lado cumentationfrancaise.fr/brp/notices/034000725.shtml.

While multiple and overdetermined, the causes of this fragility have been principally attributed to the effects of postwar immigration from France's former imperial holdings. Discussions of the contemporary crisis repeatedly signal the threat of "identitarian" or "communitarian" withdrawal, to which failed social integration of ethnically and racially marked immigrants, and most notably of their children, who are legally French, has given rise. In debates surrounding the law, these structural and historical social problems appeared in specific, embodied form, namely the veiled Muslim girl, on the one hand, and the men and boys purportedly responsible for her subjection, on the other. The fate of the Republic once again hinges on the formation of these adolescents. Their perceived social and sexual deviance motivated the new law's defense of *laïcité* and of the school as a crucible of citizenship. In the process, the fashioning of proper masculinity and femininity, and, in turn, of the relationship between men and women, played a prominent role in framing this wider discussion about the present and future harmony and cohesion of the French nation.

As in the Third Republic, the integration of citizens into the French social body has been at the core of these discussions of secularism in public schools. According to the Stasi Commission, "today's *laïcité* is confronted with the difficulty of forging unity while respecting social diversity." Its report further urged that "when *laïcité* is in crisis, French society struggles to offer a common destiny."[2] In virtually all recent accounts, the principle of equality between men and women is, now, integral to this vision of a "common destiny," and hence what it means to be a French citizen. In his mission statement to the Commission, President Jacques Chirac named "the equality of the sexes and the dignity of woman" as central to *laïcité*."[3] The Commission's report, in turn, proclaimed, "*laïcité* thus touches upon national identity, the cohesion of the social body, the equality between men and women, education, etc."[4] Thus, while coeducation or "*mixité*" was first introduced in France in the early 1960s, and then, only as a result of financial constraints, rather than as a pedagogical tenet, it is now upheld as foundational to the school's mission.[5] The preservation of this principle, and more specifically, the protection of Muslim girls from the menace of sexist and sexual violence is one of the stated goals of the law banning them from wearing headscarves to school. For this reason, many prominent feminists and feminist organizations lent support to the legislation, despite its paradoxical call for the exclusion of girls who chose to wear headscarves from school.

2. Ibid.
3. Ibid.
4. Ibid.
5. Françoise Gaspard, "Femmes, foulards, et République," in *Le foulard islamique en questions*, ed. Charlotte Nordmann (2004), 78.

Indeed, the Stasi Commission's report highlighted the threat that Islamic fundamentalism poses both to *laïcité* and to girls and women who are "children of immigrants" and often inhabitants of isolated social housing complexes in the suburbs. As they describe, "Young women find themselves victims of a resurgence of sexism which expresses itself in diverse pressures and by verbal, psychological, or physical violence. Male youths force them to wear concealing and asexual clothing, to lower their glance when they see a man; if they fail to conform, they are stigmatized as 'whores.' " From the perspective of the Commission, the "veil" gives young women "the protection that, paradoxically, the Republic should guarantee them."[6] In their view, girls who opt to wear head covering are, in fact, victims of sexualized violence, of, that is, predatory young men, whose religious and sexual perversity lead them to treat uncovered women like prostitutes. The "veil" is here associated with violation and mutilation, as it, in theory, forces girls to cover over their femininity. As one socialist deputy, Conchita Lacuey, remarked, "to hide one's hair is to renounce a part of one's femininity and one's identity."[7] The "veil" is, at the same time, a symptom of the sexual and cultural deviance of male youths who, while most often children of North African immigrants, are legally French. The "veiled girl" and the "Arab boy" embody respective poles of improper femininity and masculinity.[8] Although now operating in a different political and social context, these tropes recall, in notable ways, the images of "Arab" perversity that were mobilized during the era of France's imperialist "civilizing mission."

Thus, while not always stated explicitly, questions of both gender and sexuality are intimately bound up with how issues of "integration," ethnic and religious diversity, and the norms of French citizenship have been framed by the debate surrounding the "veil." They returned repeatedly in the National Assembly, when deputies were given the occasion to comment on the proposed law. Jean-Michel Debernard, the head of the Commission des affaires culturelles, familales, et sociales, thus cited the threat of "masculine aggression" in the implicitly Muslim immigrant communities of the suburbs. "It is in the *cités* and in the *quartiers* given over to identitarian withdrawal that the condition of women is most degraded and masculine

6. Commission de réflexion sur l'application du principe de laïcité dans la République, *Rapport*.

7. Assemblée nationale, *Application du principe de laïcité dans les écoles, collèges et lycées publiques (February 3)* (2004 [cited 2005]); available from http://www.assemblee-nationale.fr/12/cra/2003–2004/149.asp.

8. For a more extended discussion, see Nacira Guénif-Soulimas and Eric Macé, *Les féministes et le garçon arabe* (2004), 59–95. As well as Saïd Bouamama, *L'affaire du foulard islamique: la production d'un racisme respectable* (2004), 74–84. See also Jean Baubérot, *Laïcité 1905–2005, entre passion et raison* (2004); Caroline Ford, *Divided Houses: Religion and Gender in Modern France* (2005) 138–149; Françoise Gaspard and Farhad Khosrokhavar, *Le foulard et la République* (1995); Joan Scott, "Symptomatic Politics: The Banning of Islamic Headscarves in French Public Schools." *French Politics, Culture, and Society* 23, no. 3 (2005). And see the following edited collections: Alain Houziaux, ed., *Le voile que cache-t-il?* (2004); Charlotte Nordmann, ed., *Le foulard islamique en questions* (2004).

constraint is heaviest. Young women are the objects of sexist pressures which force them to wear clothing judged to be sufficiently modest and to lower their glances." It is, as a result, "at school that this essential acquisition—the equality between men and women—must be learned and lived. Boys must learn to respect girls whatever their choice of clothing."[9] The Gaullist deputy, Jean Leonetti, similarly proclaimed, "the respect for the equality of right between men and women commands the interdiction, in educational establishments, of a veil destined to hide women from men's view in order not to excite their desire."[10] The "veil," in other words, signals an insufficiently regulated and improperly schooled male desire; this desire, in turn, operates as a synecdoche for the violent and uncivil behavior of ethnically marked male youths.

My point is, obviously, not to deny or condone the reality of sexist and sexual violence against women, a violence that recent studies in France suggest, are not restricted to any milieu.[11] It is rather to suggest how, in these discussions, the "communitarianism" associated with both Islamic fundamentalism and suburban juvenile delinquency has been metonymically linked with an excessive masculinity, which connotes at once aggressive heterosexuality and problematic homosociality. Emblematic of at once too much difference and not enough, the purported "communitarianism" of these children of North African immigrants is figured as a sexualized threat to both the unity and the diversity or "*mixité*" of the social body. This language of sexual deviance and the menace it is supposed to represent symbolizes and pathologizes their failed social integration. While based on the implicit threat of masculine aggression, the law, in aiming to protect girls, actually regulates their bodies, paradoxically excluding those who would appear to be the most visible "victims." It attacks, in other words, the "ostensible" symptom, rather than structural and historical causes, which might be more rightly located, not in adolescent perversity, but in an insufficiently worked through relationship to the nation's colonial and postcolonial past. Rather than addressing these questions, however, the law and the debates surrounding it conjured the specter of a deviant, aggressive masculinity and an overly passive, victimized femininity as foreign to and incompatible with French citizenship. They have, in turn, served to reinforce a national and republican fantasy of egalitarian because complementary heterosexuality.[12] While the law purportedly aims to further integration, it has reinforced presuppositions that children of North African immigrants, who are in most cases, legally French, fail to conform to this

---

9. Assemblée nationale, *Avis presenté au nom de la Commission des affaires culturelles, familiales et sociales sur le projet de loi n. 1378* (2004 [cited 2005]); available from http://www.assemblee-nationale.fr/12/rapports/r1382.asp.

10. Assemblée nationale, *Application du principe de laïcité dans les écoles, collèges et lycées publiques (February 3)*.

11. Clarisse Fabre and Eric Fassin, *Liberté, égalité, sexualités* (2003), 130.

12. See ibid., 138–39.

desirable model of sexual harmony. The debates surrounding the law illustrate with great clarity the complex relationship between citizenship as a legal status and as a cultural and political norm.

The contemporary insistence on the necessity and desirability of *"mixité"* is markedly different from the social vision set forth by the pedagogues and politicians of the early Third Republic. It nonetheless reveals how gendered conceptions of sexual desire and its proper regulation continue to shape the meaning of citizenship and social integration. It has been my aim throughout this book to question how implicit assumptions of heterosexuality have worked historically to organize society in theoretically equitable, productive, and harmonious ways. Such idealizations, I suggest, entail an attribution of social value to certain lives and certain subjects over others, in ways that are marked by gender and sexuality, but also by class, race, religion, and ethnicity. The project of rethinking the political and social centrality of heterosexuality does not entail blind anti-normativity or radical individualism. It calls, instead, for a transformation of the presumptive norms of citizenship, including how and whether it should be sexed.

Bibliography

Reviews and Journals Consulted

Annales de dermatologie et de syphilographie
Annales des maladies vénériennes
Année sociologique
Bulletin administratif du ministère de l'instruction publique
Bulletin bi-mensuel de la Société de médecine militaire française [BSMMF]
Bulletin de l'Académie de médecine
Bulletin de la Société française de la prophylaxie sanitaire et morale [BSFPSM]
Bulletin de la Société française de philosophie
Bulletin officiel de la Ligue des droits de l'homme
Bulletin universitaire de l'Académie d'Alger
Gazette des tribunaux
La Cocarde
Journal officiel
Journal officiel de Madagascar et Dépendences [JOMD]
Libres entretiens
Paris médical
Presse médicale
Prophylaxie antivénérien
Receuil Dalloz
Revue blanche
Revue bleue
Revue des deux mondes
Revue d'hygiène
Revue générale des sciences pures et appliqués
Revue internationale de l'enseignement
Revue du monde musulman
Revue pédagogique
Revue philosophique de la France et de l'étranger
Revue scientifique de la France et de l'étranger
Revue universitaire
Le Temps

Primary Sources

Assemblée nationale. *Application du principe de laïcité dans les écoles, collèges et lycées publiques (3 February)* 2004 [cited 2005]. Available from http://www.assemblee-nationale.fr/12/cra/2003–2004/149.asp.

———. *Avis presenté au nom de la Commission des affaires culturelles, familiales et sociales sur le projet de loi n. 1378* 2004 [cited 2005]. Available from http://www.assemblee-nationale.fr/12/rapports/r1382.asp.

Avril de Sainte-Croix, Ghenia. *Une morale pour les deux sexes.* Paris: Dupont, 1900.

Barni, Jules. *La morale dans la démocratie suivi du Manuel républicain: Présentation de Pierre Macherey.* Paris: Kimé, 1992.

Barrès, Maurice. *Sensations de Paris—Ces messieurs—Ces Dames: 52 croquis par nos meilleurs artistes.* Paris: C. Dalou, 1888.

———. *Scènes et doctrines du nationalisme.* Paris: Félix Juven, 1902.

———. *Les déracinés (1897).* Paris: Gallimard, 1988.

———. *Mes cahiers, 1896–1923.* Edited by Guy Dupré. Paris: Plon, 1994.

Benoist, Gustave. *De l'instruction des indigènes dans la province de Constantine.* Paris: Hachette, 1886.

Benoit-Lévy, Edmond, and F.-B. Bocandé. *Manuel pratique pour l'application de la loi sur l'instruction obligatoire.* Paris: Cerf, 1882.

Bérenger, Henry. *L'effort.* Paris: Armand Colin, 1893.

———. *La France intellectuelle.* Paris: Armand Colin, 1899.

———. "La crise du fonctionnarisme en France." In *Les prolétaires intellectuelles en France,* edited by Henry Bérenger, 51–99. Paris: Éditions de La Revue, 1901.

———. "Les prolétaires intellectuels en France." In *Les prolétaires intellectuels en France,* edited by Henry Bérenger, 1–51. Paris: Éditions de La Revue, 1901.

Bert, Paul. *Lettres de Kabylie: La politique algérienne.* Paris: Alphonse Lemerre, 1885.

Bertillon, Jacques. *Le problème de la dépopulation.* Paris: Armand Colin, 1897.

Bonzon, Jacques. *Le crime et l'école.* Paris: Guillaumin, 1896.

Bourgeois, Léon. *Solidarité.* 2nd ed. Paris: Armand Colin, 1897.

Bourgeois, Léon, and Alfred Croiset. *Essai d'une philosophie de la solidarité: Conférences et discussions (1901–1902).* Edited by École des hautes études sociales. Paris: Alcan, 1902.

Bourget, Paul. *Un crime d'amour.* Paris: Alphonse Lemerre, 1898.

———. *Essais de psychologie contemporaine.* Paris: Gallimard, 1993.

Bréal, Michel. *Quelques mots sur l'instruction publique en France.* Paris: Hachette, 1872.

Brieux, Eugène. *Théâtre complet de Brieux: Les avariés—Les hannetons—La petite amie.* Vol. 6. Paris: Libraire Stock, 1923.

Brouardel, Paul. *Le secret médical.* 2nd ed. Paris: J.-B. Ballière, 1893.

Buisson, Ferdinand. "Distribution des prix aux cours normaux de la Société pour l'instruction élémentaire (28 juillet 1883, à la Sorbonne)." In *Conférences et causeries pédagogiques,* edited by Musée pédagogique, 73–87. Paris: Charles Delagrave, 1888.

———. *Conférence sur l'enseignement intuitif (31 août 1878).* Paris: Delagrave, 1897.

———. "Le devoir présent de la jeunesse." In *Morale sociale,* edited by Émile Boutroux, 231–54. Paris: Alcan, 1899.

———. "Éducation de la volonté." *Revue pédagogique* 35, no. 10 (1899): 310–45.

———. *Le vote des femmes.* Paris: H. Dunod & E. Pinat, 1911.

———, ed. *Dictionnaire de pédagogie et d'instruction primaire, 1re partie.* Vols. 1, 2. Paris: Hachette, 1887.

Burdeau, Auguste. *L'Algérie en 1891: Rapport et discours à la Chambre des députés.* Paris: Hachette, 1892.

———. *Devior et patrie: Notions de morale et d'éducation civique.* Paris: Alcide Picard et Kaan, 1893.

Cavaillon, André. *L'armement anti-vénérien en France*. Préface de Prof. Pinard. Paris: Mouvement sanitaire, 1928.

Chevalier, Julien. *De l'inversion sexuel au point de vue médico-légal*. Paris: Doin, 1885.

———. *Une maladie de la personnalité: L'inversion sexuelle*. Paris: Stock, 1893.

Combes, Émile. *L'instruction primaire des indigènes: Rapport fait au nom de la Commission chargée d'examiner les modifications à introduire dans la législation et dans l'organisation des divers services de l'Algérie*. Paris: P. Mouillot, 1892.

Commenge, O. *Les maladies vénériennes dans les armées anglaise, française et russe*. Paris: G. Masson, 1895.

Commission de la dépopulation. *Procès-verbaux: Sous-commission de la natalité*. Melun: Imprimerie administrative, 1902.

Commission de réflexion sur l'application du principe de laïcité dans la République. *Rapport au président de la République* 2003 [cited 2005]. Available from http://www.ladocumentationfrancaise.fr/brp/notices/034000725.shtml.

Commission extraparlementaire du régime des moeurs. *Procès verbaux des séances*: Melun: Imprimerie administrative, 1909.

Cousin, Victor. *Du vrai, du beau et du bien*. Paris: Didier, 1853.

Crawley, Ernest. "Sexual Taboos: A Study in the Relations of the Sexes." *Journal of the Anthropological Institute of Great Britain and Ireland* 24 (1895): 116–25; 219–35; 430–36.

———. *The Mystic Rose: A Study of Primitive Marriage and of Primitive Thought in Its Bearing on Marriage (1902)*. 2nd ed. Vol. 1. London: Methuen, 1927.

Convers, Francis. "Le secret médical dans les lois modernes récentes: Le secret médical dans l'armée." Doctorate medicine, Lyon, 1913.

Croiset, Alfred, ed. *L'éducation morale dans l'université (École des hautes études sociales, 1900–1901)*. Paris: Alcan, 1901.

Debove, Georges Maurice, and Dr. A.-F. Plicque. *Hygiène*. Edited by Félix Martel. Paris: Delagrave, 1906.

des Cilleuls, Alfred. *Histoire de l'enseignement libre dans l'ordre primaire en France*. Paris: Victor Retaux, 1898.

Dieu, M. le Médecin Inspecteur. *Rapport sur l'evolution et la prophylaxie des maladies vénériennes dans l'armée française*. Edited by Ministère de l'Intérieur et des Cultes. Melun: Imprimerie administrative, 1903.

Dumont, Arsène. *Dépopulation et civilisation*. Paris: Lecrosnier et Babé, 1890.

———. "Rapport sur l'âge au mariage et son influence sur la natalité." In *Commission de la dépopulation: Sous-commission de la natalité*. Melun: Imprimerie administrative, 1902.

Dupuy, Adrien. *L'état et l'université ou la vraie réforme de l'enseignement secondaire*. Paris: Cerf, 1890.

Dupuy, J. Th. *Le dogme du secret médical (essai de réfutation): Étude de médecine légale, d'hygiène sociale et de morale professionelle*. Paris: F. R. de Rudeval, 1903.

Durkheim, Émile. "Cours de science sociale: Leçon d'ouverture." *Revue internationale de l'enseignement* 8, no. 1 (1888): 23–48.

———. "Suicide et natalité: Étude de statistique morale." *Revue philosophique de la France et de l'étranger* 26, no. 11 (1888): 446–63.

———. "La prohibition de l'inceste et ses origines." *Année sociologique* 1 (1898): 1–70.

———. "Rôle des universités dans l'éducation sociale du pays." In *Congrès international de l'éducation sociale*, 128–38. Paris: Alcan, 1901.

———. *Le suicide*. Paris: Presses universitaires de France, 1930.

———. *Leçons de sociologie: Physique du moeurs et du droit*. Paris: Presses universitaires de France, 1950.

———. *Montesquieu et Rousseau: Précurseurs de la sociologie*. Paris: M. Rivière, 1953.

———. *L'éducation morale*. Paris: Presses universitaires de France, 1963.

———. "La prohibition de l'inceste et ses origines." In *Journal sociologique*, edited by Jean Duvignaud, 37–101. Paris: Presses universitaires de France, 1969.

———. "Review of Anna Lampérière *Le rôle social de la femme*." In *Journal sociologique*, edited by Jean Duvignaud, 391. Paris: Presses universitaires de France, 1969.

———. "Review of Fouillée, *Les éléments sociologiques de la morale* (1905–1906)." In *Journal sociologique*, edited by Jean Duvignaud, 568–84. Paris: Presses universitaires de France, 1969.

———. "Communauté et société selon Tönnies (1889)." In *Textes 1*, edited by Victor Karady, 383–90. Paris: Éditions de minuit, 1973.

———. "Evolution juridique en France à l'époque monarchique (1904)." In *Textes 3*, edited by Victor Karady, 330–34. Paris: Éditions de minuit, 1973.

———. "Individualism and the Intellectuals." In *Émile Durkheim on Morality and Society*, edited by Robert N. Bellah, 43–57. Chicago: University of Chicago Press, 1973.

———. "The Intellectual Elite and Democracy." In *Émile Durkheim on Morality and Society*, edited by Robert N. Bellah, 58–60. Chicago: University of Chicago Press, 1973.

———. "Introduction à la sociologie de la famille (1888)." In *Textes 3*, edited by Victor Karady, 9–34. Paris: Éditions de minuit, 1973.

———. "La famille conjugale (1892)." In *Textes 3*, edited by Victor Karady, 35–49. Paris: Éditions de minuit, 1973.

———. "Le problème religieux et la dualité de la nature humaine (1913)." In *Textes 2*, edited by Victor Karady, 23–59. Paris: Éditions de minuit, 1973.

———. *Les règles de la méthode sociologique*. 18e ed. Paris: Presses universitaires de France, 1973.

———. "Mariage et sexualité primitifs selon Crawley (1903)." In *Textes 3*, edited by Victor Karady, 94–102. Paris: Éditions de minuit, 1973.

———. "Organisation et vie du corps social selon Schaeffle (1888)." In *Textes 2*, edited by Victor Karady, 355–77. Paris: Éditions de minuit, 1973.

———. "Origine du mariage dans l'espèce humaine d'après Westermarck (1895)." In *Textes 3*, edited by Victor Karady, 70–92. Paris: Éditions de minuit, 1973.

———. "Origines du testament romain (1910)." In *Textes 3*, edited by Victor Karady, 65–68. Paris: Éditions de minuit, 1973.

———. "The Principles of 1789 and Sociology." In *Émile Durkheim: On Morality and Society*, edited by Robert N. Bellah, 34–42. Chicago: University of Chicago Press, 1973.

———. "Sociology in France in the Nineteenth Century." In *Émile Durkheim: On Morality and Society*, edited by Robert N. Bellah, 3–22. Chicago: University of Chicago Press, 1973.

———. "Débat sur le mariage et le divorce (1909)." In *Textes 2*, edited by Victor Karady, 206–15. Paris: Éditions de minuit, 1975.

———. "La définition du fait moral." In *Textes 2*, edited by Victor Karady, 257–88. Paris: Éditions de minuit, 1975.

———. "Le divorce par consentement mutuel (1906)." In *Textes 2*, edited by Victor Karady, 181–97. Paris: Éditions de minuit, 1975.

———. *De la division du travail social*. 11e ed. Paris: Presses universitaires de France, 1986.

———. *L'évolution pédagogique en France*. Paris: Presses universitaires de France, 1990.

———. *Sociologie et philosophie*. Paris: Presses universitaires de France, 1996.

Engels, Frederick. *The Origin of the Family, Private Property, and the State*. New York: International, 1975.

Enquête sur l'enseignement secondaire: Procès-verbaux des dépositions. Vol. 1. Paris: Imprimerie de la Chambre des Députés, 1899.

Espinas, Alfred. *Des sociétés animales: Étude de psychologie comparée.* Paris: Ballière, 1877.

Ferry, Jules. *Discours et opinions de Jules Ferry.* Edited by Paul Robiquet. Vol. 4. Paris: Armand Colin, 1896.

Fiaux, Louis. *L'organisation actuelle de la surveillance médicale de la prostitution est-elle susceptible d'amélioration.* Bruxelles: H. Lamertin, 1899.

———. *Enseignement populaire de la moralité sexuelle.* Paris: Alcan, 1908.

———. *L'armée et la police des moeurs: La biologie sexuelle du soldat.* Paris: Alcan, 1917.

Fonssagrives, Joseph (Abbé). *Conseils aux parents et aux maîtres sur l'éducation de la pureté.* Paris: Charles Poussielegue, 1902.

Fouillée, Alfred. *L'enseignement au point de vue national.* Paris: Hachette, 1891.

———. *Tempérament et caractère selon les individus, les sexes et les races.* Paris: Alcan, 1895.

———. *Les études classiques et la démocratie.* Paris: A. Colin, 1898.

———. *La France au point de vue moral.* Paris: Alcan, 1900.

———. *Les éléments sociologiques de la morale.* 2nd ed. Paris: Alcan, 1905.

Fournier, Alfred. *Syphilis et mariage: Leçons professées à l'Hôpital Saint-Louis.* Paris: Masson, 1880.

———. "Danger social de la syphilis." In *Compte rendu des séances,* edited by Conférence internationale pour la prophylaxie de la syphilis et des maladies vénériennes. Brussels: Lamertin, 1899.

Frary, Raoul. *La question du latin.* 2nd ed. Paris: L. Cerf, 1885.

Garnier, Pierre. *Célibat et célibataires: Caractères, dangers et hygiène chez les deux sexes.* Paris: Garnier, 1889.

Gréard, Octave. *L'esprit de discipline dans l'éducation—Mémoire présentée au Conseil académique dans la séance du 26 juin 1883.* Paris: Delalain, 1883.

———. *Education et instruction-Enseignement secondaire.* 2nd ed. Vol. 1. Paris: Hachette, 1889.

Guyot, Yves. *La préfecture de police.* Paris: Administration du journal *La Lanterne,* 1879.

———. *La prostitution.* Paris: G. Charpentier, 1882.

———. *La police.* Paris: G. Charpentier, 1884.

Hegel, G. W. F. *Philosophy of Right.* Translated by T. M. Knox. Oxford: Oxford University Press, 1971.

———. *Phenomenology of Spirit.* Translated by A. V. Miller. Oxford: Oxford University Press, 1977.

Hygiène des hommes de troupe. Paris: Henri Charles-Lavauzelle, 1909.

Janet, Paul. *La morale.* Paris: Delagrave, 1874.

Jeanmaire, Charles. *L'idée de la personnalité dans la psychologie moderne.* Toulouse: Privat, 1882.

Jeanselme, Édouard. "Maladies vénériennes." In *Traité d'hygiène: Étiologie et prophylaxie des maladies transmissibles par la peau et les muqueuses externes,* edited by A. Chantemesse and E. Mosny, 601–708. Paris: Baillière, 1911.

Joyeux, B. *Le péril vénérien et la prostitution à Hanoi.* Hanoi: Imprimerie d'Extrême-Orient, 1930.

Kant, Immanuel. *Groundwork of the Metaphysics of Morals.* Translated by H. J. Paton. New York: Harper and Row, 1956.

———. *The Metaphysics of Morals.* Translated by Mary Gregor. Cambridge: Cambridge University Press, 1996.

———. *Critique of Practical Reason.* Translated by Mary Gregor. Cambridge: Cambridge University Press, 1997.

Kermogard, Pauline. "Les écoles maternelles." In *Les écoles maternelles*, edited by Marie Matrat and Pauline Kermogard. Paris: Hachette, 1889.

Lacapère, Georges. *La syphilis arabe (Maroc, Algérie, Tunisie)*. Paris: Doin, 1923.

Lacassagne, Alexandre. *Dictionnaire encyclopédique des sciences médicales*. Edited by Raige-Delorme and Dechambre. Vol. 22. Paris, 1865–1889, s.v. "Péderastie," 239–59.

Lagneau, Gustave. "Du secret médical relativement aux maladies vénériennes." *Extrait du Bulletin de la Société de médecine légale*, (12 July 1869).

———. *Remarques démographiques sur le célibat en France*. Paris: Compte rendu de l'Académie des sciences morales et politiques, 1885.

———. *Du surmenage intellectuel et de la sédentarité dans les écoles*. Paris: Compte rendu de l'Académie des sciences morales et politiques, 1887.

Laprade, Victor de. *L'éducation homicide: Plaidoyer pour l'enfance (nouvelle édition)*. Paris: Didier, 1868.

Laupts, Dr (Georges Saint-Paul). *Perversion et perversité sexuelles*. Paris: Georges Carré, 1896.

LeGendre, Dr. P. "Le rôle du médecin scolaire." In *Premier congrès d'hygiène scolaire et de pédagogie physiologique*, edited by Ligue des médecins et des familles pour l'hygiène scolaire, 11–45. Paris: Masson, 1903.

Legrain, Dr. Maurice. *Des anomalies de l'instinct sexuel et en particulier des inversions du sens génital*. Paris: G. Carré, 1896.

Lubbock, John. *The Origin of Civilization and the Primitive Condition of Man: Mental and Social Condition of Savages*. London: Longmans, Green, 1882.

Lycées et collèges des jeunes filles: Documents, rapports et discours. Paris: Cerf, 1888.

Maneuvrier, Édouard. *L'éducation de la bourgeoisie sous la République*. Paris: Cerf, 1888.

———. *Commission pour les études des améliorations à introduire dans le régime des établissements d'enseignement secondaire: 4e sous-commission*. Paris: Imprimerie nationale, 1889.

Marion, Henri. *Leçons de morale*. Paris: Armand Colin, 1882.

———. *Leçons de psychologie appliquée à l'éducation*. Paris: Armand Colin, 1882.

———. *De la solidarité morale: Essai de psychologie appliquée*. 2nd ed. Paris: Ballière, 1883.

———. *L'éducation dans l'université*. Paris: Armand Colin, 1892.

———. *L'éducation des jeunes filles*. Paris: Armand Colin, 1902.

Ministère de l'instruction publique. *Commission pour l'étude des améliorations à introduire dans le régime des établissements d'enseignement secondaire*. Paris: Imprimerie nationale, 1888.

———. "Enseignement secondaire: Instructions et règlements." *Bulletin administratif du ministère de l'instruction publique*, no. 922 (supplément) (1890): 415–640.

Morgan, Lewis Henry. *Ancient Society; or, Researches in the Lines of Human Progress from Savagery, through Barbarism to Civilization*. New York: Henry Holt, 1877.

Parent-Duchâtelet, A.-J.-B. *La prostitution à Paris au 19e siècle; Texte présenté et annoté par Alain Corbin*. Paris: Seuil, 1981.

Perrier, Edmond. *Les colonies animales et la formation des organismes*. Paris: G. Masson, 1881.

Pichon, Ernest-Jean-François. "Les maladies vénériennes aux colonies—Leur prophylaxie dans l'armée coloniale." Doctorate medicine, Bordeaux, 1905.

Pinard, Alphonse, and Charles Richet. "Rapport sur les causes physiologiques de la diminution de la natalité en France (séance 10 décembre)." In *Commission de la dépopulation: sous-commission de la natalité*. Melun: Imprimerie administrative, 1902.

Plan d'études et programmes de l'enseignement primaire des indigènes en Algérie. Paris: Hachette, 1890.

Plisson, L. *Le secret médical dans l'armée*. Paris: Librarie militaire R. Chapelot, 1908.

Queyrat, Auguste, and Just Sicard de Plauzoles, eds. *Manuel d'éducation prophylactique contre les maladies vénériennes.* Edited by Comité national de propagande d'hygiène sociale et d'éducation prophylactique. Paris: Maloine, 1922.
Renan, Ernest. *L'islamisme et la science (conférence faite à la Sorbonne le 29 mars 1883).* Paris: Calman Lévy, 1883.
Rodes, Jean. *Adolescents: Moeurs.* Paris: Mercure de France, 1904.
Rommel (Alfred Duplessin), Dr. *Au pays de la revanche.* Geneva: Librarie Stapelmohr, 1886.
Rossignol (Roger Debury), Georges. *Un pays de célibataires et de fils uniques.* Paris: E. Dentu, 1896.
Rousseau, Jean-Jacques. *Émile or On Education.* Translated by Allan Bloom. New York: Basic Books, 1979.
Rouvier, Frédéric (Père). *La révolution maîtresse d'école: Étude sur l'instruction laïque, gratuite et obligatoire.* Avignon: Seguin Frères, 1880.
Saint-Maurice, C. *Pétition à MM. les députés contre l'instruction obligatoire, par un ami de l'instruction.* Paris: Dentu, 1880.
Sansterre (ouvrier agricole), Jean. *Qu'est-ce que l'enseignement laïque, gratuit et obligatoire? La vexation, l'absurdité, le despotisme.* Montpellier: Hamelin frères, 1880.
Sénat, Commision d'étude des questions algériennes. *Dépositions du 1er mai au 20 juillet 1891.* Paris: P. Mouillot, 1891.
Simon, Jules. *La réforme de l'enseignement secondaire.* 2nd ed. Paris: Hachette, 1874.
Smith, W. Robertson. *Kinship and Marriage in Early Arabia.* Cambridge: Cambridge University Press, 1885.
———. *Lectures on the Religion of the Semites.* Edinburgh: Adam and Charles Black, 1889.
Spencer, Herbert. *The Principles of Sociology: Domestic Institutions (1885).* 3rd ed. Vol. 3. New York and London: D. Appleton, 1910.
Spuller, Eugène. "La République et l'enseignement (1884)." In *Éducation de la démocratie: Troisième série de conférences populaires,* edited by Eugène Spuller. Paris: Alcan, 1892.
Taine, Hippolyte. *Les origines de la France moderne: Le régime moderne* vol. 2, *Église, École.* Paris: Hachette, 1894.
Thibierge, Georges. *Syphilis et déontologie.* Paris: Masson, 1903.
———. *La syphilis et l'armée.* Paris: Masson, 1917.
Turgeon, Charles. *Le féminisme français: L'émancipation politique et familiale de la femme.* Paris: Libraire de la Société du receuil général des lois et des arrêts, 1902.
Valabrègue, Jules. *Commentaire sur l'obligation de l'instruction primaire à l'usage des maires, des commissions municipales scolaires et des directeurs des établissements d'instruction.* Paris: Hachette, 1883.
Valentino, Charles. *Le secret professionel en médecine: Sa valeur sociale.* Paris: Naud, 1903.
Vallès, Jules. *Le bachelier* (1881). Paris: GF-Flammarion, 1970.
Vignon, Louis. *La France en Algérie.* Paris: Hachette, 1893.
Villot, Étienne Cécile Édouard. *Moeurs, coutumes, et institutions des indigènes de l'Algérie.* 3rd ed. Algiers: Adolphe Jourdain, 1888.
Westermarck, Édouard. *Origine du mariage dans l'espèce humaine.* Translated by Henry de Varigny. Paris: Guillaumin, 1895.

Secondary Sources

Accampo, Elinor A., Rachel G. Fuchs, and Mary Lynn Stewart, eds. *Gender and the Politics of Social Reform in France, 1870–1914.* Baltimore: Johns Hopkins University Press, 1995.

Adler, K. H. *Jews and Gender in Liberation France.* Cambridge: Cambridge University Press, 2003.

Ageron, Charles-Robert. *Les algériens musulmans et la France (1871–1919).* Vol. 1. Paris: Presses universitaires de France, 1968.

Aisenberg, Andrew R. *Contagion: Disease, Government, and the "Social Question" in Nineteenth-century France.* Stanford: Stanford University Press, 1999.

———. "Syphilis and Prostitution: A Regulatory Couplet in Nineteenth-century France." In *Sex, Sin, and Suffering: Venereal Disease and European Society since 1870,* edited by Roger Davidson and Lesley A. Hall, 15–28. London: Routledge, 2001.

Alaimo, Kathleen. "Shaping Adolescence in the Popular Milieu: Social Policy, Reformers, and French Youth, 1870–1920." *Journal of Family History* 17, no. 4 (1992): 419–38.

———. "Adolescence, Gender and Class in Educational Reform in France: The Development of *Enseignement Primaire Supérieur,* 1880–1910." *French Historical Studies* 18, no. 4 (1994): 1025–55.

Aldrich, Robert. "Homosexuality in the French Colonies." In *Homosexuality in French History and Culture,* edited by Jeffrey Merrick and Michael David Sibalis, 201–18. New York: Harrington Press, 2001.

Allen, Ann Taylor. "Feminism, Venereal Disease, and the State in Germany, 1890–1918." *Journal of the History of Sexuality* 4, no. 1 (1993): 27–50.

Antomarchi, Véronique. *Politique et famille sous la Troisième République, 1870–1914.* Paris: L'Harmattan, 2000.

Ariès, Philippe. *Centuries of Childhood: A Social History of Family Life.* Translated by Robert Baldick. New York: Vintage, 1960.

Audoin-Rouzeau. *L'enfant de l'ennemi (1914–1918).* Paris: Aubier, 1995.

Auspitz, Katherine. *The Radical Bourgeoisie: The Ligue de l'enseignement and the Origins of the Third Republic, 1866–1885.* Cambridge: Cambridge University Press, 1982.

Avon, Philippe. "Contribution à l'histoire des maladies vénériennes dans l'armée française—Prophylaxie et traitement." Doctorate medicine, Lyon, 1968.

Barberis, Daniela S. "The First *Année sociologique* and Neo-Kantian Philosophy in France." Ph.D. diss., University of Chicago, 2001.

Barnes, David S. *The Making of a Social Disease: Tuberculosis in Nineteenth-century France.* Berkeley: University of California Press, 1995.

Barrows, Susanna. *Distorting Mirrors: Visions of the Crowd in Late-Nineteenth-Century France.* New Haven: Yale University Press, 1981.

Baubérot, Jean. "Note sur Durkheim et la laïcité." *Archives des sciences sociales des religions* 69, no. 1 (1990): 151–56.

———. *La morale laïque contre l'ordre moral.* Paris: Seuil, 1997.

———. *Laïcité 1905–2005, entre passion et raison.* Paris: Seuil, 2004.

Becchia, Alain. "Les milieux parlementaires et la dépopulation de 1900 à 1914." *Communications (Dénatalité: L'antériorité française (1800–1914))* 44 (1986): 201–46.

Bederman, Gail. *Manliness and Civilization: A Cultural History of Gender and Race in the United States, 1880–1917.* Chicago: University of Chicago Press, 1995.

Berenson, Edward. *The Trial of Madame Caillaux.* Berkeley: University of California Press, 1992.

Berlière, Jean-Marc. *La police des moeurs sous la Troisième République.* Paris: Seuil, 1992.

Bernheimer, Charles. *Figures of Ill Repute: Representing Prostitution in Nineteenth-century France.* Cambridge: Harvard University Press, 1989.

Bernstein, Laurie. *Sonia's Daughters: Prostitutes and Their Regulation in Imperial Russia.* Berkeley: University of California Press, 1995.

Besnard, Philippe. "Durkheim et les femmes ou *Le suicide* inachevé." *Revue française de sociologie* 14 (1973): 27–61.

———. "The *Année sociologique* team." In *The Sociological Domain: The Durkheimians and the Founding of French Sociology,* edited by Philippe Besnard, 11–39. Cambridge: Cambridge University Press, 1983.

Birnbaum, Pierre. "French Sociologists between Reason and Faith: The Impact of the Dreyfus Affair." *Jewish Social Studies* 2, no. 1 (1995): 1–35.

Blanckaert, Claude. "La crise de l'anthropométrie: Des arts anthropotechniques aux dérives militantes." In *Les usages de l'anthropologie: Discours et pratiques en France (1860–1940),* edited by Claude Blanckaert, 97–198. Paris: L'Harmattan, 2001.

Blévis, Laure. "La citoyenneté française au miroir de la colonisation: Étude des demandes de naturalisation des 'sujets français' en Algérie coloniale." *Genèses,* no. 53 (2003): 25–47.

Bleys, Rudi. *The Geography of Perversion: Male-to-male Sexual Behavior Outside the West and the Ethnographic Imagination, 1750–1918.* New York: New York University Press, 1995.

Blum, Carol. *Strength in Numbers: Population, Reproduction, and Power in Eighteenth-century France.* Baltimore: Johns Hopkins University Press, 2002.

Bompaire-Evesque, Claire. "Paris, centre de la vie politique dans 'Le roman de l'énergie nationale' de Maurice Barrès." *Cahiers de l'Association Internationale des Études Françaises* 42 (1990): 63–75.

Bonnell, Victoria E., Lynn Hunt, and Richard Biernacki, eds. *Beyond the Cultural Turn: New Directions in the Study of Society and Culture.* Berkeley: University of California Press, 1999.

Borie, Jean. *Le célibataire français.* Paris: Sagitaire, 1976.

Borneman, John. "Until Death Do Us Part: Marriage/Death in Anthropological Discourse." *American Ethnologist* 23, no. 2 (1996): 215–35.

Bouamama, Saïd. *L'affaire du foulard islamique: La production d'un racisme respectable.* Paris: Geai bleu, 2004.

Boulogne, Jean Claude. *Histoire du célibat et des célibataires.* Paris: Fayard, 2004.

Brandt, Allan M. *No Magic Bullet: A Social History of Venereal Disease in the United States since 1880.* Oxford: Oxford University Press, 1987.

Brooks, John I. "Philosophy and Psychology at the Sorbonne, 1885–1913." *Journal of the History of the Behavioral Sciences* 29, no. 2 (1993): 123–45.

———. *The Eclectic Legacy: Academic Philosophy and the Human Sciences in Nineteenth-century France.* Newark: University of Delaware Press, 1998.

Brubaker, Rogers. *Citizenship and Nationhood in France and Germany.* Cambridge: Harvard University Press, 1992.

Bullard, Alice. *Exile in Paradise: Savagery and Civilization in Paris and the South Pacific, 1790–1900.* Stanford: Stanford University Press, 2000.

Butler, Judith. *Gender Trouble: Feminism and the Subversion of Identity.* New York: Routledge, 1990.

———. *The Psychic Life of Power.* Stanford: Stanford University Press, 1997.

———. *Antigone's Claim: Kinship between Life and Death.* New York: Columbia University Press, 2000.

———. *Undoing Gender.* New York: Routledge, 2004.

Canguilhem, Georges. *Le normal et le pathologique.* Paris: Presses universitaires de France, 1966.

Carol, Anne. *Histoire de l'eugénisme en France: Les médecins et la procréation, 19ᵉ–20ᵉ siècle.* Paris: Seuil, 1996.

Caron, Jean-Claude. "Young People in School: Middle and High School Students in France and Europe." In *A History of Young People in the West,* vol. 2, *Stormy Evolution to Modern Times,* edited by Giovanni Levi and Jean-Claude Schmidt, 117–73. Cambridge: Belknap Press, 1997.

———. À l'école de la violence. Paris: Aubier, 1999.

Carroll, David. French Literary Fascism: Nationalism, Anti-Semitism, and the Ideology of Culture. Princeton: Princeton University Press, 1995.

Chamboredon, Jean-Claude. "Émile Durkheim: Le social, objet de science: Du moral au politique?" Critique 40, no. 445–46 (1984): 460–531.

Chanet, Jean-François. L'école républicaine et les petites patries. Paris: Aubier, 1996.

Charle, Christophe. La crise littéraire à l'époque du naturalisme. Paris: Presses de l'École normale supérieure, 1979.

———. "La lutte des classes en littérature: L'étape de Paul Bourget and Vérité d'Émile Zola." In Les écrivains et l'affaire Dreyfus, edited by Gérald Leroy. Paris: Presses universitaires de France, 1983.

———. "Le beau mariage d'Émile Durkheim." Actes de la recherche en sciences sociales, no. 55 (1984): 45–49.

———. Dictionnaire biographique des universitaires aux 19ᵉ et 20ᵉ siècle: La Faculté des lettres de Paris. Vol. 1. Paris: Éditions du Centre national des recherches scientifiques, 1985.

———. Les élites de la République, 1880–1900. Paris: Fayard, 1987.

———. Naissance des 'intellectuels', 1880–1900. Paris: Éditions de minuit, 1990.

———. "La magistrature intellectuelle de Taine." In Taine au carrefour des cultures du 19ᵉ siècle, edited by Stéphane Michaud, 111–25. Paris: Bibliothèque nationale de France, 1996.

Charnay, Jean Paul. Société militaire et suffrage politique en France depuis 1789. Paris: SEVPEN, 1964.

Childers, Kristen Stromberg. Fathers, Families, and the State in France, 1914–1945. Ithaca: Cornell University Press, 2003.

Choquette, Leslie. "Degenerate or Degendered? Images of Prostitution and Homosexuality in the French Third Republic." Historical Reflections/Reflexions Historiques 23, no. 2 (1997): 205–28.

Clancy-Smith, Julia. "Islam, Gender, and Identities in the Making of French Algeria, 1830–1963." In Domesticating the Empire: Race, Gender, and Family Life in French and Dutch Colonialism, edited by Julia Clancy-Smith and Frances Gouda, 154–74. Charlottesville: University Press of Virginia, 1998.

Clark, Linda. The Rise of Professional Women in France: Gender and Public Administration. Cambridge: Cambridge University Press, 2000.

Clark, Terry Nichols. Prophets and Patrons: The French University and the Emergence of the Social Sciences. Cambridge: Harvard University Press, 1973.

Clarke, Eric O. Virtuous Vice: Homoeroticism and the Public Sphere. Durham: Duke University Press, 2000.

Coffin, Judith. The Politics of Women's Work: The Paris Garment Trades, 1750–1915. Princeton: Princeton University Press, 1996.

Cohen, Ed. Talk on the Wilde Side: Toward a Genealogy of a Discourse on Male Sexualities. New York: Routledge, 1993.

Cole, Joshua. The Power of Large Numbers: Population, Politics, and Gender in Nineteenth-century France. Ithaca: Cornell University Press, 2000.

Colonna, Fanny. Instituteurs algériens: 1883–1939. Paris: Presses de la Fondation nationale des sciences politiques, 1975.

Conklin, Alice L. A Mission to Civilize: The Republican Idea of Empire in France and West Africa. Stanford: Stanford University Press, 1997.

———. "Colonialism and Human Rights, A Contradiction in Terms? The Case of France and West Africa, 1895–1914." American Historical Review 103, no. 2 (1998): 419–42.

Copley, Antony. *Sexual Moralities in France, 1780–1980: New Ideas on the Family, Divorce, and Homosexuality.* London: Routledge, 1989.

Corbin, Alain. "Le péril vénérien au début du siècle: Prophylaxie sanitaire et prophylaxie morale." *Recherches* 11, no. 29 (1977): 245–83.

———. *Les filles de noce.* Paris: Aubier, 1978.

Crépin, Annie. *La conscription en débat: Le triple apprentissage de la nation, de la citoyenneté, de la République: 1789–1889.* Arras: Artois presses université, 1998.

Crubellier, Maurice. *L'enfance et la jeunesse dans la société française, 1800–1950.* Paris: Armand Colin, 1979.

Curtis, Sarah A. *Educating the Faithful: Religion, Schooling, and Society in Nineteenth-century France.* DeKalb: Northern Illinois University Press, 2000.

Datta, Venita. *Birth of a National Icon: The Literary Avant-Garde and the Origins of the Intellectual in France.* Albany: State University of New York Press, 1999.

Daughton, James P. "The Civilizing Mission: Missionaries, Colonialists, and French Identity, 1885–1914." Ph.D. diss., University of California, Berkeley, 2002.

Davidson, Arnold I. *The Emergence of Sexuality: Historical Epistemology and the Formation of Concepts.* Cambridge: Harvard University Press, 2001.

Davidson, Roger, and Lesley A. Hall. *Sex, Sin, and Suffering: Venereal Disease and European Society since 1870.* London: Routledge, 2001.

Davy, Georges. "La famille et la parenté d'après Durkheim." In *Sociologues d'hier et d'aujourd'hui,* 81–122. Paris: Presses universitaires de France, 1950.

Dean, Carolyn J. *The Frail Social Body: Pornography, Homosexuality, and Other Fantasies in Interwar France.* Berkeley: University of California Press, 2000.

Déloye, Yves. *École et citoyenneté: L'individualisme républicain de Jules Ferry à Vichy: controverses.* Paris: Presses de la Fondation nationale des sciences politiques, 1994.

Delumeau, Jean, and Daniel Roche, eds. *Histoire des pères et de la paternité.* Paris: Larousse, 1990.

Derczansky, Alexandre. "Note sur la judéité de Durkheim." *Archives de sciences sociales des religions* 69, no. 1 (1990): 157–60.

Desan, Suzanne. *The Family on Trial in Revolutionary France.* Berkeley: University of California Press, 2004.

Desvages, Hubert. "L'enseignement des musulmans d'Algérie sous le rectorat de Jeanmaire: Le rôle de l'école." *Mouvement social* 70 (1970): 109–42.

Dickinson, Edward Ross. "The Men's Christian Morality Movement in Germany, 1880–1914: Some Reflections on Politics, Sex, and Sexual Politics." *Journal of Modern History* 75, no. 2 (2003): 59–110.

Digeon, Claude. *La crise allemande de la pensée française (1870–1914).* Paris: Presses universitaires de France, 1959.

Dijkstra, Bram. *Idols of Perversity: Fantasies of Feminine Evil in Fin-de-siècle Culture.* New York: Oxford University Press, 1986.

Ditz, Toby L. "The New Men's History and the Peculiar Absence of Gendered Power: Some Remedies from Early American Gender History." *Gender and History* 16, no. 1 (2004): 1–35.

Donzelot, Jacques. *The Policing of Families.* Translated by Robert Hurley. Baltimore: Johns Hopkins University Press, 1979.

———. *L'invention du social: Essai sur le déclin des passions politiques.* Paris: Seuil, 1994.

Doty, C. Stewart. *From Cultural Rebellion to Counterrevolution: the Politics of Maurice Barrès.* Athens: Ohio University Press, 1976.

Elwitt, Sanford. *The Making of the Third Republic: Class and Politics in France, 1868–1884.* Baton Rouge: Louisiana State University Press, 1975.

———. *The Third Republic Defended: Bourgeois Reform in France, 1880–1914.* Baton Rouge: Louisiana State University Press, 1986.

Engelstein, Laura. *The Keys to Happiness: Sex and the Search for Modernity in Fin-de-siècle Russia.* Ithaca: Cornell University Press, 1992.

Evans, David. "Tackling the 'Hideous Scourge': The Creation of the Venereal Disease Treatment Centers in Early Twentieth-century Britain." *Social History of Medicine* 5, no. 3 (1992): 413–33.

Ewald, François. "A Concept of Social Law." In *Dilemmas of Law in the Welfare State,* edited by Gunther Teubner, 40–75. Berlin: Walter de Gruyther, 1985.

———. *L'état providence.* Paris: Grasset, 1986.

———, ed. *Naissance du Code civil: La raison du législateur.* Paris: Flammarion, 1989.

Fabiani, Jean-Louis. *Les philosophes de la république.* Paris: Éditions de minuit, 1988.

———. "Métaphysique, morale, sociololgie: Durkheim et le retour à la philosophie." *Revue de métaphysique et de morale,* no. 1–2 (1993): 175–91.

Fabre, Clarisse, and Eric Fassin. *Liberté, égalité, sexualités.* Paris: Belfond, 2003.

Filloux, Jean-Claude. "Il ne faut pas oublier que je suis fils de rabbin." *Revue française de sociologie* 17, no. 2 (1976): 259–66.

———. "Personne et sacré chez Durkheim." *Archives des sciences sociales des religions* 69 (1990): 41–53.

———. *Durkheim et l'éducation.* Paris: Presses universitaires de France, 1994.

Forth, Christopher E. *The Dreyfus Affair and the Crisis of French Manhood.* Baltimore: Johns Hopkins University Press, 2004.

Foucault, Michel. *Discipline and Punish: The Birth of the Prison.* Translated by Alan Sheridan. New York: Vintage, 1979.

———. *The History of Sexuality, Volume I: An Introduction.* Translated by Robert Hurley. New York: Vintage, 1980.

———. *Les anormaux: Cours au Collège de France, 1974–1975.* Edited by François Ewald and Alessandro Fontana. Paris: Gallimard, 1999.

Fout, John C. "Sexual Politics in Wilhelmine Germany: The Male Gender Crisis, Moral Purity, and Homophobia." *Journal of the History of Sexuality* 2, no. 3 (1992): 388–421.

Ford, Caroline. *Divided Houses: Religion and Gender in Modern France.* Ithaca: Cornell University Press, 2005.

Fraisse, Geneviève. *Reason's Muse: Sexual Difference and the Birth of Democracy.* Translated by Jane Marie Todd. Chicago: University of Chicago Press, 1994.

Fuchs, Rachel. *Poor and Pregnant in Paris: Strategies for Survival in the Nineteenth Century.* New Brunswick: Rutgers University Press, 1992.

———. "France in Comparative Perspective." In *Gender and the Politics of Social Reform in France, 1870–1914,* edited by Elinor A. Accampo, Rachel Fuchs, and Mary Lynn Stewart, 157–87. Baltimore: Johns Hopkins University Press, 1995.

———. "Seduction, Paternity, and the Law in Fin-de-siècle France." *Journal of Modern History* 72, no. 4 (2000): 944–89.

Furet, François, and Mona Ozouf. *Lire et écrire: L'alphabétisation des Français de Calvin à Jules Ferry.* Paris: Éditions de minuit, 1977.

Gane, Mike. "Durkheim: Woman as Outsider." In *The Radical Sociology of Durkheim and Mauss,* edited by Mike Gane, 85–132. London: Routledge, 1992.

Garaud, Marcel. *La révolution française et la famille.* Paris: Presses universitaires de France, 1978.

Garb, Tamar. *Bodies of Modernity: Figure and Flesh in Fin-de-siècle France.* London: Thames and Hudson, 1998.

Gaspard, Françoise, and Farhad Khosrokhavar. *Le foulard et la République.* Paris: Découverte, 1995.

———. "Femmes, foulards, et République." In *Le foulard islamique en questions,* edited by Charlotte Nordmann, 72–80. Paris: Éditions Amsterdam, 2004.

Gasparini, Eric. *La pensée politique d'Hippolyte Taine.* Aix-en-Provence: Presses universitaires d'Aix-Marseille, 1993.

Gibson, Mary. *Prostitution and the State in Italy, 1860–1915.* 2nd ed. Columbus: Ohio State University Press, 2000.

Gildea, Robert. *Education in Provincial France, 1800–1914: A Study of Three Departments.* Oxford: Clarendon Press, 1983.

Gillis, John R. *Youth and History: Tradition and Change in European Age Relations, 1770–Present.* New York: Academic Press, 1974.

Girardet, Raoul. *La société militaire de 1815 à nos jours.* Paris: Perrin, 1998.

Goldstein, Jan. "Foucault and the Post-Revolutionary Self: The Uses of Cousinian Pedagogy in Nineteenth-century France." In *Foucault and the Writing of History,* edited by Jan Goldstein, 99–134. Oxford: Basil Blackwell, 1994.

———. " 'Saying I': Victor Cousin, Caroline Angebert, and the Politics of Selfhood in Nineteenth-century France." In *Rediscovering History: Politics, Culture, and the Psyche,* edited by Michael Roth, 240–75. Stanford: Stanford University Press, 1994.

———. *The Post-Revolutionary Self: Politics and Psyche in France, 1750–1850.* Cambridge: Harvard University Press, 2005.

Grayzel, Susan R. "Mothers, Marraines, and Prostitutes: Morale and Morality in First World War France." *International History Review* 19, no. 1 (1997): 66–82.

Greenberg, Louis M. "Bergson and Durkheim as Sons and Assimilators." *French Historical Studies* 9, no. 4 (1976): 619–34.

Grew, Raymond, and Patrick J. Harrigan. *School, State, and Society: The Growth of Elementary Schooling in Nineteenth-century France.* Ann Arbor: University of Michigan Press, 1991.

Guénif-Soulimas, Nacira, and Eric Macé. *Les féministes et le garçon arabe.* Paris: L'aube, 2004.

Guerrand, R. H. *Lycéens révoltés, étudiants révolutionnaires au 19e siècle.* Paris: Éditions du temps, 1969.

Guillaume, Pierre. *Le rôle social du médecin depuis deux siècles, 1800–1945.* Paris: Association pour l'étude de l'histoire de la sécurité sociale, 1996.

Gullickson, Gay. *Unruly Women: Images of the Commune.* Ithaca: Cornell University Press, 1996.

Guy, Donna J. *Sex and Danger in Buenos Aires: Prostitution, Family, and Nation in Argentina.* Lincoln: University of Nebraska Press, 1991.

Guyard, Marius-François. "Barrès et la Révolution française: La leçon des *Déracinés.*" In *Barrès: Une tradition dans la modernité,* edited by André Guyaux et al., 131–37. Paris: Librairie Honoré Champion, 1991.

Halpérin, Jean-Louis. *L'impossible Code civil.* Paris: Presses universitaires de France, 1992.

Halley, Janet. "Reasoning about Sodomy: Act and Identity in and after Bowers v. Hardwick." *Virginia Law Review* 79, no. 7 (1993): 1721–80.

Harris, Ruth. *Murders and Madness: Medicine, Law, and Society in the Fin-de-siècle.* Oxford: Oxford University Press, 1989.

———. " 'The Child of the Barbarian': Rape, Race and Nationalism in France during the First World War." *Past and Present* 141 (1993): 170–206.

Harrison, Carol E. *The Bourgeois Citizen in Nineteenth-century France: Gender, Sociability, and the Uses of Emulation.* Oxford: Oxford University Press, 1999.

Harrison, Mark. "The British Army and the Problem of Venereal Disease in France and Egypt during the First World War." *Medical History* 39 (1995): 133–58.

Harsin, Jill. *Policing Prostitution in Nineteenth-century Paris.* Princeton: Princeton University Press, 1985.

——. "Syphilis, Wives, and Physicians: Medical Ethics and the Family in Late Nineteenth-Century France." *French Historical Studies* 16, no. 1 (1989): 72–95.

Hawkins, M. J. "Durkheim on Occupational Corporations: An Exegesis and Interpretation." *Journal of the History of Ideas* 55, no. 3 (1994): 461–81.

Hayat, Pierre. *La passion laïque de Ferdinand Buisson.* Paris: Kimé, 1999.

Hayward, J. E. S. "Solidarity: The Social History of an Idea in Nineteenth-century France." *International Review of Social History* 4, no. 2 (1959): 261–84.

——. "The Official Social Philosophy of the French Third Republic: Léon Bourgeois and Solidarism." *International Review of Social History* 6, no. 1 (1961): 19–48.

Hazareesingh, Sudhir. *From Subject to Citizen: The Second Empire and the Emergence of Modern French Democracy.* Princeton: Princeton University Press, 1998.

Héritier, Françoise. *Two Sisters and Their Mother.* Translated by Jeanine Herman. New York: Zone Books, 2002.

Hershatter, Gail. *Dangerous Pleasures: Prostitution and Modernity in Twentieth-century Shanghai.* Berkeley: University of California Press, 1997.

Hesse, Carla. *The Other Enlightenment: How French Women Became Modern.* Princeton: Princeton University Press, 2001.

Heuer, Jennifer. *The Family and the Nation: Gender and Citizenship in Revolutionary France, 1789–1830.* Ithaca: Cornell University Press, 2005.

Higonnet, Patrice. "The Harmonization of the Spheres: Goodness and Dysfunction in the Provincial Clubs." In *The French Revolution and the Creation of Modern Political Culture,* edited by Keith Michael Baker, 117–37. Oxford: Pergamon, 1994.

Hildreth, Martha L. *Doctors, Bureaucrats, and Public Health in France, 1888–1902.* New York: Garland, 1986.

Hill, Andreas. " 'May the Doctor Advise Extramarital Intercourse?': Medical Debates on Sexual Abstinence in Germany, c. 1900." In *Sexual Knowledge, Sexual Science,* edited by Roy Porter and Mikulas Teiche, 284–302. Cambridge: Cambridge University Press, 1994.

Horne, Janet A. *A Social Laboratory for Modern France.* Durham: Duke University Press, 2000.

Horvath-Peterson, Sandra. *Victor Duruy and French Education: Liberal Reform in the Second Empire.* Baton Rouge: Louisiana State University Press, 1984.

Houziaux, Alain, ed. *Le voile que cache-t-il?* Paris: Les editions de l'atelier, 2004.

Hull, Isabel V. *Sexuality, State, and Civil Society in Germany, 1700–1815.* Ithaca: Cornell University Press, 1996.

Hunt, Lynn. *The Family Romance of the French Revolution.* Berkeley: University of California Press, 1992.

——. "Male Virtue and Republican Motherhood." In *The French Revolution and the Creation of Modern Political Culture,* edited by Keith Michael Baker, 195–208. Oxford: Pergamon, 1994.

——. "Forgetting and Remembering: The French Revolution Then and Now." *American Historical Review* 100, no. 4 (1995): 1119–35.

——. ed. *The New Cultural History.* Berkeley: University of California Press, 1989.

Isambert, François-A. "Durkheim: une science de la morale pour une morale laïque." *Archives des sciences sociales des religions* 69 (1990): 129–46.

Isambert-Jamati, Viviane. "Une réforme des lycées et collèges: Essai d'analyse sociologique de la réforme de 1902." *Année sociologique* 20 (1969): 9–60.

——. *Crises de la société, crises de l'enseignement: sociologie de l'enseignement secondaire français.* Paris: Presses universitaires de France, 1970.

Jones, Robert Alun. "Robertson Smith, Durkheim and Sacrifice: An Historical Context for *The Elementary Forms of Religious Life.*" In *Émile Durkheim: Critical Assessments*, edited by Peter Hamilton, 376–404. London: Routledge, 1990.

———. "Durkheim, Realism, and Rousseau." *Journal of the History of the Behavioral Sciences* 32, no. 4 (1996): 330–53.

———. *The Development of Durkheim's Social Realism.* Cambridge: Cambridge University Press, 1999.

Karady, Victor. "The Durkheimians in Academe: A Reconsideration." In *The Sociological Domain: The Durkheimians and the Founding of French Sociology,* edited by Philippe Besnard, 71–89. Cambridge: Cambridge University Press, 1983.

———. "Les professeurs de la République: Le marché scolaire, les réformes universitaires et les transformations de la fonction professorale à la fin du 19ᵉ siècle." *Année sociologique* 47–48 (1983): 90–112.

———. "Durkheim et les débuts de l'ethnologie universitaire." *Actes de la recherche en sciences sociales* 74 (1988): 23–32.

Katz, Jonathan. *The Invention of Heterosexuality.* New York: Dutton, 1995.

Kerber, Linda. "The Paradox of Women's Citizenship: The Case of Martin vs. Massachusetts, 1805." *American Historical Review* 97, no. 2 (1992): 349–78.

Kloppenberg, James T. *Uncertain Victory: Social Democracy and Progressivism in European and American Thought, 1870–1920.* Oxford: Oxford University Press, 1986.

Kuper, Adam. "Durkheim's Theory of Primitive Kinship." *British Journal of Sociology* 36, no. 2 (1985): 224–37.

———. *The Invention of Primitive Society: Transformations of an Illusion.* London: Routledge, 1988.

———. "Incest, Cousin Marriage, and the Origin of the Human Sciences in Nineteenth-century England." *Past and Present* 174, no. 1 (2002): 158–83.

Kushner, Howard I. "Suicide, Gender, and Fear of Modernity in Nineteenth-century Medical and Social Thought." *Journal of Social History* 26, no. 2 (1992): 461–90.

La Vopa, Anthony J. "Thinking about Marriage: Kant's Liberalism and the Peculiar Morality of Conjugal Union." *Journal of Modern History* 77, no. 1 (2005): 1–34.

LaCapra, Dominick. *Émile Durkheim: Sociologist and Philosopher.* Ithaca: Cornell University Press, 1972.

———. "History, Reading, and Critical Theory." In *History and Reading: Tocqueville, Foucault, French Studies,* 21–72. Toronto: University of Toronto Press, 2000.

Lacroix, Bernard. *Durkheim et le politique.* Montreal: Presses de la fondation nationale des sciences politiques, 1981.

Lamanna, Mary Ann. *Émile Durkheim on the Family.* London: Sage, 2002.

Lambelet, André J. "A Reluctant Reconciliation: Army Officers, Conscription, and Democratic Citizenship in the French Third Republic, 1870–1940." Ph.D. diss., University of California, Berkeley, 2001.

Landes, Joan B. *Women and the Public Sphere in the Age of the French Revolution.* Ithaca: Cornell University Press, 1988.

Laqueur, Thomas. *Making Sex: Body and Gender from the Greeks to Freud.* Cambridge: Harvard University Press, 1990.

Le Naour, Jean-Yves. *Misères et tourments de la chair durant la Grande Guerre: Les moeurs sexuelles des Français, 1914–1918.* Paris: Aubier, 2002.

Lefebvre, Thierry. "Syphilis et automédication au tournant du siècle." *Revue de l'histoire de la pharmacie,* no. 306 (1995): 43–51.

Lehmann, Jennifer M. *Durkheim and Women.* Lincoln: University of Nebraska Press, 1994.

Lehning, James R. *To Be a Citizen: The Political Culture of the Early Third Republic.* Ithaca: Cornell University Press, 2001.

Lenoir, Rémi. *Généalogie de la morale familiale.* Paris: Seuil, 2003.

Lévi-Strauss, Claude. *The Elementary Structures of Kinship*. Boston: Beacon Press, 1970.

Levine, Philippa. *Prostitution, Race, and Politics: Policing Venereal Disease in the British Empire*. New York: Routledge, 2003.

Loeffel, Laurence. *La question du fondement de la morale laïque sous la IIIᵉ République (1870–1914)*. Paris: Presses universitaires de France, 2000.

Logue, William. *From Philosophy to Sociology: The Evolution of French Liberalism, 1870–1914*. DeKalb: Northern Illinois University Press, 1983.

———. *Charles Renouvier: Philosopher of Liberty*. Baton Rouge: Louisiana State University Press, 1993.

Löwy, Ilana. "Les 'faits scientifiques' et leur public: L'histoire de la détection de la syphilis." *Revue de synthèse* 1, no. 1 (1995): 27–54.

Luc, Jean-Noël. *L'invention du jeune enfant au 19ᵉ siècle: De la salle d'asile à l'école maternelle*. Paris: Belin, 1997.

———, ed. *La petite enfance à l'école, 19–20ᵉ siècles: textes officiels présentés et annotés*. Paris: Economica, 1982.

Lukes, Steven. *Émile Durkheim: His Life and Work*. New York: Harper and Row, 1972.

Margadant, Jo Burr. *Madame le professeur: Women Educators in the Third Republic*. Princeton: Princeton University Press, 1990.

Matlock, Jann. *Scenes of Seduction: Prostitution, Hysteria and Reading Difference in Nineteenth-century France*. New York: Columbia University Press, 1994.

Maugue, Annelise. *L'identité masculine en crise au tournant du siècle, 1871–1914*. Paris: Rivages, 1987.

Mayeur, Françoise. *L'enseignement secondaire des jeunes filles sous la Troisième République*. Paris: Presses de la fondation nationale des sciences politiques, 1977.

———. *Histoire générale de l'enseignement et de l'éducation en France: de la Révolution à l'Ecole républicaine*. Vol. 3. Paris: Nouvelle librairie de France, 1981.

———. "La femme dans la société selon Jules Ferry." In *Jules Ferry, fondateur de la République*, edited by François Furet, 79–89. Paris: Éditions de l'École des hautes études sociales, 1985.

Mayeur, Jean-Marie. "Jules Ferry et laïcité." In *Jules Ferry, fondateur de la République*, edited by François Furet, 147–60. Paris: Éditions de l'École des hautes études sociales, 1985.

———. *La question laïque, 19ᵉ–20ᵉ siècle*. Paris: Fayard, 1997.

McBride, Theresa. "Divorce and the Republican Family." In *Gender and the Politics of Social Reform in France, 1870–1914*, edited by Elinor A. Accampo, Rachel G. Fuchs, and Mary Lynn Stewart, 59–81. Baltimore: Johns Hopkins University Press, 1995.

McLaren, Angus. *Sexuality and Social Order: The Debate over the Fertility of Women and Workers in France, 1770–1920*. New York: Holmes and Meier, 1983.

———. *The Trials of Masculinity: Policing Sexual Boundaries, 1870–1930*. Chicago: University of Chicago Press, 1997.

Merllié, Dominique. "Les rapports entre la *Revue de métaphysique* et la *Revue philosophique*: Xavier Léon, Théodule Ribot, Lucien Lévy-Bruhl." *Revue de métaphysique et de morale*, no. 1–2 (1993): 59–90.

Miller, Julia. "The 'Romance of Regulation': The Movement against State-regulated Prostitution in France, 1871–1948." Ph.D. diss., New York University, 2000.

Mucchielli, Laurent. *La découverte du social: Naissance de la sociologie en France (1870–1914)*. Paris: Éditions de la découverte, 1998.

Muller, Detlef K., Fritz Ringer, and Brian Simon, eds. *The Rise of the Modern Educational System: Structural Change and Social Reproduction, 1870–1920*. Cambridge: Cambridge University Press, 1987.

Murard, Lion, and Patrick Zylberman. *Hygiène dans la République*. Paris: Fayard, 1996.

Neubauer, John. *The Fin-de-siècle Culture of Adolescence*. New Haven: Yale University Press, 1992.

Nicolet, Claude. *L'idée républicaine en France (1789–1924): Essai d'histoire critique*. Paris: Gallimard, 1994.

Nora, Pierre. "Le *Dictionnaire de pédagogie* de Ferdinand Buisson: Cathédrale de l'école primaire." In *Les lieux de mémoire: La République*, edited by Pierre Nora, 353–78. Paris: Gallimard, 1984.

Nord, Philip. "The Welfare State in France, 1870–1914." *French Historical Studies* 18, no. 3 (1994): 821–38.

———. The Republican Moment: Struggles for Democracy in Nineteenth-century France. Cambridge: Harvard University Press, 1995.

Nordmann, Charlotte, ed. *Le foulard islamique en questions*. Paris: Éditions Amsterdam, 2004.

Norris, Katharine H. "Reinventing Childhood in Fin-de-siècle France: Child Psychology, Universal Education and the Cultural Anxieties of Modernity." Ph.D. diss., University of California, Berkeley, 2000.

Nye, Robert A. "Degeneration, Neurasthenia and the Culture of Sport in Belle Époque France." *Journal of Contemporary History* 17, no. 1 (1982): 51–68.

———. *Crime, Madness and Politics in Modern France: The Medical Concept of National Decline*. Princeton: Princeton University Press, 1984.

———. "Heredity, Pathology, and Psychoneurosis in Durkheim's Early Work." In *Émile Durkheim: Critical Assessments*, edited by Peter Hamilton, 234–76. London: Routledge, 1990.

———. "The History of Sexuality in Context: National Sexological Traditions." *Science in Context* 4, no. 2 (1991): 387–406.

———. *Masculinity and Male Codes of Honor in Modern France*. Oxford: Oxford University Press, 1993.

O'Brien, Justin. *The Novel of Adolescence in France: The Study of a Literary Theme*. New York: Columbia University Press, 1937.

Offen, Karen. "The Second Sex and the Baccalauréat in Republican France, 1880–1924." *French Historical Studies* 13, no. 2 (1983): 252–86.

———. "Depopulation, Nationalism, and Feminism in Fin-de-siècle France." *American Historical Review* 89, no. 3 (1984): 648–76.

Oosterhuis, Harry. *Stepchildren of Nature: Krafft-Ebing, Psychiatry, and the Making of Sexual Identity*. Chicago: University of Chicago Press, 2000.

Outram, Dorinda. *The Body and the French Revolution: Sex, Class and Political Culture*. New Haven: Yale University Press, 1989.

Ozouf, Mona. *L'école, l'église, et la République, 1871–1914*. Paris: Armand Colin, 1963.

Paillard, Yves-Georges. "Les recherches démographiques sur Madagascar au début de l'époque coloniale et les documents de 'l'AMI'." *Cahiers d'études africaines* 27, no. 1–2 (1987): 17–42.

Pateman, Carole. *The Sexual Contract*. Cambridge: Polity Press, 1988.

Pedersen, Jean E. "Something Mysterious: Sex Education, Victorian Morality, and Durkheim's Comparative Sociology." *Journal of the History of the Behavioral Sciences* 34, no. 2 (1998): 135–51.

———. "Sexual Politics in Comte and Durkheim: Feminism, History, and the French Sociological Tradition." *Signs* 27, no. 1 (2001): 229–63.

———. *Legislating the French Family: Feminism, Theater, and Republican Politics, 1870–1920*. New Brunswick: Rutgers University Press, 2003.

Pedersen, Susan. *Family, Dependence, and the Origins of the Welfare State: Britain and France, 1915–1945*. Cambridge: Cambridge University Press, 1993.

Peiss, Kathy. *Cheap Amusements: Working Women and Leisure in Turn-of-the-century New York*. Philadelphia: Temple University Press, 1987.

Peneff, Jean. *Écoles publiques, écoles privées dans l'ouest, 1880–1950*. Paris: Éditions L'Harmattan, 1987.

Peniston, William. *Pederasts and Others: Urban Culture and Sexual Identity in Nineteenth-century Paris*. New York: Harrington Park Press, 2004.

Pernot, Denis. "Paris, province pédagogique." *Romantisme* 21, no. 83 (1994): 107–17.

———. *Le roman de socialisation, 1889–1914*. Paris: Presses universitaires de France, 1998.

Perrot, Michelle. "The New Eve and the Old Adam: Changes in French Women's Condition at the Turn of the Century." In *Behind the Lines: Gender and the Two World Wars*, edited by Margaret Randolph Higonnet, Jane Jenson, and Sonya Michel. New Haven: Yale University Press, 1987.

———. "Dans le Paris de la Belle Epoque, les 'Apaches,' premières bandes de jeunes." In *Les ombres de l'histoire: Crime et châtiment au XIXᵉ siècle*, 351–64. Paris: Flammarion, 2001.

Pick, Daniel. *Faces of Degeneration: A European Disease, c. 1848–c. 1918*. Cambridge: Cambridge University Press, 1989.

Pickering, W. S. F. "The Enigma of Durkheim's Jewishness." In *Debating Durkheim*, edited by W. S. F. Pickering and H. Martin, 10–39. London: Routledge, 1994.

Pinto, Louis. "Le détail et la nuance: La sociologie vue par les philosophes dans la *Revue de métaphysique et de morale*, 1893–1899." *Revue de métaphysique et de morale*, no. 1–2 (1993): 141–74.

Pitt, Alan. "The Irrationalist Liberalism of Hippolyte Taine." *Historical Journal* 41, no. 4 (1998): 1035–53.

Plott, Michèle. "The Rules of the Game: Respectability, Sexuality, and the *Femme Mondaine* in Late-Nineteenth-century Paris." *French Historical Studies* 25, no. 3 (2002): 531–56.

Porch, Douglas. *The March to the Marne: The French Army, 1871–1914*. Cambridge: Cambridge University Press, 1981.

Proschan, Frank. "Eunuch Mandarins, *Soldats mamzelles*, Effeminate Boys, and Graceless Women: French Colonial Constructions of Vietnamese Genders." *GLQ* 8, no. 4 (2002): 435–67.

———. " 'Syphilis, Opiomania, and Pederasty': Colonial Construction of Vietnamese (and French) Social Diseases." *Journal of the History of Sexuality* 11, no. 4 (2002): 610–36.

Prost, Antoine. *Histoire de l'enseignement en France, 1800–1967*. Paris: Armand Colin, 1968.

Quétel, Claude. *History of Syphilis*. Translated by Judith Braddock and Brian Pike. Baltimore: Johns Hopkins University Press, 1990.

Rabinow, Paul. *French Modern: Norms and Forms of the Social Environment*. Cambridge: MIT Press, 1989.

Ralston, David B. *The Army of the Republic: The Place of the Military in the Political Evolution of France, 1871–1914*. Cambridge: MIT Press, 1967.

Rambaud, Vital. "Barrès et 'le sens du relatif'." *Mesure* 4 (1990): 183–96.

Rauch, André. *Le premier sexe: Mutation et crise de l'identité masculine*. Paris: Hachette, 2000.

Reddy, William M. *The Navigation of Feeling: A Framework for the History of Emotions*. Cambridge: Cambridge University Press, 2001.

Reid, Martine. "L'Orient liquidé (Barrès, *Les déracinés*)." *Romanic Review* 83, no. 3 (1992): 379–88.

Rhoades, Michelle K. " 'No Safe Women': Prostitution, Masculinity, and Disease in France during the Great War." Ph.D. diss., University of Iowa, 2001.

Rigaud, Louis. "L'école en Algérie (1880–1862)." In *L'école en Algérie: 1830–1862*, edited by Association "Les Amis de Max Marchand de Mouloud Ferdoun et de leurs Compagnons," 23–73. Paris: Paublisud, 2001.

Ringer, Fritz. *Fields of Knowledge: French Academic Culture in Comparative Perspective.* Cambridge: Cambridge University Press, 1992.

Rioux, Jean-Pierre. *Nationalisme et conservatisme: La Ligue de la patrie française.* Paris: Éditions Beauchesne, 1977.

Roberts, Mary Louise. *Civilization without Sexes: Reconstructing Gender in Postwar France, 1917–1927.* Chicago: University of Chicago Press, 1994.

———. *Disruptive Acts: The New Woman in Fin-de-siècle France.* Chicago: University of Chicago Press, 2002.

Ronsin, Francis. *Les divorciaires: Affrontements politiques et conceptions du mariage dans la France du 19ᵉ siècle.* Paris: Aubier, 1991.

———. "Une aventure de jeunesse de sociologie: Les relations entre le divorce et le suicide." *Revue d'histoire moderne et contemporaine* 42, no. 2 (1995): 292–312.

Rosanvallon, Pierre. *L'état en France de 1789 à nos jours.* Paris: Seuil, 1990.

———. *Le sacre du citoyen: histoire du suffrage universel en France.* Paris: Gallimard, 1992.

———. *Le modèle politique français: La société civile contre le jacobinisme à nos jours.* Paris: Seuil, 2004.

Rosario, Vernon A. "Pointy Penises, Fashion Crimes, and Hysterical Mollies: The Pederasts' Inversions." In *Homosexuality in Modern France*, edited by Jeffrey Merrick and Bryant T. Ragan Jr. Oxford: Oxford University Press, 1996.

———. *The Erotic Imagination: French Histories of Perversity.* Oxford: Oxford University Press, 1997.

Roynette, Odile. *"Bons pour le service": L'expérience de la caserne en France à la fin du 19ᵉ siècle.* Paris: Belin, 2000.

Rubin, Gayle. "The Traffic in Women: Notes on the 'Political Economy' of Sex." In *Feminism and History*, edited by Joan Scott, 105–51. Oxford: Oxford University Press, 1996.

Saada, Emmanuelle. "Citoyens et sujets de l'empire français: Les usages du droit en situation coloniale." *Genèses*, no. 53 (2003): 4–24.

Schafer, Sylvia. *Children in Moral Danger and the Problem of Government in Third Republic France.* Princeton: Princeton University Press, 1997.

———. "Between Paternal Right and the Dangerous Mother: Reading Parental Responsibility in 19th-century French Civil Justice." *Journal of Family History* 23, no. 2 (1998): 173–89.

Schneewind, J. B. *The Invention of Autonomy: A History of Modern Moral Philosophy.* Cambridge: Cambridge University Press, 1998.

Schneider, William H. *Quantity and Quality: The Search for Biological Regeneration in Twentieth-century France.* Cambridge: Cambridge University Press, 1990.

Schorske, Carl E. *Fin-de-siècle Vienna: Politics and Culture.* New York: Vintage Books, 1981.

Schultheiss, Katrin. *Bodies and Souls: Politics and the Professionalization of Nursing in France, 1880–1922.* Cambridge: Harvard University Press, 2001.

Scott, Joan W. *Gender and the Politics of History.* New York: Columbia University Press, 1988.

———. *Only Paradoxes to Offer: Feminism and the "Rights of Man" in France, 1789–1940.* Cambridge: Harvard University Press, 1996.

――――. *Parité: Sexual Equality and the Crisis of French Universalism*. Chicago: University of Chicago Press, 2005.

――――. "Symptomatic Politics: The Banning of Islamic Headscarves in French Public Schools." *French Politics, Culture, and Society* 23, no. 3 (2005): 106–27.

Sedgwick, Eve. *Epistemology of the Closet*. Berkeley: University of California Press, 1990.

Seeley, Paul. "O Sainte Mère: Liberalism and the Socialization of Catholic Men in Nineteenth-century France." *Journal of Modern History* 70, no. 4 (1998): 862–91.

Seigel, Jerrold. *Bohemian Paris: Culture, Politics, and the Boundaries of Bourgeois Life, 1830–1930*. New York: Penguin, 1986.

――――. "Autonomy and Personality in Durkheim: An Essay on Content and Method." *Journal of the History of Ideas* 48, no. 3 (1987): 483–507.

Serman, William. *Les officiers français dans la nation, 1848–1914*. Paris: Aubier, 1982.

Sewell, William H. *Work and Revolution in France: The Language of Labor from the Old Regime to 1848*. Cambridge: Cambridge University Press, 1980.

――――. "Le citoyen/la citoyenne: Activity, Passivity, and the Revolutionary Concept of Citizenship." In *The French Revolution and the Creation of Modern Political Culture*, edited by Colin Lucas, 105–23. Oxford: Pergamon Press, 1988.

Shapiro, Ann-Louise. *Housing the Poor of Paris, 1850–1902*. Madison: Wisconsin University Press, 1985.

――――. *Breaking the Codes: Female Criminality in Fin-de-siècle Paris*. Stanford: Stanford University Press, 1996.

Sheradin, Kristin A. "Reforming the Republic: Solidarism and the Making of the French Welfare State, 1871–1914." Ph.D. diss., University of Rochester, 2000.

Shope, Janet Hinson. "Separate but Equal: Durkheim's Response to the Woman Question." *Sociological Inquiry* 64, no. 1 (1994): 23–36.

Showalter, Elaine. *Sexual Anarchy: Gender and Culture at the Fin-de-siècle*. New York: Viking, 1990.

Sibalis, Michael David. "The Regulation of Male Sexuality in Revolutionary and Napoleonic France, 1789–1815." In *Homosexuality in Modern France*, edited by Jeffrey Merrick and Bryan T. Ragan Jr. Oxford: Oxford University Press, 1996.

Silverman, Debora. *Art Nouveau and the Fin-de-siècle in France: Politics, Psychology, and Style*. Berkeley: University of California Press, 1989.

――――. "The 'New Woman,' Feminism and the Decorative Arts in Fin-de-siècle France." In *Eroticism and the Body Politic*, edited by Lynn Hunt, 144–63. Baltimore: Johns Hopkins University Press, 1991.

Sirinelli, Jean François. "Littérature et politique: Le cas Burdeau-Bouteiller." *Revue historique* 272, no. 1 (1984): 91–111.

Smith, Bonnie. *Ladies of the Leisure Class: The Bourgeoises of Northern France in the Nineteenth Century*. Princeton: Princeton University Press, 1981.

Sohn, Anne-Marie. "The Golden Age of Male Adultery: The Third Republic." *Journal of Social History* 28, no. 3 (1995): 469–90.

Sonn, Richard. *Anarchism and Cultural Politics in Fin-de-siècle France*. Lincoln: University of Nebraska Press, 1989.

――――. "The Early Political Career of Maurice Barrès: Anarchist, Socialist, or Protofascist?" *Clio* 21, no. 1 (1991): 41–60.

Soucy, Robert. *Fascism in France: the Case of Maurice Barrès*. Berkeley: University of California Press, 1972.

Stepan, Nancy Leys. "Race, Gender, Science, and Citizenship." *Gender and History* 10, no. 1 (1998): 26–52.

Sternhell, Zeev. *Maurice Barrès et le nationalisme français*. Paris: Presses de la fondation nationale des sciences politiques, 1972.

Stewart, Mary Lynn. *Women, Work, and the French State: Labour Protection and Social Patriarchy, 1879–1919*. Kingston: McGill-Queen's University Press, 1989.

Stewart, Suzanne R. *Sublime Surrender: Male Masochism at the Fin-de-siècle*. Ithaca: Cornell University Press, 1998.

Stock-Morton, Phyllis. *Moral Education for a Secular Society: The Development of Morale Laïque in Nineteenth-century France*. Albany: State University of New York Press, 1988.

Stoler, Ann Laura. *Race and the Education of Desire: Foucault's History of Sexuality and the Colonial Order of Things*. Durham: Duke University Press, 1995.

———. *Carnal Knowledge and Imperial Power: Race and the Intimate in Colonial Rule*. Berkeley: University of California Press, 2002.

Stone, Judith F. *Sons of the Revolution: Radical Democrats in France 1862–1914*. Baton Rouge: Louisiana State University Press, 1996.

Storra-Lemarre, Annie. *L'enfer de la Troisième République: Censeurs et pornographes (1881–1914)*. Paris: Imago, 1990.

———. *La République des faibles: Les origines intellectuelles du droit républicain, 1870–1914*. Paris: Armand Colin, 2005.

Stovall, Tyler. "The Color Line behind the Lines: Racial Violence in France during the Great War." *American Historical Review* 103, no. 3 (1998): 737–69.

———. "Love, Labor, and Race: Colonial Men and White Women in France during the Great War." In *French Civilization and Its Discontents*, edited by Tyler Stovall and Georges Van Den Abbeele. Lanham, MD: Lexington Books, 2003.

Strenski, Ivan. *Durkheim and the Jews of France*. Chicago: University of Chicago Press, 1997.

Strumhinger, Laura S. *What Were Little Girls and Boys Made Of? Primary Education in Rural France, 1830–1880*. Albany: State University of New York Press, 1983.

Suleiman, Susan Rubin. *Authoritarian Fictions: The Ideological Novel as Literary Genre*. New York: Columbia University Press, 1983.

Suny, Ronald Grigor, Patrick Brantlinger, and Richard Handler. "Review Essays: What's beyond the Cultural Turn?" *American Historical Review* 107, no. 5 (2002): 1475–1520.

Sussman, George D. *Selling Mothers' Milk: The Wet-Nursing Business in France, 1715–1914*. Urbana: University of Illinois Press, 1982.

Sydie, R. A. "Sex and the Sociological Fathers." *Canadian Review of Sociology and Anthropology* 31, no. 2 (1994): 117–38.

Talbott, John E. *The Politics of Educational Reform in France, 1918–1940*. Princeton: Princeton University Press, 1969.

Tamagne, Florence. "Adolescence et homosexualité: Pratiques, discours et représentations (1850–1945)." *Adolescence* 19, no. 1 (2001): 321–32.

Taraud, Christelle. *La prostitution coloniale*. Paris: Payot, 2003.

Terry, Jennifer. *An American Obsession: Science, Medicine, and Homosexuality in Modern Society*. Chicago: University of Chicago Press, 1999.

Thébaud, Françoise. *Quand nos grand-mères donnaient la vie: La maternité en France dans l'entre-deux-guerres*. Lyon: Presses universitaires de Lyon, 1986.

Thiercé, Agnès. *Histoire de l'adolescence*. Paris: Belin, 1999.

Thompson, Elizabeth. *Colonial Citizens: Republican Rights, Paternal Privilege, and Gender in French Syria and Lebanon*. New York: Columbia University Press, 2000.

Thompson, Victoria Elizabeth. "Creating Boundaries: Homosexuality and the Changing Social Order in France, 1830–1870." In *Homosexuality in Modern France*, edited by Jeffrey Merrick and Bryant T. Ragan, 102–27. Oxford: Oxford University Press, 1996.

Thullier, Guy. *Bureaucratie et bureaucrates en France au 19e siècle*. Edited by École pratique des hautes études. Geneva: Droz, 1980.

Tiersten, Lisa. *Marianne in the Market: Envisioning Consumer Society in Fin-de-siècle France*. Berkeley: University of California Press, 2001.

Tiryakian, Edward A. "Sexual Anomie, Social Structure, Societal Change." *Social Forces* 59, no. 4 (1981): 1025–53.

Toews, John. "Intellectual History after the Linguistic Turn: the Autonomy of Meaning and the Irreducibility of Experience." *American Historical Review* 92, no. 4 (1987): 879–907.

Tomkins, S. M. "Palmitate or Permanganate: The Venereal Prophylaxis Debate in Britain, 1916–1926." *Medical History* 37 (1993): 382–98.

Tosh, John. "Hegemonic Masculinity and the History of Gender." In *Masculinities in Politics and War,* edited by Stefan Dudnik, Karen Hagemann, and John Tosh, 41–58. Manchester: Manchester University Press, 2004.

Toth, Stephen A. "Desire and the Delinquent: Juvenile Crime and Deviance in Fin-de-siècle French Criminology." *History of the Human Sciences* 10, no. 4 (1997): 45–63.

Turin, Yvonne. "Instituteurs et colonisation en Algérie au 19ᵉ siècle." *Revue historique* 234, no. 2 (1965): 353–74.

Villey, Raymond. *Histoire du secret médical*. Paris: Seghers, 1986.

Vogt, W. Paul. "The Uses of Studying Primitives: A Note on the Durkheimians, 1890–1940." *History and Theory* 15, no. 1 (1976): 33–44.

Walkowitz, Judith. *Prostitution and Victorian Society: Women, Class, and the State*. Cambridge: Cambridge University Press, 1982.

———. *City of Dreadful Delight: Narratives of Sexual Danger in Late-Victorian London*. Chicago: University of Chicago Press, 1992.

Weber, Eugen. "Pierre de Coubertin and the Introduction of Organised Sport in France." *Journal of Contemporary History* 5, no. 2 (1970): 3–26.

———. "Gymnastics and Sports in Fin-de-siècle France: Opium of the Classes." *American Historical Review* 76, no. 1 (1971): 70–98.

———. *Peasants into Frenchmen: The Modernization of Rural France, 1870–1914*. Stanford: Stanford University Press, 1976.

Weil, Rachel. *Political Passions: Gender, the Family, and Political Argument in England, 1680–1714*. Manchester: Manchester University Press, 1999.

Weill, Georges. *Histoire de l'enseignement secondaire en France (1802–1920)*. Paris: Payot, 1921.

Weisz, George. *The Emergence of Modern Universities in France, 1863–1914*. Princeton: Princeton University Press, 1983.

———. "The Republican Ideology and the Social Sciences: The Durkheimians and the History of Social Economy at the Sorbonne." In *The Sociological Domain: The Durkheimians and the Founding of French Sociology,* edited by Philippe Besnard, 90–119. Cambridge: Cambridge University Press, 1983.

Wishnia, Judith. *The Proletarianizing of the Functionnaires: Civil Service Workers and the Labor Movement under the Third Republic*. Baton Rouge: Louisiana State University Press, 1990.

Wiegman, Robyn. "Object Lessons: Men, Masculinity, and the Sign Women." *Signs* 26, no. 2 (2001): 355–88.

Zeldin, Theodore. "The Conflict of Moralities: Confession, Sin, and Pleasure in the Nineteenth Century." In *Conflicts in French Society: Anticlericalism, Education, and Morals in the Nineteenth Century,* edited by Theodore Zeldin, 13–50. London: George Allen and Unwin, 1970.

Index

adolescents, 29–30, 39–41, 42
  colonial natives as, 58, 59–60, 68
  education and, 48–49, 60, 73
  as minors, 15, 188
  problem of, 29–30, 39–41, 44
  prostitution and venereal disease, 187–88,
    192–93, 196–204, 206, 210–11, 218
  sexual abstinence and, 198, 201
  sexual consciousness in, 189, 195–96,
    206, 211
  sexual deviance and, 19, 43–48, 49–50,
    122
Aicard, Jean, 69
Aisenberg, Andrew, 193
Algerians
  as adolescents, 58, 59–60, 68
  culture/religion of, 60, 64–65, 246
  domination/civilizing of, 62–68
  education, 13–14, 19, 44, 58–59, 60–68
  family/marriage in, 59, 64–67
  morality and, 64–65, 67
  women in, 66–67
André, Louis, 218–19
anomie, 133, 152, 153–55, 158, 165, 182
  bacheliers and, 88, 96–98, 100–102,
    107–10
  bachelors and, 71–72, 107–8, 182, 196
  materialism and, 153
Arabs. *See* Algerians
Ariès, Philippe, 73
Les avariés (Brieux), 202–4
Avril de Saint-Croix, Ghenia, 191, 192, 200

baccalauréat, 14, 69, 71, 89, 90
  reform of, 75–76, 105, 123
bacheliers
  anomie and, 88, 96–98, 100–102, 107–10

immorality and, 11, 86–87, 88, 97–100,
    107
  materialism and, 88, 114, 116–17
  modern life and, 105–7
  as nonproductive workers, 75, 82, 86,
    89–90, 98, 101, 104, 109–10, 112
  prostitution and, 11, 98–100
  social integration of, 85, 87–88, 97–98,
    100, 107
bachelors, 14, 71, 114, 121
  anomie and, 71–72, 107–8, 182, 196
  as criminals, 206–10, 211
  education and, 88, 110
  homosexuality and, 121
  individualism and, 88, 114, 116–18, 134
  materialism and, 88, 114, 116–17,
    119–20
  prostitution and venereal disease, 206–10,
    211
  soldiers as, 214
  suicide and, 108, 134, 150, 154
Bachofen, Jacob, 169, 170
Balzer, Félix, 234, 235–36
Barni, Jules, 30
Barrès, Maurice, 74, 85, 107, 110, 112, 125,
    141
  anti-Semitism and, 93–94
  Les déracinés, 90–93, 96–102, 109, 112,
    126, 196
  Kantianism and, 90–94, 96
Barthélemy, Toussaint, 190, 196, 222
Bérenger, Henry, 106–10, 112, 117
Bérenger, Réné, 190, 205–7
Bernard, Léon, 241
Bernard, Paul, 64
Bert, Paul, 224
Berthélemy, Henry, 159

Berthelot, Marcelin, 63, 104–6
Bertillon, Jacques, 114, 116, 119–20, 134, 150
  suicide and divorce, 154–55
Bertillon, Louis Adolphe, 150
biological determinism, 150–51, 154–55, 170–71
biological science, philosophy vs., 178–80
birth rate, 112–21
  delayed marriage and, 116–17
  divorce and, 154
  education and, 69, 110, 119
  illegitimacy and, 214
  individualism and, 118–20
  infant health and, 177, 178
  materialism and, 119–20, 134
  prostitution and, 111
  social capillarity, 116–20
  suicide and, 134, 150
  venereal disease and, 114
  women and, 113
Bodin, E., 236
Bonald, Louis de, 128
Boulanger, Georges, 70
Bourgeois, Léon, 49, 76, 129, 130, 161
Bourget, Paul, 85, 91, 107
Boutroux, Émile, 74, 90, 143, 163
Bréal, Michel, 77, 79, 89
Brieux, Eugène, 202–4, 221, 222
Brissaud, 212–13, 221, 223
Broca, Paul, 151
Brouardel, Paul, 194
Brunetière, Ferdinand, 176
Buisson, Ferdinand, 4, 17, 30–31, 45, 80, 127, 143, 244
  adolescence, 29–30, 39–41, 44
  colonial education, 59, 61, 63–64
  discipline and will, 33–35, 38–39, 50
  intuition, 31, 32, 33, 34
  mandatory education, 23
  moral education, 31–32
  morality and virility, 239–40
  socialization and education, 35, 37, 38, 39–41, 56, 57
  women's suffrage, 182–83
Burdeau, Auguste, 65, 80
bureaucracy
  birth rate and, 118, 120
  déclassement and, 75, 82, 86, 89, 98, 101, 104, 109–10, 112, 120
  rise of, 110, 112
Burlureaux, Charles, 216, 223, 224, 225, 228, 230
Butler, Josephine, 191

Carle, 230
Carnot, Sadi, 70
Chambon, Jeanne, 159

Charle, Christophe, 85
Chauvel, Paul, 216, 221
Chevandier law (1892), 201
Chirac, Jacques, 245
citizenship, 2, 3, 4–5, 12
  adults vs. minors, 15
  education and, 4–5, 9, 11, 17–18, 35, 244–48
  gender equality/complementarity, 182–83, 245–46, 247–48
  hygiene and, 213–14
  independence vs. social embeddedness, 70–72
  individual rights vs. social good, 186, 189, 191–95, 205–6, 220–23, 240, 241
  integration of outsiders, 244–48
  as male, 2–3, 6, 7, 11, 240, 243
  marriage and, 1–2, 5, 55, 221, 240–41, 243
  medical privacy and, 189, 193–95
  as noncolonial, 5, 15, 62
Cole, Joshua, 113
colonial natives
  as adolescents, 58, 59–60, 68
  culture/religion of, 60, 64–65, 230, 246
  as degenerate, 223, 224, 227, 229–30, 237, 246
  family/birth rate regulations, 227, 228
  homosexuality, 229, 230
  medical training/facilities, 228, 229
  as minors, 15, 188, 213, 227
  modesty, 229–30
  prostitution and, 67, 215, 224, 227
  venereal disease, 223–30, 237–38
  See also Algerians
Colonna, Fanny, 62–63
Combes, Émile, 58–59, 60, 67
communitarianism, 245, 247
Compayré, Gabriel, 80
Comte, Auguste, 127, 128, 162
Conklin, Alice, 63
Constant, Benjamin, 128
Constitution (1875), 2
Contagious Disease Acts, 191, 214, 215
Corbin, Alain, 186–87, 190
Cousin, Victor, 30, 31, 128
Crawley, Ernest, 171–72
Un crime d'amour (Bourget), 92
Croiset, Alfred, 80, 130

Darwin, Charles, 169
Davy, Georges, 136
Debernard, Jean-Michel, 246
Declaration of the Rights of Man, 127, 240
degeneracy theory, 150, 154–55
De la division du travail social (Durkheim), 125, 138–43, 145–48, 150, 181
  philosophy vs., 163, 164
De la solidarité morale (Marion), 44–50

Déloye, Yves, 49
Les déracinés (Barrès), 90–98, 100–102,
     109, 112, 126
Descent of Man (Darwin), 169
Desjardins, Paul, 159
*Dictionnaire de pédagogie et de l'instruction
     publique* (Buisson), 17, 18, 31, 45
  discipline, 33
  intuition, 32
  mandatory education, 23
  paternal moral authority, 27–28, 38
Discourse on the Origin of Inequality
     (Rousseau), 127
division of labor
  biological, 144–45, 148
  See also organic solidarity
divorce, 154–55, 157, 158–60, 181, 183
Doléris, Jacques Amedée, 177–79, 183
Dreyfus Affair, 70, 129, 130, 176
  army reform and, 214, 215, 218, 231
  Barrès and, 91, 94, 102
  individual rights and, 186
Dumont, Arsène, 116–19
Dupuy, Adrien, 84
Durkheim, Émile, 45, 126–28
  anomie, 131, 133, 152, 153–55, 158, 165,
     182
  divorce, 154–55, 157, 158–60, 181, 183
  incest taboo, 15, 167–76
  individualism vs. filiation, 141, 144
  kinship, 171, 172
  as male-oriented, 131, 135, 157, 159–60
  mind vs. body, 151–53, 155–57
  organizations, professional, 142, 146, 153
  paternal/religious authority, 126, 135,
     136, 138, 139–41
  personhood, 176
  primitive vs. modern society, 137–39, 145,
     146–47, 148–49, 150, 168
  religion/totemism, 167, 168, 171, 172–77,
     179, 180–81
  the sacred, 167, 176–77, 179, 180–82
  social rules and morality, 143, 148, 150,
     152–53, 161, 162–68, 174–75
  social rules and morality, hygiene vs., 179,
     180–81
  social vs. biological explanations, 150–51,
     154–55, 170–71, 172, 173
  suicide, 134, 135, 149–57, 158, 165
  traditional vs. modern society, 125–26,
     133–36, 138, 139–41, 144
  women and marriage, 131, 135, 136,
     146–47, 151–52, 155–59, 175, 182
  women and taboos, 171–72, 175
  See also organic solidarity; sociology
Durkheim, Émile, and marriage, 5, 14–15,
     126, 134, 135–43, 160, 169–70
  birth rate and, 134–35

exogamy, 168, 170, 171, 173–74
  organic solidarity and, 145–49, 156–57,
     161–62, 173
  passion, 146, 175
  the sacred and, 176–77, 179, 180–82
  as self-sacrifice, 143–44
  sexual regulation and, 149, 152, 153–56,
     157–60, 165, 168, 173–74, 201
  sexual regulation and sex education, 177,
     179–81
  suicide and, 149–57, 165
Duruy, Victor, 75

école maternelles, 35–37
education
  coeducation, 245, 247–48
  of colonial natives, 13–14, 19, 44, 58–59,
     60–68
  integration of outsiders, 244–48
  as secular, 4, 9, 13, 21–22, 25–27, 33, 36,
     74, 75, 244
  sexuality and, 11, 13
  as social policy, 12–13, 17–18, 40–41
  of women, 35, 37, 51–52, 54, 66–67, 80,
     245
education, primary school
  bureaucracy and, 110
  lower grades, 37–38
  as mandatory, 22–25
  morality and citizenship, 4–5, 9, 11,
     17–18, 25–27, 33, 40–42, 45–46
  as nonelite, 13, 22, 25
  nursery schools, 35–37
  paternal authority and, 9, 18, 23–28, 41,
     87
  republican reforms, 13, 21–29, 35–37
  sentiment/affect vs. coercion, 13, 18–19,
     21, 23, 24, 28–29, 33–37, 40–41, 43
  sentiment/affect vs. reason, 29, 56, 68
  as socialization, 9, 22, 35–37, 38–41
  teachers, men vs. women, 35–38, 40–41
education, secondary school, 14, 73, 77
  boarding schools, 47–48, 73–74, 75–84,
     91
  as class-preserving, 108–9, 112
  as democratizing, 73, 75, 78, 89
  discipline, 48–49, 76–77, 79, 81–82
  elite, 22
  as emasculating, 71, 77, 80, 83–86, 89,
     90–96, 97–99, 122
  family vs. state, 77–79, 85–86, 87–89,
     92–93, 196–97
  hygiene and, 83
  independent thinking vs. social embedded-
     ness, 70–71, 90–96, 107, 109, 123
  morality and, 74
  reforms, 48–49, 74–77, 80–96, 102–3,
     105–12, 123

education, secondary school (*continued*)
    self-moderation and citizenship, 49, 81–82
    sentiment/love vs., 56, 69, 108
    sexual deviance and, 19, 43, 47–48, 77, 82, 83–84, 92
    socialization and, 85–86, 87–88, 92–93, 107, 123
    universalism vs. filiation, 90–96, 123
    See also baccalauréat; bacheliers
education, secondary school, curriculum
    modern vs. classical tracks, 75–76, 89, 104, 123
    physical education, 77, 79, 83
    science vs. literature tracks, 89, 104–7, 123
    sex education, 177–79, 195–204, 218
L'éducation morale (Durkheim), 165–66
L'effort (Bérenger), 107–9
Ehrlich, Paul, 201, 231
Émile (Rousseau), 29
Engels, Friedrich, 168–69
Espinas, Alfred, 128, 144, 145, 148

Fabriani, Jean-Louis, 164
Faivre, Paul, 239
Falloux law (1850), 21, 23
family. *See* marriage
femininity. *See* gender roles, female
femininization of men, 69, 71, 77, 80, 83–86, 89, 90–96, 97–99, 122
Le féminisme français (Turgeon), 182
Ferrier, J., 221–22
Ferry, Jules, 21, 30, 45, 70, 219, 244
    affect and education, 28
    colonial education, 59, 61
    early childhood education, 35–36, 41
    mandatory education, 23, 24–25
    religion vs. public morality, 26–27
Ferry laws (1882), 21–23, 26
Fiaux, Louis, 191, 204–5, 207
filiation
    individualism vs., 141, 144
    occupations and, 141–42
    solidarity and, 163
    universalism vs., 90–96, 123
Fison, Lorimer, 138
Fonssagrives, Abbé, 197
Forth, Christopher, 93
Foucault, Michel, 7, 77, 187
Fouillée, Alfred, 1–2, 104, 162, 213
Fourier, Charles, 128
Fournier, Alfred, 185, 186, 190, 191–92, 196–202, 206, 223
Frary, Raoul, 75
Frazer, James, 171
Freud, Sigmund, 6

Galliéni, Joseph, 224, 227–28, 229
Garnier, Pierre, 114, 121

Gaucher, Ernest, 222, 234, 235, 236
gender roles, female, 9, 245
    education and, 28–29, 35–41
    evolution of, 146–47, 171–73, 175
    feminism and, 71, 113–14, 182–83, 191, 200
    sentiment/love and, 28–29, 35–41, 51–52, 56
    sexual consciousness in, 189
    in socialization, 3, 11, 28–29, 35–41
    as wives/mothers, 9, 37, 38, 41, 55, 113–14, 154
    as wives/mothers (Durkheim), 131, 151–52, 156–57, 175
    See also prostitution; women; women and law
gender roles, male, 8, 11–12, 245, 247
    as citizens, 2–3, 6, 7, 11
    communitarianism and, 247
    evolution of, 146–47
    forcefulness and, 37–38
    heterosexuality, 1–3, 5, 7, 8, 10–12, 72, 84
    as husbands and fathers, 8, 15, 55, 71, 118, 147–48, 156, 161–62, 182, 187
    morality and, 4–5, 8
    patriarchy and, 9, 18, 23–28, 41, 87, 135, 197
    sexual consciousness in, 189
    See also adolescents; bachelors; men
Godart, Justin, 236, 237, 239
Gougerot, 238, 239
Gréard, Octave, 37, 80
Guyot, Yves, 191

Hayem, Henri, 206–7
heterosexuality, 175–77, 179–81, 198, 241–42, 243, 246–47
    incest taboo and, 168, 174, 175
    male gender roles and, 1–3, 5, 7, 8, 10–12, 72, 84
    organic solidarity and, 145–49, 161–62, 173–74, 175
    See also homosexuality; marriage
The History of Sexuality (Foucault), 7, 187
homosexuality, 10, 11, 84, 121, 230
    colonial natives, 229, 230
    in schools, 19, 43, 47–48, 77, 82, 83–84, 92
    solidarity and, 173
Honnorat, André, 116, 119
Howitt, A. W., 138
Hunt, Lynn, 6
hygienic science, 177–79, 183
    See also public health

"Individualism and the Intellectuals"
    (Durkheim), 176

Islam, 60, 64–65, 230, 244–45
  gender differences, 66–67, 245–48

Janet, Paul, 23–24, 30, 31, 32
Jeanmaire, Charles, 61–62
Jeanselme, Édouard, 225
Judaism, 93–94, 126

Kant, Immanuel, 30, 39, 53, 166–67, 180,
    181
  Marion's critique of, 53–54
  marriage, 143–44, 180
  reason and morality, 31–33, 34, 38, 50,
    143
Kantian philosophy
  as dangerous, 90–96
  Durkheim and, 128–29, 165–67, 175, 180
Karady, Victor, 169
Kermogard, Pauline, 36

LaCapra, Dominick, 145
Lacassagne, Alexandre, 47
Lagneau, Gustave, 114, 214
Lamennais, Félicité de, 128
Laprade, Victor, 77, 79, 89
Laupts, Dr. (Georges Saint-Paul), 83–84
Lavisse, Ernest, 80, 106, 204
LeBon, Gustave, 145, 147
Le Chapelier law (1791), 127
Legrain, Maurice, 47, 121
Legrand, R., 220–21
Leonetti, Jean, 247
Le Pileur, Louis, 190, 207, 210, 222
Lépine, Louis, 190
Le Play, Ferdinand, 138
Leroux, Pierre, 128
Letourneau, Charles, 138, 150–51, 154, 155
Liard, Louis, 80, 204
liberal approach to education, 23, 24, 33,
    43, 45–46, 48
Littré, Émile, 162
Loi sur la protection des enfants du premier
    âge (1874), 209
Lubbock, John, 171
Luc, Jean-Noël, 36
Lyautey, Hubert, 218
lyceé. *See* education, secondary school

Madagascar, colonial policies, 227–29
Maistre, Joseph de, 128
Maneuvrier, Édouard, 82–83, 86, 89
Margueritte, Paul and Victor, 158
Marion, Henri, 45, 89, 127
  adolescence and deviance, 44–45, 46–48,
    49–50
  authoritarian regimes, 46
  education and citizenship, 45–46
  education of girls, 51–52, 54

family, conjugal, 54–56, 58
Kant critique, 53–54
love/affect and morality, 50–54, 56–57,
    144
political/sexual repression, 46–47, 49
reason and morality, 50–54, 56–57, 59,
    80–81, 144
solidarity and moral action, 54, 128, 143,
    240
marriage
  as affect and reason, 51, 54, 56, 58,
    143–44
  civilization and, 5, 54–55, 58
  class and, 108–9, 117–18
  conjugal family, 5, 54–56, 58
  conjugal family (Durkheim), 126, 131,
    135–43, 145–49, 151
  evolution of, 136, 137–40, 146–49,
    169–70
  exogamy, 168, 170, 171, 173–74
  gender roles, 1–3, 5, 6, 13, 55–56, 147–48
  gender roles (Durkheim), 131, 136,
    146–47
  health and, 150–51
  heterosexuality, 1–3, 5, 51, 58
  as natural, 116–17, 120–21, 140, 151
  in other cultures, 5, 54, 55, 59, 64–67
  patriarchal family, 135, 138, 139–40
  as self-sacrifice, 143
  socialization in, 1, 21, 54–55, 56, 88, 196
  social vs. individual contract, 139–41, 159
  solidarity and, 145–49, 156–57, 161–63
  suicide and, 149–57, 165
  See also bachelors; divorce; Durkheim,
    Émile, and marriage
masculinity. *See* gender roles, male
masculinization of women, 113–14
materialism
  anomie and, 153
  bachelors/*bacheliers* and, 88, 114,
    116–17, 119–20
Maurras, Charles, 85
McLennan, John Ferguson, 169, 170, 171
medical rationality, 177
men
  femininization of, 69, 71, 77, 80, 83, 84,
    85–86, 89, 90–96, 97–99, 122
  law and, 208–10, 211
  See also gender roles, male
Ménard, Louis, 96
Mercier, V., 206, 207–8
Metchnikoff, Elie, 231, 232, 233
military
  civilian workers, 220–23, 238
  in colonies, 215, 223–30
  doctors in, 216, 218
  homosexuality, 230
  length of service, 231

military (*continued*)
  as minors, 15, 188, 212–13, 227, 231
  prostitution and, 213, 215, 220, 232,
    235–36, 238
  recreational activities, 219
  reforms, 214–19, 220–24, 231
  sexual abstinence and rape, 235–36
  sexuality and, 213
  World War I, 234–38
military and venereal disease, 225, 226,
    234
  education and, 215–16, 218–19, 220,
    225, 231–32, 233, 237
  medical privacy and, 216, 218, 221,
    232
  screening and treatment, 220–21, 225,
    227, 231, 232–33, 236–37
  World War I, 234–38
Morgan, Lewis Henry, 138, 169, 170, 171
Murard, Lion, 236

Nana (Zola), 191
Naquet, Alfred, 154, 158
Nye, Robert, 7–8, 47

occupations, 89–90, 141–42
  See also bureaucracy
organic solidarity, 126, 129, 130–31, 137,
    138–39, 144
  division of labor, 130, 137, 141, 144,
    145–48
  incest/homosexuality and, 173
  marriage and, 145–49, 156–57, 161–62,
    173
  philosophical solidarity and, 161
Origines de la France contemporaine
  (Taine), 84–85, 88, 89

Parent-Duchâtelet, A.-J.-H., 190
Pateman, Carol, 6
patriarchy, 6, 135, 197
  education and, 9, 18, 23–28, 38, 41, 87
  religious authority and, 126, 135, 136,
    138, 139–41
La pavé d'amour (Aicard), 69
Pécaut, Félix, 80
pedagogy. *See* education
Pedersen, Jean, 157
Pernot, Denis, 90
Perrier, Edmond, 144, 145, 148
Petit, Paul, 220–21, 222, 223, 227, 228
Pinard, Adolphe, 114, 239, 240–41
Pinto, Louis, 164
pornography, 197–99
Pour no fils quand ils auront 17 ans
  (Fournier), 198–202
Pourquéry de Boisserin, Joseph-Gaston, 60,
    65–66
Prévost, Marcel, 182

prostitution
  abolitionist movement, 185–86, 191, 200,
    204–5, 222, 235
  bacheliers and immorality, 11, 98–100
  birth rate and, 111
  in colonies, 67, 215, 224, 227
  as dangerous, 200–201, 202
  as immoral, 191
  marriage vs., 8, 15, 55, 71, 118, 147–48,
    156, 161–62, 182, 186
  military and, 213, 215, 220, 232, 235–36,
    238
  regulation of, 15, 185–87, 188, 189,
    190–93, 195, 200, 207
  as state sanctioned, 191, 215
  See also public health
public health, 15–16
  adult vs. minors, 15, 188, 212–13, 227, 231
  birth rate/infant health, 177, 178
  civilian naval workers, 220–23
  law and, 189, 205–10
  medical privacy and, 189, 193–95, 216,
    218, 221
  morality vs., 209
  wet nurses, 208–9
  See also military; military and venereal
    disease; prostitution; venereal disease

Queyrat, Auguste, 239, 241

racialist anthropology, 150–51
Rausch, André, 76
Les règles de la méthode sociologique
  (Durkheim), 168
religion
  authority and, 126, 135, 136, 138, 139–41
  education and, 4, 9, 13, 21–22, 25–27,
    33, 36, 74, 75, 244–48
  Islam, 60, 64–65, 230, 244–45
  public morality and, 26–27
  totemism, 167, 168, 171, 172–77, 179,
    180–81
Renan, Ernest, 59–60
Renouvier, Charles, 31
Revolution of 1789, 2, 6–7, 127, 129
Ribot, Alexandre, 105
Ribot, Théodule, 33, 141
Ribot Commission (1899), 105–6, 112
Richet, Charles, 114
Ringer, Fritz, 89
Roberts, Mary Louise, 93
Rousseau, Jean-Jacques, 29, 116, 127,
    128–29, 148
Roussel, Théophile, 209
Roux, Émile, 231, 232, 233

Saint-Claire Deville, Henri, 48, 77
Saint-Simon, Henri de, 127
Schaeffle, Albert, 137

Schmoll, Louis, 208
sex education, 177–81, 195–204, 218
sexuality, 15, 84, 167–76, 244
  abstinence, 198, 201, 233–34, 235–36
  adolescence and deviance, 19, 43–48,
    49–50, 187
  consciousness and, 189
  incest, 92, 170–71, 173
  individual and social order, 187–88
  marriage and suicide, 149–57, 165
  perversion and civilization, 116–17, 121
  pornography, 197–99
  puberty and, 30, 58
  social vs. natural, 131, 179, 198, 202
  theories of, 6–8, 10–11, 15–16, 121,
    187
  See also homosexuality; prostitution
Sicard de Plauzoles, Just, 239, 241
Simon, Jules, 76, 79
Simonin, J., 216
Smith, W. Robertson, 171, 172
social capillarity, 116–20
The Social Contract (Rousseau), 148
Société de médicine militaire française
  (SMMF), 232
Société française de prophylaxie sanitaire et
  morale (SFPSM), 186, 189, 190,
    192–93, 210–11
sociology
  development of, 127–29, 131, 136–38,
    149–50, 164–65, 168–69
  individual vs. state, 127–28
  morality and, 137
  philosophy vs., 142–43, 161–68
  politics and, 129
  social vs. natural, 131
  traditional vs. modern society, 125–26,
    133–36, 137, 138, 139–41, 144
  See also Durkheim, Émile; organic solidar-
    ity; solidarity
Solidarism, 128–31, 161–62
solidarity
  filiation and, 163
  hygiene and, 224, 230
  marriage and, 145–49, 156–57, 161–63
  moral action and, 54, 128, 143, 240
  philosophical, 129, 130, 161
  reproduction and, 162
  See also organic solidarity
Spencer, Herbert, 137, 140, 169
Stasi, Bernard, 244, 245–46
suffrage, 2, 17
  women's, 3, 182–83, 192
suicide, 134, 135
  bachelors and, 108, 134, 150
  divorce and, 154–55, 157, 158
  marriage and, 149–57, 165
Suicide (Durkheim), 134, 149–57, 165, 166,
  168

Suleiman, Susan, 100
syphilis. *See* venereal disease

Taine, Hippolyte, 100–101, 107, 110
  state-education critique, 74, 84–89, 91, 93
Taraud, Christelle, 224
Tarde, Gabriel, 150
Thibierge, Georges, 194
Tönnies, Ferdinand, 137
totemism, 167, 168, 171, 172–77, 179,
  180–81
Trielle, Alcide, 217
Turgeon, Charles, 182–83

venereal disease, 15, 177, 178, 185, 187–88,
  189
  birth rate and, 114
  education and, 189, 195–204, 210–11,
    215–16, 218–19, 239–41
  medical privacy and, 189, 193–95, 216,
    218, 221
  moral education and, 239–41
  as national menace, 192–93, 196, 239
  post–World War I, 239–42
  scientific advances, 230–31
  sexual abstinence and, 198, 201, 233–34,
    235–36
  treatments, 201, 215, 231, 239
  World War I, 188, 213, 234–35
  See also military and venereal disease
Vignon, Louis, 66
Villey, Raymond, 193
Vincent, Louis, 221
Le vote des femmes (Buisson), 182

Wagner, Charles, 107
Waitz, Theodor, 145
Waldeck-Rousseau, René, 218
Waldeck-Rousseau law (1884), 110
Wassermann, August von, 231
Westermarck, Edward, 169, 170
Wishnia, Judith, 110
women
  birth rate and, 113
  colonial natives, 66–67
  education and, 35–38, 51–52, 54, 66–67,
    80, 245
  masculinization of, 113–14
  suffrage, 3, 182–83, 192
  taboos and, 171–72, 175
  See also gender roles, female
women and law, 3, 4–5, 6, 9, 41, 247–48
  individual rights and, 191–92, 193–95,
    200, 207
  venereal disease and, 189, 193–95,
    208–10, 211, 222

Zola, Émile, 91, 191
Zylberman, Patrick, 236